ON LOVE

VICTORINE TEXTS IN TRANSLATION
Exegesis, Theology and Spirituality from the Abbey of St Victor

2

Grover A. ZINN
Editor in Chief

Hugh FEISS OSB
Managing Editor

On Love

A Selection of Works of Hugh, Adam, Achard, Richard,
and Godfrey of St Victor

Hugh Feiss OSB
ed.

BREPOLS

© 2011, Brepols Publishers n.v., Turnhout, Belgium.

D/2011/0095/16

ISBN 978-2-503-53459-6

Printed in the E.U. on acid-free paper.

Godfrey of St Victor, 'Microcosm', self-portrait.
Paris, Bibliothèque nationale de France, lat. 14515, fol. 106v

Michaeli, fratri optimo

TABLE OF CONTENTS

PREFACE

The Abbey of St Victor at Paris was one of the major centers for biblical interpretation, theological reflection, spiritual guidance, and liturgical practice/innovation in the twelfth century and beyond. The Editorial Board of the series *Victorine Texts in Translation* is pleased to present this volume in a continuing series of publications offering English translations (often for the first time) of a wide range of writings by authors resident at or formed at the Abbey.

The past several decades have seen a renaissance in the study of the Victorines, with a number of recent studies, the inception of a French translation series, a dedicated monograph series published with Brepols, the establishment of the Hugo von Sankt Viktor Institut, and a Colloquium in Paris celebrating the 900th anniversary of the founding of the Abbey. The translated texts presented in this series form an American counterpart to these initiatives. Our series aims to make Victorine texts more accessible to a wider English-speaking audience. *Victorine Texts in Translation* uses the latest critical Latin texts being published in the *Corpus christianorum continuatio medievalis* or, where both necessary and possible, uses Latin texts that are improvements over the texts collected and published in the *Patrologia latina* of Migne. Introductions to each volume and each work translated give the intellectual and historical background for understanding the work. Each text is also annotated.

The planning and execution of this project have been a community effort from the beginning. Our plans crystallized at a meeting hosted by Michael Signer at the University of Notre Dame. His recent death was a great loss to us and to Victorine and Jewish-Christian studies.

The members of the editorial board have shared the decisions of what to translate, done some of the translations, and reviewed together the work at each stage of the way. We have been joined by a number of other scholars engaged in Victorine studies who have offered translations or suggestions.

The subtitle of this series, *Exegesis, Theology and Spirituality from the Abbey of St Victor*, uses categories developed in the centuries following the flourishing of Victorine thought in the twelfth century.

However, these categories indicate well the breadth of the Victorines' interests. For them, and for their predecessors, what is today understood as "theology" often occurred in the context of scriptural interpretation and was intertwined with spirituality and liturgy. This integrated vision is one contribution that the Victorines can make for contemporary readers.

Luc Jocqué, our Editor at Brepols and a distinguished scholar in the field of Victorine studies, has been a guiding light and insightful commentator on the project since the beginning. We are indebted to him for his trust in this project and his assistance in bringing it to fruition.

Planning and translation are in place for additional volumes, so we can promise that there will soon be more Victorine works in English translation. Each volume will be generally topical, as is this one *On Love*, with some works translated in their entirety, while for other works selected passages will be translated. A variety of genres will be included in each volume, from exegesis, to theological treatises, spiritual writings, and liturgical poetry.

The works contained in this volume *On Love* make it obvious how deeply immersed the Victorines were in the thought and language of the Latin Bible. Virtuosi of the Word, they drew on all the historical and scientific knowledge available to them to understand the Sacred Scriptures. Volume Three of this series will present texts in which the canons of St Victor and their associates elaborate their theories of biblical interpretation.

This series was launched and continues with the conviction that the Victorine authors are important not only for understanding the intellectual and spiritual currents of the twelfth and thirteenth centuries in particular, but also for the contribution they can make to the intellectual, religious and spiritual life of the present century.

Grover A. Zinn
Oberlin College

ACKNOWLEDGMENTS

This second volume of the series, *Victorine Texts in Translation*, has come to be through the work of the very dedicated editorial board, who vetted the individual sections and then the complete document. The work that Boyd Taylor Coolman and Dale Coulter did in editing the first volume of the series made editing this second volume easier. Franklin Harkins, of the editorial board, Juliet Mousseau, Andrew Kraebel, and Vanessa Butterfield graciously and skillfully undertook translations of works by Hugh, Adam, and Richard of St Victor. Christopher Evans, also a member of the editorial board, prepared preliminary editions of the Latin texts of two of Hugh's most important works. Joanne Draper vetted the introduction and Lynell Jutila some of the texts. However, the greatest contributor to editing the book project was Lucy Stamm, who painstakingly, with loving care for detail, edited the entire manuscript. We are immensely grateful to her. The deficiencies that remain despite their help are the responsibility of the editor.

Our dealings with Luc Jocqué, a distinguished Victorine scholar and our editor with Brepols, have been most cordial and helpful. He has shown immense patience and given unfailing support to our undertaking. He has worked with Gary Brandl of New City Press to bring out a paperback edition in the United States. We are grateful to both of them.

Thirty years ago, Père Jean Châtillon took Rainer Berndt, SJ, Patrice Sicard, CR, and the editor of this volume on a tour of Victorine sites around Paris. With his copy of Fourier Bonnard's history of the abbey and order of St Victor in hand, he took us to the Victorine churches and priories of Amponville, Ury, Puiseaux, Villiers-le-Bel and to the Victorine abbeys of Saint-Vincent of Senlis and La Victoire. Père Châtillon's enthusiasm was infectious. All us who study and love the Victorines owe a great debt to him, and to the two scholars who traveled with us that day, who have carried on his work.

ABBREVIATIONS

GCS	*Die griechischen christlichen Schriftsteller der ersten drei Jahrhunderte* (Berlin and Leipzig, 1897–).
JTS	*Journal of Theological Studies* (London/Oxford, 1900–).
MS	*Mediaeval Studies* (Toronto: Pontifical Institute of Mediaeval Studies, 1939–).
NPNF	*Select Library of the Nicene and Post-Nicene Fathers* (New York, 1887–92; Grand Rapids: Eerdmans, 1978).
Oeuvre 1	*L'oeuvre de Hugues de Saint-Victor*, 1, Latin text by H. B. Feiss and P. Sicard, trans. (French) D. Poirel, H. Rochais, and P. Sicard, intro., notes, and appendices D. Poirel, Sous le Règle de saint Augustin (Turnhout: Brepols, 1997).
Oeuvre 2	*L'oeuvre de Hugues de Saint-Victor*, 2, intro., trans., and notes by B. Jollès, Sous le Règle de saint Augustin (Turnhout: Brepols, 2000).
PL	*Patrologiae cursus completus sive bibliotheca universalis, integra, uniformis, commoda, oeconomica, omnium ss. Patrum, doctorum scriptorumque ecclesiasticorum qui ab aevo apostolico ad Innocentii III tempora floruerunt . . . series Latina*, ed. J.-P. Migne, 221 vols. (Paris, 1844–64).
PLS	*Patrologiae cursus completus*, a J. P. Migne editus, Parisiis, 1844. *Series latina. Supplementum*. Ed. A. Hamman. 5 vols. (Paris: Garnier, 1958–).
RBen	*Revue Bénédictine* (Maredsous, 1885–).
RTAM	*Recherches de théologie ancienne et médiévale* (Louvain, 1929–96), now RTPM.
RTPM	*Recherches de théologie et philosophie médiévale* (Leuven: Peeters, 1997–), formerly RTAM.
SB	*Spicilegium Bonaventurianum* (Grottaferrata: Editiones Collegii S. Bonaventurae, 1963–).
SBO	*Sancti Bernardi Opera*, ed. J. Leclercq, C. H. Talbot, and H. M. Rochais, 9 vols. (Rome: Editiones Cistercienses, 1957–98).
SC	*Sources Chrétiennes* (Paris: Cerf, 1942–).
Schmitt	*Anselmi Opera Omnia*, ed. F. S. Schmitt (Edinburgh: Thomas Nelson, 1938–68). Reprinted with Spanish translation in *Obras completas de San Anselmo*, 2 vols., ed. Julian Alameda. (Madrid: Biblioteca de Autores Cristianos, 1951–53).

TPMA	Textes philosophiques du Moyen Age (Paris: J. Vrin, 1958–).
VTT	Victorine Texts in Translation (Turnhout: Brepols, 2010–).

VICTORINE AUTHORS[1]

WILLIAM OF CHAMPEAUX

Introd.	*Introductiones dialecticae secundum Wilgelmum and secundum G. Paganellum*, ed. Yukio Iwakuma: in *Cahiers de l'Institut du Moyen Age Grec et Latin* 63 (1993): 57–114.
Sententiae	*Sententiae*, ed. Odon Lottin: *Psychologie et morale aux xiiᵉ et xiiiᵉ siècles*, 5: *Problèmes d'histoire littéraire. L'école d'Anselme de Laon et de Guillaume de Champeaux* (Gembloux: J. Duculot, 1959), 189–227.

GILDUIN OF ST VICTOR

Accentibus	*Libellus de accentibus cum Prologo*, ed. Luc Jocqué and Dominique Poirel, "De Donat à Saint-Victor: un 'De accentibus' inédit," *La tradition vive. Mélanges d'histoire des textes en l'honneur de Louis Holtz*, ed. Pierre Lardet (Turnhout: Brepols, 2003), 181–92.

HUGH OF ST VICTOR

Adnot. in Pent.	*Adnotationes elucidatoriae in Pentateuchon*, PL 175.29–86 [*Notes on the Pentateuch*].
Adnot. in Jud.	*Adnotatiunculae elucidatoriae in librum Judicum*, PL 175.87–96. [*Notes on Judges*].
Adnot. in Reg.	*Adnotationes in librum Regum*, PL 175.95–114 [*Notes on Kings*].

---

[1] * indicates doubtful authenticity.

Adnot. in Threnos   *Adnotatiunculae in Threnos Jeremiae*, PL 175.255–322 [*Notes on Lamentations*].

Archa Noe   *De archa Noe* (*De arca Noe morali*), ed. P. Sicard, CCCM 176 (Turnhout: Brepols, 2001): 3–117 [*Ark of Noah*, tr. a Religious of C.S.M.V. [Sr. Penelope Lawson], in Hugh of Saint-Victor, *Selected Spiritual Writings* (New York: Harper and Row, 1962), 45–153].

Arrha   *De arrha animae*, ed. Karl Müller, *Hugo von St. Viktor, Soliloquium de arrha animae und De vanitate mundi.* Kleine Texte für Vorlesungen und Übungen 123 (Bonn, 1913), 1–26; ed. and tr. Sicard, et. al., *Oeuvre*, 1:226–83; tr. Vincenzo Liccaro, *Didascalicon, I doni della promessa divina, L'essenza dell'amore, Discorso in lode del divino amore* (Milan: Rusconi, 1987); [*Betrothal-Gift of the Soul*, tr. F. Sherwood Taylor, *The Soul's Betrothal-Gift* (Westminster, England: Dacre Press, 1945); tr. Kevin Herbert, *Soliloquy on the Earnest Money of the Soul*, Medieval Philosophical Texts in Translation 9 (Milwaukee: Marquette University Press, 1956); tr. Feiss, VTT 2:183–232].

Assumpt.   *Pro Assumptione Virginis*, ed. and tr. B. Jollès, *Oeuvre*, 2:112–61 [*Assumption of the Virgin*].

BM Virg.   *De beatae Mariae virginitate*, ed. and tr. B. Jollès, *Oeuvre*, 2:182–253 [*Virginity of Mary*].

Cant. BM.   *Super Canticum Mariae*, ed. and tr. Jollès, *Oeuvre*, 2:24–91 [*On the Canticle of Mary*].

Chronicon   *Chronicon vel de tribus maximis circumstantiis gestorum*, partial editions, ed. W. M. Green, "Hugo of St Victor, *De tribus maximis circumstantiis gestorum*" *Speculum* 18 (1943): 484–93; ed. G. Waitz, "Chronica quae dicitur Hugonis de Sancto Victore," *Monumenta Germaniae Historica, Scriptores* 24 (Hanover, 1879): 88–97; "Hugues de Saint-Victor lexicographe," ed. Roger Baron, *Cultura neolatina*, 16 (1956): 109–45 [*Chronicon*, partially tr. Mary Carruthers, "The Three Best Memory Aids," in *The Medieval Craft of Memory: An Anthology of Texts and Pictures*, ed. Mary Carruthers and Jan M. Ziolkowski (Philadelphia: University of Pennsylvania, 2002), 32–40].

Decalogum   *Institutiones in Decalogum*, PL 176.9–15 [*Instructions on the Decalogue*].

Didasc.   *Didascalicon*, ed. C. H. Buttimer (Washington: The Catholic University Press, 1939) [*Didascalicon*, trans. and intro.

J. Taylor (New York: Columbia University Press, 1991); ed. and tr. Thilo Offergeld, Hugo von Sankt Viktor, *Didascalicon de Studio Legendi/Studienbuch*, Fontes Christiani 27 (Freiburg: Herder, 1997); tr. Vincenzo Liccaro, *Didascalicon, I doni della promessa divina, L'essenza dell'amore, Discorso in lode del divino amore* (Milan: Rusconi, 1987); tr. Michel Lemoine, Hugues de Saint-Victor, *L'Art de lire/Didascalicon*. Sagesses chretiennes (Paris: Cerf, 1991).

Diligens scrutator   Ralf Stammberger, "*Diligens scrutator sacri eloquii*: An Introduction to Scriptural Exegesis by Hugh of St Victor Preserved at Admont Library (MS 671)," *Manuscripts and Medieval Culture: Reform and Renewal in Twelfth-Century Germany*, ed. Alison I. Beach, Medieval Church Studies 13 (Turnhout: Brepols 2007), 272–83 [*Diligent Investigator*].

Egredietur   *Super "Egredietur uirga,"* ed. and tr. B. Jollès, *Oeuvre*, 2:270–86 [*A Shoot Will Come Forth*].

Ep. 1   *Epistola 1 ad Ranulphum de Mauriaco* (= *Misc.* 1 67), PL 176.1011 [*Letter 1 to Ranulph de Mauriaco*, tr. Feiss, in introduction to VTT 2:67].

Ep. 2   *Epistola 2 ad Ranulphum de Mauriaco, De solutione quatuor quaestionum*, PL 176.1011–14 [*Letter 2 to Ranulph de Mauriaco*].

Ep. 3   *Epistola 3 ad Joannem Hispalensem Achiepiscopum*, PL 176.1014–18 [*Letter 3 to Archbishop John*].

Epitome   *Epitome Dindimi*, in Hugh of St Victor, *Opera propaedeutica*, ed. Roger Baron, Publications in Mediaeval Studies (Notre Dame, IN: University of Notre Dame Press, 1966), 187–247 [*Epitome of Dindimus*].

Eulogium   *Eulogium sponsi et sponsae* (*De amore sponsi ad sponsum*), PL 176.987–94 [*Praise of the Bridegroom*, partially tr. A Religious of the C.S.M.V., *The Divine Love: The two treatises* De Laude Caritatis and De Amore Sponsi ad Sponsam *by Hugh of St Victor*, (London: A. R. Mowbray & Co., 1956), 26–38; partially tr. Richard A. Norris, Jr., in *The Song of Songs: Interpreted by Early Christian and Medieval Commentators*, The Church's Bible (Grand Rapids: Eerdmans, 2003), 167–72; tr. Feiss, VTT 2:113–136].

Grammatica   *De grammatica*, ed. Baron, *Opera propaedeutica*, 75–163 [*On Grammar*].

In Hier. cael.   *Commentariorium in hierarchiam caelestem*, PL 175.923–1154 [*Commentary on the Celestial Hierarchy*].

In Eccl.   *In Salomonis Ecclesiasten homiliae*, PL 175.113–256 [*Homilies on Ecclesiastes*].

Inst. nov.   *De institutione novitiorum*, ed. and tr. P. Sicard, et. al., *Oeuvre*, 1:18–114 [*Instruction of Novices*].

Lament.   *Adnotatiunculae elucidatoriae in Threnos Jeremiae*, PL 175.255–322 [*On Lamentations*].

Laude car.   *De laude caritatis*, ed. and tr. P. Sicard, *Oeuvre*, 1:182–207; tr. Vincenzo Liccaro, *Didascalicon, I doni della promessa divina, L'essenza dell'amore, Discorso in lode del divino amore* (Milan: Rusconi, 1987); [*On the Praise of Charity*, tr. A Religious of the C.S.M.V., *The Divine Love*, 9–24; tr. Joseph McSorley, *Hugh's Praise of Love* (Patterson, NJ: St Anthony Guild Press, 1941), first printed in *Catholic World* 72 (1901): 727–37; tr. Harkins, VTT 2:151–68].

Libellus   *Libellus de formatione arche* (*De arca Noe mystica*), ed. P. Sicard, CCCM 176 (Turnhout: Brepols, 2001): 121–62 [*Little Book on Forming the Ark*, tr. Jessica Weiss, *A Little Book about Constructing Noah's Ark*, in Caruthers and Ziolkowski, eds., *Medieval Craft of Memory*, 41–70].

Mappa   *Descriptio mappe mundi*, ed. P. Gautier Dalché (Paris: Études Augustiniennes, 1988), with corrections and additions suggested in Gautier Dalché, "La Descriptio mappe mundi de Hugues de Saint-Victor: retractatio et additamenta," in J. Longère, ed., *L'abbaye Parisienne de Saint-Victor au Moyen Âge*, Bibliotheca Victorina 1 (Turnhout: Brepols, 1991), 143–79 [*Description of the Map of the World*].

Maria porta   *Maria porta*, ed. and tr. Jollès, *Oeuvre* 2:282 [*Mary as Gate*].

Meditatione   *De meditatione*, ed. and tr. Baron, *Six opuscules spirituels*, SC 155 (Paris: Cerf, 1969): 44–59 [*On Meditation*].

*Misc.   *Miscellanea*, PL 177.469–900 (Many are not authentic; those by Hugh of St Victor are concentrated in Books 1 and 2), PL 177.469–588) [*Miscellanea*].

Orat. dom.   *De oratione dominica*, PL 175.774–89 [*On the Lord's Prayer*].

Potestate   *De potestate et uoluntate Dei*, PL 176.839–42 [*The Power and Will of God*].

Quat. volunt.   *De quatuor voluntatibus*, PL 176.841–46 [*The Four Wills of Christ*].

Quid vere	*Quid vere diligendum sit*, ed. and tr. Baron, *Six opuscules*, 94–99 [*What Truly Should be Loved?* tr. Butterfield, VTT 2:169–82].
Quinque sept.	*De quinque septenis*, ed. and tr. Baron, *Six opuscules*, 100–19 [*The Five Sevens*].
Practica	*Practica geometriae*, ed. Baron, *Opera propaedeutica*, 15–64 [*Practical Geometry*, tr. Frederick A. Homann, Mediaeval Philosophical Texts in Translation, 29 (Milwaukee: Marquette University Press, 1991)].
Sacr. dial.	*De sacramentis dialogus*, PL 176.17–42 [*Dialogue on the Sacraments*].
Sacr.	*De sacramentis christianae fidei*, PL 176.173–618; ed. Rainer Berndt, Corpus Victorinun, Textus historici 1 (Münster: Aschendorff, 2008 [*On the Sacraments of the Christian Faith (De Sacramentis) of Hugh of Saint Victor*, trans. R. Deferrari (Cambridge, MA: The Mediaeval Academy of America, 1951; repr. Eugene, OR: Wipf & Stock, 2007); *Über die Heiltümer des christlichen Glaubens*, tr. Peter Knauer, ed. Rainer Berndt, Corpus Victorinum, Schriften 1 (Münster: Aschendorff, 2010)].
Sapientia	*De sapientia Christi*, PL 176.845–56 [*The Wisdom of Christ*].
Script.	*De scripturis et scriptoribus sacris*, PL 175.9–28 [*On Sacred Scriptures and their Authors*, partially tr. Denys Turner, *Eros and Allegory*, CS 156 (Kalamazoo: Cistercian, 1995), 267–74].
Sent. div.	*Sententiae de divinitate*, ed. Piazzoni, "Ugo di San Vittore 'auctor' delle 'Sententiae de divinitate,'" *Studi Medievali*, 3rd series, 23 (1982): 861–955 [*Sentences of Divinity*, tr. C. Evans, VTT 1:111–77].
Sent. liber	"Le *Liber Magistri Hugonis*," ed. D. van den Eynde, *Franciscan Studies* 23 (1963): 268–99.
Sent. mag.	"*Sententiae magistri Hugonis Parisiensis*," ed. L. Ott, RTAM 27 (1960): 29–41.
Sent. quel.	"Quelques recueils d'écrits attribués à Hugues de Saint-Victor," ed. O. Lottin, RTAM 25 (1958): 248–84.
Sent. quest.	"Questions inédits de Hugues de Saint-Victor," ed. O. Lottin, RTAM 26 (1959): 177–213; 27 (1960): 42–60.
Sent. rep.	P. Sicard, "Repertorium Sententiarum quae in saeculi XII Hugonis de Sancto Victore operum codicibus inveniuntur," *Sacris erudiri* 32 (1991): 171–221.

Septem donis	*De septem donis Spiritus sancti*, ed. and tr. Baron, *Six opuscules*, 120–33 [*The Seven Gifts of the Holy Spirit*].
Spir. dijud.	*De eo quod spiritualis dijudict omnia, et de judicio veri et boni* = *Miscellanea* 1.1, PL 177.469–77 [*The Spiritual Person Judges All*].
Subst. dilect.	*De substantia dilectionis*, ed. and tr. Baron, *Six opuscules*, 82–93; tr. Vincenzo Liccaro, *Didascalicon, I doni della promessa divina, L'essenza dell'amore, Discorso in lode del divino amore* (Milan: Rusconi, 1987); [*On the Substance of Love*, tr. A Religious of the C.S.M.V., Hugh of Saint-Victor, *Selected Spiritual Writings*, 187–91; tr. Butterfield, VTT 2:139–48].
Tribus diebus	*De tribus diebus*, ed. D. Poirel, CCCM 177 (Turnhout: Brepols, 2002): 3–70 [ed. and tr. Vincenzo Liccaro, *I tre giorni dell'invisbile luce; L'unione del corpo e dello spirito*. Classici della Filosofia Cristiana 6 (Florence: Sansoni, 1974), 15–181; *On the Three Days*, tr. Feiss, VTT 1:61–102].
Tribus rerum	*De tribus rerum subsistentiis*, ed. C. H. Buttimer, *Didascalicon*, 134–35 [*The Three Subsistences*].
Unione	*De unione spiritus et corporis*, ed. A. Piazzonni, "Il *De unione spiritus et corporis* di Ugo di San Vittore," *Studi Medievali*, 21 (1980): 861–88; ed. and tr. Vincenzo Liccaro, *I tre giorni dell'invisbile luce; L'unione del corpo e dello spirito*. Classici della Filosofia Cristiana 6 (Florence: Sansoni, 1974), 182–242 [*The Union of Spirit and Body*].
Vanitate	*De vanitate mundi*, ed. PL 176.703–39; ed. Karl Müller, *Hugo von St. Viktor, Soliloquium de arrha animae und De vanitate mundi*. Kleine Texte für Vorlesungen und Übungen 123 (Bonn: A. Marcus and E. Weber, 1913), 26–48 (Books 1 and 2) [*The Vanity of the World*, tr. A Religious of the C.S.M.V. [Sr. Penelope Lawson] in Hugh of Saint-Victor, *Selected Spiritual Writings*, 157–82].
Verbo Dei	*De Verbo Dei*, ed. and tr. R. Baron, *Six opuscules*, 60–81 [*The Word of God*].
Verbo inc.	*De Verbo incarnato collationes tres*, PL 177.320–24 [*Incarnate Word*].
Virtute orandi	*De virtute orandi*, ed. H. Feiss, tr. P. Sicard, et. al. *Oeuvre* 1:126–61 [*The Power of Prayer*].

ADAM OF ST VICTOR

Sequentiae | *Sequentiae*, ed. Jean Grosfillier, *Les sequences d'Adam de Saint-Victor: Étude littéraire (poétique et rhétorique). Textes et traductions, commentaires*, Bibliotheca Victorina 20 (Turnhout: Brepols, 2008): 252–481; ed. E. Misset and P. Aubry, *Les proses d'Adam de Saint-Victor, texte et musique* (Paris: 1900); ed. G. Dreves and Clemens Blume, *Analecta Hymnica*, vols. 54 and 55 (Leipzig: 1915, 1922); ed. and tr. Bernadette Jollés, *Quatorze proses du XIIe siècle à la louange de Marie*, Sous la Règle de saint Augustin (Turnhout: Brepols, 1994) [ed. and tr. Digby Wrangham, Adam of St Victor, *Liturgical Poetry*, 3 vols. (London: Kegan Paul, Trench, 1881) ed. and tr. Juliet Mousseau, Dallas Medieval Texts (Leuven: Peeters, 2011)].

ANDREW OF ST VICTOR

Hept. | *Expositio super Heptateuchum*, ed. Charles Lohr and Rainer Berndt, CCCM 53 (Turnhout: Brepols, 1986) [*On the Heptateuch*].

Reg. | *Expositio Hystorica in Librum Regum*, ed. F. A. van Liere, CCCM 53A (Turnhout: Brepols, 1996) [*Commentary on Samuel and Kings*, tr. F. A. van Liere, CCT 3 (Turnhout: Brepols, 2010)].

Salom. | *Expositiones historicae in Libros Salomonis*, ed. Rainer Berndt, CCCM 53B (Turnhout: Brepols, 1991) [*Commentary the Books of Solomon*].

Ezech. | *Expositio in Ezechielem*, ed. Michael Signer, CCCM 53E (Turnhout: Brepols, 1991) [*Commentary on Ezekiel*].

Danielem | *Expositio super Danielem*, ed. Mark A. Zier, CCCM 53F (Turnhout: Brepols, 1990) [*Commentary on Daniel*].

XII prophetas | *Expositio super duodecim prophetas*, ed. F. A. van Liere and M. A. Zier, CCCM 53G (Turnhout: Brepols, 2007) [*Commentary on the Twelve Minor Prophets*].

ACHARD OF ST VICTOR

Discretione | *De discretione animae, spiritus et mentis,* ed. G. Morin, "Un traité faussement attribué à Adam de Saint-Victor," *Aus*

der Geisteswelt des Mittelalters, BGPTMA, Supplementband 3/1 (Münster: Aschendorff, 1935), 251–62; ed. N. M.
Häring, "Gilbert of Poitiers, Author of the 'De discretione
animae, spiritus et mentis' commonly attributed to Achard
of Saint Victor," MS 22 (1960): 148–91 [*On the Distinction
of Soul, Spirit and Mind*, tr. H. Feiss, Achard of Saint Victor, *Works*, CS 165 (Kalamazoo: Cistercian Publications,
2001): 353–74].

Serm.   De unitate Dei et pluralitate creaturarum, ed. and tr.

Serm.   *Sermons inédits*, ed. Châtillon, TPMA 17 (Paris: J. Vrin,
1970) [*Sermons*, tr. H. Feiss, *Works*, 59–351; *Sermon 5*,
tr. Feiss, VTT 2:247–59].

Unitate   *De unitate Dei et pluralitate creaturarum*, ed. and tr.
E. Martineau, (Saint-Lambert des Bois: Franc-Dire, 1987)
[*On the Unity of God*, tr. H. Feiss, *Works*, 375–480].

RICHARD OF ST VICTOR

XII patr.   *De duodecim patriarchis* (*Benjamin Minor*), ed. J. Châtil-
lon, *Les douze patriarches ou Beniamin minor*, SC 419
(Paris: Cerf, 1997) [*The Twelve Patriarchs*, tr. Clare Kirch-
berger, Richard of Saint-Victor, *Selected Writings* (New
York: Harper, 1955), 78–128; tr. Grover Zinn, Richard of
St Victor, *The Twelve Patriarchs, The Mystical Ark, Book
Three of the Trinity*, Classics of Western Spirituality (New
York: Paulist, 1979), 51–147].

*Abdiam   *In Abdiam*, PL 175.371–406 [*On Obadiah*]

Ad me clamat   *Ad me clamat ex Seir*, ed. J. Ribaillier, Richard de Saint-
Victor, *Opuscules théologiques*, TPMA 15 (Paris: J. Vrin,
1967): 256–80 [*He Calls to Me from Seir*].

Adnot. Psalm.   *Mysticae adnotationes in Psalmos*, PL 196.265–402 [*Mystical Notes on the Psalms*].

Apoc.   *In Apocalypsim*, PL 196.683–888 [*On the Apocalypse*].

Apprehendet   *Apprehendet messis vindemiam*, ed. B. Hauréau, *Notices et
extraits de quelques manuscripts latins de la Bibliothèque
Nationale*, 5 vols. (Paris: C. Klincksieck, 1890–93), 1:116–17
[*Harvest*].

Arca Moys.   *De arca Moysi* (*De arca mystica; Benjamin major*), ed.
Marc-Aeilko Aris, *Contemplatio: Philosophische Studien
zum Traktat Benjamin Maior des Richard von St. Victor*.

Mit einer verbesserten Edition des Textes, Fuldaer Studien 6 (Frankfurt am Main: Josef Knecht, 1996) [*Ark of Moses*, tr. Grover Zinn, *Twelve Patriarchs, The Mystical Ark, Book Three of the Trinity*, Classics of Western Spirituality (New York: Paulist, 1979) 149–343].

*Cant.
In Cantica canticorum explanatio, PL 196.405A–534A [*Explanation of the Song of Songs*].

Carb.
Carbonum et cinerum, ed. J. Châtillon, *Trois opuscules spirituels de Richard de Saint-Victor* (Paris: Études augustiniennes, 1986), 253–63 [*Coals and Ashes*].

Causam
Causam quam nesciebam, ed. Châtillon, *Trois opuscules*, 201–21 [*A Cause I Did Not Know*].

Comp. Christi
De Comparatione Christi ad florem et Mariae ad virgam, PL 196.1031–32 [*Comparing Christ to a Flower and Mary to a Branch*].

Concord.
De concordantia temporum, PL 196.241–56 [*Comparative Chronology*].

Decl. nonn. diff.
Declarationes nonnullarum difficultatum Scripturae, ed. J. Ribaillier, *Opuscules théologiques*, 201–14 [*Resolutions of Some Difficulties in Scripture*].

Diff. pecc.
De differentia peccati mortalis et venialis, ed. Ribaillier, *Opuscules théologiques*, 291–93 [*The Difference between Mortal and Venial Sin*].

Diff. sac.
De differentia sacrificii Abrahae a sacrificio Beatae Mariae Virginis, PL 196.1043–60 [*The Difference between the Sacrifices of Abraham and Mary*].

Egyptus est
Egyptus est uita secularis, ed. Hauréau, *Notices et extraits*, 1:243 [*Egypt Is Secular Life*].

Emman.
De Emmanuele, PL 196.601–66 [*On Emmanuel*].

Erud.
De eruditione hominis interioris, PL 196.1229–1366 [*Instruction of the Interior Person*].

Exterm.
De exterminatione mali et promotione boni, PL 196.1073–1116 [*On Exterminating Evil and Promoting Good*].

Gem. pasch.
Sermo in die pasche, PL 196.1059–74 [*Twofold Pasch*]. (This sermon is a conflation of two sermons, one for Palm Sunday, one for Easter; only the first is by Richard.)

Illa die
In illa die, ed. Châtillon, *Trois opuscules*, 123–52 [*On That Day*].

In medio
In medio annorum, PL 196.401–4 [*In the Midst of the Years*].

*Joel	*In Joel*, prologue ed. A. Wilmart, "Le commentaire sur le prophète Nahum attribué à Julien de Tolède," *Bulletin de littérature ecclésiastique*, 23 (1922): 276–78, rest of text in PL 175.321–72 [*On Joel*].
Jud. pot.	*De iudiciaria potestate in finali et universali iudicio*, ed. Ribaillier, *Opuscules théologiques*, 142–54 [*The Power of Judgment*].
LE	*Liber exceptionum*, ed. Jean Châtillon, TPMA, 5 (Paris: J. Vrin, 1958) [*Book of Notes*].
Mater mentis	*Tolle puerum et matrem eius . . . Mater mentis puritas*, ed. Hauréau, *Notices et extraits*, 1:116 [*Take the Child . . . The Mother*].
Med. Plagis	*De meditandis plagis quae circa finem mundi evenient* (PL 196.201–12 [*Meditating on the Plagues*]
*Misc.	*Miscellanea* 4.43–47 (PL 177.721–25); *Miscellanea* 4.52 (PL 177.726–27); *Miscellanea* 5.4 (PL 177.753–54); *Miscellanea* 6.14 (PL 177.817–19); *Miscellanea* 6.27 (PL 177.826–27); *Miscellanea* 6.28 (PL 177.827–30); *Miscellanea* 6.33 (PL 177.831–36); Jean Châtillon, "Autour des *Miscellanea* attribué à Hugues de Saint-Victor. Note sur la redaction brève de quelques ouvrages ou opuscules spirituels de prieur Richard," *Revue d'ascétique et de mystique* 25 (1949): 299–305 [*Miscellanea*].
Misit Her.	*Misit Herodes rex manus* (PL 141.277–306) [*Herod the King*].
Missione	*De missione Spiritus sancti sermo*, PL 196.1017–32 [*Sermon on the Sending of the Holy Spirit*].
*Nahum	*In Nahum*, PL 96.705–58 + A. Wilmart, "Le commentaire sur le prophète Nahum attribué à Julien de Tolède," *Bulletin de littérature ecclésiastique*, 23 (1922): 262–65 [*On Nahum*].
Nonn. alleg.	*Nonnullae allegoriae tabernaculi foedoris*, PL 196.191–202 [*Some Allegories on the Tabernacle of the Covenant*, tr. G. Zinn, *Twelve Patriarchs*, 344–70].
*Pascha	*Sermo in die Pascha*, PL 196.1067–74 [*Sermon on Easter*].
Post sex annos	*Post sex annos*, ed. Hauréau, *Notices et extraits*, 1.112–14 [*After Six Years*].
Pot. lig.	*De potestate ligandi et solvendi*, ed. Ribaillier, *Opuscules théologiques*, 77–110 [*The Power to Bind and Loose*].
Proles	*Tolle puerum et matrem eius . . . Proles de uirgine matre*, ed. Hauréau, 1.116 [*Take the Child . . . The Offspring*].

Quat. grad.	*De quatuor gradibus violentae caritatis*, ed. and tr. G. Dumeige, *Ives, Épître à Séverin sur la charité; Richard de Saint-Victor, Les quatre degrés de la violente charité*, TPMA 3 (Paris: J. Vrin, 1955): 126–77 [*On the Four Degrees of Violent Love*, partially translated Clare Kirchberger, Selected Writings, 213–33; tr. A. Kraebel, VTT 2:261–300].
Quest.	*De quaestionibus Regulae sancti Augustini solutis*, ed. M. Colker, *Traditio* 18 (1962): 201–23 [*Questions on the Rule of St Augustine*].
Quid eis	*Quid eis dabis, Domine?* ed. Hauréau, *Notices et extraits*, 1.118–19 [*What Will You Give Them?*].
Quomodo Christus	*Quomodo Christus ponitur in signum populorum* (PL 196.523–28) [*How Christ Is a Sign for the Peoples*].
Quomodo Spiritus	*Quomodo Spiritus Sanctus est amor Patris et Filii*, ed. Ribaillier, *Opuscules théologiques*, 164–66 [*How the Holy Spirit is the Love of Father and Son*].
Ramis	*Sermo in ramis palmarum*, PL 196.1059–67 [*Sermon on Palm Sunday*].
Sanct. hodie	*Sanctificamini hodie*, ed. Hauréau, 1.243 [*Be Sanctified Today*].
Sac. David	*De sacrificio David prophetae et quid distet inter ipsum et sacrificium Abrahae patriarchae*, PL 196.1031–42 [*On the Sacrifice of David*].
Serm. cent.	*Sermones centum*, PL 177.899–1210 [*One Hundred Sermons*].
*Serm. Greg.	*Sermo in honorem Gregorii Magni*, partially ed. Jean Châtillon in "Contemplation, action et predication d'après un sermon inédit de Richard de Saint-Victor en l'honneur de saint Grégoire-le-Grand," *L'homme devant dieu*, Mélanges offerts au Père de Lubac, Theologie 5–58 (Paris: Aubier, 1963–64), 2:89–98 [*Sermon in Honor of St Gregory*].
Sex sunt dies	*Sex sunt dies*, ed. Hauréau, 1.243 [*There Are Six Days*].
Sp. blasph.	*De spiritu blasphemiae*, ed. Ribaillier, *Opuscules théologiques*, 121–29 [*On the Spirit of Blasphemy*].
Statu	*De statu interioris hominis post lapsum*, ed. Ribaillier, AHDLMA 42 (1967): 61–128 [*On the Interior State*].
Super exiit	*Super exiit edictum ou De tribus processionibus*, ed. J. Châtillon and W.-J. Tulloch, *Richard de Saint-Victor, Sermons et opuscules spirituels inédits: L'édit d'Alexandre ou Les trios*

processions (n.p.: Desclée de Brouwer, 1951) [*On the Three Processions*].

Tab. foed.   *Expositio difficultatum suborientium in expositione tabernaculi foederis*, PL 196.211–56) [*Explanation of Difficulties regarding the Tabernacle*].

Templo   *De templo Salominis*, PL 196.223–42 [*On Temple of Solomon*].

Trin.   *De Trinitate*, ed. J. Ribaillier, TPMA 6 (Paris: J. Vrin, 1958); ed. and tr. G. Salet, *La Trinité*, SC 67 (Paris: Cerf, 1959) [*On the Trinity*, tr. C. Evans, VTT 1:209–382].

Tribus per.   *De tribus personis appropriatis in Trinitate*, ed. Ribaillier, *Opuscules théologiques*, 182–87 [*On Trinitarian Appropriations*].

Verbo Eccl.   *De illo verbo Ecclesiastici "Eleemonsina patris non erit in obliuionem,"* ed. Ribaillier, *Opuscules théologiques*, 295–96 [*The Alms of the Father*].

Verbis ap.   *De verbis apostolicis*, ed. Ribaillier, *Opuscules théologiques*, 314–17 [*The Words of the Apostle*].

Verbis Is.   *In die illa nutriet*, ed. Châtillon, *Trois opuscules* (Paris, Études Augustiniennes, 1986), 55–152 [*On that Day*].

Vis. Ezek.   *In visionem Ezechielis*, ed. Jochen Schröder, *Gervasius von Canterbury, Richard von Saint-Victor und die Methodik der Bauerfassung im 12. Jahrhundert*, 2 vols., Veröffentlichung der Abteilung Architekturgeschichte des Kunsthistorischen Instituts der Universität zu Köln 71 (Cologne: Kleikamp, 2000), 2: 372–553 (PL 196.527–606) [*The Vision of Ezekiel*].

GODFREY OF ST VICTOR

Microcosmus   *Microcosmus*, ed. Philippe Delhaye (Lille: Facultés catholiques, 1951) [partially tr. Feiss, VTT 2:301–41].

Fons   *Fons philosophiae*, ed. Pierre Michaud-Quantin, Analecta mediaevalia Namurcensia 8 (Louvain: Nauwelaerts/ Namur: Godenne, 1956) [tr. Edward Synan, *The Fountain of Philosophy* (Toronto: Pontifical Institute of Mediaeval Studies, 1972)].

Praeconium   "Praeconium Augustini," ed. Philip Damon, MS 22 (1960): 92–107.

Sermo gen. cap.	*Sermo in generali capitulo,* ed. Helmut Riedlinger, *Die Make-llosigkeit der Kirche in den lateinischen Hoheliedkommentaren des Mittelalters,* BGPTMA 38/3 (Münster: Aschendorff, 1958), 188–93 [*Sermon at a General Chapter*].
Sermo quadr.	[Fragment of a draft for a sermon for the First Sunday of Lent], ed. Françoise Gasparri, "Textes autographes d'auteurs victorins du xiie siècle," *Scriptorium* 35 (1981): 281–84.
Sermo St Victor	*Sermo de omnibus sanctis et specialiter de Sancto Victore,* partially ed. Philippe Delhaye, *Le Microcosmus de Gode-froy de Saint-Victor, Étude théologique* (Lille: Facultés catholique/Gembloux: J. Duculot, 1951), 232–33 [*Sermon for All Saints and St Victor*].
Sermo Sanct.	*Sermo in die omnium sanctorum,* ed. Delhaye, *Le Microcosmus,* 233–43 [*Sermon for All Saints*].

WALTER OF ST VICTOR

Serm. ined.	Gaulteri a Sancto Victore et quorumdam aliorum, *Sermones inediti triginta sex,* ed. J. Châtillon, CCCM 30 (Turnhout: Brepols, 1975) [*Sermons*].
Contra quat.	*Contra quatuor labyrinthos Franciae de Gauthier de Saint-Victor,* ed. P. Glorieux, AHDLMA, 19, Année 1952 (1953): 195–334 [*Against the Four Labyrinths of France*].

WRITINGS ASSOCIATED WITH ST VICTOR

Liber ordinis	*Liber ordinis Sancti Victoris Parisiensis,* ed. Luc Jocqué and Ludo Milis, CCCM 61 (Turnhout: Brepols, 1984).
Sent. divinit.	*Sententiae divinitatis,* ed. B. Geyer, *Die Sententiae divinitatis. Ein Sentenzenbuch der gilbertschen Schule, aus den Handschriften zum ersten Male herausgegen und historisch untersucht,* BGPTMA 7 (Münster: Aschendorff, 1909).
Summa Sent.	Odo of Lucca, *Summa Sententiarum,* PL 176.41–174.

JEROME

Heb. nom.   *Liber interpretationis Hebraicorum nominum*, ed. P. de La-
              garde, CCL 72 (Turnhout: Brepols, 1969): 58–161.

In Ps.   *Tractatus sive homiliae in psalmos. In Marci evangelium.
              Alia varia argumenta*, ed. G. Morin, et al. CCL78 (Turn-
              hout: Brepols, 1958).

AUGUSTINE

C. Jul. imp.   *Contra Julianum opus imperfectum*, ed. M. Zelzer, CSEL
                85/2 (Vienna: Verlag der Österreichischen Akademie der
                Wissenschaften, 2004) (PL 45.1049–1608).

C. ep. Parm.   *Contra epistolam Parmeniani*, ed. M. Petschenig, CSEL 51
                (Vienna: F. Tempsky, 1908).

C. Faust.   *Contra Faustum Manicheum* (PL 42.207–518) [*Answer to
                Faustus, A Manichean*, tr. R. Teske (Hyde Park, NY: New
                City Press, 2007)].

C. s. Ar.   *Contra sermonem Arianorum*, ed. P.-M. Hombert, CCL
                87A (Turnhout: Brepols, 2009) (PL 42.683–708).

Cat. rud.   *De catechizandis rudibus*, ed. G. Combès and J. Farges,
                Le magistère Chrétien, Oeuvres de saint Augustin 11 (Paris:
                Desclée de Brouwer, 1949): 28–147; ed. I. B. Bauer, in *De
                fide rerum invisibilium*, et alia, CCL 46 (Turnout: Brepols,
                1969) [*Instructing Beginners in Faith*, tr. Raymond Can-
                ning (Hyde Park, NY: New City Press, 2007)].

Civ. Dei   *De civitate Dei*, ed. B. Dombart and A. Kalb, CCL 47–48
                (Turnhout: Brepols, 1955) [*The City of God*, tr. H. Betten-
                son (New York: Penguin, 1986); tr. R. W. Dyson (New
                York: Cambridge, 1998)].

Conf.   *Confessiones*, ed. L. Verheijen, *Confessionum Libri XIII*,
                CCL 37 (Turnhout: Brepols, 1990): 1–273; ed. J. J.
                O'Donnell, *Confessions*, vol. 1 (Oxford: Clarendon, 1992);
                tr. Maria Boulding, (Hyde Park, NY: New City Press,
                1997); tr. H. Chadwick (New York: Oxford, 1991)].

Conl. Max.   *Conlatio cum Maximino Arianorum episcopo*, ed. P.-M.
                Hombert, CCL 87A (Turnhout: Brepols, 2001) (PL
                42.709–42).

Div. quaest. 83	*De diversis quaestionibus* LXXXIII, ed. Almut Mutzenbecher, CCL 44A (Turnhout: Brepols, 1975): 3–249 (PL 40:11–100) [tr. Boniface Ramsey, *Responses to Miscellaneous Questions* (Hyde Park, NY: New City Press, 2008)].
Doc. Chr.	*De doctrina Christiana*, ed. J. Martin, CCL 32 (Turnhout: Brepols, 1962): 1–167; ed. G. Combès and J. Farges, *Le magistère chrétien*, 168–541 [tr. Edmund Hill, *Teaching Christianity* (Hyde Park, NY: New City Press, 1996)].
En. Ps.	*Enarrationes in Psalmos*, ed. E. Dekkers and J. Fraipont, CCL 38–40 (Turnhout: Brepols, 1956) [tr. Maria Boulding, *Expositions of the Psalms*, 6 vols. (Hyde Park, NY: New City Press, 2000–2004)].
Ench.	*Enchiridion ad Laurentium de fide spe et caritate*, ed. J. Rivière, *Exposés généraux de la foi*, Oeuvres de saint Augustin 9 (Paris: Desclée de Brouwer, 1947): 102–327; ed. E. Evans, CCL 46 (Turnhout: Brepols, 1969) [tr. Bruce Harbert, *The Augustine Catechism: The Enchiridion on Faith, Hope, and Love* (Hyde Park, NY: New City Press, 2008)].
Ep.	*Epistolae*, ed. A. Goldacher, CSEL 34, 44, 57, 58 (Vienna: F. Tempsky, 1895–1923); *Epistolae ex duobus codicibus nuper in lucem prolatae*, ed. J. Divjak, CSEL 88 (Vienna: Hoelder-Pichler-Tempsky, 1981) [tr. Roland Teske, *Letters*, 4 vols. (Hyde Park, NY: New City Press, 2001–5)].
F. et symb.	*De fide et symbolo*, ed. J. Zycha, CSEL 41 (Vienna: F. Tempsky, 1900); ed. J. Rivière, *Exposés généraux*, 8–75 [ed. and tr. E. P. Meijering (Amsterdam: J. C. Gieben, 1987); tr. in *On Christian Belief* (Hyde Park, NY: New City Press, 2005)].
Gn. litt.	*De Genesi ad litteram*, ed. J. Zycha, CSEL 28.1 (Vienna: F. Tempsky, 1894): 1–456 [tr. Edmund Hill, *The Literal Meaning of Genesis* in *On Genesis* (Hyde Park, NY: New City Press, 2002), 155–506].
In 1 Jo.	*In Primam epistolam Joannis*, ed. P. Agaësse, *Commentaire de la Première Épître de S. Jean*, SC 75 (Paris: Cerf, 1994) (PL 35.1977–2062) [tr. John W. Rettig, *Tractates on the First Epistle of John*, FOC 92 (Washington, DC: The Catholic University of America, 1995): 97–277].
Jo. ev. tr.	*In Johannis evangelium tractatus*, ed. R. Willems, CCL 36 (Turnhout: Brepols, 1954) [*Tractates on the Gospel of John*, tr. John W. Rettig, FOC 78, 79, 88, 90, 92 (Washington, DC: The Catholic University of America, 1988–95)].

Lib. arb.	*De libero arbitrio,* ed. W. Green, CCL 29 (Turnhout: Brepols, 1970) (CCL 29) [tr. Mark Pontifex, *The Problem of Free Choice,* ACW 22 (Westminster, MD: Newman, 1955)].
Mor.	*De moribus ecclesiae catholicae et de moribus Manichaeorum,* ed. J. B. Bauer, CSEL 90 (Vienna: Hoelder-Pichler-Tempsky, 1992); ed. B. Roland-Gosselin, *La morale chrétienne,* Oeuvres de saint Augustin 1 (Paris: Desclée de Brouwer, 1936): 30–123 (PL 32.1309–78).
Serm,	*Sermones,* PL 38–39 [tr. Edmund Hill, *Sermons,* 11 vols. (Hyde Park, NY: New City Press, 1990–)].
Spir. et litt.	*De spiritu et littera,* ed. C. Urba and J. Zycha, CSEL 60 (Vienna: F. Tempsky, 1913). [tr. John Burnaby, in *On the Spirit and the Letter,* Library of Christian Classics 8 (Philadelphia: Westminser, 1955).]
Trin.	*De Trinitate,* ed. W. J. Mountain and F. Glorie, CCL 50, 50A (Turnhout: Brepols, 1968) [tr. Edmund Hill, *On the Trinity* (Hyde Park, NY: New City Press, 1991)].
Vera rel.	*De vera religione,* tr. K.-D. Daur, CCL 32 (Turnhout: Brepols, 1962): 171–260 [*On True Religion,* tr. J. H. S. Burleigh [Chicago: Henry Regnery, 1968; tr. in *On Christian Belief* (Hyde Park, NY: New City Press, 2005)].

Boethius

Con. phil.	*De Consolatione philosophiae,* ed. L. Bieler, CCL 94 (Turnhout: Brepols, 1984); *The Theological Tractates; The Consolation of Philosophy,* ed. and tr. H. F. Stewart, E. Rand, and I. Tester, Loeb (Cambridge: Harvard, 1952), 128–413.

Gregory the Great

Dial.	*Dialogues,* ed. A. de Vogüé, SC 160, 265 (Paris; Cerf, 1979–80). [*Dialogues,* tr. O. Zimmerman, FOC 39 (Reprinted: Washington, DC: Catholic Univeristy of America Press, 2002).
Hom. ev.	*Homiliae in Evangelia,* ed. R. Étaix, CCL 76 (Turnhout: Brepols, 1999); *Homélies sur l'Evangile,* ed. R. Étaix, et. al. SC 485, 522 (Paris: Cerf, 2005–8).

Hom. Ez.	*Homiliae in Hiezechielem,* ed. M. Adriaen, CCL 142 (Turnhout: Brepols, 1971); *Homélies sur Ézékiel,* ed. Charles Morel, SC 327, 360 (Paris: Cerf, 1986–90).
Mor.	*Moralia in Iob,* ed. M. Adriaen, CCL 143, 143A, 143B (Turnhout: Brepols, 1979–85); *Morales sur Job,* 1–2, ed. Gillet, SC32bis, (Paris: Cerf, 1989); *Morales sur Job,* 11–14, ed. A. Bocognano, SC 212 (Paris: Cerf, 1974); *Morales sur Job,* 15–16, ed. A. Bocognano, SC 221 (Paris: Cerf, 1975); *Morales sur Job,* 28–29, ed. M. Adriaen et. al., SC 476 (Paris: Cerf, 2003); *Morales sur Job,* 30–32, ed. M. Adriaen, et. al., SC 525 (Paris: Cerf, 2009).

Isidore of Seville

Etym.	*Etymologiarum sive Originum Libri XX,* ed. W. M. Lindsay, 2 vols. (Oxford: Clarendon Press, 1911); available online at http://penelope.uchicago.edu/Thayer/e/roman/texts/isidore/home.html [*Etymologies,* tr. Stephen A. Barney, et al. (New York: Cambridge, 2006)].

Bernard of Clairvaux

SBO	*Sancti Bernardi opera,* ed. Jean Leclercq, et al., 9 vols. (Rome: Editiones Cisterciensis, 1957–98).
SCC	*Sermones super Cantica canticorum,* SBO 1–2 [*On the Song of Songs,* tr. Kilian Walsh and Irene Edmonds, 4 vols, CF 4, 7, 31, 40 (Kalamazoo: Cistercian Publictions, 1971–83)].
Gradibus	*De gradibus superbiae et humilitatis,* SBO 3:13–59 [tr. M. B. Pennington, *The Steps of Humility and Pride* (Kalamazoo: Cistercian Publications, 1989).]

Peter Lombard

Sent.	*Sententiae in IV Libris Distinctae,* ed. I. Brady, SB 4–5 (Grottaferrata: Editiones Collegii S. Bonaventurae ad Claras Aquas, 1971–81 [*Sentences,* tr. Giulio Silano, 4 vols.

(Toronto: Pontifical Institute of Mediaeval Studies, 2007–10).]

Aelred of Rievaulx

Amicita   *De spiritali amicitia*, ed. A. Hoste, in *Opera ascetica*, ed. A. Hoste and C. H. Talbot, CCCM 1 (Turnhout: Brepols, 1971), 281–350 [*Spiritual Frendship*, tr. Lawrence C. Braceland, ed. Marsha L. Dutton, CF 5 (Collegeville, MN: Liturgical Press, 2010)].

Thomas Aquinas

Sum. theo.   *Summa theologiae*. Ed. Petrus Caramello. 3 vols. Turin: Marietti, 1952 [*Summa Theologica*. Tr. Fathers of the English Dominican Province. 3 vols. (New York: Benziger, 1947)].

GENERAL INTRODUCTION

Hugh Feiss OSB

> *We dare not rest the whole weight of the heart's longing in any finite good.*
>
> Gilbert Meilaender,
> "Creatures of Time and Place."[1]

> *what is this thing called love*
> *this funny thing*
> *called love*
> *just who can solve its mystery?*
> . . .
> *I ask the Lord*
> *in heaven above*
> *what is this thing*
> *called love?*
>
> Cole Porter (1929)

The Victorines do not speak of theology as an academic study or profession. They more often speak of *doctrina*, teaching as activity and content, which was an element in a vital progression from faith in hope and love to eternal life with the Triune God.[2] One learns the truth about God and about Christian love from three sources: experience, faith in divine authorities, and reasoning. These three avenues to the truth about love structure what follows. In the first two sections, which are concerned with experience and authority, the discussion will center on

---

[1]   Cited by Paul Lauritzen, "Intellectual Street Fighter: Gilbert Meilaender's Ethics of Everyday," *Commonweal*, vol. 137/10 (May 21, 2010): 15.

[2]   Richard of St Victor's theological method has received considerable scholarly scrutiny: Hugh B. Feiss, "Learning and the Ascent to God in Richard of St Victor" (STD diss., Rome: Pontificium Athenaeum Anselmianum, 1980), a shortened version of which was privately published under the same title (St Benedict, OR: [Mount Angel Abbey, 1979]); Dale M. Coulter, *Per visibilia ad invisibilia: Theological Method in Richard of St Victor (d. 1173)*, Bibliotheca Victorina 19 (Turnhout: Brepols, 2006); Elizabeth Reinhardt, "Das Theologieveständnis Richards von Sankt Viktor," in *What is "Theology" in the Middle Ages? Religious Cultures of Europe (11th–15th Centuries) as Reflected in their Self-Understanding*, ed. Mikolaj Olszewski, Archa Verbi, Subsidia 1 (Münster: Aschendorff, 2007): 85–103.

the theology of Hugh and Richard of St Victor. The third section will discuss how, in order to understand the nature, demands, and joys of love, all five authors represented in this collection apply faith-inspired reason to experience and to the authoritative teachings of Scripture as interpreted in the Church.

EXPERIENCE: HUGH OF ST VICTOR

Hugh of St Victor mentions experience a number of times. For example, he appeals to experience regarding seaworthy designs for ships[3] and notes the absence of experiential evidence for the movement of the "firmament."[4] The experience of temptation teaches the truth of the commandments.[5] Someone serious about the Christian life should have an experienced guide who fears neither error nor exhaustion.[6]

At one point, Hugh makes a theoretical distinction between ways of knowing: (1) by act, when the senses grasp something present, (2) by understanding, when something absent is thought about or something non-existent is imagined; and (3) by experience of one's internal feelings.[7] God cannot be grasped by any of these. Some things are investigated only for the sake of understanding; others pertain more especially to doing, which perfects knowledge through experience.

---

[3]   Archa Noe 1.4 (Sicard, 18.13–18 [PL 176.627A]; tr. Religious of C.S.M.V., 60–61). For texts and references on experience in Hugh's theology, see Pierre Miquel, Le vocabulaire latin de l'expérience spirituelle dans la tradition monastique et canoniale de 1050 à 1250, Théologie historique 17 (Paris: Beauchesne, 1989), 163–85.

[4]   Sacr. dial. (PL 176.21B).

[5]   Inst. nov. 7 (PL 176.933D).

[6]   Laude car. 7 (Sicard, 189 [PL 176.973A]; tr. Harkins, VTT 2:162).

[7]   Sacr. 1.10.2 (PL 176.328C): "Cum enim res quaelibet apud nos subsistant: vel per actum, quando videlicet praesentes sensu comprehenduntur, vel per intellectum, quando absentes vel etiam non existentes in similitudine sua et in imagine per intellectum capiuntur; vel etiam per experientiam, quando ea quae in nobis sunt sentiuntur a nobis, ut est gaudium, tristitia, timor et amor, quae subsistunt in nobis et sentiuntur a nobis: nullo horum modorum invisibilia Dei comprehenduntur nobis quae credi solum possunt comprehendi." ("Things of any sort subsist in us either through act, when some present object is grasped by sensation, or through understanding when absent things or even non-existent things are grasped in likeness and image through the understanding, or through experience, when we sense things within us, such as joy, sadness, fear, and love, which subsist within us and are sensed by us. We grasp the invisible things of God in none of these ways; they can only be grasped by being believed"). Throughout the introduction and notes, all translations are the author's, even if references to other English translations are provided.

Knowledge of the truth is not perfect unless the habit of virtue follows. Therefore, he [Pseudo-Dionysius] calls 'brightest doctrine,' that which consists in the habit of virtue, because the mistress of understanding is experience; and he knows virtue best who learns about it not just by hearing, but also by tasting and doing. In experience and in the habit of virtue, the knowledge of truth is made perfect.[8]

Hugh sometimes appeals to experience to understand the workings of divine love. God, like a human lover, sometimes lets the believer experience his presence; at other times God withdraws in order make the heart's desire for Him increase.[9] Hugh knew and believed that "charity never fails" (1 Cor. 13:8), but then he learned by experience how true this is.[10]

However, it is the experience of restlessness that looms largest in Hugh's understanding of human love, desire, and joy. At the beginning of his treatise *The Ark of Noah*, Hugh writes:

One time when I was sitting in the gathering of the brothers, and they were asking questions and I was answering, many things had been brought up. The conversation finally came to this. All of us together began most of all to wonder about and sigh at the instability and restlessness of the human heart. With intense desire they asked that they be shown what cause brings about such great changeability in the thoughts of the human heart, and then they urgently insisted that they be taught if there is any technique or exercise that could counter this great evil. And so we, insofar as God's inspiration enables, want to satisfy the love (*caritati*) of the brothers on both scores and to solve this knotty question on the basis of solid authority and reason.[11]

---

[8] *In Hier. coel.* 7 (PL 177.1061B): "Non enim perfectum facit cognitio veritatis, nisi habitus virtutis subsequatur. Idcirco lucidissimam doctrinam vocat, quae in habitu virtutis constat, quia magistra intelligendi experientia est; et ille optime virtutum novit, qui eam non audiendo solum, sed et gustando et faciendo didicit. In experientia et habitu virtutis, cognitio veritatis perficitur." The wider context of this statement is the distinction of three stages in the spiritual life: purgation, illumination, and perfection. It is possible to see this sort of experience of virtue as an instance of the third kind of knowledge mentioned in the previous note.

[9] *In Eccl.* 16 (PL 175.231BC); *Eulogium*, 1 (PL 176.987B; tr. Feiss, VTT 2:125).

[10] *Ep. 1, Ad Ranulphum de Mauriaco* (PL 176.1011A).

[11] *Archa Noe* 1.1 (Sicard, 3.1–12; tr. Religious of C.S.V.M., 45): "Cum sederem aliquando in conventu fratrum et, illis interrogantibus meque respondente, multa in medium prolata fuissent, ad hoc tandem deducta sunt verba ut de humani potissimum cordis instabilitate et inquietudine ammirari omnes simul et suspirare inciperemus. Cumque magno quidam desiderio exposcerent demonstrari sibi, que causa in corde hominis tantas cogitationum fluctuationes ageret, ac deinde si qua arte sive laboris cuiuslibet exercitatione huic tanto malo obviari posset summopere doceri flagitarent, nos, quantum Deo aspirante valuimus, in

In the *Ark of Noah*, and in other works, most notably his *Homilies on Ecclesiastes* and *The Vanity of the World,* Hugh examines the nature, causes, and remedies of the restlessness of the human heart. At this point what is important is his interest in the experience of such restlessness. Hugh's finds that "Solomon," the author of *Ecclesiastes*, knew by experience the vanity of seeking to find peace for his spirit in riches, pleasure, and knowledge; experience taught him that there is no secure harbor for the human heart in the changeable world.[12]

EXPERIENCE: RICHARD OF ST VICTOR

Richard of St Victor has a very high regard for experience as a source of knowledge.[13] Experiential knowledge is possible at every level of cognition, but what is most important for him is what one can learn through the experience of one's own inner life and efforts. Richard believes that people generally put more credence in what can be proven through experience than in what is arrived at by a process of reasoning.[14] Richard is not out of sympathy with this attitude, in spite of his great confidence in the power of reason.

The mind knows nothing better, more certainly, or more sublimely than what it has learned through experience. For the human soul, the proper and pre-eminent way of learning is to prove something by its own experience.[15] In matters of historical fact, as well as in the secrets

---

utroque caritati fratrum satisfacere volentes, utriusque questionis nodum ductis tam ex auctoriate quam ex ratione firmamentis solvimus."

[12] See the many references to Hugh's *Homilies on Ecclesiastes* and *The Vanity of the World* in Miquel, *Le vocabulaire latin*, 172–77.

[13] In this discussion of experience in Richard's thought, I draw on Feiss, "Learning and the Ascent to God." On Richard's idea of experience and the importance he attaches to it, see E. Cousins, "The Notion of Person in the De Trinitate of Richard of St Victor" (Ph.D. diss., Fordham University, 1966), 83–88; Gervais Dumeige, *Richard de Saint-Victor et l'idée chrétienne de l'amour* (Paris: Presses Universitaires de France, 1952), 159–60; Joseph Ebner, *Die Erkenntnislehre Richards von St. Viktor*, BGPTMA 19.4 (Munich: Aschendorff, 1917): 15–17; Miquel, *Le vocabulaire latin*, 186–200; Evans, tr. *On the Trinity*, VTT 1:356 nn. 40–42. E. Martineau, *De Unitate Dei et pluralitate creaturarum* (Saint-Lambert des Bois: Franc-Dire, 1987), 32–36, criticizes Richard's empiricism, contrasting it unfavorably with the *intellectualité* of Achard of St Victor.

[14] *Trin.* 4.8 (Ribaillier, 170.14–15; tr. Evans, VTT 1:274): "Sed magis judicant homines juxta id quod experientia probat quam juxta id quod ratiocinatio dictat." ("But people judge more according to what experience proves than according to what reasoning declares").

[15] *Erud.* 1.2 (PL 196.1235A): "Nihil autem melius, nil certius, nihilque sublimius animus agnoscit quam quod per experimentum didicit, et forte hic est proprius atque praecipuus, et

of the mystical life, the man of personal experience has particular authority.[16]

While reason can discover some things, others are the province of experience.[17] For one thing, experience gives sure knowledge of contingent things, whereas reason (or, more properly, understanding) is at home in the realm of necessary, unchanging realities.[18] Further, experience can foster knowledge of the natures of things[19] and of spiritual realities,[20] which in our present state we cannot comprehend through reasoning.[21] On the other hand, reason, utilizing the lessons of experi-

---

omnino sublimissimus humanae animae discendi modus, quando aliquid proprio experimento probamus" ("The mind knows nothing better, nothing more certainly, nothing more sublimely, than what it learns through experience, and perhaps this is the proper and preeminent and most utterly sublime way of learning for the human soul, when we prove something through our own experience"). *Erud.* 2.18 (PL 196.1317C): "Parva et parum certa est illa scientia, quam non adjuvat et confirmat rerum experientia" ("That knowledge is restricted and only slightly certain which the experience of things does not aid and confirm").

[16]   *Tab. foed.* 1.5 (PL 196.214C): "Libenter recipiatur Josephus in his quae per experientiam novit" ("Joseph is willingly received in those matters that he knows through experience"); *Arca Moys.* 5.19 (Aris, 148 [PL 196.192BC]; tr. Zinn, 343): "Melius hoc [mentis excessum] nos illorum peritia instruit, quos ad scientiae hujus plenitudinem non tam aliena doctrina quam propria experientia provexit" ("We learn about this better from the expertise of those who are brought to the fullness of this knowledge not so much by another's teaching as by their own experience"); *Adnot. Psalm.* 28 (PL 196.321A); cf. Ps.-Richard of St Victor, *In Cant.* 40 (PL 196.520AB).

[17]   *XII patr.* 79 (Châtillon, 318 [PL 196.56BC]; tr. Zinn, 136–37); *Adnot. Psalm.* 28 (PL 196.290D–291A).

[18]   *Trin.* 1.4 (Ribaillier, 89.12–15; tr. Evans, VTT 1:215): "Omnia que ceperunt esse ex tempore pro beneplacito Conditoris, possibile est esse, possibile est non esse. Unde et eo ipso eorum esse non tam ratiocinando colligitur quam experiendo probatur" ("All things which began to be in time by the good pleasure of their Creator can be and/or not be. Hence, for that very reason their being is not so much arrived at through reasoning as it is proven by experience"); *Trin.* 1.1 (Ribaillier, 86.10–12; tr. Evans, VTT 1:213): "Et temporalium quidem notitiam per ipsam experientiam apprehendimus; eternorum vero notitiam modo ratiocinando, modo credendo assurgimus" ("We gain knowledge of temporal things through our very experience; we rise to knowledge of eternal things sometimes through reasoning and sometimes through believing"); *Trin.* prol. (Ribaillier, 84.38–40; tr. Evans, VTT 1:211).

[19]   *Arca Moys.* 2.4 (Aris, 26 [PL 196.82D]; tr. Zinn, 179): "Modo autem ignorantiae tenebris involuti quoties de ea [natura rerum] aliquid quaerimus, per experientiae argumenta palpamus potius quam videmus" ("Now, however, we are enveloped in the darkness of ignorance, and whenever we seek something about it, we touch it through evidence of experience rather than see it").

[20]   *Trin.* 3.10 (Ribaillier, 145.24–25; tr. Evans VTT 1:255): "quod non capit intelligentia, persuadet michi tamen ipsa experientia" ("I am persuaded by experience about what intelligence does not grasp").

[21]   *Erud.* 2.18 (PL 196.1317B): "Multa enim quae per investigationem non possumus, per experientiam plenius et certius addiscimus" ("Many things that we cannot learn through investigation [=reasoning], we learn more fully and more certainly through experience").

ence, can reach where experience has no access.[22] However, even for those things that lie beyond experience, reason must find a springboard in experience before it can reach them.[23]

All nature is a book written by the hand of God, but human nature is so in a pre-eminent way. Experience of one's own nature can help lead the believer ultimately to contemplation of God and union with God. In the interior life of the Christian, immediate experience is particularly important in what concerns the divine presence to the soul and the resulting spiritual peace.[24] A second important role of experience in the spiritual life is educating one to knowledge of one's own limitations and of one's need for God.[25] Thirdly, experience is indispensable in the formation of conscience and moral discernment.[26]

In the effort to understand the truths of faith, human experience provides analogies and starting points for knowledge of Christian doctrine. For example, in *On the Trinity*, Richard draws on Christians' experience of the image of God in their own human nature. He states the principle clearly, utilizes it early in the book, and has recourse to it subsequently a number of times.

> In created nature we read what we ought to think or know regarding uncreated nature: every day we see how, by the operation of created nature, one existing being produces another, one existence proceeds from another. What then? Could it be that there is not, or cannot be, any such operation of nature in that most excellent uncreated nature? Thus, as often as we rise from viewing visible things to the contempla-

[22] *Arca Moys.* 1.6 (Aris, 13 [PL 196.71D], Zinn, 163): "ex invisibilibus per experientiam notis alia et alia ratiocinando colligit quae per experientiam non novit" ("from invisible things known through experience it gathers some things, and through reasoning it gathers others that it does not know through experience"); *Trin.* 5.6 (Ribaillier, 201.4-5): "Ex rebus quas per experientiam novimus, admonemur quid circa inexperta et divina querere debeamus" ("from the things that we know through experience we are admonished concerning what we ought to seek regarding divine things we have not experienced"); *XII patr.* 19 (Châtillon, 140 [PL 196.13CD]; tr. Zinn, 71); *Arca Moys.* 1.8 (Aris, 16 [PL 196.73C]; tr. Zinn, 166).

[23] *Trin.* 1.7 (Ribaillier, 92.4-7; tr. Evans, VTT 1:217).

[24] *Super exiit* 4 (Châtillon, 106.10-12); *XII patr.* 36 (Châtillon, 188 [PL 196.25C]; tr. Zinn, 90); *XII patr.* 38 (Châtillon, 198 [PL 196.27D]; tr. Zinn, 93); *Adnot. Psalm. 28* (PL 196.321A); cf. Ps.-Richard, *Cant.* 2 (PL 196.411C); *Cant.* 3 (PL 196.413B); *Cant.* 5 (PL 196.420B); *Cant.* 40 (PL 196.520AB).

[25] *Diff. sac.* (PL 196.1052D): "experientiae magisterio docearis de tua infirmitate vera sentire" ("Let the teaching of experience teach you to think truthfully about your infirmity"); *Diff. sac.* (PL 196.1052B); *Exterm.* 1.22 (PL 196.1269B); *De verbis Ap.* 2 (Ribaillier, 39).

[26] *Decl. nonn. diff.* 3.3 (Ribaillier, 208): "per propriam experientiam ad discretionem erudimur" ("we learn discernment from our own experience"); *XII patr.* 67 (Châtillon, 282 [PL 196.48AC]; tr. Zinn, 124); *Erud.* 2.18 (PL 196.1317B).

tion of invisible ones, we do nothing else than set up a sort of ladder whereby we can mentally ascend to the things which are above us. Hence, in this treatise the whole process of our reasoning will have its beginnings in the things that we know by experience.[27]

Richard speaks specifically of the experience of love. In seeking the necessary reasons for the Trinity of persons in God, the believer takes a clue from repeated experience that nothing is better; nothing brings greater happiness than love.[28]

In *On the Four Degrees of Violent Love*, Richard boldly undertakes to track the growth of Christian love of God by comparing love of God with passionate, even obsessive, erotic love. At the first stage both forms of love are good, but in the subsequent stages love of God is increasingly good whereas, as it advances through stages two to four, human love is increasingly bad.[29] To prepare the way for his discussion of passionate love of God, Richard sketches a series of remarkable vignettes about the stages of falling madly in love. His descriptions are as vivid as Catullus' poems about his love-become-hate for Lesbia or Andre Dubus III's descriptions of the obsessive and ultimately self-destructive loves of the protagonists in *House of Sand and Fog*.[30] Richard wrote at

---

[27]   *Trin.* 1.9, 10 (Ribaillier, 94.12–16, 95.12–16; tr. Evans, VTT 1:218–19): "In natura creata legimus quid de natura increata pensare vel estimare debeamus: videmus cotidie quomodo nature ipsius operatione existentia existentiam producit, et existentia de existentia procedit. Quid ergo? Numquid in illa superexcellenti natura operatio nature nulla erit aut omnino nil poterit? . . . Quotiens igitur per visibilium speculationem ad invisibilium contemplationem assurgimus, quid aliud quam quamdam velud scalam erigimus, per quam ad ea que supra nos sunt, mente ascendamus? Inde est quod in hoc tractatu omnis ratiocinationis nostre processus initium sumit ex his que per experientiam novimus." *Trin.* 3.9 (Ribaillier, 144.14–16; tr. Zinn, 382, tr. Evans, VTT 1:254): "Habet itaque homo quomodo legat et discat in seipso quid per contrarium estimare debeat de Deo suo. Conferamus in unum, si placet, que ratio ratiocinando invenit in natura divina, et ea que experientia reperit in natura humana" ("A human being has a way to read and learn in himself what by contrast he should think about his God. Let us compare, if it pleases you, what reason finds in the divine nature by reasoning with those things it discovers in human nature by experience"). See also *Trin.* 3.10 (Ribaillier, 145.28–30; tr. Zinn, 383, tr. Evans, VTT 1:255); *Trin.* 4.2 (Ribaillier, 163.7–9, 164.21–24; tr. Evans, VTT 1:268–69), for the argument that if man knows by experience things in himself which he cannot explain, how much more likely is it that he will not be able to explain things he knows or believes to be true about God, although he cannot experience them.

[28]   *Trin.* 3.3 (Ribaillier, 138.8–11; tr. Zinn, 375–76, tr. Evans, VTT 1:218–19): "Conscientiam suam unusquisque interroget procul dubio et absque contradictione inveniet quia sicut nihil caritate melius, sic nihil caritate jocundius. Hoc nos docet ipsa natura, idem ipsum multiplex experientia" ("Let each one question his consciousness: without doubt or contradiction he will find that nothing is better than love, nothing more pleasant. Nature itself teaches this to us and so does manifold experience").

[29]   *Quat. grad.* 18, 20 (Dumeige, 145, 147).

[30]   Andre Dubus III, *House of Sand and Fog* (New York: Norton, 1999). For Catullus, a helpful

a time when there was great interest in Ovid's love poetry and Constantine the African's discussion of love-sicknesses and its remedies was beginning to circulate.[31]

There are many kinds of love, but Richard's theme is "burning, seething love," whose violence wounds the heart.[32] He finds descriptions of the successive stages of such love in the poems that constitute the *Song of Songs,*[33] although even those passionate poems seem to fall short of the obsessive infatuation Richard describes. In the first stage of such love, the lover cannot contain or conceal "the boiling of his desire." He sighs and draws deep breaths; his face is "pale and pining"; only with difficulty can he turn his attention to other occupations.[34] Then, in the second stage, the lover cannot concentrate on anything else; he thinks or dreams about nothing else; he is a prisoner to his love; he finds no peace.[35] In the first stage, one could still flee from love; at this second stage one can escape only by buying one's freedom through works of mercy, even if one's mind is fixed on the beloved.[36] The third degree of love excludes all other feelings and thoughts. The beloved is everything; all else is nothing. The lover is beyond advice, common sense, and consolation.[37] He has no energy for anything but the beloved.[38] There is no relief for him except to pray for mercy and deliverance. Just as the first stage bound the lover's feelings, and the second bound his thoughts, the third binds his actions. All he can do is move

source is http://en.wikipedia.org/wiki/Poetry_of_Catullus. Richard of St Victor did not know Catullus' poems.

[31] Constantine the African, who died as a monk of Montecassino about 1087, translated a number of Arabic medical writings. He produced a paraphrase of an Arabic vademecum for physicians called *Zad al-musafir wa-qut-al-hadir,* which he entitled *Viaticum peregrinantis.* Chapter 20 of Book One discusses love-sickness ("amor qui et eros dicitur"), its causes, symptoms, and cures. On Constantine's work and its later commentators, see Mary F. Wack, *Lovesickness in the Middle Ages: The Viaticum and Its Commentaries* (Philadelphia: University of Pennsylvania Press, 1990).

[32] *Quat. grad.* 2 (Dumeige, 127): "amor ille ardens et fervens" ("that ardent and boiling love"). The *De quatuor gradibus violentiae caritatis* is translated by Andrew B. Kraebel, VTT 2:275–300. The paragraph numbers remain the same.

[33] *Quat. grad.* 4 (Dumeige, 129).

[34] *Quat. grad.* 6 (Dumeige, 131): "ut desiderii sui estus cohibere vel dissimulare omnino non valeat . . . profunde ingemiscens et longa suspiria trahens . . . vultus pallens atque tabescens" ("so that he can in no way restrain or hide the heat of his desire . . . groaning deeply and uttering long sighs . . . a pale and flushed face").

[35] *Quat. grad.* 7 (Dumeige, 133): "mentem hominis, nec ad horam quietam esse permittit" ("it allows a person's mind not even one hour of quiet").

[36] *Quat. grad.* 9 (Dumeige, 133–35).

[37] *Quat. grad.* 10 (Dumeige, 135–37).

[38] *Quat. grad.* 11 (Dumeige, 137).

his lips in prayer.[39] In the fourth degree, the passionate lover discovers that nothing can satisfy his ardent desire. He is thirsty; he drinks; yet he thirsts the more. Love has reached the stage of insatiability.[40] The lover can do nothing for himself, and no one can do anything for him directly. Others can only pray for him. Those who love each other with the violence of the fourth degree are drawn irresistibly toward each other, but are left unsatisfied; they quarrel; their love is mixed with jealousy and hate.[41] Once the lover has reached the fourth degree of violent love, he has gone beyond the narrowing and intensification of attention and feeling that occur in falling in love; he has become obsessed. In romantic love he has sought in a human being something no human being can provide; hence the ambivalence of his feelings toward the beloved.[42]

Richard sees the first degree of passionate love as proper to marriage. In marital love, the beloved should be the primary focus of one's affection. Intimate mutual love, expressed in the marriage bed, "tightens the chains of peace between those who are pledged to one another, and it renders that indissoluble and perpetual union pleasing and delightful." However, the second degree is bad because it keeps one from providing for necessities and exercising one's responsibilities. The third and fourth stages lead to bitterness and strife. In the third, the lover cannot enjoy at will what he desires; in the fourth, his insatiable longing embitters even his enjoyment of the beloved. The fourth degree is a foretaste of hell.[43]

Richard knows that in love feeling and reason do not always coincide. Sometimes, feeling draws a person toward loving something, but reason restrains him. At other times, a person loves objects by deliberate choice, although he is not drawn toward them by desire.[44]

---

[39] *Quat. grad.* 11–13 (Dumeige, 137–39).

[40] *Quat. grad.* 14 (Dumeige, 141): "insatiabilis anime sitis vel esuries non sedatur sed irritatur" ("the insatiable thirst and hunger of the soul is not calmed, but aroused").

[41] *Quat. grad.* 16 (Dumeige, 143).

[42] José Ortega y Gasset analyzed the way romantic love narrows and fixates attention. Denis de Rougement theorized that in intense romantic love the lover is seeking something that natural love cannot provide. For these ideas and the works in which they appear, see Robert G. Hazo, *The Idea of Love*, Concepts in Western Thought Series (New York: Praeger, 1967), 474, 476–77.

[43] *Quat. grad.* 19 (Dumeige, 147): "quedam forma future damnationis" ("a kind of image of future damnation").

[44] *Quad grad.* 24 (Dumeige, 151): "sepe ad aliquid diligendum trahimur ex affectione et tamen renitimur ex ratione. Et sepe multa ex proposito deliberationis diligimus que tamen per desiderii appetitum minime affectamus" ("often we are drawn to love something by feeling, but our reason restrains us. And often we love many things by choice for which we feel no desire").

For Richard of St Victor, the authority of faith along with its authoritative norms, experience, and reason interpenetrate. They are not completely independent criteria or sources of knowledge.[45] For example, when Richard examines the experience of human love, he views it as it has been transformed by faith and with the illumination that reason can give when guided by faith. For Richard the experience of human love has its roots in the mystery of the Trinity; thus the experience of human love has implications for faith, and faith has implications for human love. Richard's dialectic enables the believer who meditates with reason on experience to glimpse at the summit of human love the reflection of the Trinity. Faith remains the principle and standpoint; it transforms experience and guides and illumines reason.

AUTHORITIES

For the Victorines, the primary authority is the Sacred Scriptures. After the Scriptures, St Augustine is certainly the author who has the most impact on their thought. This section will state briefly how Hugh and Richard of St Victor think about the authority and interpretation of the Scriptures (the topic of the third volume of *Victorine Texts in Translation*). For both of them, an example will be given to illustrate how the authority of Scripture influences their thinking about love. There follows a summary of Augustine's thinking on love, which will make it possible later in this introduction to detect how the Victorines follow or develop Augustine's legacy.

THE SCRIPTURES: HUGH OF ST VICTOR

For Hugh of St Victor, the Sacred Scriptures are the authority par excellence. All other authorities are commentaries on and summaries

---

[45]   In view of *Trin.* 1.1 (Ribaillier, 86.7–87.12), one might think these three are relatively separate. There, Richard writes that there are three ways to knowledge: by experience we know temporal things, and by reasoning or believing we rise to knowledge of eternal things. However, his own methodology in *On the Trinity* is to begin with faith invested in authority, and then to seek in experience a starting point whereby he can reason toward a deeper understanding of what he believes. *Trin.* 1.10 (Ribaillier, 95.15–17): "Inde est quod in hoc tractatu omnis ratiocinationis nostre processus initium sumit ex his que per experientiam novimus" ("Hence it is that in this treatise our entire reasoning process begins from the things which we know by experience").

of scriptural truth.[46] Scripture is concerned with the truth in which lies salvation. Other writings, including the apocrypha, are not pure because they do not contain truth without error; nor are they perfect, since they do not restore the soul to true knowledge and love of God. Therefore, they are not worthy to be called "divine."

> The only Scripture that is rightly called *divine* is that which is inspired by the Spirit of God and issued by those who speak by the Spirit of God; it makes humanity divine, reforming it to the likeness of God by instructing in knowledge and exhorting to love. Whatever is taught in it is truth; whatever is commanded is goodness; whatever is promised is happiness.[47]

Other writings are concerned with God's work of creation; the subject of the divine Scripture is Christ's work of restoration. Scripture alone teaches pure and perfect truth about the knowledge and love of God. It is also unique in that parts of it have a threefold interpretation. The primary, historical sense refers to realities that in turn signify other realities. There are two such spiritual meanings: the allegorical meaning, by which visible things refer to invisible ones, and the tropological meaning, by which visible things teach what is to be done.[48]

Elsewhere, Hugh writes,

> The divine Scriptures are those that, written by cultivators of the Catholic faith, the authority of the universal church—for the strengthening of that same faith—received into the number of the divine books and

---

[46] Hugh's work, *De scripturis et scriptoribus sacris* (*On Sacred Scriptures and Their Authors*) will serve as the main source for what follows. Regarding that work and for parallels in other writings of Hugh, see Franklin T. Harkins, *Reading and the Work of Restoration: History and Scripture in the Theology of Hugh of St Victor*, Studies and Texts 167 (Toronto: Pontifical Institute of Mediaeval Studies, 2009): 142–50. For the Augustinian background of Hugh's distinction of the historical/literal meaning and the spiritual meaning(s), see Harkins, *Reading*, 150–59. Hugh's *Diligent investigator* (Stammberger, 241–83 [edition, 272–83]) covers some of the same ground as *De scripturis*, but does not include the questions of matter and authority that are discussed there. Stammberger also unravels some of the composition and manuscript history of *De scripturis et scriptoribus sacris*.

[47] *Script.* 1 (PL 175.10–11A): "Sola autem illa Scriptura jure divina appellatur, quae per Spiritum Dei aspirata est, et per eos qui Spiritu Dei locuti sunt administrata, hominem divinum facit, ad similitudinem Dei illum reformans, instruendo ad cognitionem, et exhortando ad dilectionem ipsius. In qua quidquid docetur, veritas; quidquid praecipitur, bonitas; quidquid promittitur felicitas est." On the non-canonical books, see *Script.* 11 (PL 175.18CD). The pairing of knowledge and love, and the threefold distinction—truth, goodness, and happiness/beatitude—are schemas that occur very frequently in the Victorine writers.

[48] *Script.* 2–4 (PL 175.11D–13A); cf. *Script.* 17–18 (PL 175.24AD): "De materia Sacrae Scripturae" ("the subject material of Sacred Scripture").

retained to be read. There are, besides, many others works—written at different times by religious and wise men—that, although they are not approved by the authority of the universal Church, nevertheless because they are not out of harmony with the Catholic faith and teach some useful things, are counted among the divine utterances.[49]

Because Scripture is the primary authority, Hugh is very careful to delineate what writings it includes. He divides the Old Testament into the law, the prophets, and the *agiographi*. In the *agiographi* are included the Psalms and Song of Songs. In another category are Wisdom, Sirach, Judith, Tobit, and Machabees, which, following Jerome, Hugh says are read but are not included in the canon. The New Testament is also divided into the three categories: gospels, the writings of the Apostles, and the decretals or canons. Then come the writings of the Holy Fathers: Jerome (whose arrangement of the canon of the Old Testament Hugh was following), Augustine, Ambrose, Gregory, Isidore, Origen, Bede, and numerous others. Like Wisdom, Sirach, and the other books not in Jerome's Hebrew canon, the writings of the Fathers are read but not included in the canon. The full and perfect truth mentioned above is contained in each of the books of Scripture, but none is superfluous.[50]

Thus Hugh defines the divine Scriptures as texts written under the inspiration of the Holy Spirit by cultivators of the Catholic faith, teaching without error the saving truth about the work of restoration, included in the canon of the Scriptures by the authority of the universal Church, and describing persons, events, and things that in turn signify other invisible realities. In Hugh's reckoning, the Old Testament books are those of the Hebrew canon, whereas the New Testament books include not just the apostolic writings, but also the decrees of the Church. As Wisdom and the other books Hugh excludes from the canon are closely associated with the Old Testament, so the Christian writers from Origen to Bede are closely related to the New Testament.

---

[49]   *Didasc.* 4.1 (Buttimer, 70.21–71.4; tr. Taylor, 102–3): "Scripturae divinae sunt quas, a catholica fidei cultoribus editas, auctoritas universalis ecclesiae ad ejusdem fidei corroborationem in numero divinorum librorum computandas recepit et legendas retinuit. Sunt praeterea alia quam plurima opuscula, a religiosis viris et sapientibus diversis temporibus conscripta, quae licet auctoritate universalis ecclesiae probata non sint, tamen quia a fide catholica non discrepant et nonnulla etiam utilia docent, inter divina computantur eloquia."

[50]   *Script.* 6–8 (PL 175.15A–16B). Hugh's understanding of the inspiration of the Holy Spirit is such that it can include non-Scriptural works. For some observations on this division of inspired writings, see Evans, VTT 1:161–63 nn. 17 and 20.

In the *Didascalicon*, Hugh writes that the Song of Songs is, as it were, the epithalamium or wedding song of Christ and the Church.[51] By the twelfth century, this understanding of the Song of Songs was deeply imbedded in Christian thinking. The love that unites Christ and the Church is the allegorical or doctrinal meaning of the Song of Songs. In *The Praise of the Bridegroom*, Hugh develops the moral or tropological meaning, in which the Song of Songs tells of the union of the soul with God. In developing this interpretation, Hugh draws on a tradition rooted in the writings of Origen that flowered in the *Sermons on the Song of Songs* by Hugh's contemporary, Bernard of Clairvaux.[52]

THE SCRIPTURES: RICHARD OF ST VICTOR

Richard of St Victor's theory of scriptural interpretation follows closely the thought of Hugh of St Victor. His discussion of the canon of Scriptures is adopted almost verbatim from Hugh of St Victor.[53] The Scriptures were written by the grace of the Holy Spirit.[54] As a result, they contain no error.[55] The different parts of Scripture converge in unanimous witness to God's revelation.[56] However, the Scriptures con-

---

[51]   *Didasc.* 4.8 (Buttimer, 81; tr. Taylor, 110). In this chapter Hugh is following Jerome and Isidore.

[52]   See, for example, Denys Turner, *Eros and Allegory: Medieval Exegesis of the Song of Songs*, CS 156 (Kalamazoo: Cistercian Publications, 1995); *The Song of Songs Interpreted by Early Christian and Medieval Commentators*, tr. Richard Norris, The Church's Bible (Grand Rapids, MI: Eerdmans, 2003).

[53]   *LE* 1.2.9 (Châtillon, 119.2–120.37 = Hugh of St Victor, *Script.* 6 [PL 175.15A–16B]).

[54]   *Apoc.* prol. 1 (PL 196.638B): "Liber iste per septiformem Spiritus sancti gratiam editus . . ." ("This book produced through the sevenfold grace of the Holy Spirit . . ."). The following discussion of Richard's theory of biblical interpretation is largely a summary of chapter 5 of my unpublished doctoral dissertation, "Learning and the Ascent to God in Richard of St Victor (Rome: Pontifical Athenaeum of Sant'Anselmo, 1980)."

[55]   *Viz. Ezek.* prol. (PL 196.529A): "si non facimus prophetam mentiri" ("unless we make the prophet a liar"); *Verbo Eccl.* (Ribaillier, 295); *Nonn. alleg.* (PL 196.199D): "sacra historia ab omni falsitate et fatuitate aliena" ("Sacred history is foreign to all falsehood and folly"); *Serm. cent.* 95 (PL 177.1195C): "veritas Scripturae sacrae nulla vetustate corrumpitur" ("the truth of Sacred Scripture is not corrupted by age").

[56]   *Erud.* 1.20 (PL 196.1263C): "Juvat hoc loco in considerationem adducere quomodo ista lectio et evangelica videantur sibi mystica locutione concinere" ("It will help to consider at this point how this reading and the Gospel seem to harmonize in mystic utterance"); *Erud.* 1.29 (PL 196.1280A): "Videsne, quaeso, quomodo concurrunt sibi propheticae sententiae, quomodo concordet David cum Daniele, veritas cum figura, prophetae sententia cum visione prophetica?" ("Do you see, I ask, how the prophetic statements mutually concur, how David is in harmony with Daniel, truth with figure, the prophet's statement with the prophetic vision?")

vey the progressive unfolding of revelation that reaches its definitive
stage in the New Testament. The six wings of the four living creatures
in the book of Revelation are symbols of the stages in the unfolding of
biblical revelation. The first wing is the law of nature. The second
through the fifth wings are the reading of the written law, the prophets,
the gospel law, and the apostolic teaching; the sixth wing is the knowledge of the teachers who follow after the apostles in time and explain
the obscure parts of the Scriptures.[57]

The content of the Scriptures is, as Hugh of St Victor teaches, the
work of restoration consisting of the Incarnation of the Word and all
the sacraments that pertain to it.[58] The purpose of Scripture is to trans-
mit understanding, to inspire devotion, and to nurture both contemplation and action.[59] The Scriptures are a buttress against temptation,
a mirror in which one can come to recognize the good and evil within
oneself, and a stimulus to cleansing compunction.[60]

---

[57]   *Apoc.* 2.2 (PL 196.752AB); *Apoc.* 7.10 (PL 196.885BC).

[58]   *LE* 1.2.8 (Châtillon, 119.9–11): "Taliter accedit sacra Scriptura per opus conditionis ad materiam suam, id est ad opus restaurationis" ("In this way Sacred Scripture advances through
the work of creation to its proper subject matter, which is the work of restoration"); *Serm.
cent.* 99 (PL 177.1195CD): "sacra Scriptura . . . nos utramque partem fidei, et illam scilicet qua
in Creatorem, et illam qua in Redemptorem credimus docet" ("Sacred Scripture . . . teaches
us both parts of faith, both that by which we believe in the Creator and that by which we
believe in the Redeemer"); *LE* 1.2.1 (Châtillon, 114.2–8); *Apoc.* 4.1 (PL 196.798C); *LE* 1.2.6
(Châtillon, 177.2–13); cf. Hugh of St Victor, *Sacr.* 1 prol. 3 (PL 176.184AC; tr. Deferrari, 4).

[59]   *Apoc.* 1.5 (PL 196.9718CD): "quaeramus in sacra pagina non solum eruditionem, sed etiam
aedificationem, quia illa sola utilis atque laudabilis est scientia, quam commendat comes
justitia" ("Let us seek in the sacred page not only learning, but also edification, because the
only science that is useful and praiseworthy is that which its companion justice commends");
Apoc. prol. 1 (PL 196.683BC): Richard's aim in writing the commentary on the Apocalypse—
"that you may also have from this book . . . what instructs your mind, enkindles your feelings,
and advances and leads your efforts to greater things" ("ut habeas ex hoc quoque libro . . .
quod sensum tuum erudiat, affectum accendat, studium ad majora promoveat et perdu-
cat")—parallels that of divine providence in seeing to the composition of the book, which
was given by "divine Providence for instruction and consolation" ("divina providentia ad
eruditionem et consolationem datus"); *LE* 2.1.14 (Châtillon, 230.39–40): "Esca sacram Scripturam significat, que cibus spiritalis est animarum" ("Food signifies Sacred Scripture, which
is the spiritual nourishment of souls"); *LE* 2.10.4.1 (Châtillon, 384.44–45 = *Serm. cent.* 4 [PL
177.910A]); *LE* 2.12.14 (Châtillon, 473.13–21); *Nonn. alleg.* (PL 196.199B); Ps.-Richard of St Victor, *Cant.* 23 (PL 196.474C).

[60]   *LE* 2, prol. (Châtillon, 213.10–12): "In ipsa animatur ne frangatur in adversis, solidatur ne
dissolvatur in prosperis, et sumit recordationem de preterito, cautelam de futuro" ("In it, he
is enlivened lest he be broken in adversities, solidified lest he become dissolute in prosperity,
and he receives recollection of the past and caution regarding the future"); *LE* 2.10.9 (Châtillon, 394.40–42 = *Serm. cent.* 9 [PL 177.919B]): "Speculum significat Scripturarum lectionem,
in qua anima quid in se bonum sit, quidve malum, quid honestum, quid inhonestum contemplatur" ("A mirror signifies the reading of the Scriptures, in which the soul contemplates

Like Hugh, Richard is convinced that the words of Scripture, or more accurately the realities they describe, have more than one meaning. That this should be so is not surprising, for what has flowed from the divine oracle necessarily is something great, profound, and most salutary. The same reality may have different symbolic meanings in different passages of Scripture, and different facets of things may signify the same spiritual truth. Hence, Richard gives alternative interpretations of the same text.[61] Richard distinguishes the literal and spiritual senses, divides the latter into allegorical and tropological, and sometimes adds the anagogical.[62] It is a matter of history when things, deeds, or words contained in the letter are referred to in straightforward speech. Allegory occurs when the mystic words or deeds signify the presence of Christ or of the sacraments of the Church. Tropology is a moral discourse aimed at correcting and fashioning morals with either open or figurative words. Anagogy, which literally means "what leads to higher things," is discourse that speaks of future rewards and life in heaven, either with mystic words or openly.[63] In his theory of scriptural interpretation, Richard gave a certain primacy to the literal, historical

what is good in it and what is bad, what is honorable and what is dishonorable"); *Apoc.* 1.4 (PL 196.707D): "Sicut enim aquae a sordibus lavant, ita verba Scripturarum a vitiis purgant" ("Just as water washes away stains, so the words of the Scriptures purge from vices"). Cf. Augustine, *En. Ps.* 103.1.4 (Dekkers and Fraipont, 1476.20–26 [PL 37.1338]); Gregory the Great, *Ep.* 2.50 (Ewald and Hartmann 1:152.19 = 2.52, PL 77.595C); *Hom. Ez.* 1.6.2 (Adriaen, 67 [PL 76.829BC]); *Hom. Ez.* 1.7.16–17 (Adriaen, 93.332–33, 355–56 [PL 76.848AC]); *Mor.* 2.1.1 (Gillet, 252 [PL 75.553D–554D]); *Reg. past.* 3.24 (PL 77.94A).

61 *Apoc.* 1, prol. (PL 196.685D); *Erud.* 1.26 (PL 196.1274BC); *Adnot. Psalm.* 2 (PL 196.269A); *XII patr.* 86 (Châtillon, 342 [PL 196.62AB]; tr. Zinn, 145); *XII patr.* 87, (Châtillon, 346 [PL 196.63A–64A]; tr. Zinn, 146); *Apoc.* 1.9 (PL 196.731AB); *Apoc.* 1.11 (PL 196.740CD); *Apoc.* 7.5, (PL 196.869A); *LE* 2.12.6 (Châtillon, 466.2–467.56); *Statu* 42–44 (Ribaillier, 114–17); *Emman.* 2, prol. (PL 196.633D).

62 Historical, allegorical, tropological: *Exp. diff.* 1, prol. (PL 196.211C); *LE* 1, prol., (Châtillon, 97.18–20); *LE* 1.2.3 (Châtillon, 115.2–116.21); *LE* 1.2.8 (Châtillon, 119.11–16); *LE* 2.2.12 (Châtillon, 241.29–30); *Erud.* 1.18 (PL 196.1260D); *Serm. cent.* 59 (PL 177.1080D); *Serm. cent.* 90 (PL 177.1182C); cf. Walter of St Victor, *Serm. inedit.* 4.4 (Châtillon, 34.59–74); Maurice of St Victor, *Serm. inedit.* 6.4 (Châtillon, 229.100–8); for Godfrey of St Victor, see Philippe Delhaye, *Le Microcosmus de Godefroy de Saint-Victor. Étude théologique* (Lille: Facultés catholiques, 1951), Appendix R, pp. 275–81; historical, allegorical, tropological, and anagogical: *LE* 2.3.11 (Châtillon, 258.4); *LE* 2.10.10 (Châtillon, 395.23 = *Serm. cent.* 10 [PL 177.920C]); *LE* 2.10.11 (Châtillon, 399.37–41 = *Serm. cent.* 11 [PL 177.923D]); *Serm. cent.* 95 (PL 177.1196D–1197B).

63 *Serm. cent.* 95 (PL 177.1196D–1197A): "verba coelestis oraculi vel historice, vel allegorice, vel tropologice, vel anagogice accipiuntur. . . . Anagogice, id est ad superiora ducens, locutio est quae de praemiis futuris et de vita quae est in caelis, mysticis vel apertis verbis disputat" ("The words of the heavenly oracle are taken historically, or allegorically, or tropologically, or anagogically. . . . Anagogically, that is, leading to higher things by speech dealing with future rewards and life in heaven, whether with mystical or plain words").

sense.[64] This is evident in his two-part *Book of Notes*, which is meant as a primer for those who wish to advance to the study and preaching of the Bible. Most of the first part is a compendium of world history, while the second part, devoted to the spiritual meaning of the scriptural things, people, and events is arranged historically.[65]

The authority of the Scriptures is primary in the life of the Church and of the individual Christian. Biblical authority (*auctoritas in sacra pagina*) is the source and summary of Christian faith and teaching.[66] The very letter of the Scriptures possesses authority.[67] Richard appeals to the authority of the biblical text as a matter of course in his commentaries; it is by this authority that an interpretation will stand or fall.[68]

Richard strongly affirms the authority of Scripture in a comment on the Transfiguration:

> If now you believe you see Christ transfigured, do not easily believe what you see in him or hear from him, unless Moses and Elijah concur.

---

[64] *Nonn. alleg.* (PL 196.199D): "In Scriptura sacra primum locum tenet historia" ("In Sacred Scripture, history has the first place").

[65] *LE* 1, prol. (Châtillon, 97.6–8, 15–20): "pauca vel nulla simplicitati tue sacre scripture lectionem ingredienti necessaria pretermittimus. . . . Totam scedule huius seriem in duas partes dividimus. In prima parte . . . cursum historiarum ab initio usque ad nos decurrentium. In secunda parte materiam habemus sensus allegoriarum et tropologiarum secundum subjacentis lineam historie dispositarum" ("We have omitted few or no things which are necessary for you, hitherto uninstructed, as you begin the reading of Sacred Scripture. . . . We have divided the entire sequence of this text into two parts. In the first part . . . [is] the course of history from the beginning down to our time. In the second, we have the subject matter of the meaning of the allegorical and tropological senses arranged according to the underlying historical sequence").

[66] *Apoc.* 7.2 (PL 196.826A); cf. Jerome, *In ps.* 86 (G. Morin, *Opera homiletica*, CCL78 [Turnhout: Brepols, 1958], 116.208–11 [PL 26.1149B]); Gregory, *Mor.* 2.1.1 (Gillet, 252 [PL 75.553D–554D]). See also *Apoc.*3.4 (PL 196.781B): "illi libri in quibus origo et summa fidei comprehenditur" ("those books in which are contained the origin and summit of faith"); *Arca Moys.* 1.6 (Aris, 16 [PL 196.72A]; tr. Zinn, 163); *Arca Moys.* 4.3 (Aris. 88 [PL 196.137C]; tr. Zinn, 262); *Arca Moys.* 4.17 (Aris, 109 [PL 196.156B]; tr. Zinn, 289–90); *Serm. cent.* 95 (PL 177.1196A, 1197B).

[67] *Tab. foed.* 1.11 (PL 196.220D).

[68] *Vis. Ezek.* 4 (PL 196.543A): "non nostra auctoritate, sed Scripturae attestatione probamus." ("We offer proof not by our authority, but by the testimony of Scripture"); *Vis. Ezek.* 13 (PL 196.570C): "centum cubitos secundum praedictam Scripturae auctoritatem occupabit" ("according to the aforesaid authority of Scripture, it will occupy 100 cubits"); *Misit Her.* 19 (PL 141.303B): "Sed haec opinio non mihi recipienda videtur, nisi aliquo canonicae Scripturae testimonio confirmetur" ("But it seems that I should not receive this opinion unless it is confirmed by some witness from the canonical Scriptures"); *Emman.* 1.1 (PL 196.606D): "Qui non intelligit sensum vaticinantis prophetae, credat vel sententiae exponentis evangelistae" ("Let whoever does not understand the oracle of the prophet believe the opinion of the evangelist who explains it"); *Emman.* 2.10 (PL 196.645AB).

We know that any testimony stands by the mouth of two or three. Any truth that the authority of the Scriptures does not confirm is suspect in my eyes; I do not receive Christ in His brightness, unless Moses and Elijah are standing by. . . . If Christ teaches me regarding exterior things or things interior to me, I easily accept it, since I can test these things by my own experience. But when my mind is led to the heights, . . . I do not receive Christ without a witness. No apparent revelation is ratified without the testimony of Moses and Elijah, without the authority of the Scriptures.[69]

An example of how Richard applies this theory to biblical teaching on love is his interpretation of Jesus' summary of the Law in the twofold commandment of love. The Victorines give great authority to Jesus' command to love God with all one's heart, mind, and strength, and one's neighbor as oneself. A simple example of the attention they gave to that command is *Sermon* 88 of the *One Hundred Sermons* attributed to Richard of St Victor.[70] The sermon takes as its theme Deut. 6:5: "You will love the Lord your God with all your heart, and with all your soul, and with all your strength."[71] The sermon argues that the one thing that has lasting worth is to serve God. One can have every sort of earthly advantage, but it does no good unless one serves God. If someone loves and serves God, then even if he is miserable in his life, he will pass over to eternal life. To serve God is to love God. If one loves something or someone or many things in contravention of the love of God, one must relinquish them all. The martyrs give an example when they not only hand over what is theirs but their very selves for the love of God.

We must love God because God loves us first, giving us some gifts and promising others, so that we might love God. The least of his gifts

---

[69]   *XII patr.* 81 (Châtillon, 322 [PL 196.57BD]; tr. Zinn, 138–39): In the previous chapter (*XII patr.* 80, Châtillon, 322 [PL 196.57B]; tr. Zinn, 138), Richard wrote that Christ teaches both earthly and heavenly things, "sed terrena in valle, coelestia in monte" ("but earthly things in the valley, heavenly ones on the mountain"). Now, in chapter 81 he proceeds to discuss the latter: "si jam te credis Christum videre transfiguratum, quidquid in illo videas, quidquid ab illo audias non ei facile credas, nisi occurrant ei Moyses et Elias. Scimus quia in ore duorum vel trium stat omne testimonium. Suspecta est mihi omnis veritas quam non confirmat Scripturarum auctoritas, nec Christum in sua clarificatione recipio, si non assistant ei Moyses et Elias. . . . Si Christus docet me de rebus exterioribus vel de intimis meis facile recipio, utpote in his quae comprobare possum proprio experimento; verum ubi ad alta mens ducitur . . . non recipio Christum sine teste, nec rata poterit esse quamlibet verisimilis revelatio sine attestatione Moysis et Eliae, sine Scripturarum auctoritate"); cf. Augustine, *Contra Ep. Man.* 5.6 (PL 42.176).

[70]   PL 177.1177C–1179A.

[71]   See also, Deut. 11:1; 13:3 (Vulg.); 30:6; Sir. 7:32 (Vulg.); Matt. 22:37; Luke 10:27.

is this entire world and everything it contains. The second gift he gives us is that he made us in his image and likeness, a great and wonderful gift. A third gift is the grace of redemption, which came through the death of his Son. The gift that God promises is future glory. Thus we have from God four good gifts: creation, nature, grace, and glory.

We should love God with all our heart, soul, strength, and mind, that is, wisely, devoutly, bravely, and without forgetfulness. "And you should love your neighbor as yourself"[72] in good deeds, good advice, and intention. In all of these ways, let us love our neighbor on the way, whom we are going to have as our companion in heaven.

In this sermon, there is no hint of a conflict between altruistic love of God and neighbor and seeking eternal life. The *Liber pancrisis*, the most authentic collection of the teachings of the school of Anselm of Laon (d. 1117), declares that because it is a law of nature, the command to love God above all things and one's neighbor as oneself is one of the few Old Testament commands that remain binding under the New Covenant. In interpreting the twofold command, the *Liber pancrisis* maintains "we must love God, not on account of some reward which we expect from him, but for his own sake."[73] Elsewhere the *Liber pancrisis* distinguishes sharply between three forms of loving God: sons of God who seek him for his own sake, mercenaries who serve him in expectation of a reward, and slaves who seek God out of fear.[74] An anonymous author of the later twelfth century, invoking the authority of Anselm of Laon, writes that one should love God even if God were stern and willed one's damnation.[75] It will be apparent that the Victorines, like

---

[72] Matt. 22:39; 19:19; Luke 10:27; Jas. 2:8; Lev. 19:18.
[73] *Liber pancrisis,* 201, cited in Cédric Giraud, *Per verba magistri: Anselme de Laon et son école au xiiᵉ siècle*, Bibliothèque d'histoire culturelle du Moyen Âge 8 (Turnhout: Brepols, 2010): 315: "Caritas est motus animi ad diligendum Deum propter Deum et se et proximum propter Deum. Deum enim debemus diligere non propter aliquod premium quod ab eo expectemus, sed propter ipsum solum" ("Charity is the movement of the soul to love God on account of God and oneself and one's neighbor on account of God. We ought to love God not on account of any reward that we expect from him, but only for his own sake"). On the commands of the Old Testament, see *Liber pancrisis* 51, cited in Giraud, 250: "Secundum precepta vero non cessat lex ex toto. Illa enim precepta naturalia, ut de dilectione Dei et proximi, et ibi et hic sunt. Secundum tamen illa alia precepta que pertinent ad sacramenta illa, ut custodies sabbatum, et similia, cessat" ("As far as precepts are concerned, the law does not cease completely. Those precepts that arise from nature, such as those about love of God and neighbor, pertain to both then and now. However, regarding those other precepts that pertain to the sacraments of that time, such as keeping Sabbaths and the like, the law ceases").
[74] *Liber pancrisis,* 335, cited in Giraud, 315.
[75] *Anonymi auctoris saeculi XII Expositio in epistolas Pauli*, ed. Rolf Peppermüller, BGPTMA 68 (Münster: Aschendorff, 2005), 66–67, cited in Giraud, 316.

St Thomas Aquinas, do not think that there is a contradiction between loving God for his own sake and the search for happiness through union with God. Perhaps one could think of a spouse loving her husband for his sake but also as a source of her own delight.

St Augustine

Hugh of St Victor is called "the second Augustine."[76] Apart from the Bible, St Augustine is the primary authority for Hugh's theological thinking. This is true of his theology of love and of the theologies of love of his twelfth-century successors at St Victor.[77] Love is a topic to which Augustine returns over and over. He writes no theoretical treatise specifically devoted to love, but his *Sermons on the First Letter of John* are extended reflections on biblical teaching on love. What follows are some key elements of Augustine's understanding of love, with emphasis on those that influence the Victorines. Many quotations from Augustine's works are given in the notes in both Latin and English; pondering such passages—as the Victorines do—is an excellent way to immerse oneself in Augustine's thinking on love.[78]

In *On the City of God* (AD 413/427) Augustine writes that there is not a clear distinction in the meanings of *amor*, *caritas*, and *dilectio*. In the supreme authority, the Sacred Scriptures, which Augustine cites in Latin, all three of these can be used interchangeably for good or evil kinds of love.[79] However, in his somewhat earlier *Sermons on the First*

[76] Thomas de Cantimpré, *Bonum universale de proprietatibus apum*, 2.16, cited by Joseph de Ghellinck, *Le mouvement théologique du XIIᵉ siècle*, 2nd ed. (Paris: Desclée de Brouwer, 1938), 185.

[77] Dumeige, *Richard de Saint-Victor*, 27–31.

[78] For Augustine's understanding of love and a bibliography on the topic, see T. J. van Bavel, "Love," in *Augustine through the Ages: An Encyclopedia*, ed. Allan D. Fitzgerald (Grand Rapids: Eerdmans, 1999), 509–16; Etienne Gilson, *The Christian Philosophy of Saint Augustine*, tr. L. E. M. Lynch (New York: Random House, 1960), 165–69; Dany Dideberg, *Saint Augustin et la Première Épître de saint Jean: Une théologie de l'agapè*, Théologie historique 34 (Paris: Beuchesne, 1975).

[79] *Civ. Dei* 14.7 (Dombart and Kalb, 422; tr. O'Meara, 557): "Nonulli arbitrantur aliud esse dilectionem sive caritatem, aliud amore. Dicunt enim dilectionem accipiendam esse in bono, amorem in malo. . . . Sed scripturas religionis nostrae, quarum auctoritatem ceteris omnibus litteris anteponimus, non aliud dicere amorem, aliud dilectionem vel caritatem insinuandum fuit" ("Some think that *dilectio* and *caritas* are one thing and *amor* another. They say that *dilectio* is to be taken in a good sense, and *amor* in a bad sense. . . . But here the task was to show that the Scriptures of our religion, whose authority we put before all other writings, do not say that *amor* is one thing and *dilectio* or *caritas* another"). Here O'Meara translates

Letter of John (AD 407), he does note that *dilectio* usually indicates laudable kinds of love while *amor* is used to refer to carnal love.[80]
Love determines who a person is. It creates a fundamental distinction between those who are good and those who are evil. Those who love with true love are born of God. Those who love their neighbor whom they see also see God, because they see charity itself, and God dwells within them.[81] "Each person lives from his love, either well or badly." Those live well who are "warmed by a love for the spiritual and intelligible good, and not by cupidity for bodily illusions."[82]
Love is an inclination, impetus, or striving for something desired. Love is a restless desire for the object of the heart's longing.[83] Love draws us out of ourselves: *delectatio* is the attractive power of outside reality that draws us without physical coercion.[84] Love itself is to be

---

caritas as charity, *dilectio* as fondness, and *amor* as love. See *Civ. Dei* 15.22 (Dombart and Kalb, 488; tr. O'Meara, 637): "Huius igitur caritatis, hoc est dilectionis et amoris, ordine perturbato . . ." ("When this order of charity, that is, of affection and love, was disturbed . . ."); *Mor.* 1.15.24 (Rivière, 60 [PL 32.1321–2]): "Nam quid erit aliud optimum hominis, nisi cui inhaerere et beatissimum. Id autem est solus Deus, cui haerere certe non valemus, nisi dilectione, amore, caritate" ("For what besides to be joined to Him will be the best and blessed thing for a human being. That object is God alone, to whom we certainly cannot be joined except by affection, love, and charity").

[80] *In 1 Jo.* 8.5 (Agaësse, 346 [PL 35.2058]; tr. Rettig, 233): "Omnis dilectio, sive quae carnalis dicitur, quae non dilectio, sed magis amor dici solet (dilectionis enim nomen magis solet in melioribus rebus dici, in melioribus accipi)" ("Every *dilectio*, whether it be carnal, in which case it is usually called not *dilectio* but *amor* [for the word *dilectio* is more usually spoken and taken regarding better things]").

[81] *In 1 Jo.* 2.14.5 (Agaësse, 180 [PL 35.1997]; tr. Rettig, 158): "talis est quisque, qualis ejus dilectio" ("As a person loves, so he is"). *In 1 Jo.* 5.7 (Agaësse, 261–61 [PL 35.2016]; tr. Rettig, 192–93): "Dilectio ergo sola discernit inter filios Dei et filios diaboli. . . . Qui habent caritatem, nati sunt ex Deo, qui non habent, non sunt nati ex Deo. . . . Si enim fratrem quem vides dilexeris, simul videbis et Deum: quia videbis ipsam caritatem, et intus inhabitat Deus" ("Love alone distinguishes the sons of God and the sons of the devil. . . . Those who have charity are born of God; those who do not have it are not born of God. . . . For if you love the brother whom you see, at the same time you will also see God, because you will see charity itself and God dwells within").

[82] *C. Faustum* 5.11 (PL 42.228): "ex amore suo quisque vivit, vel bene vel malo. Vos autem si spiritualis atque intelligibilis boni charitate, ac non corporalium phantasmatum cupiditate arderetis" ("everyone lives from his love, either well or badly. If you are warmed by love of a spiritual and intelligible good and not by cupidity for bodily illusions").

[83] *Conf.* 1.1.1 (O'Donnell, 3; tr. Boulding 39): "fecisti nos ad te et inquietum est cor nostrum donec requeiscat in te" ("you have made us toward yourself and our heart is restless until it rests in you").

[84] *En. Ps.* 39:11 (Dekkers and Fraipont, 433–34): In the race of which Paul writes in 1 Cor. 9:24, all run and all receive a crown. "Qui prior venerit, expectat ut cum posteriore coronetur. Agonem quippe istum non cupiditas, sed caritas facit; omnes currentes amant se, et ipse amor cursus est" ("The one who arrives first waits so that he can be crowned with the one who comes later. Charity, not cupidity makes this contest; all those who run love themselves, and

desired, but not the sordid love by which the soul seeks to love things inferior to it for their own sakes. This latter, which is better called cupidity, is the root of all evils. One should stake one's love on something that cannot be taken away from the one loving and enjoying it.[85]

By the dynamism of love, the lover seeks to become one with its object.[86] At all levels—the love of a Christian for God, the love of friend to friend, the sexual love of man and woman—love couples or tries to couple lover and loved object.[87] If one loves the eternal God, one will remain for eternity with God to whom one is joined by love.[88]

---

love itself is the race"); *Jo. ev. tr.* 26.4–5 (Willems, 261–62): pleasure (*voluptas, delectatio*) draws both the senses and the mind; one is drawn by a chain on the heart ("cordis vinculo trahitur").

[85] *Div. quaest. 83*, 35.1 (Mutzenbecher, 50): "Nihil aliud est amare quam propter se ipsam rem aliquam appetere. Num igitur propter se ipsum amor appetendus est, cum quando desit quod amatur, ea sit indubitata miseria? Deinde cum amor motus quidam sit, neque ullus sit motus nisi ad aliquid, cum quaerimus quid amandum sit, quid sit illud ad quod moveri operat quaerimus. Quare si amandus est amor, non utique omnis amandus est. Est enim et turpis amor, quo animus se ipso inferiora sectatur, quae magis proprie cupiditas dicitur, omnium scilicet malorum radix. Et ideo non amandum est quod amanti et fruenti auferri potest" ("To love is nothing else than to desire something for its own sake. Now therefore, when love is sought for its own sake, when what is loved ceases to be, is not the result undoubted misery? Then, since love is a kind of motion, and there is no motion that is not toward something, when we seek what is to be loved, we seek that toward which love strives to move. For this reason, if love is loved, not all love is to be loved. For there is a base love, by which the soul goes after things inferior to itself. That love is more properly called cupidity. It is the root of all evils. And, therefore, one ought not love what can be taken away from the one who loves and enjoys it"). *Mor.* 1.15.24 (Rivière, 60 [PL 32.1321–2]), cited above, note 79.

[86] *De ordine* 18.48 (PL 32.1017): "Amici quid aliud quam unum esse conantur? Et quanto magis unum, tanto magis amici sunt. . . . Quid amor omnis? Nonne unum vult fieri cum eo quod amat, et si ei contingat, unum cum eo fit. Voluptas ipsa non ob aliud delectat vehementius, nisi quod amantia sese corpora in unum coguntur" ("What do friends strive for other than to be one? The more they are one, the more they are friends. . . . What is every love? Does it not wish to become one with what it loves and, if it reaches that, it becomes one with it? Physical desire itself does not delight passionately over anything else except that loving bodies are joined together in one").

[87] *Trin.* 8.10.14 (Mountain and Glorie, 290–91): "Amor autem alicuius amantis est, et amore aliquid amatur. Ecce tria sunt, amans et quod amatur et amor. Quid est ergo amor nisi quaedam vita duo aliqua copulans vel copulari appetens, amantem scilicet et quod amatur? Et hoc etiam in extremis carnalibusque amoribus ita est. . . . Quid amat animus in amico nisi animum. Et illic igitur tria sunt, amans et quod amatur et amor." ("Love is of some lover. And by love something is loved. So notice there are three things: lover, what is loved, and love. What is love except a kind of life joining two things or seeking to join them, namely, the lover and that which is loved. And this is the way it is even in extreme carnal loves. . . . What is it that the mind loves in a friend if not his mind. And so there are three things: lover, and what is loved, and love").

[88] *In 1 Jo.* 2.14 (Agaësse, 180 [PL 35.1997], Rettig, 158): "Tenete potius dilectionem Dei, ut quomodo Deus est aeternus, sic et vos maneatis in aeternum: quia talis est quisque, qualis ejus

Augustine distinguishes between the things that we use and the things that we enjoy. "To enjoy is to adhere by love to something for its own sake. To use is to refer something that comes into use toward obtaining what you love, provided the latter is to be loved. For unlawful use ought rather to be called abuse or misuse."[89] We are exiles in this world traveling toward our true home where happiness lies. We ought not to become so enamored of traveling through this beautiful world that we lose interest in our destination.[90] Beatitude is to be found only in God, our final end, and all else must be seen as means to this end. Only God is to be enjoyed. This distinction between "enjoy" (*frui*) and "use" (*uti*) spells out an order of love. It does not mean that one can take no joy in the beauty of the spring, nor does it mean that people are merely means to an end. What it means is that our hearts can rest only in the absolute Good and infinite Love, which is God; if we try to find rest in some other object we are not acting within the order inherent in creation, and we will not be happy.[91]

Every virtue is a form of love. The fruit of the Spirit is love, and from that love—as from a root or source—arise joy, peace, and the other virtues.[92] Virtue is ordered love; that is, love aligned with the God-given

---

dilectio est" ("Hold rather to the love of God, so that just as God is eternal, so you too can remain unto eternity, because as a person's love is, so he is").

[89]   *Doc. Chr.* 1.4.4 (Martin 8; tr. Hill, 107): "Frui enim est amore alicui rei inhaerere propter se ipsam. Uti autem, quod in usum venerit, ad id, quod amas obtinendum referre, si tamen amandum est. Nam usus inlicitus, abusus potius vel abusio nominandus est."

[90]   *Doc. Chr.* 1.4.4 (Martin, 8; tr. Hill, 107–8).

[91]   Gilson, *The Christian Philosophy of Saint Augustine*, 166–67; van Bavel, "Love," 513. Here is an example: *Doc. Chr.* 1.33.37 (Martin, 27; tr. Hill, 122): "Cum autem homine in deo frueris, deo potius quam homine frueris, illo enim frueris, quo efficeris beatus, et ad eum te pervenisse laetaberis, in quo spem ponis, ut venias. . . . Si vero inhaeseris atque permanseris, finem in ea ponens laetitiae tuae, tunc vere et proprie frui dicendus es; quod non faciendum est nisi in illa trinitate, id est summo et incommutabili bono" ("When you enjoy a human being in God, you enjoy God rather than the human being. You will be enjoying the one by whom you are made happy, and you will rejoice that you have reached him in whom you place your hope, that you may come to him. . . . If you cling and stand fast, putting the goal of your joy in it, then truly and properly you may be said to enjoy it; because nothing is to be enjoyed except that Trinity, that is, the highest and incommutable Good"); *Conf.* 1.1.1 (O'Donnell, 3; tr. Boulding, 39): "fecisti nos ad te et inquietum est cor nostrum donec requiescat in te" ("you made us [with a deep yearning] toward yourself, and our heart is restless until it rests in you").

[92]   *Jo. ev. tr.* 87.1 (Willems, 544): "Unde et apostolus Paulus . . . fructus, inquit, spiritus caritas est: ac deinde cetera tamquam ex isto capite exorta et religata contexuit, quae sunt, gaudium, pax, longanimitas, benignitas, bonitas" ("Hence the Apostle Paul . . . says, 'The fruit of the Spirit is charity': and then he connected to it the rest as sprung from this source and bound to it. They are: joy, peace, patience, kindness, goodness"); *En. Ps.* 51.12 (Dekkers and Fraipont, 631): "Radix nostra caritas nostra, fructus nostri opera nostra: opus est ut opera tua de cari-

nature and destiny of human beings created and recreated in the image and likeness of God: "It seems to me that a short and true definition of virtue is the ordering of love"; for this reason, in the holy Song of Songs the Spouse of Christ, the City of God, sings, 'Order love in me.'"[93] The four cardinal virtues are varieties of ordered love.[94]

Augustine names four suitable objects of love: God, our neighbors, ourselves, and our bodies. Love of ourselves and of our bodies is so natural there is no need for an explicit commandment to do so.[95] His belief in the Incarnation and the resurrection of the body prompts him to affirm the love of one's body.[96] Beyond these four kinds of licit love

---

tate procedant, tunc est radix tua in terra viventium" ("Charity is our root: it is necessary that your works proceed from charity, for then your root is in the land of the living").

[93] *Civ. Dei* 15.22 (Dombart and Kalb, 488; tr. O'Meara, 637): "Unde mihi videtur, quod definitio brevis et vera virtutis ordo est amoris; propter quod in sancto cantico canticorum cantat sponsa Christ, civitas Dei: 'Ordinate in me caritatem'" ("Hence, it seems to me that the short and true definition of virtue is the ordering of love. For this reason in the holy Song of Songs, the Spouse of Christ, the City of God, sings: 'Order love in me'"); *Doc. Chr.* 1.27.28 (Martin, 22; tr. Hill, 118): "Ille autem iuste et sancte vivit . . . qui ordinatam habet dilectionem, ne aut diligat, quod non est diligendum, aut non diligat, quod diligendum est, aut amplius diligat, quod minus diligendum est, aut aeque diligat, quod vel minus vel amplius diligendum est, an minus vel amplius quod aeque diligendum est" ("He lives in a just and holy manner . . . who has ordered love, so that he does not love what is not to be loved nor does he love what is to be loved either more or less than it should be loved, or love equally what ought to be loved less or more, or love less or more what ought to be loved equally"). For further references see Richard of St Victor, *Trin.* 3.2, (Ribaillier, 136–37; tr. Evans, VTT 1:248–49, and 369–70 note 195).

[94] *Mor.* 1.15.25 (Rivière, 60–61 [PL 32.1322]: "nihil omnino esse virtutem affirmaverim, nisi summum amorem Dei" ("I would affirm that virtue is nothing else than the supreme love of God").

[95] *Doc. Chr.* 1.35.39 (Martin, 29; tr. Hill, 123): "ut se quisque diligat, praecepto non opus est" ("there is not need of a command that one love oneself"); *Doc. Chr.* 1.24.24 (Martin, 19, tr. Hill, 116): "Nemo ergo se odit" ("Therefore, no one hates himself"); *Trin.* 14.14.18 (Mountain and Glorie, 445–46; tr. Hill, 384): "Qui ergo se diligere novit deum diligit; qui vero non diligit deum etiam si se diligit, quod ei naturaliter inditum est, tamen non inconvenienter odisse se dicitur" ("Whoever knows how to love himself loves God; whoever does not love God even if he loves himself, something that is naturally innate, can rightly be said to hate himself"); *Ench.* 20.76 (ed. Rivière, 238; tr. Arand, 75–76).

[96] *Civ. Dei.* 1.13 (Dobart and Kalb, 14; tr. O'Meara, 22): "nullo modo ipsa spernenda sunt corpora, quae utique multo familiarius atque coniunctius quam quaelibet indumenta gestamus. Haec enim non ad ornamentum vel adiutorium, quod adhibitur extrinsecus, sed ad ipsam naturam hominis pertinent" ("in no way should we despise human bodies, which are worn much more intimately and closely than any clothes. They do not pertain to decoration or help which is extrinsic, but to the very nature of the human being"); *En Ps.* 149.18 (Dekkers and Fraipont, 2058): "Posset dici et corpus nostrum carcer, non quia carcer est quod fecit Deus, sed quia poenale est mortale. . . . Tota ista forma, status, incessus, membra ordinata, sensuum dispositiones, . . . omnis haec compago et fabricae distinctio, non potuit fieri nisi a Deo. . . . Corpus enim tuum fecit Deus bonum, quia bonus est" ("One could say

are both the illicit will to dominate others, and excessive craving for physical things. One should not try to subject to oneself human beings who ought to be subject only to God, nor should one who ought to serve God become subservient to physical things.[97]

So love of God and love of neighbor are crucial. The twofold command to love God and neighbor sums up all Scripture. The Sacred Scriptures aim to teach the love of that Reality which is to be enjoyed, and the love of those who can enjoy that Reality with us, that is, God and neighbor.[98] Christ became a human being, incarnate as our neighbor, in order to show us how much God loves us,[99] to show us Love in Person.[100] God is love,[101] and love is the likeness of God in us. Love draws us to him and, as our love increases, we become more like God.[102]

---

that our body is a prison, not because what God made is a prison, but because it [has become subject to] punishment and death. . . . All the form, stature, diversity, ordered members, arrangements of the senses, . . . all the connection and diversity of structure, could be brought about only by God . . . for God made your body good, because He is good").

[97] *Doc. Chr.* 1.23.23–1.24.24 (Martin, 18–19; tr. Hill, 115–16); *Conf.* 2.6.14 (O'Donnell, 21; tr. Boulding, 71): "Ita fornicatur anima, cum avertitur abs te et quaerit extra te ea quae pura et liquida non invenit, nisi cum redit ad te" ("A soul commits fornication when it turns away from you and seeks outside of you things that it does not find pure and clear, except by returning to you").

[98] *Doc. Chr.* 1.35.39–36.40 (Martin, 29; tr. Hill, 123–24).

[99] *Cat. rud.* 4.7–8 (Combès and Farges, 30–36).

[100] *In 1 Jo 10.5* (Agaësse, 420 [PL 35.2059]; tr. Rettig, 268): "'Finis enim Legis Christus est.' . . . Et quid est, 'finis Christus?' Quia Christus Deus, et finis praecepti charitas, et Deus charitas" ("'The end of the Law is Christ.' . . . And why is Christ the end? Because Christ is God, and the end of the commandment is love, and God is love").

[101] *In 1 Jo.* 8.14 (Agaësse, 368 [PL 35.2044]; tr. Rettig, 244): "Amplius tibi non potuit dilectio commendari, quam ut diceretur Deus. . . . 'Deus dilectio est. Et qui manet in dilectione, in Deo manet, et Deus in eo manet.' Vicissim in se habitant, qui continet et qui continetur. Habitas in Deo, sed ut contineraris: habitat in te Deus, sed ut te contineat, ne cadas." ("Love could not be more emphatically commended to you than it is when it is said to be God. . . . 'God is love, and whoever remains in love remains in God, and God remains in him.' They dwell in each other reciprocally; one holds and one is held. You dwell in God, but so that you are held; God dwells in you, but so that he holds you, so you may not fall").

[102] *Mor.* 1.11.18 (Rivière, 48 [PL 32.1319]): "Secutio igitur Dei, beatitatis appetitus est: consecutio autem, ipsa beatitas. At eum sequimur diligendo, consequimur vero, non cum hoc omnino efficimur quod est ipse, sed ei proximi, eumque mirifico et intelligibili modo contingentes, ejusque veritate et sanctitate penitus illustrati atque comprehensi" ("Striving for God is desire for beatitude; attaining God is beatitude itself. We strive for him by loving, we attain him, not when we are made completely what he is, but when we are made near him, connected to him in a wonderful and intelligible way, completely illumined and encompassed by his truth and holiness"); *Mor.* 1.14.23 (Rivière, 58 [PL 32.1321]): "Fit ergo per caritatem ut conformemur Deo" ("It comes about through love that we are conformed to God").

At the same time, we become more aware of God's utter mystery.[103]
Since God is love, God indwells in us as love.[104]
Love of God is impossible without love of neighbor. Both the Old
Testament and Jesus command love of neighbor, and whoever loves
God does what God commands. To love God is to participate in God's
love for all human beings, whom he created.[105] More important still is
the bond that unites all in Christ:

> Whoever loves the Son also loves the sons of God. Which sons of God?
> The members of the Son of God. By loving one becomes a member,
> and, through love one becomes part of the fabric of the Body of Christ.
> And there will be one Christ loving Himself. For when the members
> love each other, He loves his body. . . . Therefore, when you love the
> members of Christ, you love Christ; when you love Christ, you love
> the Son of God; when you love the Son of God, you love the Father.
> Love cannot be divided.[106]

---

[103] *En. Ps.* 99.5–6 (Dekkers and Fraipont, 1396): "Inquantum autem in te caritas crescit, efficiens
te et revocans te ad similitudinem Dei, pertendit usque inimicos; ut sis ei similes qui facit
solem suum origi non super bonos tantum. . . . Quantum accedes ad similitudinem, tantum
proficis in caritate, et tanto incipis sentire Deum . . . et ibi sentis dici non posse quod sentis"
("Insofar as love grows in you, shaping you in the likeness of God and recalling you to it, love
extends even to enemies, so that you are like him who makes his sun rise not just on the
good. . . . The more you advance in love, the more you approach God's likeness and the more
you grow in awareness of God . . . and there you become aware that you cannot express that
awareness").

[104] *In 1 Jo.* 8.14 (Agaësse, 368 [PL 35.2044]; tr. Rettig, 244), cited above, note 101.

[105] *Jo. ev. tr.* 87.1 (Willems, 544): "Neque enim vera dilectione diligeremus invicem, nisi diligentes
Deum. Diligit enim unusquisque proximum tamquam seipsum, si diligit Deum" ("We do
not love each other with true love unless we love God. For each one loves his neighbor as
himself if he loves God"); *In 1 Jo.* 8.10 (Agaësse, 360 [PL 35.2042]; tr. Rettig, 241): "Si ergo
optas, diligendo inimicum, ut sit frater tuus; cum eum diligis, fratrem diligis. . . . Sic et nos
Deus amavit peccatores" ("If therefore you so choose that by loving your enemy he may be
your brother, when you love him you love a brother. . . . Thus has God loved us sinners"); *En.
Ps.* 102.13 (Dekkers and Fraipont, 1463): "Occurrit tibi homo peccator, duo nomina dixi; haec
duo nomina non superflua sunt; duo nomina aliud quod homo, aliud quod peccator; quod
homo opus est Dei; quod peccator, opus hominis est; da operi Dei, noli operi hominis"
("A man, a sinner, comes your way. I just used two nouns: these two nouns are not redundant;
one indicates that he is a man, the other that he is a sinner; that he is a man is the work of
God; that he is a sinner is the work of the man. Give to the work of God, not to the work of
the man").

[106] *In 1 Jo.* 10.3 (Agaësse, 414 [PL 35.2055–6]; tr. Rettig, 165): "Nec potest quisquam diligere
Patrem, nisi diligat Filium; et qui diligit Filium, diligit et filios Dei. Quos filios Dei? Membra
Filii Dei. Et diligendo fit et ipse membrorum, et fit per dilectionem in compage corporis
Christi: et erit unus Christus amans seipsum. . . . Cum ergo membra Christi diligis, Christum
diligis; cum Christum diligis, Filium Dei diligis; cum Filium Dei diligis, et Patrem diligis.
Non potest ergo separari dilectio" ("No one can love the Father unless he loves the Son.
Whoever loves the Son also loves the sons of God. Which sons of God? The members of the

Extend your love throughout the whole world, if you wish to love Christ, because the members of Christ are located throughout the world.[107]

Loving one's neighbor, loving God, and loving love are intimately connected.[108] Without loving God, it is impossible to love one's neighbor as one should love oneself, that is, so that one's neighbor may reign with Christ. Those who love each other in order to have God truly love themselves; and so, in order to love themselves, they love God.[109] Love of neighbor encompasses care of soul and body.[110]

Although we love only God as the ultimate goal and happiness of our existence, we do not love others as mere objects to be consumed or as sources of pleasure. Loving others is to wish them true happiness. We love them not as a source of pleasure or as things to be consumed, but with benevolence, which wills their good and happiness without expecting some other profit. Love itself is never diminished in being expended. In some way the purest love is for people on whom we have nothing to bestow, for then we are not tempted to feel superior over them or to dominate them.[111]

Son of God. And by loving he himself becomes a member, and by love he is fitted into the body of Christ. And there will be one Christ loving himself. . . . Therefore, when you love the members of Christ, you love Christ; when you love Christ, you love the Son of God; when you love the Son of God, you also love the Father. Love cannot be divided up").

[107] *In Jo.* 10.8 (Agaësse, 430 [PL 35.2060]; tr. Rettig, 273): "Extende charitatem per totum orbem, si vis Christum amare; quia membra Christi per orbem jacent."

[108] *Trin.* 8.8.12 (Mountain and Glorie, 286–89; tr. Hill. 253–54).

[109] *Jo. ev. tr.* 83.3 (Willems, 536): "Utquid enim diligit nos Christus, nisi ut regnare possimus cum Christo? Ad hoc ergo et nos invicem diligamus. . . . Qui autem se propter habendum Deum diligunt, ipsi se diligunt; ergo ut se diligant, Deum diligent" ("To what purpose does Christ love us, if not that we can reign with Christ? Let us therefore love each other for this same purpose. . . . However, those who love themselves in order to have God, love themselves; therefore in order that they may love themselves, they will love God").

[110] *Mor.* 1.26.52 (Rivière, 98 [PL 32.1332]): "Homo igitur, ut homini apparet, anima rationalis est mortali atque terreno utens corpore. Partim ergo corpori, partim vero animae homini benefacit qui proximum diligit. Ad corpus quod pertinet medicina nominata, . . . sed etiam cibus et potus, tegmen et tectum, defensio denique omnis atque munitio" ("As he appears to a man, a man is a rational soul using a mortal or earthly body. Someone who loves his neighbor benefits a man, partly in his body and partly in his soul. To the body pertain what is termed medicine, . . . but also food and drink, covering and a roof, and finally every kind of defense and protection").

[111] *In 1 Jo.* 8.5 (Agaësse, 346–48 [PL 35.2058–9]; tr. Rettig, 233–34): "Omnis dilectio, fratres charissimi, utique benevolentiam quamdam habet erga eos qui diliguntur. . . . Et quidquid ad cibandum amamus, ad hoc amamus, ut illud consumatur, et nos reficiamur. Numquid sic amandi sunt homines, tanquam consumendi? Sed amicitia quaedam benevolentiae est. . . . Opera misericordiae cessabunt; numquid ardor charitatis exstinguetur? Germanius amas felicem hominem, cui non habes quod praestes; purior ille amor erit, multoque sincerior.

The history of world revolves around love, two cities defined by whether their love is God-centered or self-centered—one subject to God and turned toward neighbor, the other seeking its private interest and looking for domination:

> There are two loves: of which one is holy and the other unclean; one social, the other private; one considers the common utility for the sake of the heavenly community, the other subjugates even what is common to its own power by arrogating dominion to itself; one is subject to God, the other seeks to rival God; one is peaceful, the other unruly; one is calm, the other seditious; one prefers the truth to the praise of the wayward, the other is avid for praise of any sort; one is friendly, the other envious; one wishes for his neighbor what he wishes for himself, the other wishes to subject his neighbor to himself; the one rules his neighbor to benefit his neighbor; the other rules him for his own benefit. These existed previously in the angels: one in the good angels, and the other in the bad. They distinguish two cities in the human race, according to the wonderful and ineffable providence of God, who guides and orders all that he creates. One city is of the just, the other of the unjust; they advance through time intermingled, but they will be separated at the last judgment.[112]

Nam si praestiteris misero, fortassis extollere te cupis adversus eum, et eum tibi vis esse subjectum; qui auctor est tui beneficii. Ille indiguit, tu impertitus es; quasi major videris quia tu praestitisti, quam ille cui praestitum est. Opta aequalem, ut ambo sub uno sitis cui nihil praestari potest" ("Dearly beloved brothers, certainly all love has some kind of benevolence toward those who are loved. . . . And whatever we love to eat, we love it so that it may be consumed and we may be nourished. Are people to be loved in the same way, as things to be consumed? Rather, friendship is a kind of benevolence. . . . Works of mercy will cease, but will the ardor of love be extinguished? You love more truly a fortunate man to whom you do not have anything that you may give; such a love will be more pure and much more sincere. For if you give something to a needy person, perhaps you wish to flaunt yourself in comparison with him, and you want the one who is the occasion for your beneficence to be subject to you. He was needy, you bestowed; because you have bestowed, you seem somehow greater than he to whom the bestowal was made. Wish for an equal, so that you both may be under one on whom nothing can be bestowed"). *In 1 Jo.* 6.2–4 (Agaësse, 278–84 [PL 35.2019–21]; tr. Rettig, 199–202, with a note on the meaning of "benevolentia").

[112] *Gn. Litt.* 11.15 (Zycha, 347–48): "Hi duo amores—quorum alter sanctus et alter immundus; alter socialis, alter privatus, alter communi utilitati consulens propter supernam societatem, alter etiam rem communem in potestatem propriam redigens propter adrogantem dominationem, alter subditus, alter aemulus deo, alter tranquillus, alter turbulentus, alter pacificus, alter seditiosus, alter veritatem laudibus errantium praeferens, alter quoquo modo laudis avidus, alter amicalis, alter invidus, alter hoc volens proximo quo sibi, alter subicere proximum sibi, alter propter proximi utilitatem regens proximum, alter propter suam—praecesserunt in angelis, alter in bonis, alter in malis, et distinxerunt conditas in genere humano civitates duas sub admirabili et ineffabili providentia dei, cuncta, quae creat, administrantis et ordinantis, alteram iustorum, alteram iniquorum, quarum etiam quadam temporali conmixtione peragitur saeculum, donec ultimo iudicio separentur."

Fifty times in his works, Augustine quotes 1 John 4:18: "There is no fear in love, but perfect love drives out fear."[113] The sign of advance in Christian love is the reduction of fear; the sign of perfection in love is the absence of fear.[114] Fear pertains to the old man not yet fully emancipated from sin; love pertains to the new man reborn into the freedom of Christ.[115]

Love then is the root of all Christian existence, virtue, and action. "Love and do what you will; if you are silent, be silent because of love; if you shout out, shout out because of love; . . . let the root of love be within; from this root only good can come into existence."[116]

Augustine's teaching profoundly shapes the Victorines' understanding of love. Next to the Bible, he is their most important authority. He provides the framework within which they work, even if they sometimes alter or question that framework. There are elements within his framework that seem problematic. Some of these the Victorines address; others they do not. Here are examples, some of which will be discussed in this introduction.

Augustine's understanding of the relationship between body and soul, and his notion that the soul loves the body as something beneath itself, both seem problematic. Godfrey is uncomfortable with Augustine's explanation of the union of body and soul, and he modifies Augustine's thought on love of the body. The distinction between "to use" (*uti*) and "to enjoy" (*frui*)—whatever nuances Augustine sometimes gives it—seems to imply it is wrong to enjoy finite things, so that all that is not God is only a tool or occasion for loving God. The Victorines

---

[113]   Dideberg, *Saint Augustin*, 190–201.

[114]   *Div. quaest. 83*, 36.1 (Mutzenbecher, 54): "Signum provectus eius [caritatis] est imminutio timoris; signum perfectionis eius nullus timor, quia et radix est omnium malorum cupiditas, et consummata dilectio foras mittit timorem" ("The sign of [charity's] advancing is the diminishment of fear; the sign of its perfection is no fear, because the root of all evils is base desire, and consummated love casts out fear").

[115]   *Civ. Dei*, 14.9 (Dombart and Kalb, 429; tr. O'Meara, 565–66); *En. Ps.* 127, 7–9 (Dekkers and Fraipont, 1871–74), where following a version of Ps. 18:10 (Vulg.), Augustine distinguishes a (servile) fear of pain or punishment from "chaste" (*castus*) fear—the latter fears that the Bridegroom will delay, the former that he will come. Chaste fear does not want to lose the embrace of the Bridegroom whom it loves.

[116]   *In 1 Jo.* 7.8 (Agaësse, 328 [PL 35.2033]; tr. Rettig, 223 and note): "Dilige, et quod vis fac: sive taceas, dilectione taceas; sive clames, dilectione clames; . . . radix sit intus dilectionis, non potest de ista radice nisi bonum existere." Here Augustine alludes to the literal sense of "existere," ex + stare, to stand out from. Cf. Richard of St Victor, *Trin.* 4.16 and 22 (Ribaillier, 178–79, 187–88; tr. Evans, VTT 1:280–81, 287–88).

generally avoid this distinction. The notion of ordered love, again in spite of Augustine's nuances, seems to imply that one should measure out love to other people according to their worth, which seems to make God's love for fallen humankind disordered. While accepting the notion of ordered love, the emphasis that Richard and Achard give to divine compassion makes it clear that love is not measured solely according to the moral goodness of the person loved. Some claim that a eudaemonistic understanding of love such as Augustine's makes all human love, even of God, selfish. Hugh argues that it does not. In Augustine's theory, the non-rational, non-evaluative, passionate side of love seems undervalued; Richard and Godfrey assign it more scope and worth. Augustine writes of love of self, but other authorities, followed by Richard of St Victor in his work *On the Trinity*, teach that love requires another as its object.[117]

There are three problematic features of Augustine's thought on love that the Victorines do not seem to question. These concern, respectively, loving others, the world, and oneself. As Joseph Lienhard writes, "Augustine was the first Christian writer to elaborate a theory of Christian friendship,"[118] yet friendship scarcely appears in his treatments of Christian love. How, then, is friendship to be integrated into a general theory of Christian love? The second problem concerns how, within Augustine's schema, it is possible to love material things. Finally, loving oneself does not seem to be quite as automatic as Augustine asserts; there are other forms of self-hate besides violating God's commandments.

Beyond the scope of this volume, there is Augustine's vastly influential and very complex teaching on marriage that has been controversial from his time to ours. Hugh of St Victor elaborates a theology of marriage, and Godfrey praises the contribution of married people to the Church.

---

[117] *Trin.* 3.2 (ed. Ribaillier, 136–37; tr. Evans, VTT 1:248–49, 369, notes 193–94); Hugh of St Victor, *Arrha*, 11 (Sicard, 232; tr. Feiss, VTT 2:206–7). References to *On the Betrothal-Gift of the Soul* are to the paragraph numbers in VTT 2.

[118] Joseph T. Lienhard, "Friendship, Friends," in *Augustine through the Ages*, 372–73, who writes that friendship is always important to Augustine. At least from the time he writes the *Confessions* (397/401) Augustine thinks of friendship as a gift of the Spirit, which "adds attraction and delight to the Christian charity owed to all." For his mature ideas on friendship see, for example, *Conf.* 4.4.7–4.12.19 (O'Donnell, 35–40); *Trin.* 9.6.11 (Mountain and Glorie, 302–3, tr. Hill, 276–77); *Civ. Dei* 19.8 (Dombart and Kalb, 672–73; tr. O'Meara, 862–63).

FAITHFUL REASON SEEKING TO UNDERSTAND LOVE

Pondering with the eyes of faith the authoritative teaching of the
Scriptures, St Augustine, and other Christian authorities, and, drawing
on their own experience, Hugh, Richard, and Godfrey of St Victor, pen
writings in which they seek to understand the nature, possibilities, and
risks of love and to instruct and exhort their readers about love. Other
Victorines, such as Achard and Adam, do not compose treatises or
meditations on love, but love is an integral part of their thought and
writing. In the process, the Victorines systematize and reshape the
broader Christian tradition of which they are a part. The sections that
follow will summarize and then analyze what each Victorine thinks
about love.

HUGH OF ST VICTOR

Hugh gives us a hint about why he writes so often about love. Human beings never tire of speaking about what they want very much.[119]
The Bridegroom can speak to the bride of nothing but love.[120] Hugh's
writing about love is like a bellows blowing on the fire of his readers'
love.[121]

The titles of Hugh's works reflect the various Latin words for love:
On the Praise of Charity (caritatis); The Love (amore) of the Bridegroom;
On the Substance of Love (dilectionis). He observes elsewhere that in
the Bible caritas and dilectio are often synonyms.[122] His cover letter to
On the Praise of Charity evokes dilectio,[123] and after praising the caritas
of the Biblical saints,[124] he refers to the dilectio celebrated in the Song
of Songs[125] and to the force of amor that enables martyrs to give their
lives for God's sake.[126] Dilectio makes a choice between caritas and cu-

---

[119] Eulogium 1 (PL 176.987B). Almost all the works of Hugh of St Victor referred to in this section
       are in VTT 2.
[120] Eulogium 7 (PL 176.989C).
[121] Laude car. 1 (Sicard, 182).
[122] Hugh discusses the words for love in Sacr. 1.13.12 (PL 176.545D–550C), where he refutes those
       who would distinguish caritas, which they say can never be lost, from dilectio, which can be
       lost.
[123] Laude car. 1 (Sicard, 182).
[124] Laude car. 2 (Sicard, 182).
[125] Laude car. 3 (Sicard, 184).
[126] Laude car. 4 (Sicard, 184–86).

piditas.[127] As he reaches the end of his praise of charity, Hugh again uses all three words synonymously.[128] One is left with the impression that while in Hugh's usage *caritas* is inherently and unchangeably good, even divine, *dilectio* can be directed at what is good or bad, since it connotes choice. However, Hugh is drawn by the usage of the Latin Scriptures to employ the two words almost synonymously. *Amor* is a broader term, which has the same range as the English "love"; that is, *amor* can take the forms of love of God, love of neighbor, and love (*cupiditas*) of money or sensual pleasure. All romantic or erotic love is *amor*, but not all such love is *caritas* or *dilectio*, although it can be.[129]

Love is the life of the heart.[130] It is a fire seeking kindling so that it may turn into a blaze.[131] When it does burn hot, it can purify or consume.[132] Since love is life of the heart, one cannot be truly alive without it; certainly, without love no one can be happy.[133] Each human being loves to love and to be loved.[134] From love comes everything that is from us, whether good or bad.[135] A formal definition of love is "a delight of someone's heart toward something on account of something."[136] If the heart has not yet attained the object of its love, love is desire in motion; when it has attained its object, love is enjoyment at rest.[137] Love is unquenchable, stronger than death.[138]

---

[127] *Laude car.* 4, 6–8 (Sicard, 184–92, especially 188.99–103). Even if my conjecture that the title of *Quid vere dilegendum est* is a question is mistaken, the use of *dilectio* in the title connotes choice.

[128] *Laude car.* 15 (Sicard, 198).

[129] These three terms for "love" present the translator with dilemmas. There are also other words that overlap with these three: e.g., *pietas, affectus, affectio*. The most pressing issue is how to translate "*caritas.*" "Charity" is a cognate for "*caritas,*" but "charity" has a different nuance in ordinary English usage. In his introduction to *On the Praise of Charity*, Franklin T. Harkins gives a cogent rationale for the practice he adopts of translating "*caritas*" consistently as "charity." Other translators in this volume vary their translations of these terms, taking their cue from context, and giving the Latin words in parentheses where this seems helpful. Their introductions to the translations take up this question of vocabulary.

[130] *Quid vere* 1 (Baron, 94); *Arrha* 3 (Sicard, 226).

[131] *Arrha* 13, 19 (Sicard, 232, 238).

[132] *Subst. dilect.* 1 (Baron, 82).

[133] *Arrha* 9 (Sicard, 230).

[134] *Laude car.* 1 (Sicard, 182); *Arrha* 17, 39 (Sicard, 236, 254–56); Augustine, *Conf.* 3.1 (O'Donnell, 23).

[135] *Subst. dilect.* 1 (Baron, 82).

[136] *Subst. dilect.* 5 (and 8), (Baron, 86.48–49 and 90.97–98): "amor est delectatio cordis alicuius ad aliquid propter aliquid."

[137] *Subst. dilect.* 5, 8, 9 (Baron, 86, 90); *Quid vere* 2 (Baron, 94).

[138] *Laude car.* 5, 3 (Sicard, 186–88, 184).

Love is a singular, unique movement, which divides into two streams, charity and cupidity.[139] "When love takes the form of cupidity, desire directs the heart; when it has the form of charity, the heart directs desire."[140] If desire directs the heart, human beings are carried by the tide of their desires, and love cascades downward through passion toward exterior things. If faith in the heart directs love toward interior or eternal things, love rises upward.[141] Hence, love (*diligere, dilectum*) requires choice (*eligere, electum*).[142] However, as will be clear, Hugh regularly moves to more complex analyses, which take him beyond this simple dichotomous choice between charity and cupidity.

Since love is a movement, human beings are never at rest until they enjoy an object that fully satisfies their desire. As beings endowed with immortality, they seek an eternal object; if such an object does not exist, they are condemned to eternal misery.[143] As beings whose desire is boundless, they seek a perfect, infinite Good.[144] Anything less will leave them still desiring and seeking, but loving union with an eternal and perfect Good brings the peaceful enjoyment of eternal beatitude.[145]

And so a human being finds herself loving all the good things of the earth, but she cannot embrace any one of them above all the rest, for she knows that all are limited and fleeting. The created object of her love may cease to exist or something may come along that she loves more.[146] As she recognizes, seeks, and strives to possess the perfect, eternal Good,[147] her love moves from the many to the One.[148] Human life on earth is then a voyage on a stormy sea in which love can be ordered, a directed impetus toward the Good, or disordered, a careening toward evil.[149] There are three possibilities: one can be in the sea, without faith, tossed by waves of desire; or one can be in the ship of faith, but headed for shipwreck because lured by transitory goods; or one can

---

[139] *Subst. dilect.* 3 (Baron, 84).
[140] *Subst. dilect.* 1 (Baron, 82).
[141] *Subst. dilect.* 1 (Baron, 82); *Quid vere* 4–5 (Baron, 96–98); *Arrha* 7 (Sicard, 228).
[142] *Arrha* 5, 72, *et passim* (Sicard, 226–28, 284); *Laude car.* 6 (Sicard, 188).
[143] *Arrha* 9 (Sicard, 230).
[144] *Quid vere* 2 (Baron, 94).
[145] *Subst. dilect.* 6 (Baron, 86).
[146] *Arrha* 6–7 (Sicard, 228).
[147] *Arrha* 71 (Sicard, 283).
[148] *Eulogium* 20 (PL 176.994A).
[149] *Subst. dilect.* 3, 5, 8, 9, 10, 13 (Baron, 84, 86, 90, 92).

be securely on board the ship of faith, steering by the love of eternal Good.[150]

In another metaphor, Hugh describes human life as a race run by the impetus of love. The human being ought to choose the road of justice and run it with those who love and seek justice. This is the road that leads to the Author of righteousness. The choosing, the running, and the arriving are all the work of charity. Charity is the road and the guide, but charity is also the goal because God is charity. Whoever has charity has God. God dwells in her and she in God.[151] As she runs—with the impetus of God-given charity, under the guidance of God's love, toward God who is love—she has as companions others in whose progress she rejoices.[152] Having been moved to praise and wonder by the world, which God has made, she runs from it—good as it is—to turn inward toward God.[153] Love is disordered if she runs in conformity with the world, that is, if she lets the ups and downs of earthly existence determine her happiness and sorrow.[154] Insofar as the world is a siren that can draw the love toward shipwreck, Christian life requires a turning from the world, a renunciation: flee, trample, curb, subdue, despise, and reject "the world!"[155] Only in God is there complete joy.[156] She should love the gifts of God as given by him, and love God for herself and herself for God.[157]

In *The Praise of the Bridegroom*, Hugh gives other threefold divisions of human beings in love. In their desire or attachment toward earthly things and pleasures, they may restrict themselves to what is absolutely necessary, or they may aim to satisfy bodily desire, or they may seek to maximize pleasures—a sequence of best, good, bad. Again,

---

[150] *Quid vere* 5 (Baron, 96–98).
[151] *Laude car.* 7–9, 14 (Sicard, 188–92, 196–98).
[152] *Subst. dilect.* 11 (Baron, 92); *Sacr.* 2.13.6 (PL 176.528D): "Geminam nobis sacra Scripura charitatem commendat; Dei videlicet et proximi. Charitatem Dei ut sic ipsum diligamus ut in ipso gaudeamus. Charitatem proximi ut sic ipsum diligamus, non ut in ipso, sed ut cum ipso gaudeamus in Deo" ("Sacred Scripture commends to us a twofold charity—love of God and of neighbor: love of God so that we may love Him in such a way that we rejoice in Him; love of neighbor, so that we may love him not so that we rejoice in him, but so that we may rejoice with him in God"). We love our neighbor so that we may run with him and arrive together at God, in whom is our rest (PL 176.529A). If we love the wisdom of some person, we cannot do that unless we love Wisdom itself (PL 176.529B).
[153] *Subst. dilect.* 9 (Baron, 90); *Eulogium* 11 (PL 176.990AB).
[154] *Subst. dilect.* 12 (Baron, 92).
[155] *Laude car.* 2–4 (Sicard, 182–86); *Eulogium* 20 (PL 176.994A).
[156] *Laude car.* 6, 8 (Sicard, 188–92).
[157] *Arrha* 18 (Sicard, 236).

there are the baptized who are carnal and worldly, the baptized who are not carnal but are not raised up, and the baptized who are raised up toward God. The latter are the prime targets of the devil's attacks, and so they need patience.[158]

No one can be happy loving only herself with a miserable and solitary love. Love wishes to pour itself out on an equal.[159] On the one hand, one is neither happy nor human if one spurns the peace of community.[160] On the other hand, one should love oneself, for the beauty of the self surpasses that of all physical things.[161] God is supremely One and wants humanity—united to Him—to be one as well. Those in the Body of Christ are united to the One by their love, and through love of each other they are one with each other.[162] As a result, whatever belongs to one belongs to all, so that what one person does not obtain in himself, he possesses through love of his neighbor. The good of all becomes wholly the good of each.[163] Spiritual love (*caritas*) is not a commodity that is lessened by the participation of many; in fact, it becomes better in a singular way when it is common to all. God's love is present to each and would not be more for one person if that person were the only one. God's love for each is unique, but not private; single, but not solitary; participated, but not divided; singular for all, and complete for each.[164] The same is true of Hugh's love for the recipients of his *Soliloquy*: that it is addressed to one particular person in a community does not mean that his love for others is lessened.[165]

In these works, Hugh does not write about friendship explicitly, but his correspondence and covering letters declare his love for his friends. Of one correspondent, he asks for nothing but the gift of love.[166] His

---

158   *Eulogium* 13–18 (PL 176.990D–992D).
159   *Arrha* 11 (Sicard, 230–32).
160   *Quid vere* 1 (Baron, 94); *Arrha* 9, 11 (Sicard, 230–32).
161   *Arrha* 10, 12 (Sicard, 230, 232; tr. Feiss, VTT 2:207). In *Sacr.* 2.13.7 (PL 176.531C–534A), Hugh ponders why there is no command to love oneself. Following Augustine, he writes that a human being naturally loves himself. God made both his body and his soul good, and so he should love both. Love of the body aims at its physical well-being; love of the soul aims at its goodness. To love the soul is to love its good, and God is its good. One does not love God to wish him good, but one loves God as one's good. Whoever loves God, has God and enjoys God.
162   *Sacr.* 2.13.11 (PL 176.544A): "Ergo charitas unitas est Ecclesiae" ("Therefore, charity is the unity of the Church").
163   *Subst. dilect.* 7 (Baron, 88); *Arrha* 2, 26 (Sicard, 226, 246); *Eulogium* 16 (PL 176.991D).
164   *Arrha* 27–28 (Sicard, 246–48).
165   *Arrha* 2 (Sicard, 236).
166   *Laude car.* 1 (Sicard, 182).

letter to Ranulph de Mauriaco is evidence of the value he puts on friendship:

To beloved brother R, from Hugh, a sinner.

"Love (*caritas*) never fails" (1 Cor. 13:8).[167] I heard this and knew that it was true. Now, dearest brother, experience has concurred, and I know clearly that love never fails. I had set out from home, and I came to you in a foreign land, but it did not seem foreign because I found friends there. I do not know whether I first made friends or was made one. I found love (*caritas*) there, and I loved (*dilexi*) her. I could not grow tired of her, because she was sweet to me. I filled the little sack of my heart, and I was sorry that it was small and could not hold all of her. I filled it as much as I could. I filled completely what I had, but I could not take all that I found. I accepted as much as I could. Loaded with its great worth I did not feel its weight, because my burden uplifted me. Now, after completing a long journey, I find that my sack is still full. It is not diminished, because "love never fails." In it, dearest brother, I find first, among other things, my memory of you, and, from it, I have sealed this letter. I hope that you are safe and sound in the Lord. Repay me this love and pray for me. The Lord Jesus Christ be with you. Amen.[168]

---

[167] In *Sacr.* 2.13.11 (PL 176.539–545C), Hugh refutes those who cite this verse to claim that once one has charity one never loses it. Hugh argues that the text refers to the perdurance and perfection of charity in heaven.

[168] (PL 176.1011AB): "Dilecto fratri R. Hugo peccator. 'Charitas nunquam excidit' (1 Cor. 13:8). Audieram hoc et sciebam quod verum erat. Nunc autem, frater charissime, experimentum accessit, et scio plane quod charitas nunquam excidit. Peregre profectus eram, et veni ad vos in terram alienam; et quasi aliena non erat, quoniam inveni amicos ibi: sed nescio an prius fecerim, an factus sim. Tamen inveni illic charitatem, et dilexi eam; et non potui fastidire, quia dulcis mihi erat; et implevi sacculum cordis mei, et dolui quod angustus inventus est, et non valuit capere totam: tamen implevi quantum potui. Totum implevi quod habui, sed totum capere non valui quod inveni. Accepi ergo quantum capere potui, et onustus pretio pretioso pondus non sensi, quoniam sublevabat me sarcina mea. Nunc autem longo itinere confecto, adhuc sacculum meum plenum reperio, et non excidit quidquam ex eo, quoniam 'charitas nunquam excidit' (1 Cor. 13:8). Illic ergo, frater charissime, inter caetera memoria tui primum inventa est, et signavi ex ea litteras istas, cupiens te sanum esse et salvum in Domino. Tu ergo vicem repende dilectionis, et ora pro me. Dominus Jesus Christus tecum sit. Amen." Hugh does write of friendship briefly in *Sacr.* 2.13.6 (PL 176.529C–530A): one loves a friend because he has God. One loves a friend because he is good and just, and where goodness and justice are, there is God. One loves enemies who are not good, so that they may become good. He continues: "If God is truly loved, He is loved wherever He is found: in Himself, in the neighbor, inside and outside, above and below, far away and nearby" ("Si vere diligitur, diligitur ubicunque invenitur. In seipso, in proximo, intus et foris, et sursum et deorsum, longe et prope" [PL176.530D]).

Love is the origin of everything.[169] Charity is the road and the goal, and charity is God. The road of charity runs both ways, raising humankind to God and bringing God down to humankind.[170] Out of generous love, God created everything.[171] God created rational, spiritual beings to share in God's own happiness. God joined the rational creature to Himself so the creature could desire, embrace, and enjoy the infinite Good.[172] Charity drew the Son of God to the manger and the cross in order to call humankind back to the way.[173] The Groom came to the bride to call her to Himself.[174] Christ, the Good Samaritan, came down to where humanity lay half-dead, assumed their lot, suffered, conquered, and restored.[175] All of this manifests the affection of divine charity and serves to elicit humanity's love for God.[176]

Divine charity showers gifts of grace on the soul. These gifts are tokens of love: betrothal-gifts. Some—like the elements, the four seasons, being, and form—are gifts shared in common by all creatures. Others, the gifts of restoration, are special to the baptized. Still others are singular gifts, given to one person alone.[177] Even one's economic status, whether wealthy or poor, or one's intelligence or simplicity, can also be seen as God's gifts.[178] Since being, beauty, life, grace, and position in life are all divine gifts, the believer should be thankful and moved to love her unseen Spouse.[179]

God is love, so to have charity is to have the Trinity dwelling in oneself.[180] The logic of this is that charity comes to the believer through the sending of the Holy Spirit. The Holy Spirit is co-eternally God. Charity is given to those whom God loves very much. Unlike other gifts, charity is not given to anyone who is evil. The presence of charity is made clear by obvious signs.[181] The lover becomes like the object of her love.[182]

---

[169]   *Arrha* 61 (Sicard, 272).
[170]   *Laude car.* 9–10 (Sicard, 192–94).
[171]   *Arrha* 61 (Sicard, 274).
[172]   *Subst. dilect.* 6 (Baron, 86).
[173]   *Laude car.* 11 (Sicard, 194).
[174]   *Eulogium* 10 (PL 176.990A).
[175]   *Arrha* 43 (Sicard, 258).
[176]   *Arrha* 43 (Sicard, 258); *Laude car.* 11 (Sicard, 194–96).
[177]   *Arrha* 14–68, Sicard, 234–80; *Eulogium* 2–3 (PL 176.987B–988B).
[178]   *Eulogium* 3 (PL 176.987D–988B); *Arrha* 60–62 (Sicard, 270–74).
[179]   *Eulogium* 3, 6 (PL 176.988B, 989C).
[180]   *Laude car.* 16 (Sicard, 200); *Eulogium* 5 (PL 176.989AB).
[181]   *Laude car.* 13–15 (Sicard, 196–200).
[182]   *Arrha* 13 (Sicard, 232).

How one chooses to love determines whether a person is morally good or bad. All the commandments start from love.[183] Neither the human being as such, nor love, nor the things she loves can ever be bad; but she can love good things badly.[184] If love is the life of the soul, then lovelessness is death. Even if one loves badly, one is at least alive. But if one loves not at all, but lives in ill-will, malice, and bitterness, one is dead.[185] Put another way, to sin against the Father is to sin out of weakness; to sin against the Son is to sin out of ignorance; but to sin against the Holy Spirit is to sin against love itself.[186]

Charity is the source of all the virtues and their fruits; it drives out sinful habits and attitudes.[187] As Hugh writes, "The limbs of the virtues cannot be alive without the body of God's love. All the virtues make one body, whose head is charity."[188] The inspiration of the Holy Spirit makes the bride fruitful with virtues, her offspring.[189] The person alive with charity is big-souled and humble.[190] Charity is expressed in good works and loves the good works of others.[191]

The impetus of love keeps on moving as long as one is on earth; the Church is the great hall where one is prepared to reach the King's private chamber and the delights of nuptial union with Him.[192] Of that final consummation, the bride has a foretaste; she holds something in an embrace of love that she hopes will never end. Invisibly and incomprehensibly, she receives an earnest of the full and perfect union to come.[193]

When one compares Hugh's writings on love with those of St Augustine, the first thing one notes is that Hugh writes five works devoted to love. Only one, *The Praise of the Bridegroom*, is a commentary on a

---

[183] *Laude car.* 9 (Sicard, 192); *Sacr.* 2.13.11 (PL 176.546D): "rursum alibi dicitur: 'Habe charitatem et fac quidquid vis'" ("Elsewhere it is said, 'Have charity and do what you want'").

[184] *Subst. dilect.* 5 (Baron, 86).

[185] *Eulogium* 4–5 (PL 176.989AB).

[186] *Eulogium* 5 (PL 176.989AB); *Sacr.* 2.13.11 (PL 176.547D): "Nos charitatem non habemus, nisi inquantum Spiritum sanctum habemus" ("We have charity only to the extent that we have the Holy Spirit").

[187] *Laude car.* 15 (Sicard, 198–200); In *Sacr.* 2.13.11 (PL 176.539D), Hugh refers to those who say that *caritas* is the virtue of virtues, and that therefore no virtue is meritorious if charity is lacking.

[188] *Script.* 1 (PL 175.10): "Membra virtutum viva esse non possunt sine corpore charitatis Dei. Omnes virtutes unum corpus faciunt; cujus corporis caput charitas est."

[189] *Eulogium* 2 (PL 176.987C).

[190] *Eulogium* 4 (PL 176.988C).

[191] *Laude car.* 15 (Sicard, 198–200).

[192] *Arrha* 57 (Sicard, 268).

[193] *Arrha* 69–70 (Sicard, 280–82).

Scriptural text; the others are specifically about love. Augustine writes often about love, but he does not write works specifically about it.

Secondly, in these five works, with the exception of *In Praise of Charity*, Hugh does not make use of the dichotomy use/enjoy (*uti/frui*). *In Praise of Charity* is also the only work that exhorts the reader to despise and flee the world. In these five works, Hugh's emphasis is less on avoiding the dangers of cupidity than on directing the dynamism of love toward true and eternal joy. Although Hugh does refer to the contrast between *cupiditas* and *caritas*, the trend of his thinking about love seems to be toward analyses that are more complex.

If the declarations of his letters are not just rhetorical extravagances, Hugh clearly shares the twelfth-century taste for friendship. However, he does not analyze friendship. He believes that love of neighbor is inseparable from love of God and that one must travel to God with others. He argues with some subtlety that human beings are so interconnected that God's gift to one is a gift to all and to each.

On the Betrothal-Gift of the Soul and *The Praise of the Bridegroom* use romantic, spousal love as a metaphor for the love between the soul and God. In this, Hugh's thought parallels that of St Bernard and other writers of his time. Hugh's interpretation is theocentric, rather than Christocentric, individual rather than communal, in that the Bridegroom is God, not Christ, and the bride is the soul, rather than the Church—though elsewhere Hugh certainly develops a rich Christology and ecclesiology. Although Hugh speaks of turning inward in order to journey upward toward God, the Good—in which the heart rests in enjoyment and enjoys rest—is Charity; and wherever there is Charity, there is God.

Adam of St Victor

Adam of St Victor received his formation elsewhere, although he had close ties with St Victor. Richard of St Victor, citing Adam's sequence, *Ave virgo singularis mater*, refers to him as a "famous poet."[194] Adam seems to have been cantor at Notre-Dame in Paris from about

---

[194] *LE* 2.10.4 (Châtillon, 384 = *Serm. cent.* 4 [PL 177.910D–911A]). The verses he cites can be found in Jean Grosfillier, *Les sequences d'Adam de Saint-Victor: Étude littéraire (poétique et rhétorique). Textes et traductions, commentaires*, Bibliotheca Victorina 20 (Turnhout: Brepols, 2008), 399.9–24, 400.65–72 = Jollès, 60.9–62.24, 68.65–70.72.

1107 to 1134, when he moved to St Victor. He died about 1146. Adam shares the Victorines' interest in canonical reform that promoted communal life for the clergy, but his poetry does not show marked influence from his contemporary, Hugh of St Victor.[195]

Adam of St Victor's surviving works are sequences for liturgical use, not theological treatises.[196] However, Adam's sequences enable the care-

[195] On Adam's identity and his concern for canonical reform, see Margot Fassler, "Who Was Adam of St Victor? The Evidence of the Sequence Manuscripts," *Journal of the American Musicological Society* 37 (1984): 233–69; *Gothic Song: Victorine Sequences and Augustinian Reform in Twelfth-Century Paris* (New York: Cambridge University Press, 1993).

[196] Adam's sequences will be cited from Grosfillier's edition by the number Grosfillier assigns them and by line. Grosfillier, 855–68, who edits the sequences from Victorine liturgical books, concludes that Adam probably did not write sequences 4, 8, 38, and 44 and he considers sequences 10, 11, 37, 40, 45, 50, and 52 not certainly Adam's. In addition, there are three Marian sequences, which are not in the Victorine liturgical books and which Grosfillier does not discuss, that seem likely to be Adam's. For these Marian antiphons, see Adam de Saint-Victor, *Quatorze proses du xiiᵉ siècle à louange de Marie*, ed. Bernadette Jollès, Sous la Règle de saint Augustin 1 (Turnhout: Brepols, 1994): *Ave mater Iesu Christi* [*Hail, Mother of Jesus Christ*] (44–55), *Lux advenit veneranda* [*The Venerable Light Is Approaching*] (162–78), and *Nato nobis Salvatore* [*To the Savior Born for Us*] (180–89). These three sequences do not speak much of love; they will be referred to by title, then by the page and line in Jollès edition. To facilitate reference to other editions of Adam's sequences, here are the first lines of the poems cited by number from Grosfillier:

1   *In natale Salvatoris* (*On the Birthday of the Savior*). Christmas
3   *Gratulemur ad festivum* (*Let us Rejoice on the Feast*) (VTT 2:237–39) John the Evangelist
7   *In excelsis canitur* (*In the Heights Is Sung*) Feast of the Circumcision of Christ
9   *Virgo mater Salvatoris angelorum* (*Virgin Mother of the Savior* [*Pleasing to the Choir*] *of Angels*) Epiphany
12 *Templum cordis adornemus* (*Let Us Adorn the Temple of the Heart*) Purification of Mary
13 *Ecce dies celebris* (*Behold, the Celebrated Day*) Easter Monday
15 *Salve dies dierum Gloria* (*Hail Day, Glory of Days*) Easter Wednesday
16 *Sexta passus feria* (*Having Suffered on the Sixth Day*) Easter Friday
20 *Lux iocundus lux insignis* (*Light Delightful, Remarkable Light*) Pentecost Monday
21 *Qui procedis ab utroque* (*You Who Proceed from Both*) (VTT 1:190–93) Pentecost Tuesday
22 *Simplex in essentia* (*Simple in Essence*) (VTT 2:240–42) Pentecost Thursday
24 *Quam dilecta tabernacula* (*How Beloved Are the Tents*) Dedication of a Church
26 *Ex radice caritatis* (*From the Root of Charity*) Reception of Relics of St Victor
27 *Ad honorem tuum, Christe* (*To Your Honor, O Christ*) John the Baptist
31 *Ecce dies triumphalis* (*Behold, the Triumphal Day*) St Victor
33 *Prunis datum* (*Placed on the Coals*) St Lawrence
34 *Ave Virgo singularis / porta* (*Hail, Singular Virgin, Gate*) Assumption of Mary
35 *Ave Virgo singularis / mater* (*Hail, Singular Virgin, Mother*) Assumption of Mary
36 *Gratulemur in hac die* (*Let Us Celebrate on This Day*) Assumption of Mary
38 *Eterni festi gaudia* (*The Joys of the Eternal Feast*) St Augustine
39 *Salve mater Salvatoris / vas* (*Hail, Mother of the Savior, Vessel*) Nativity of Mary
40 *Iocundare plebs fidelis* (*Let the Faithful People Be Glad*) Evangelists
41 *Laus erumpat ex affectu* (*Praise Breaks Forth from Feeling*) St Michael
44 *Gaude Syon que diem recolis* (*Rejoice, Sion, As You Recall the Day*) St Martin
45 *Vox sonora nostri choris* (*The Sweet Sound of Our Choir*) St Catherine

ful reader to discover the lineaments of Adam's thinking about love.[197] In her introduction to the sequences in this volume, Juliet Mousseau sums up the teaching on love in the sequences translated here and in the first volume of this series. The Holy Spirit is the love of Father and Son, and the mission of the Holy Spirit on earth is to move and heal human hearts. Love brings freedom from the law and from fear. Those whom the Spirit heals become healers in their turn. In what follows, these themes will be related to what an examination of all Adam's sequences tells us about his theology of love.

Adam writes his sequences to be sung on feast days. This leads naturally to themes of harmony and concord among those singing, concord in the Church universal, and harmony between heaven and earth.[198] Another theme evoked by the purpose of the sequences is an emphasis on praise to God for his mighty works. In fact, the heart of Adam's message is the phrase, "Glory be to the Head and concord to the members." In celebrating Christ's paschal mystery and the death of the martyrs, Adam celebrates fortitude and victory over the forces of death and evil. The *armor* of chivalry may have given way to the *amour* of romance in the twelfth century, but Adam's sequences celebrate heroic and triumphant virtue more than passionate love.[199] A classical term for such steadfast virtue was *pietas*, conscientious fulfillment of one's duties toward God, community, and family. Adam often uses *pietas* in

---

46 *Exultemus et letemur* (*Let Us Exult and Rejoice*) St Andrew
47 *Cor angustum dilatemus* (*Let Us Expand Our Narrow Heart*) Apostles
48 *Stola regni laureatus* (*Crowned with Laurels and a Royal Robe*) Apostles
51 *O Maria stella maris* (*O Mary, Star of the Sea*) Blessed Virgin Mary
53 *Animemur ad agonem* (*Let Us Rouse Ourselves for the Struggle*) St Agnes

[197] Of the Latin words for love—*caritas, amor, dilectio, affectus/affectio* and *pietas/pius*—only *pietas/pius* figures in Grosfillier's subject index.

[198] For example, "armonia": 1.4 (Grosfillier, 252); 15.41 (Grosfillier, 312); 26.22 (Grosfillier, 358); 38.2 (Grosfillier, 412); 41.37 (Grosfillier, 426); "Concordia / concordare": 7.4 (Grosfillier, 280); 7.47 (Grosfillier, 282); 13.53 (Grosfillier, 306); 15.42, (Grosfillier, 312); 36.16 (Grosfillier, 405). Adam's choice of vocabulary and themes is also influenced by the requirements of meter and rhyme. For example, he likes to pair "electus/eligo, dilectus/diligo," a usage that highlights the element of choice in Christian love: 3.11 (Grosfillier, 263); 12.34–35 (Grosfillier, 300); 24.1–3 (Grosfillier, 348).

[199] Nicholas Ostler, *Ad Infinitum: A Biography of Latin* (London: Harper, 2007), 179–80. The sequence in honor of St Agnes, 53.37 (Grosfillier, 472), refers to her love-crazed tormentor as "blinded by love" ("cecus amans"); not unfittingly, he is suffocated by a demon. Adam does write that it was their love that enabled the martyrs to bear their sufferings: 44.46–49 (Grosfillier, 443): "Et quecumque fiunt ei / sustinet amore Dei " ("And whatever things happen to him, he sustains by the love of God"); 33.77–81 (Grosfillier, 392).

his sequences. In his usage, it also connotes an element of parental or filial devotion or care.[200] Unlike Hugh, who applies the *Song of Songs* to the love between God and the soul, Adam applies it almost exclusively to the love between Christ and the Church, his spiritual and special bride.[201] Christ has dowered his Church with gifts, above all the gift of the Holy Spirit,[202] who is the bond of the love between Father and Son and the author of *pietas*.[203] The saints are groomsmen who lead the bride to the embrace of her King.[204] Those singing the sequences pray that they may rest on the bed with their beloved and sing psalms, for the nuptials are nigh.[205] After her martyrdom, St Agnes, joined to her heavenly Spouse, consoles her parents and invites them to rejoice.[206]

---

[200] 12.14 (Grosfillier, 299): "puer pius, mater pia" ("loving boy, loving mother"); 9.8 (Grosfillier, 287): "piis cum muneribus" ("with loving gifts"); 35.47–48, (Grosfillier, 402): "pietate, tu, materna nos in imo respice" ("by your maternal loving-kindness look on us below"); 39.57 (Grosfillier, 419): "Salve mater pietatis" ("Hail, Mother of loving-kindness"); 46.26 (Grosfillier, 446): "doctor pius" ("loving teacher"); 46.57 (Grosfillier, 448): "pie pastor animarum" ("kind pastor of souls"); 51.1–3 (Grosfillier, 465): "Ave Maria, stella maris, pietate singularis, pietatis oculo" ("Hail Mary, star of the sea, singular in love, with the eye of love"); 51.46 (Grosfillier, 467): "solo nutu pietatis" ("by just a loving nod"); *Lux advenit veneranda* (Jollès, 164.19–20: "viscerosa pietate" ("deep-felt love"); 47.13–15 (Grosfillier, 450): "Paulus, tuba veritatis, / cultum suadet pietatis, obstat ydolatrie" ("Paul, trumpet of truth, preached the practice of loving-kindness, he opposed idolatry"). John's power was great, but his *pietas* toward the suffering was no less great: 3.26–28 (Grosfillier, 264): "non minoris pietatis erat tribulantibus" ("his loving-kindness toward the troubled was no less").

[201] 9.57 (Grosfillier, 291: "Astat sponsa regi nato" ("The bride attends the new-born king"); 9:65–66 (Grosfillier, 291): "sponsa spiritualis vero sponso specialis" ("a spiritual bride, special to her true spouse").

[202] 20.7–9 (Grosfillier, 329): "Christus misit quem promisit, pignus sponse quam revisit die quinquagesima" ("Christ sent the One whom he promised, the pledge to the bride whom he revisits on the fiftieth day:"); 48.36 (Grosfillier, 456): "cuius dos est gratia" ("whose dowry is grace").

[203] 20.65 (Grosfillier, 333): "auctor ipse pietatis" ("the very author of loving-kindness"); 21.7 (Grosfillier, 334): "Amor Patris filiique" ("the love of the Father and the Son").

[204] 48.25–27 (Grosfillier, 455): "Paranimphi nove legis / ad amplexum novi Regis / sponsam ducunt regiam" ("The groomsmen of the New Law lead the royal bride to the embrace of the new King"); 27.17 (Grosfillier, 362): "paranimphus sponsi" ("groomsmen of the spouse").

[205] 24.67–71 (Grosfillier, 351): "Iam in lecto / cum dilecto / quiescamus / et psallamus, / assunt enim nuptie" ("Now on the couch, with the beloved, we rest and we sing; the wedding is at hand").

[206] 53.54–58 (Grosfillier, 473): "stans ad dexteram gloriaris / et parentes consolaris, / invitans ad gaudia. Ne te flerent ut defunctam / iam celesti sponso iunctam" ("standing at the right you are glorified, and you console your parents, inviting them to joy. They are not to weep over you as though you were dead, for you now are joined to your heavenly spouse").

Love and affection move the assembled faithful to sing.²⁰⁷ The faithful express their love in purity, signs, and speech.²⁰⁸ As they celebrate
the victory of Christ and the saints, they receive a foretaste of the joys
to come.²⁰⁹ Many of the sequences end with a prayer expressing hope
for eternal joy and rest.²¹⁰

In keeping with his emphasis on the victory of Christ and the saints,
Adam sometimes sees life as a struggle between love of the world and
love of Christ, from which the saints emerge victorious.²¹¹ They pass
from the law of fear to the law of love, which makes them worthy of
the gift of perfect liberty.²¹² The foretaste of heavenly joy draws the
Christian away from the seductive love of the world.²¹³ The saints run
toward God with love and through love.²¹⁴ John the Evangelist is carried
like an eagle on the two wings of charity into the purer divine light.²¹⁵
The risen Christ places those whom he loves in glory, in that lasting
love than which nothing is better.²¹⁶

---

²⁰⁷ 26.1–3 (Grosfillier, 357): "Ex radice caritatis, / ex affectu pietatis, / psallat hec ecclesia" ("From
the root of charity, from the feeling of loving-kindness, let this church sing"); 41.1 (Grosfillier,
424): "Laus erumpat ex affectu" ("Let praise break forth from feeling").

²⁰⁸ 3.17–19 (Grosfillier, 264): "Intus ardens caritate, / foris lucens puritate, / signis et eloquio"
("Burning within with charity, shining outside with purity, signs, and speech").

²⁰⁹ 26.49 (Grosfillier, 359): "Pregustamus cordis ore" ("Let us have a foretaste with the mouth of
the heart"); 40.69–70 (Grosfillier, 423): "Horum rivo debriatis / sitis crescat caritatis" ("For
us intoxicated by their source, let the thirst of charity grow").

²¹⁰ For example, 27.80 (Grosfillier, 365): "Per te frui / Christus sui / det nobis praesentia"
("Through you may Christ grant us to enjoy his presence"); 36.84–86 (Grosfillier, 408): "nos
concedas in hoc mari / ut post mortem munerari / digni simus requie" ("grant to us on this
sea, to be worthy after death to receive the gift of rest"); 40.69–72 (Grosfillier, 423): "Horum
rivo debriatis / sitis crescat caritatis / ut superne claritatis / perfruamur gaudiis" ("For us
intoxicated by their source, let the thirst of charity grow, so that we may enjoy the joys of
heavenly splendor"); 45.71–72 (Grosfillier, 444): "et hic nobis gaudeat / illi nos in gloria" ("and
let her rejoice with us here below that we may rejoice with her in glory").

²¹¹ 12.46–48 (Grosfillier, 301): "Omnis amor aut deponi / prorsus solet, aut postponi / tuum
nutrientibus" ("All other love is abandoned or utterly set aside by those who nurture love for
you"); 21.52–54 (Grosfillier, 337); 26.68–69 (Grosfillier, 360); 31.8–12, 16–17 (Grosfillier, 380).

²¹² 22.23, 28–29, 54–56 (Grosfillier, 341–42).

²¹³ 26.49–52 (Grosfillier, 359): "Pregustemus cordis ore, / ut interno nos sapore / revocemur ab
amore / mundi seductorio" ("Let us have a foretaste with the mouth of the heart, so that by
that internal savor we may be called back by love from the seduction of the world"); 35.13
(Grosfillier, 399): "Sirenes voluptatis" ("the Sirens of pleasure").

²¹⁴ 9.7, 50 (Grosfillier, 287, 290).

²¹⁵ 40.37–40 (Grosfillier, 422): "Sed Iohannes ala bina / caritatis, aquilina / forma, fertur in
divina / puriori lumine" ("But John with the two wings of charity, in the shape of an eagle, is
carried into the divine by a purer light"). Godfrey of St Victor will greatly expand on this
image.

²¹⁶ 16.4–6 (Grofillier, 314): "collocat in gloria / quos dilexit" ("he places in glory those he loved");
34.77–78 (Grosfillier, 398): "caritatem permansuram / qua nichil est melius" ("lasting charity,

For Adam, then, the Holy Spirit, who is the bond of love between Father and Son, is sent into the hearts of the faithful. Moved by *pietas*, they are in harmony with each other and sing the praises of Christ. Christ dowers his bride, the Church, with the gifts of the Spirit. By their love-inspired fortitude in suffering, Christ and the martyrs conquer death. Christians struggle to break free from the love of the world and the flesh and the law of fear, in order to live by the law of love and run with love toward Christ.

ACHARD OF ST VICTOR

Achard, who was probably from England, was elected abbot of St Victor in 1155 and appointed bishop of Avranches in 1161. He died there in 1170/71. He is buried near Avranches in the Premonstratensian Abbey of La Lucerne, which he helped to establish.

Achard's surviving writings include fifteen sermons, some of them expanded to treatises,[217] a highly theoretical work, *On the Unity of God and the Plurality of Creatures*,[218] and a treatise, *On the Difference of Soul, Spirit, and Mind*.[219]

Unlike Hugh, Richard, and Godfrey, Achard of St Victor has not left us a meditation or treatise on love. None of his fifteen sermons is devoted primarily to love. However, love is mentioned in almost all of them; if the threads of love were removed from them, all that would remain is a heap of unraveled words. To find out what he thinks about

than which nothing is better"); 39.55–56 (Grosfillier, 419): "ardor indeficiens / immortalis caritas" ("indefatigable ardor, immortal charity").

[217] Achard de Saint-Victor, *Sermons inédits*, ed. Jean Châtillon, TPMA 17 (Paris: Vrin, 1970); English translation in Feiss, Achard of St Victor, *Works*, Cistercian Studies 165 (Kalamazoo: Cistercian Publications, 2001): 59–351. These sermons are the subject of the only comprehensive study of Achard's work to date, Jean Châtillon, *Théologie, spiritualité et métaphysique dans l'oeuvre oratoire d'Achard de Saint-Victor*, Études de Philosophie Médiévale 58 (Paris: Vrin, 1969). Châtillon's study was written before the publication of Achard's work *On the Unity of God*, cited in the note 218.

[218] Achard de Saint-Victor, *L'unité de Dieu et la pluralité des créatures*, ed. and tr. Emmanuel Martineau (Saint-Lambert des Bois: Authentica, 1987), which is the object of a thorough philosophical analysis by Mohammad Ilkhani, *La philosophie de la création chez Achard de Saint-Victor* (Bruxelles: Ousia, 1999); English translation, Feiss, *Works*, 379–480.

[219] *De discretione animae, spiritus et mentis*, ed. G. Morin, "Un traité faussement attribué à Adam de Saint-Victor," *Aus der Geisteswelt des Mittelalters*, BGPTMA, Supplementband 3/1 (Münster: Aschendorff, 1935): 251–62; ed. N. M. Häring, "Gilbert of Poitiers, Author of the 'De discretione animae, spiritus et mentis' commony attributed to Achard of Saint Victor," MS 22 (1960): 148–91; tr. Feiss, "On the Distinction of Soul, Spirit and Mind," *Works*, 353–74.

love we can begin with *Sermon* 5, translated below, find the references to love, and follow those threads into Achard's other sermons.

Achard uses three words for love almost interchangeably. *Amor* is the most general term; alone of the three words it can have both good forms (e.g., *amor boni*) and bad ones (e.g., *amor mundi*).[220] *Dilectio* has almost the same range of meanings, but is used primarily for love of neighbor and love of God, reflecting the way it is used in Jesus' command to love God and neighbor. *Caritas* is the love—divine, concerned for the good of the other, and self-sacrificing—that led Christ to come to humankind in lowly human form and die on its behalf. Two other terms are noteworthy. *"Pietas"* is used of the filial love of the Son for the Father and of the Father's paternal love for the Son.[221] The Son came to earth in filial love and obedience toward the Father. Like the other Victorine authors included in this volume, Achard does not refer often to *"amicitia,"* the love of friendship. One notable exception occurs in *Sermon* 14, where Christ comes interiorly to the martyr—who accepts death in order to please the Truth—and speaks to him, not as Lord to servant, but as neighbor (*vicinus*) to neighbor and friend (*amicus*) to friend.[222] Love causes one to feel compassion for Christ in his sufferings,[223] just as love is the root of compassion for one's neighbor.[224]

In his sermons, Achard does not use the contrast *uti/frui,* which played such a big role in Augustine's theology of love. Achard uses the word *frui* to describe the joy of divine contemplation. Christ's humanity enjoyed the fullness of this contemplation throughout his life on earth, and Adam and Eve enjoyed it before they sinned.[225] Now on earth some may have a foretaste of this joy, but only in the life to come

---

[220] *Serm.* 13.23 (Châtillon, 154); *Serm.* 9.3 (Châtillon, 105): "amans equos vanitatis" ("loving the horses of vanity"); *Serm.* 13.8 (Châtillon, 142): "amor casto amori odibilis" ("a love hateful to chaste love"). All of Achard's sermons are translated in Feiss, *Works,* but it seems sufficient here to give references to the Latin edition, because the numbers of the sermons and their paragraphs are the same in both the Latin and the English versions.

[221] In *Sermon* 13.15–16 (Châtillon, 149–50), Achard writes that piety and justice can be thought of as identical in God. Hence, the Incarnation can be thought of not just as the result of divine piety vanquishing divine justice, but of divine justice, so to speak, conquering itself. In *Sermon* 15.8 (Châtillon, 208), he writes of the Spirit's gift of piety as "a certain loving and devout affection toward God, arising from love, not from fear" ("a spiritu pietatis, id est, cujusdam pie et devote in Deum affectionis, ex amore videlicet, non ex timore").

[222] *Serm.* 14.14 (Châtillon, 187–88).

[223] *Serm.* 15.14 (Châtillon, 215).

[224] *Serm.* 13.28 (Châtillon, 162–64).

[225] *Serm.* 5.4 (Châtillon, 71).

will they enjoy perfectly divine goodness, perfectly understood and loved.[226] Achard consistently associates love and joy. At one point, he lists seven joys that flow from perfect charity.[227]

This love is to be understood in a Trinitarian and Christological context. God is supreme power, wisdom, and goodness.[228] Everything that exists manifests the image or vestige of the Trinity: of the Father through its being, of the Son through its beauty, of the Spirit through its usefulness. The rational creature is uniquely God's image: she can understand him from whom she has her being, and love him whom she has understood,[229] or, alternatively, she can know, love, and enjoy God.[230] God's goodness is greater than human iniquity. Christ was drawn to us by his boundless love for us (*caritas nimia in nos*). He was drawn by cords of charity, not ours but his, for he loved us first. God the Father so loved the world that he sent his only Son, and the Son so loved the world that he gave himself even unto death.[231]

Love (*caritas*) is Christ's supreme attribute.[232] It was filial devotion to his Father (*pietas*) and his great love (*dilectio*) that moved him to descend from equality with the Father and to receive the form of a slave, putting on our form in order to save us.[233] His piety (*pietas*) came to redeem our impiety;[234] his loving-kindness (*pietas*) filled him as he went to the Mount of Olives and then to his suffering and death. When he was in agony in the garden, he expressed his love by the drops of blood that flowed from his body. When he hung on the cross, he expressed his love (*dilectio*) in each wound on his body.[235] His love (*caritas*) and that of the Father are equal, but to us the Son's love seems

---

[226]   *Serm.* 1.5 (Châtillon, 31); *Serm.* 3.4 (Châtillon, 52); *Serm.* 8.2 (Châtillon, 94); *Serm.* 13.32 (Châtillon, 165): "cum bonitate perfecte intellecta et dilecta fruitur perfecte, eam perfecte contemplando et in ea perfecte delectando" ("when goodness is perfectly understood and love is enjoyed perfectly, by contemplating it perfectly and delighting in it perfectly"); Serm. 15.7 (Châtillon, 239). Achard's use of "uti" is usually neutral. One echo of Augustine's terminology occurs in a play on words in *Sermon* 15.8 (Châtillon, 208): "eoque magis estimat sibi licere uti mundo nunc quo in ejus usu minus abutitur seipso" ("to the extent that in using the world he now abuses himself less, he judges it is more permissible for him to use it").

[227]   *Serm.* 13.30–31 (Châtillon, 163).

[228]   *Serm.* 5.1 (Châtillon, 67).

[229]   *Serm.* 9.4 (Châtillon, 105–6).

[230]   *Serm.* 1.3 (Châtillon, 29); *Serm.* 9.6 (Châtillon, 107); *Serm.* 13.32 (Châtillon, 165).

[231]   *Serm.* 15.1–2 (Châtillon, 200–1).

[232]   *Serm.* 5.2 (Châtillon, 69).

[233]   *Serm.* 5.3 (Châtillon, 69–70), drawing on Phil. 2:6–18.

[234]   *Serm.* 5.5 (Châtillon, 72).

[235]   *Serm.* 5.2 (Châtillon, 68–69).

greater.[236] Very frequently, Achard returns to the incarnate Son's Paschal Mystery, a signal of his great humility and love (*dilectio*). "Who by thinking about it is not set on fire . . . and inflamed with the fire of divine love?"[237]

Knowledge and love go hand in hand. The Cherubim ("fullness of knowledge") and Seraphim ("ardent") are so named because of the excellence of their knowledge and love.[238] Following the teaching and example of Christ's disciples, we come to Jesus in knowledge of the truth and love (*amor*) of virtues.[239] We should know all Christ's mysteries through faith and delight in them through love.[240] As grace is the form of nature, the virtue of charity is what gives shape and merit to the virtues. The true food of the feelings and of willing is love of virtue.[241] Love (*caritas*) surpasses all other virtues. It rules over all of them. Without charity, every other virtue is unfruitful and without merit.[242] Pagans lack charity.[243] Love brings unity to a person; he becomes one in charity, one in love (*dilectione*) of God and neighbor.[244] Through faith and love, the saints become one with God—not in nature or person—but in justice or glory.[245]

Although Achard does not seem to identify charity and the Holy Spirit, the Holy Spirit is closely associated with the bestowal of love. Charity is given at baptism through the Holy Spirit.[246] Charity is the cement of the Holy Spirit, which binds Christians together.[247] At Pentecost, the Spirit filled the disciples with charity and love.[248]

---

[236] *Serm.* 5.3 (Châtillon, 70).
[237] *Serm.* 6.5 (Châtillon, 80): "quis, inquam, est, qui non ex tali consideratione accendatur, et igne divini amoris inflammetur" ("who, I say, is it who is not aroused by such a consideration and inflamed with the fire of divine love"). See also *Serm.* 15.1 (Châtillon, 200–1).
[238] *Serm.* 5.1 (Châtillon, 67–68).
[239] *Serm.* 5.5 (Châtillon, 72). For this pairing of (the light of) knowledge and (the warmth of) love, see *Serm.* 2.1–3 (Châtillon, 37–40); *Serm.* 13.32 (Châtillon, 165).
[240] *Serm.* 4.8 (Châtillon, 65).
[241] *Serm.* 8.2 Châtillon, 94).
[242] *Serm.* 5.2 (Châtillon, 69).
[243] *Serm.* 11.2 (Châtillon, 118–19): A venial sin is one that coexists with charity and with its remedy; a mortal sin makes one worthy of eternal death. Hence, in pagans and those who do not yet have faith in the Savior, no sin is venial, because they have no remedy. Achard is not explicit about what the remedy is; presumably, it is the grace of baptism and the gift of faith that bring remission of sins.
[244] *Serm.* 4.3 (Châtillon, 58–59).
[245] *Serm.* 1.5 (Châtillon, 33).
[246] *Serm.* 10.1 (Châtillon, 109).
[247] *Serm.* 13.27 (Châtillon, 160).
[248] *Serm.* 12.4 (Châtillon, 126).

Christ loves God and neighbor most perfectly[249] and taught his disciples to do the same. Achard quotes the Lord's twofold commandment of love of God and love of neighbor six times in his fifteen sermons.[250] By this twofold commandment, Christ taught about love of neighbor, converting us from wickedness of heart to love of neighbor.[251] This commandment inculcates three kinds of charity that are not rendered so that they may no longer be due, but so that they may always be due. One must love God, neighbor, and self, that is, what is above one, what is next to one, and what one is. Scripture indicates how one should love oneself: by ruling oneself in this life so that one might live happily in heaven. To discipline oneself is not to hate oneself, but truly to love oneself. One loves one's neighbor by keeping the twofold Golden Rule: do not do to others what you do not want done to yourself, and what you want another to do to you (for example, the corporal works of mercy) do that to your neighbor. No one can love his neighbor unless he also loves God, but no one reaches the perfection of love unless he first loves his neighbor.[252]

In *Sermon* 13, Achard develops an elaborate allegory about building the dwelling place of God. Such a dwelling needs stones that are flat on four sides. This leads him to speak of many "fours," such as the four cardinal virtues and the four beatitudes of Luke 6:20–22. He then speaks of the foursquare love of God: with one's whole heart, mind, soul, and strength, that is, fervently, wisely, perseveringly, and abundantly.[253]

Seeking a fourfold pattern in the commandment to love one's neighbor as oneself, Achard formulates a simple syllogism:

(1) Whoever does not love God, loves iniquity.
(2) Whoever loves iniquity, hates himself (Sir. 19:6 Vulg.).
(3) Therefore, if you love God, you love yourself.

Loving oneself, then, is foursquare: it consists in loving God with one's whole heart, mind, soul, and strength. Love of neighbor wills that the neighbor love God fervently, wisely, unceasingly, and sufficiently.[254]

---

[249] *Serm.* 1.6 (Châtillon, 34).
[250] Matt. 22:37–39: *Serm.* 1.6 (Châtillon, 34); *Serm.* 3.3 (Châtillon, 47, 49); *Serm.* 10.6 (Châtillon, 113); *Serm.* 13.21 (Châtillon, 153–54); *Serm.* 15.12, 15 (Châtillon, 212, 215–16).
[251] *Serm.* 5.4 (Châtillon, 72).
[252] *Serm.* 10.6 (Châtillon, 112–13).
[253] *Serm.* 13.18–21 (Châtillon, 151–53).
[254] *Serm.* 13.22 (Châtillon, 153–54).

This leads to a stark contrast: either love God or love the world. Hammer and chisel must be applied to the love of the world, a love unformed and deformed. First, perverse habits and actions must be pounded away; then, gradually, feelings and thoughts can be polished so that what was carnal becomes spiritual.[255]

A little later, Achard treats fraternal charity with more nuance. There are six surfaces on a stone that is well formed for the edifice of fraternal charity. These six surfaces are like the hands of charity. Charity plus her six arms are the seven columns of the house of virtue, the house of love. Those arms reach in all directions. Charity is embraced

> from the superior through obedience, from the inferior through providence, from the right through encouragement, from the left through compassion, from the front through imitation, from the back through exhortation. These are, as it were, the six arms of fraternal charity, which, according to the works of the six days, are extended exteriorly in good works toward the neighbor. However, interiorly divine charity remains simple and undivided, rooted in the ground of the heart.[256]

At the beginning of the spiritual itinerary, fear has a necessary role. A first step is to move from a false sense of security into fear of the Lord.[257] Gradually, love grows and fear diminishes until finally perfect charity casts out fear.[258] Similarly, at first one loves purity of heart in order to avoid punishment, but then one comes to love purity for its own sake.[259]

Achard is very fond of schemas that map the path of spiritual progress. One that he elaborates tracks the passage from fear to love through

---

[255] *Serm.* 13.24 (Châtillon, 156).
[256] *Serm.* 13.28 (Châtillon, 161): "sic igitur, juxta sex lapidis quadrati superficies, quasi sex ulnis caritatis in omnem terra effuse, lapides vivos a superiori complectitur per obedientiam, ab inferiori per providentiam, a dextris per congratulationem, a sinistris per compassionem, ab anteriori per imitationem, a posteriori per exhortationem. Hec sunt caritatis fraterne velut sex brachia, quibus secundum opera sex dierum exterius in operibus bonis extenditur ad proximum. Caritas autem divina interius in cordis radice simplex manet et indivisa."
[257] *Serm.* 5.5 (Châtillon, 72).
[258] *Serm.* 15.7–8 (Châtillon, 207–8), the gist of which is, "ex Domini timore qui est initium sapientie. Is siquidem timor inchoat, sed castus consummat, permanens in seculum seculi et in caritate consistens perfecta, que foras initialem illum timorem mittit, imprimis dumtaxat necessarium" ("by the fear of the Lord, which is the beginning of wisdom. This fear occurs in the beginning, but chaste fear occurs at the end, remaining forever and consisting in perfect love, which casts out that initial fear, which, however, was necessary at the beginning").
[259] *Serm.* 13.30 (Châtillon, 163).

a series of transformations, which Achard parallels to transfigurations in Jesus' life. First, there is the transfiguration of penitence, which mirrors the Lord's passion. In this transfiguration, the soul dies to sin, the world, and self-will. Then comes the transfiguration of justice, when someone does good, no longer out of fear of punishment but out of love (*amore*) of justice and desire for heaven.[260] This second transfiguration corresponds to the resurrection. In a third transfiguration, corresponding to the Lord's appearances after the Resurrection, the Christian humbly hides his interior renewal. He needs to do this until charity becomes deeply rooted. The fourth transfiguration, recalling the Lord's Ascension, occurs through meditation on God's works of creation and restoration, the sacraments, God's commands and promises, and the last things. The fifth transfiguration recalls the Pentecost; it occurs in contemplation. In the sixth transfiguration, the soul descends from the heights of contemplation to action, coming with Christ from the bosom of the Father into the seventh transfiguration, which occurs through emulation of Christ's example of compassion for the weak.[261]

According to another schema, some people go through the motions of spiritual reading of the Scriptures and the sacraments, but without any love for Christ (*nullo amore circa Christum*). Others have some love (*aliquid dilectionis*), but not enough to drive out carnal feelings (*carnales affectiones*); one cannot say without qualification that they have the love of God (*amorem Dei*) who wishes always to be "sole and supreme" (*semper solus vel summus*). Others study the Scriptures for money or vainglory. Finally, there are those "who are moved by great love for the humanity of Christ, either in the Scriptures or in the recep-

---

[260]   In *Serm.* 12.6–8 (Châtillon, 128–130), Achard proceeds to describe eight more transfigurations in the itinerary of the Christian: (8) repetition of contemplation (paralleling the Lord's Transfiguration on the Mount); (9) the example of a good life that brings restoration to the weak = sacramental transfiguration; (10) death, (11) separation of body and soul which leads to a wonderful renewal; (12) the general resurrection; (13) the resurrection of the body, which (14) brings great joy to the saints; and finally (15) there is the transfiguration of heaven and earth. For the transition from fear to love, see also *Serm.* 10.3 (Châtillon, 111): "ex compunctione amor" ("from compunction comes love"); *Serm.* 12.4 (Châtillon, 126): "ex timore compunctio, ex compunctione amor" ("from fear comes compunction, from compunction comes love"); *Serm.* 13.28 (Châtillon, 160); *Serm.* 14.21 (Châtillon, 193) draws the following parallels: creation/justice/fear; divine governance/wisdom/veneration; consummation/goodness/love; *Serm.* 15.7 (Châtillon, 207).
[261]   *Serm.* 12.5–6 (Châtillon, 126–27).

tion of the body and blood of Christ. Only these receive worthily, and in receiving are made members of Christ."[262]

Nothing can separate the Christian from the love of Christ.[263] Love is stronger than death.[264] In heaven we will enjoy the love of God without ever tiring of it.[265] A foretaste of such love comes in contemplation. Then the purified mind, led not by its own presumption but by inclination (*instinctu*) of God's Spirit,

> is completely inflamed with the ineffable warmth of divine love to see the face of God and, as though having put off the weight of the flesh, by the force of charity and the attraction of internal sweetness is completely rapt, dilated, and raised up.
> ... It tries to burst forth completely into contemplation and, as it were, to cross over entirely into God.[266]

However, Achard's mapping of the spiritual journey again takes a surprising turn. During life on earth, contemplative union with God is not a final resting place. When one has deserted sin, worldly aims, immoderate desires, one's own will, and has preferred faith to the insistent claims of reason, when one has left behind even oneself and service to others in order to become one spirit with God and to rest in God, one is configured to Christ. Like him, one will be led by burning charity to go from the Creator to his creatures, from God to neighbor. Charity will move one to leave the reading, prayer, tranquility, purity of soul, continuous meditation, contemplation, and wonder—that brought one to ecstatic union with God—in order to devote oneself to one's neighbor.[267] After resting in the arms of Christ, her spouse, the soul follows him, taking up the form of a servant as his love and ex-

[262] *Serm.* 4.4 (Châtillon, 59): "qui magna dilectione circa humanitatem Christi afficiuntur, vel in scripturis, vel in perceptione corporis et sanguinis Christi. Hi soli digne percipiunt, et sumendo membra Christi efficiuntur" ("who are moved with great love for the humanity of Christ, either in the Scriptures or in receiving the body and blood of Christ. These alone receive worthily and by receiving are made members of Christ").

[263] Rom. 8:35, 38–39; *Serm.* 14.15 (Châtillon, 188).

[264] *Serm.* 8.2 (Châtillon, 94).

[265] *Serm.* 2.3 (Châtillon, 40).

[266] *Serm.* 14.22 (Châtillon, 194): "ad faciem Dei videndam estu ineffabili amoris divini tota inflammatur et, quasi mole deposita carnis, vi caritatis et attractu interne dulcedinis tota raptatur, dilatatur atque sublevatur . . . tota nititur in contemplationem ipsam erumpere et quasi in Deum tota transire." See also *Serm.* 3.3 (Châtillon, 50); *Serm.* 2.4 (Châtillon, 40).

[267] *Serm.* 15.1–38 (Châtillon, 199–243).

ample and the bond of fraternal charity urge. At God's command and in imitation of Christ, one leaves God on account of God.[268]

RICHARD OF ST VICTOR

Love is a theme that pervades Richard's extensive writings on Christian life. Two of his works make noteworthy contributions to the theology of love. *The Four Degrees of Violent Love* unfolds the stages of the passionate love of God, which lead from focusing the mind on God, through affective delight in God, to ecstatic union, and beyond that to configuration to Christ in his self-emptying love for humanity. This last stage of self-emptying love parallels the teaching of Achard. Richard's *On the Trinity* is an original attempt, drawing on the theology of St Anselm, to understand the three persons in the one God in terms of love. This discussion will consider Richard's understanding of love under three headings: (1) love in the ascent toward God, (2) the four degrees of passionate love of God, and (3) love in God.

According to Richard, God creates the consciousness of the human person (*mens*) with two fundamental capabilities by which he travels toward God: cognition, by which he is God's image, and love, by which he is God's likeness. In his *mens*, knowing and loving, the human being is a created image of the Trinity.[269] Sin darkened reason, extinguished

---

[268] *Serm.* 15.36 (Châtillon, 240–41).

[269] *LE* 1.1.1, (Châtillon, 104.4–12 = *Serm. cent.* 70 [PL 177.1190CD]): "Fecit autem eam ad imaginem . . . suam secundum cognitionem veritatis, ad similitudinem suam secundum amorem virtutis. Ad imaginem suam secundum intellectum, ad similitudinem suam secundum affectum . . . ut per hoc quod facta esset ad imaginem Deum cognosceret et per hoc quod facta esset ad similitudinem Dei Deum diligeret, et cognoscendo et diligendo Deum possideret, et possidendo beata esset. Sicut enim in uno elemento igne duo sunt inter se diversa et a se prorsus remota, scilicet splendor et calor, nec splendor est calor, nec calor est splendor, quia splendor lucet et videtur, et calor ardet et sentitur . . . ita in spirituali creatura imago Dei et similitudo Dei inter se diversa sunt et a se quodammodo remota. Nam secundum illud originale bonum quo facta est ad imaginem Dei, ipsa spiritualis creatura elucet ad cognitionem, et secundum illud bonum quo facta est ad similitudinem Dei, calet ad dilectionem" ("He made him in His own image . . . in knowledge of the truth, His likeness in love of virtue; His image in understanding, His likeness in affectivity . . . so that by the fact that he was made in God's image he might know God, and made in His likeness he would love Him, and by knowing and loving God would possess Him, and possessing Him would be happy. By way of comparison, in the one element of fire there are two quite distinct and separate aspects, brightness and heat. Brightness is not heat, nor is heat brightness, for brightness shines and is seen, whereas heat warms and is felt. . . . So, in the spiritual creature the image of God and the likeness of God are distinct and rather separate. Through that original endowment by which he is made in God's image, the spiritual creature is enlightened in knowing and

84 GENERAL INTRODUCTION

love, and robbed humankind of bodily immortality, leaving it subject to necessity and death.[270] Christ came to restore reason and love.

Richard of St Victor has great confidence in the capacity of re- deemed reason. He sometimes distinguishes reason (ratio), under- standing (intellectus), and intelligence (intelligentia). Reason investigates, proves, and explains. Reason knows the things of the natu- ral world. It judges them according to their intrinsic natures and prop- erties.[271] Understanding feels, sees, and experiences. Understanding intuits the inner reality of its object with a gaze free from all distrac- tion.[272] Intelligentia is the summit of human cognition; in it, a human being's highest cognitive ability is focused on the highest object, on Truth itself.[273]

Like Hugh, Richard believes that the human heart is filled with a longing that the whole world cannot fill. Therefore, the unifying object of all one's affective life, the focus of one's love, the aim of one's freedom, should be God, in whom alone one can find happiness. When this perfect integration is achieved, then a human being is all that she can and should be—fully herself and the likeness of God.[274]

through the divine likeness he warms up with love." For the meaning of "mens," see *Erud.* 1.3 (PL 196.1235D): "Quae, inquam, est illius principalis in anima (humanae videlicet mentis) vita, nisi intentio bona?" ("What, I say, is the life of that principal factor in the soul, namely, of the human *mens*, if not a good intention?"); *Erud.* 1.19 (PL 196.1261B): "mens est principale hominis interioris" ("the *mens* is the chief thing in a human being"); *Arca Moys.* 4.20 (Aris, 115–16 [PL 196.162]; tr. Zinn, 297–99); cf. Ps.-Richard of St Victor, *Cant.* 15 (PL 196.450A); *In Nahum* 38 (PL 96.725A).

270 *LE* 1.1.3 (Châtillon. 105.2–15); *Emman.* 2.26 (PL 196.660D–661A); *Adnot. Psalm. 121* (PL 196.365C); *Statu*, prol. (Ribaillier, 61). See L. M. De Rijk, "Some Notes on the Twelfth-Century Topic of the Three (Four) Human Evils and of Science, Virtue and Techniques as their Rem- edies," *Vivarium* 5 (1967): 8–15.

271 *Decl. nonn. diff.* 1 (Ribaillier, 201).

272 *Arca Moys.* 3.9 (Aris, 66–67 [PL 196.118D–119A]; tr. Zinn, 234–35); *XII patr.* 87 (Châtillon, 344 [PL 196.62C]; tr. Zinn, 146–47); *Arca Moys.* 3.6 (Aris, 63–64 [PL 196.117AB]; tr. Zinn, 231–32); cf. Ps.-Richard of St Victor, *In Cant.* 1 (PL 196.411BC).

273 *Trin.* 2.2 (Ribaillier, 109.10–12; tr. Evans, 228–29): "Constat itaque Deum veracem esse, et hoc ipsum est ei ex veritate. Veritas igitur non est aliud aliquid quam ipse." ("It is established that God is truthful, and God is that by truth itself. Truth is nothing other than God"). See Salet, *Trinité*, 472.

274 *Adnot. Psalm. 80* (PL 196.327C): "totus mundus desiderium cordis implere non valet" ("all the world cannot fill up the desire of the heart"); *Super exiit* 2 (Châtillon, 48.20–24): "Luce clarius constat quia nemo unquam vere beari poterit sine participatione illius boni quod nec oculus vidit nec auris audivit, nec in cor hominis ascendit, quod nemo nisi ex divina revela- tione cognoscit" ("It is clearer than daylight that no one could ever be truly happy without participating in that good which eye has not seen and ear has not heard, which has not arisen in man's heart, which no one knows apart from divine revelation"); *Erud.* 1.31 (PL 196.1282D– 1283A): "Homo bonus factus est, et ad bonitatem creatus est. . . . Si ergo charitate ferves, et

As there are two natures in the human being, spirit and body, and two levels of knowing, reason and sensation, so there are two affective movements, spiritual and bodily. As created by God, the flesh and its movements were not evil or unruly. The affective elements of man's bodily nature are the feet by which the soul walks. They remain necessary and good, even though because of sin they tend to run away with the spirit instead of being at its service.[275] They must be brought into line with reason's direction.[276]

Desire takes two forms: appetite (*appetitus*) and feeling (*affectus*). Appetite is an inclination or drive to attain an object that is perceived as giving pleasure. It arises spontaneously, takes the form of a striving for pleasure, attains its goal temporarily in satiety, and then gives rise once again to desire. In this way, it is insatiable.[277] Feeling (*affectio, affectus*) is a more complex element of human experience. Like appetite, it is closely connected with the senses (*sensualitas*). At the same time, however, it may become a dimension of the highest spiritual activities.

in boni dilectione permanes . . . et tu ipse es . . . id quod, et ad quod factus es et esse debes" ("Humankind was made good and created for good. . . . If you are afire with charity and steadfast in love of the good . . . you are also . . . what you were made to be and ought to be"); *LE* 2.11.4 (Châtillon, 445.12–13); *Missione* (PL 196.1027D–1028AB); *Serm. cent.* 61 (PL 177.1089B); *Arca Moys.* 5.8 (Aris, 133 [PL 196.177C]; tr. Zinn, 321); cf. Ps.-Richard, *In Cant.* 10 (PL 196.436D).

[275] *Statu* 8 (Ribaillier, 71): "Sicut enim a pedibus corpus circumfertur, sic a carnali desiderio animus exagitatur atque circumducitur" ("Just as the body is carried around by the feet, so the mind is agitated and led around by carnal desire"); Ps.-Richard, *In Nahum* 83 (PL 96.751A); *In Abdiam* (PL 196.383BC): "Quando sermo divinus in carnem invehitur, non natura sed culpa arguitur. . . . Sicut enim in homine duae sunt naturae, spiritus scilicet et caro, ita duo motus, quibus utrumque movetur" ("When the divine word was carried into the flesh, it was not nature but guilt that was censured. . . . Just as there are two natures in a human being, namely spirit and flesh, so there are two movements, by which each is moved"). On the *affectiones* as feet, see John F. Callahan, *Augustine and the Greek Philosophers* (n.p.: Villanova University Press, 1967), 47–74; Châtillon, ed., *Sermones ineditos*, 285 note.

[276] *Ad me clamat* 3 (Ribaillier, 258): "desideria carnis de carnis quidem necessitate surgunt" ("desires of the flesh arise from the need of the flesh"); *Adnot. Psalm. 28* (PL 196.310C): after distinguishing the desires which arise from the deliberation of reason from those which arise without such deliberation, Richard observes, "et sunt quidem ex utroque genere alia bona, alia mala" ("so that of both kinds some are good and others bad"); *Erud.* 2.23 (PL 196.1322D): "irrationabilia desideria sub rationis magisterio coercere" ("to force irrational desires under the tutelage of reason"); *Erud.* 2.18 (PL 196.1217A); *Adnot. Psalm. 80* (PL 196.328A). "Desiderium" is a broad and complex term in Richard's writings. For some of its various meanings, see Dumeige's comments in his edition of *Quat. grad.*, 196–97.

[277] *Statu* 10 (Ribaillier, 73–74); cf. *XII patr.* 5–6 (Châtillon, 100–6 [PL 196.5CD]; tr. Zinn, 57–59); *Erud.* 2.30 (PL 196.1281A).

For example, perfect love involves not just a rational choice, but feeling as well.[278]

The feelings of the heart are innumerable. They all have their source in a basic affectivity (*affectio; cordis affectus*).[279] Richard employs several lists of the basic affects. He utilizes the classical division into four basic ones: "love, hate, joy, and sorrow are the four principal feelings (*affectiones*), from which all other desires, wishes, aims, and feelings draw their origin."[280] There is also an expanded list in the *Twelve Patriarchs*: "The principal feelings which arise in turn from the soul's one affectivity are seven in number: hope and fear, joy and sorrow, hate,

---

[278]   *Decl. nonn. diff.* 1 (Ribaillier, 201); *XII patr.* 5 (Châtillon, 100–104 [PL 196.4C–5C]; tr. Zinn, 57–58); *XII patr.* 25 (Châtillon, 156–58 [PL 196.18A]; tr. Zinn, 77–78); *Serm. cent.* 39 (PL 177.1000A).

[279]   *Statu* 9 (Ribaillier, 71): "Quis, quaeso, digne exponere possit quot modis se affectus humanus variare consuevit? . . . per diversa rapitur et multiformiter varietur cordis affectus" ("Who, I ask, can properly explain in how many ways human affect usually varies? . . . The affect of the heart is pulled by different things and varies in many ways"); *LE* 2.1.14 (Châtillon, 230.58): "caritas in affectu cordium" ("charity in the affect of hearts"); *Arca Moys.* 3.22 (Aris, 81 [PL 196.132A]; tr. Zinn, 253): "Sed quis omnes humanae affectionis qualitates enumeret?" ("But who could list all the forms of human feeling?") Generally, *affectio* and *affectus* in the singular refer to man's affective life, in contrast to *ratio* and *intellectus*: Gregory, *Mor.* 20.31.61 (Adriaen, 1047 [PL 76.174A]): "Intellectus vero cum intenditur, ei in Deum ardentior affectus aperitur" ("When the understanding is focused on God, the affect opens unto God more fervently"); *Mor.* 24.8.15 (Adriaen, 1198 [PL 76.294BC]): "quos a bestiis ratione distinguit. . . . At contra hi qui carnali affectioni succumbunt, non jam homines, sed jumenta nominantur" ("He distinguishes them from beasts because of their reason. . . . On the contrary, these who succumb to carnal feeling are not called men any longer, but beasts"). See, for example, Richard of St Victor, *Adnot. Psalm. 121* (PL 196.363B). In the plural, the two words (*affectus, affectiones*) refer to the various tendencies, feelings, and inclinations of human affectivity: *XII patr.* 7 (Châtillon, 108–10 [PL 196.6BC]; tr. Zinn, 60–61). On these terms, see Dumeige, *Quat. grad.*, 192–93; J. Châtillon, "Cordis affectus au moyen âge," *DS* 2:2288–2300; J. Châtillon, ed., *Sermons et opuscules*, 1:1vii–1viii; John T. Noonan, "Marital Affection in the Canonists," *Studia Gratiana* 12 (1967): 487; J. Longère, introduction to *XII patr.*, 46–48.

[280]   *Statu* 34 (Ribaillier, 102): "Amor itaque et odium, gaudium et dolor quatuor principales affectiones sunt ex quibus cetera omnia desideriorum, voluntatum, votorum, affectionumque originem trahunt" ("Love and hate, joy and sorrow are the four principal feelings from which all other desires, willings, choices, and feelings draw their origin"); *Misit Herodes* 6 (PL141.284A–187C) lists *cupiditas, metus, dolor, gaudium* (desire, fear, sorrow, joy); *Statu* 9, (Ribaillier, 72); Augustine, *Civ. Dei* 14.7.2 (Dombart and Kalb, 422.41–44 [PL 41.410]): "Amor ergo inhians habere quod amatur, cupiditas est, id autem habens eoque fruens laetitia; fugiens quod ei adversatur, timor est, idque si acciderit sentiens tristitia est" ("Love longing to have what is loved is cupidity; but love having and enjoying it is joy; love fleeing what opposes it is fear; and if love feels that what is opposed to it has occurred, it is sadness"); Hugh of St Victor, *Libellus* 4 (Sicard, 140.53–141.55 [PL 176.692C]); Adam of St Victor, *Superne matris gaudia* 49.17–20 (Grosfillier, 460): "Confusa sunt hic omnia, / spes, metus, meror, gaudium / Vix hora vel dimidia / fit in celo silentium" ("Here all things are confused together, / hope, fear, sadness, and joy. / There is scarcely a half hour / of silence in heaven"); Pierre Courcelle, "La culture antique d'Absalon de Saint-Victor," *Journal des Savants* (année 1972): 279–80.

love, and shame."²⁸¹ Feelings may be good or bad, depending on
whether they are in accord with reason; that is, ordered to the right
object and kept in the right measure.²⁸² In the present life, the gradual
recovery of the power to implement one's liberty and to rule over one's
appetites and feelings is from first to last a gift of grace.²⁸³

One can plot the Christian life as a passage—nurtured by reading,
meditation, prayer, and good works—from compunction to contemplation and compassion. Love is woven into each facet of this passage.
To begin with, the reality of sin requires that compunction be a part of
every Christian life. At the heart of compunction lies sorrow for sin
and devotion.²⁸⁴

God, who inspired the writing of Sacred Scripture, inspires the
reader to understand the spiritual content of what was written.²⁸⁵ The

---

²⁸¹ *XII patr.* 7 (Châtillon, 108 [PL 196.6B]; tr. Zinn, 60): "Principales ergo affectus septem sunt
qui ab una animi affectione alternatim surgunt. Spes videlicet et timor, gaudium et dolor,
odium, amor et pudor" ("There are seven principal feelings which arise at different times
from the single affectivity of the mind, namely, hope, fear, joy and sorrow, hate, love and
shame").

²⁸² *XII patr.* 7 (Châtillon, 108 [PL 196.6B]; tr. Zinn, 59–60): "Siquidem nihil aliud est virtus quam
animi affectus ordinatus et moderatus. Ordinatus quidem, quando illud est ad quod esse
debet; moderatus, quando tantus est quantus esse debet" ("Thus, a virtue is nothing else than
an ordered and measured affect of the mind: ordered when it is directed to what it should be
directed, measured when it is as great as it should be"); *Super exiit* 4 (Châtillon, 102.20–22):
"Affectiones itaque tue contra te veniunt, quando sunt inordinate, tibi veniunt quando sunt
ordinate" ("Therefore, your feelings come against you when they are disordered; they come
for you when they are ordered"); *Erud.* 2.18 (PL 196.1317A): "carnales affectiones sub rigore
disciplinae restringimus" ("we restrain carnal feelings with rigorous discipline"); *XII patr.* 29
(Châtillon, 172 [PL 196.21A]; tr. Zinn, 83): "nam quidquid affectio cordis usurpat ad laudem
sui, rectius sane ratio retorquet ad gloriam Dei" ("for whatever the affect of the heart usurps
to its own praise, reason rightly twists back toward the glory of God"); Ps.-Richard of St Victor, *In Nahum* 25 (PL 96.719CD); *In Nahum* 66 (PL 96.737C).

²⁸³ *Arca Moys.* 3.24 (Aris, 84 [PL 196.133C, 134D]; tr. Zinn, 257): "Absque dubio quidquid boni
in bonorum cordibus agitur, septiformis ille Spiritus per inspirantem gratiam operatur . . .
omnium voluntates ad voluntatis suae arbitrium sine aliqua coactione inclinat. . . . Superius
iam assignavimus quam sint multiplices vel multiformes, humani cordis affectus. Hos utique
ille Domini Spiritus cotidie in electis paulatim contemperat, et in unam harmoniam confor-
mat" ("Without doubt, whatever good is done in the hearts of good people is the work of that
sevenfold Spirit through his inspiring grace. . . . He inclines the wills of all to the judgment
of His will without any force. . . . Above we indicated already how multiple and multiform
are the feelings of the human heart. These the Spirit of the Lord daily moderates in the elect
and forms together in a single harmony"); *Erud.* 2.30 (PL 196.1281C); *Erud.* 3.31 (PL 196.1329D–
1330A).

²⁸⁴ Richard connects compunction with *devotio* in *Erud.* 1.18 (PL 196.1259AB); *Adnot. Psalm. 136*
(PL 196.375A); *Pot. lig.* 25 (Ribillier, 110); he relates it to tears in *Erud.* 1.18 (PL 196.1259AB);
Erud. 1.10 (PL 196.1280D); *Adnot. Psalm. 25* (PL 196.286B); *Adnot. Psalm. 34* (PL 196.367A).

²⁸⁵ *Erud.* 2.6 (PL 196.1305AB): "Absque dubio nunquam proprie Scripturarum sacrarum inter-
pretatio fit, sine ejus magisterio, qui eas inspiravit" ("Without doubt, interpretation of the

Spirit has also inspired the Church's teachers in the reading of the Scriptures, so that now the divine books are already glossed by the readings, meditations, and discussions of perfect teachers.[286] The fruits of reading are gained only by one who reads with aims in harmony with the goals of Scripture, which was written so that readers would love religion, preserve unity, and have charity.[287] Reading dispels the illusion of falsehood and the wickedness of evil, and leads to genuine or perfect knowledge of the truth and love of goodness.[288]

The meditation that follows on reading takes diverse forms; whatever nourishes the mind, stirs up devotion, and builds up the soul can be utilized.[289] Every sincere Christian seeks to nourish his consciousness toward good desires by means of spiritual meditations.[290] Meditation leads to prayer.[291] Devotion, fervent love, is the heart of prayer.[292]

Sacred Scriptures is never properly done without the teaching of the One who inspired them"); *Apoc.* 1.10 (PL 196.733D–734B).

[286]   *LE* 2.10.22 (Châtillon, 416.12–16 = *Serm. cent* 22 [PL 177.940AB]): "Scias agros istos, scilicet libros divinos, ab optimis agricolis per multos labores bene cultos, id est a perfectis doctoribus per multas afflictiones, vigilias, lectiones, meditationes, disputationes, bene emendatos, bene glosatos, et compositos" ("You should know that these fields, namely the divine books, have been well emended, well glossed, and composed by accomplished teachers through many afflictions, vigils, readings, meditations, and disputations"). Particularly in his *Book of Notes*, Richard makes use of this work of predecessors. He draws especially on the biblical glosses, Bede, Isidore, and Hugh of St Victor.

[287]   *Quid eis* (Hauréau 1.118).

[288]   *LE* 2, prol. (Châtillon, 221.9–11).

[289]   *Arca Moys.* 4.21 (Aris, 117.25–27 [PL 196.164B]; tr. Zinn, 301); *Trin.* prol. (Ribaillier, 79.3–4; tr. Evans, 209); *Erud.* 2.16 (PL 196.1315B); Ps.-Richard, *Cant.* 33 (PL 196.499D); *Cant.* 16 (PL 196.451D–452A).

[290]   *Erud.* 2.18 (PL 196.1317A): "et cogitationes nostras in morum circumspectione occupamus, et per spirituales meditationes omnes sensus nostros in bonis desideriis nutrimus" ("and we occupy our thoughts with moral examination, and through spiritual meditations we nurture all our perceptions in good desires").

[291]   *Erud.* 1.7 (PL 196.1243A): "Scimus autem, quia intime et devote nunquam mens orat, quae se ad devotionem studiosis praemeditationibus prius non excitat. Hi sunt verae devotionis socii inseparabiles, circumspectae, discretae, et providae cogitationes. Sine hujusmodi enim sociis et cooperatoribus, quaelibet nostra devotio non novit vel valet orare quomodo oportet" ("However, we know that the mind never prays interiorly and devoutly, if it does not first arouse itself to devotion with zealous preparatory meditations. These are the inseparable companions of true devotion: circumspect, discerning, and foreseeing thoughts. Without comrades and cooperators of this sort, our devotion is neither able nor knowledgeable enough to pray as it should"). It is meditation in the sense of pondering one's moral life that Richard especially associates with prayer; see *Erud.* 1.12 (PL 196.1248B–1249B).

[292]   *Erud.* 1.42, PL 196.1296D–1297B. According to Hugh of St Victor, *Virtute orandi* 7 (Feiss, 136–38 [PL 176.980A,D]), petitionary prayer has two elements: the object of the request and the devotion of the petitioner, which is the essential element. Sometimes the petitioner is so moved with devotion that the greatness of her love causes her to forget her petition. Ultimately prayer leaves discourse behind and becomes pure prayer which turns into wordless

It inspires confession of faults, prayer for forgiveness, and praise of God's mercy.[293]

Prayer leads to action: growth in virtue, asceticism,[294] compassion for others,[295] and acceptance of suffering in love for Christ, who suffered for humanity's salvation.[296] Charity is the queen of the virtues; without it, the virtues lose their value.[297] God loved us first, giving us many gifts,[298] above all the gift of Christ.[299] Love of God may be servile at the beginning, but it should become filial.[300] Love of God is inseparable from love of neighbor, whether friend or enemy.[301] Love of neighbor should take three forms: desire, word, and good works.[302] Love (*caritas*) is the cement of the Church.[303]

There are three causes that may lead one beyond action and prayer into ecstasy: great devotion, great wonder, and great exultation. In intense devotion, the mind is so inflamed by love that it is volatilized and rises toward the heights. In great wonder, the mind, divinely illumined and rapt in amazement at the highest beauty, is raised above itself. In intense joy and exultation the mind is, so to speak, drunk with an abundance of interior sweetness.[304] In ecstasy (*mentis excessus; mentis alienatio*), as everywhere in human life, the fire which illumines the mind to see also enkindles the will to love. In this consuming and ecstatic union with God, the Christian's will is utterly in harmony with the divine will. Having glimpsed eternal joys in contemplation, the soul burns with desire to possess them. Whoever burns with these desires

praise (*in jubilum*); see also *Virtute orandi* 12–14 (Feiss, 146–60 [PL 176.981D–988A]).

[293] *Erud.* 1.14 (PL 196.1251A): "Triplex sit officium verae et perfectae devotionis. Primum est confessio criminis, secundum postulatio miserationis, tertium glorificatio miserentis" ("The role of true and perfect devotion is threefold: first, confession of sin; second, request for mercy; third, glorification of the one who is merciful").

[294] *Statu* 35 (Ribaillier, 104–5); *XII patr.* 3 (Châtillon, 96.19–20 [PL 196.3B]; tr. Zinn, 55); *XII patr.* 39 (Châtillon, 202.52–54 [PL 196.28D]; tr. Zinn, 94); Adam of St Victor, 26.41–44 (Grosfillier, 359): "Dulcor iste non sentitur / in scissuris mentium / nec in terra reperitur / suave viventium" ("One does not sense this sweetness in divided minds, nor in the lands of soft living").

[295] *LE* 2.10.19 (Châtillon, 411.24–25 = *Serm. cent.* 19 [PL 177.935B]); *Serm. cent.* 60 (PL 177.1083CD).

[296] *Exterm.* 1.6 (PL 196.1084BD); *Carb.* 4 (Châtillon, 257.106–118).

[297] *LE* 2.10.5 (Châtillon, 387.60–61 = *Serm. cent.* 10, [PL 177.912C]); *Adnot. Psalm. 44* (PL 196.321D–322D); *Serm. cent.* 58 (PL 177.1077A); *Serm. cent.* 78 (PL 177.1146D).

[298] *LE* 2.3.4 (Châtillon, 252).

[299] *Illa die* 13 (Châtillon, 149–50).

[300] *LE* 2.10.10 (Châtillon, 396–98 = *Serm. cent.* 10, PL 177.921A–922C).

[301] *LE* 2.10.4 (Châtillon, 383.9–12, 31–35 = *Serm. cent.* 4 [PL 177.909B, D]); *LE* 2.1.15 (Châtillon, 231); *Serm. cent.* 39 (PL 177.999D); *Verbis ap.* 1 (Ribaillier, 318).

[302] *LE* 2.10.10 (Châtillon, 397 = *Serm. cent.* 10 [PL 177.922C]); *Serm. cent.* 97 (PL 177.1202A).

[303] *LE* 2.10.1 (Châtillon, 375.11–13 = *Serm. cent.* 1 [PL 177.901B]).

[304] *Arca Moys.* 5.5 (Aris, 129 [PL 196.174C]; tr. Zinn, 316–17).

is also filled with mercy and compassion for others.[305] A person is lifted up to contemplation of divine truth by the love of God; then the love of neighbor draws him back.[306] Such is the conclusion of *On the Four Degrees of Violent Love.*

Richard's description of four stages in the experience of infatuation and obsessive love of another human being was detailed above. While the final three stages of such love become increasingly worse, the final stages of violent love for God become progressively better. Christ taught that one should love God with heart, soul, and mind. In the first stage of violent love of God, one loves that way, but not totally. In the second stage, one loves God with all one's heart, that is, one loves God as the result of reflection and deliberation. In the third stage, one loves God with all one's soul, that is, with deep feeling (*affectio*) and desire. To love with all one's heart is the result of studied concentration (*ex studio*); to love with all one's soul is the result of choice (*pro voto*). In some earthly loves, desire precedes deliberation, but that is never the case in love of God.[307] Love of God is a deliberate choice before it becomes an ecstatic delight.[308]

---

[305] *Apoc.* 7.6 (PL 196.871D).

[306] *Adnot. Psalm.* 28 (PL 196.317C): "Qui enim per semitam veritatis ascenderant, per misericordiae tramitem descendunt. . . . Amor Dei rapit eos sursum; amor proximi retrahit eos deorsum" ("Those who had ascended by the path of truth, descend by the way of mercy. . . . The love of God snatches them upward; the love of neighbor draws them back down"); *Apoc.* 1.4 (PL 196.705B).

[307] *Quat. grad.* 20–25 (Dumeige, 146–53). Citations are given here according to the Latin text. The same paragraph numbering is used in the English translation by Andrew Kraebel in this volume.

[308] Pierre Rousselot, *Pour l'histoire du problème de l'amour au Moyen Âge*, BGPTMA 6/6 (Münster; Aschendorff, 1908), tr. Alan Vincelette, *The Problem of Love in the Middle Ages: A Historical Contribution*, Marquette Studies in Philosophy 24 (Milwaukee: Marquette University Press, 2001), contended that there were two theories of love in the Middle Ages. Simply put, he maintained that the "physical" theory of love, exemplified by Hugh of St Victor and St Thomas Aquinas, taught that true love of self and love of God and neighbor are identical, because benevolent love for others brings happiness and fulfillment to the lover. By contrast, Rousselot described an "ecstatic" theory of love, exemplified by Abelard and Richard of St Victor, according to which love was irrational and in contradiction with the self's inclination for happiness. A number of authors have questioned this assessment of Richard of St Victor's theory of love. For example, Dumeige, *Richard de Saint-Victor*, 119–25, cites *Emman.* 2.24 (PL 196.659A): "What was supremely sweet to him, he found worthy of supreme love, and what he judged to be loved supremely, he clung to with the highest love" ("Quod enim illi summe dulce fuit, summa dilectione dignum invenit, et quod summe diligendum judicavit, summa illi dilectione inhaesit") and notes Richard's habit of joining knowledge and love and seeing them as mutually reinforcing; Fernand Guimet, "*Caritas ordinata* et *amor discretus* dans la théologie trinitaire de Richard de Saint-Victor," *Revue de Moyen Âge latin*, 4 (1948): 234–36; Jean Châtillon, "Les quatres degrés de la charité d'après Richard de Saint-

The first degree of violent love of God is like an engagement; the second, like a wedding; the third, like sexual union; the fourth, like childbirth.[309] Again, in the first degree of violent love, the soul thirsts for the experience of internal sweetness that comes from tasting how sweet the Lord is; in the second, the soul moves toward God in thirst when it desires to be raised above itself in contemplation in order to see God; in the third, it thirsts into God when, in ecstasy, it forgets itself and passes completely into God; in the fourth, it thirsts as God does when it leaves its own will behind and commits itself completely to the Lord.[310] In the first degree, God enters the soul and the soul returns to itself. In the second degree, the soul ascends above itself and is raised to God. In the third degree the soul raised to God passes totally into God. In the fourth degree, the soul goes out for God's sake and descends beneath itself. In the first stage, it enters through meditation; in the second, it ascends through contemplation; in the third, it is led into jubilation; in the fourth, it goes out because of compassion.[311] The more the love of God trumps all other loves, the more the soul is filled with joy.[312]

In the first stage, God does not show his presence, but God fills the soul with delight and desire to hear and see more. In the second stage, this desire is answered by grace so that the soul flies on the eagle's wings of contemplation and experiences great delights, which it never forgets. The brightness it sees captures its attention. In the third degree of violent love of God, the mind is snatched up into the abyss of divine light and forgets all else, even itself. Gazing on God's beauty, it passes over into the divine glory. Like iron in a furnace, the mind becomes liquified and incandescent; it knows the secrets of divine Wisdom and becomes one spirit with God. It is totally at the disposal of the divine will.[313]

At this point, Richard's argument takes a Christological turn as the soul becomes configured to the divine Wisdom become flesh. Like molten metal, the soul is ready to take on the image of the mold into

Victor," *Revue d'ascétique et de mystique*, 20 (1939): 262–64. For further discussion see, Hazo, *Idea of Love*, 95–160, and Thomas M. Osborne, Jr., *Love of Self and Love of God in Thirteenth-Century Ethics* (Notre Dame: University of Notre Dame Press, 2005), 25–31, 94–105, though neither discusses Richard of St Victor. Rousselot, I believe, misinterpreted Richard of St Victor.

[309]   *Quat. grad.* 26 (Dumeige, 153).
[310]   *Quat. grad.* 28 (Dumeige, 155).
[311]   *Quat. grad.* 29 (Dumeige, 157).
[312]   *Quat. grad.* 31 (Dumeige, 159).
[313]   *Quat. grad.* 32–41 (Dumeige, 159–71).

which God wishes to pour it. That mold is Christ, who did not cling to the form of God, but humbly emptied himself, taking on the form of a servant, becoming obedient even to death on the cross. Greater love than this no one can have. In this fourth stage then, conformed to Christ, violent love of God leads the soul away from God's presence. As it died to self in ecstasy, now it rises in compassion. It is impassible insofar as it rejoices to suffer in Christ.[314]

Richard's *On the Four Degrees of Violent Love* is clearly a literary and theological tour de force. This short summary cannot do justice to the richness of his biblical allusions and citations, in which he draws especially on the Song of Songs and the Psalms. In this work, Richard uses almost interchangeably three words for love: *caritas, dilectio,* and *amor*.[315] *Amor* is the most general term of the three: it is one of the fundamental feelings or inclinations (*affectiones*) of the soul, by which it moves and is moved. *Amor* is the dynamism of being, drawing the subject toward others for good or ill. Richard often refers to it as a fire:[316] a purifying fire, a source of liquefaction, or a boiling cauldron. *Caritas,* which translates the Greek New Testament's *agape,* has no corresponding verbal form. *Caritas* is an interior dynamism, received from God. *Caritas* by nature dilates; it is expansive; it creates personal bonds with others.[317] Most often, Richard reserves *dilectio/diligere* for God's love for human beings and for human beings' love of God and neighbor, both of which are the manifestations of the divine nature, which is *caritas.*

If love is the fundamental dynamism and life of the human spirit, and the human being is made in God's image and likeness, then it stands to reason that love is to be found in God. In his work *On the Trinity,* Richard looks for reasons why God is three and one. He sets out to consruct a ladder of contemplation by which one can take up eagle's wings and fly to the heavenly realm, following in the footsteps of Christ who sent us the Spirit to empower us to ascend after him. In that heavenly realm he finds that God is love.[318]

---

[314] *Quat. grad.* 42–47 (Dumeige, 171–77).

[315] Gervais Dumeige, *Ives, Épître a Séverin sur la charité; Richard de Saint-Victor, Les quare degrés de la violente charité,* Textes philososphiques du Moyen Âge, 3 (Paris: Vrin, 1955): 194–95, 197; Pierluigi Cacciapuoti, *"Deus existentia amoris." Teologia della carità e teologia della Trinità negli scritti di Riccardo di San Vittore († 1173),* Bibliotheca Victorina 9 (Turnhout: Brepols, 1998): 112–78. The rest of this paragraph draws on these two sources.

[316] For examples from Richard's works, see Dumeige, *Ives,* 110 note 2 and 194–95.

[317] *Quomodo Christus* (PL 196.526BC); *Super Exiit* 4 (Châtillon, 106); Cacciapuoti, *Teologia,* 119.

[318] *Trin.* prol. (Ribaillier, 82; tr. Evans, 210). For another summary of Richard's teaching on love

In the first book of *On the Trinity*, Richard shows that the supreme substance, God, exists from itself and from eternity. God is one. God's wisdom and power are supremely perfect and identical with the God-head. In book two, Richard argues that God is the supreme and perfect good. From this he derives new arguments that God is utterly simple.[319] In book three, Richard moves from the divine unity to a consideration of the divine plurality. If God is supreme goodness then in God supreme love (*caritas*) cannot be wanting, for nothing is better or more perfect than *caritas*. One who loves himself with a private love (*amor*) is not rightly said to have *caritas*, for love (*amor*) must tend toward another in order to be *caritas*.[320] So, where there is not a plurality of persons, there is no *caritas*.[321] Supreme *caritas* must be directed at a supreme object, otherwise it would be disordered; hence there must be a plurality of persons in God.[322]

However, it is not enough for the divine goodness and happiness that there be a second person to whom the first communicates his infinite greatness. The two of them require a third person as the joint object (*condilectum*) of their shared benevolence with whom they can share the delights of their charity.[323] If there are only two persons, there is in each a love for the other, but not the joy of a shared love (*condilectio, concordialis caritas, consocialis amor*) for a third.[324]

Finally, Richard, reworking Boethius, defines a person as an incommunicable ex-istence, that is, an incommunicable standing forth into

in *On the Trinity*, see Dumeige, *L'idée*, 69–109.

[319] *Trin.* 2.16–18 (Ribaillier, 123–25).

[320] Richard here cites Gregory the Great, *Hom. ev.* 1.17.1 (Étaix, 141.117 [PL 76.1139A]); tr. Evans, VTT 1:369 note 193, where further references are given). Dumeige, *L'idée*, 40–41, observes that Richard thought every person naturally loves himself and esteems himself. Richard seems to think this a necessary and good form of love, though it is only a beginning: *Erud.* 1.21 (PL 196.1265). Love of self can easily mislead one, if it is not restrained: *Arca Moys.* 4.9 (Aris, 96 [PL 196.144D]; tr. Zinn, 272–73); *Adnot. Psalm.* 25 (PL 196.277A); *Exterm.* 1.14–15 (PL 196.1082BC).

[321] Cf. Achard of St Victor, *Unitate* 1.5 (Martineau, 74; tr. Feiss, 382).

[322] *Trin.* 3.2 (Ribaillier, 136–37; tr. Evans, 248–49).

[323] *Trin.* 3.14–15 (Ribaillier, 149–51; tr. Evans, 259–60). Richard seems to be skirting the idea that a love that is exclusively between two can be tainted with selfishness, even jealousy. On the Porta di Erclano at Pompeii there is an inscription that reflects much painful human experience: "Amamus—invidemus" ("We love—We are jealous"), cited in Richard A. LaFleur, *Scribblers, Sculptors, and Scribes* (New York: Collins, 2010), 3. One could develop the idea that divine love is utterly free of jealousy and so lacks the human tendency toward exclusive possessiveness, and hence is *condilectio*. Richard mentions jealousy in his description of the awful fourth stage of passionate human love in *Quat. grad.* 16. In *Arrha*, 21–28, "Self" convinces "Soul" that God's love for her is not diminished because God loves others as well.

[324] *Trin.* 3.20 (Ribaillier, 154–55; tr. Evans, 263–64).

being. In the Trinity, there is one who does not proceed from (literally: stand forth into being from) another, but has another proceeding from him. There is a second who proceeds from another, but has another proceeding from him. There is a third who proceeds from another, but has no one proceeding from him. The first of these possesses the fullness of gratuitous love (*gratuitus amor*); the third possesses the fullness of owed love (*debitus amor*); the second possesses the fullness of both gratuitous and owed love.[325]

Love, then, stems from God—three persons who are one in power, wisdom, and goodness and related by love bestowed, returned, and shared. If, as seems likely, *On the Trinity* is one of Richard's last works,[326] he did not have the opportunity to reflect on human love and community in the light of what reason shows must be the place of love in God.[327] However, in the sixth book of *On the Trinity*, Richard does say that it is fitting that the third person of the Trinity be called the Holy Spirit. One speaks of a group of people having the same "spirit," that is, loving the same object. The Father and Son breathe out the Holy Spirit as the joint expression of their love. They breathe that same Spirit into the hearts of the saints. The Spirit is a gift given to human beings when love is poured into their hearts.[328] By loving God and neighbor with true charity, human beings manifest the likeness of God.[329]

GODFREY OF ST VICTOR

The first volume of this series contained translations of Victorine texts on the Trinity and Creation. Those texts emphasized the role of love in the inner life of the Trinity as well as the divine kindness that led the Triune God to create a world in which human beings, made in God's image and likeness, mirror the power, wisdom, and goodness of God. Human beings, then, are a particularly apt point of reference for thinking about God. This framework is in the background of Godfrey's

---

[325] *Trin.* 5.16–19 (Ribaillier, 214–17; tr. Evans, 310–12); cf. *Verbis ap.* 9 (Ribaillier, 337).

[326] Cacciapuoti, *Teologia*, 89–90.

[327] Among modern efforts to do so, see Ewert H. Cousins, "The Notion of Person in the De Trinitate of Richard of Saint Victor" (PhD diss., Fordham University, 1966); "A Theology of Interpersonal Relations," *Thought*, 45 (1970): 56–82.

[328] *Trin.* 6.9–10, 14 (Ribaillier, 237–39, 245–46; tr. Evans, 327–29, 333–34).

[329] *LE* 2.10.23 (Châtillon, 418 = *Serm. cent.* 23, PL 177.942A).

Microcosm, and he sometimes refers to it specifically.[330] In the background, also, is the whole drama of sin and redemption as explicated by the Augustinian tradition. Godfrey does not quarrel with that tradition, but he prefers to emphasize not the devastation of sin, but the power of grace. His focus is on the dignity of the human being, which the Son of God made his own in order to show and elicit divine charity. Godfrey is concerned, not with speculation about the primordial forms or the process of creation, but with the result of God's creative love that endows human beings with gifts of nature and grace.

Among those gifts are the senses, the imagination, and the primary affects of sorrow, fear and hope, joy and sorrow, hate and love, confidence and modesty. These perceptive abilities, feelings, and impulses are natural and good, though they need to be ordered and moderated by reason and circumspection. All of them are natural to human beings;[331] all are capable of being informed by charity. The Holy Spirit can dispose these emotions through charity to accomplish great things. In particular, charity can bring love upward toward imageless contemplation and a foretaste of heavenly joy.[332] Charity, then, is a grace, the work of the Holy Spirit, which purifies and transforms the natural impulses of love. Grace does not eliminate the gifts and impulses of nature but purifies and enhances them.[333] Good works done in the body are spiritual because the Spirit animates them.[334]

Having thus set the stage, Godfrey allows divine Charity to explain herself, first in a conversation that takes place after a banquet that she provides and then when she appears in a vision as a bird with six wings. In the first discourse, there is a fourfold division of love: love of what is beneath (our bodies), love of ourselves, love of neighbor, and love of God.[335] In the second discourse, Charity corrects this to a sixfold division: love of body and soul, love of friend and enemy, love of God and the God-man.[336] It is striking that Godfrey does not speak directly of love of the world around us, its flowers and stones or food and drink.

---

[330] *Microcosmus*, 82–83, 207, 227, 228–29, 235. References to the *Microcosmus* will be given by the paragraph numbers in Delhaye's edition.
[331] *Microcosmus*, 140.
[332] *Microcosmus*, 139.
[333] *Microcosmus*, 169–70, 202.
[334] *Microcosmus*, 191.
[335] *Microcosmus*, 142.
[336] *Microcosmus*, 208, 211–12, 224.

He refers to love of the physical world only in reference either to love
of one's body and soul or to active charity toward one's neighbor.

Godfrey is particularly detailed and eloquent in his discussion of
love of one's own body.[337] Godfrey thinks of body and soul as partners,
working together. The soul, moved by the Spirit, nurtures good
thoughts and feelings in the senses and imagination and at times lifts
them upward, whereas the body enables the will to act in the world.
Showing a delicate sense of what is humanly possible and swimming
against the tide of theological opinion in his time, Godfrey says that,
although spontaneous impulses and desires are sometimes unruly and
enticements to sin, they are not in themselves sinful unless one consents to them. Such impulses need to be ordered by charity; if they
cannot be eliminated, they can at least be contained.[338] Body and soul
are related as man and wife, inhabitant and home, rider and mount,
traveling companions, and coheirs. Godfrey's insistence on ordered
love of one's own flesh is somewhat startling now and was in Godfrey's
time as well. Medieval authors tend to use "flesh" (caro) in a negative
way. In this, they follow St Paul, but whereas Paul thought of "flesh" not
as the body but as all within a person that draws him or her to sin, later
authors tend to come close to equating "flesh" and "body."[339] The connotations of carnalis ("carnal" in English) are then of sinful appetites
that arise in the flesh. Godfrey defends himself against possible critics
of his affirmation of the flesh by saying that charity requires that all
love be ordered. Jesus said we should love our neighbors as ourselves,
and we are soul and body, one person, one human being. Although by
mutual agreement soul and body are separated by death, they will be
reunited forever.[340]

It is not easy to distinguish clearly what Godfrey says of love of one's
body from what he says about love of one's soul—perhaps because he
did not have an adequate philosophical framework in which to formu-
late his understanding of their close association, such as Aristotelian
philosophy would provide in the next century. Love of the soul involves
ordering one's inclinations and desires because, unless one provides
them with boundaries, like water they will run downhill toward vani-

[337] Microcosmus, 154–66, 209–10, 214.
[338] Microcosmus, 105–28, 167–70, 191, 215.
[339] James D. G. Dunn, The Theology of Paul the Apostle (Grand Rapids: Eerdmans, 1998) 51–78.
[340] Microcosmus, 155, 220–21.

ties and vain curiosity. However, under the warmth of charity they rise like water vapor toward the sun.[341]

Godfrey does not define what charity is, but he thinks of it as love patterned (ordered and moderated) after the self-giving love of Christ, who considered no one his enemy and was willing to die as a friend for all.[342] In the form of love of neighbor, charity seeks what others need rather than what they deserve.[343] Here again, charity is transformative. As Seneca wrote, we are social animals.[344] We are naturally inclined to love our neighbors, relatives, and families. When we work together with people, bonds of love are created that bring security and pleasure.[345] Family bonds and neighborliness can and should be expressions of charity. An ordinary, blameless life is a path to salvation and an adornment of the Church. Not all saints are martyrs or monks.[346] Those in positions of authority have a special duty to love their neighbor in practical ways, just as Christ did, even to the giving of their lives.[347]

When Godfrey turns to love of God and love of the God-man, Lady Charity warns him that here especially he needs the interplay of boldness, humility, and modesty. These virtues need one another if they are to be ordered. Circumspection sees to that ordering.[348] In fact, since the one Spirit inspires charity, which informs all the virtues, the virtues are all interconnected. Armed with both boldness and humility, Godfrey can rightly approach, understand, and explain the third level of human love, love for God and the God-man.[349]

Lady Charity tells Godfrey that before he dares to consider the love of God, he is to recollect himself, to gather in his scattered thoughts and desires and concentrate on what is above.[350] Now that Godfrey has been exercised in the first four kinds of loving, Lady Charity has left him. It is up to him to reach toward the last two kinds of love, love of

[341] *Microcosmus*, 167, 215.
[342] *Microcosmus*, 216–18, 241, 82–103.
[343] *Microcosmus*, 176–77.
[344] Seneca *De beneficiis*, 7.1.7 (Seneca, *Moral Essays*, ed. John W. Basore [Cambridge: Harvard University Press, 1964] 3:458), cited by Godfrey, *Mirocosmus*, 172 (Delhaye, 192.7) and 216 (Delhaye, 236.4).
[345] *Microcosmus*, 172–74.
[346] *Microcosmus*, 196, 207.
[347] *Microcosmus*, 222–23.
[348] *Microcosmus*, 205.
[349] *Microcosmus*, 180–82.
[350] *Microcosmus*, 204.

God and love of the God-man, perhaps because they are the realm of grace and experience. When he has kissed her three times, he is ready to fly in ordered love to the Lord. From now on, he will direct all he does to Him, and he will nurture the same ordered love in his neighbor.[351]

In a remarkable passage, Godfrey describes the fifth and sixth kinds of love, love of God and love of the God-man, which constitute the bond of sweetest affection by which the human being is bound to God immediately, ineffably, and inseparably. *Immediately*, that is, without any intermediary, for he loves God directly, not through or because of anything else. It is a mutual bond. The human being is eternally beloved before he loves in time; by being loved, he is enabled to love. *Ineffably*, because only the soul who has experienced it can know how sweet this bond of love is. Even after experiencing this love, she cannot express it because it is the Holy Spirit,[352] to which no human affection is similar. Still, desiring to express what it experiences, the holy soul uses the metaphor of a bride aglow with desire for her husband; she then experiences the sweetness of attaining what she desires. Although nothing in human affections is similar to or sweeter than spousal love, even such spousal love is not comparable to love of God. *Inseparably*, because when Christ personally took up human nature, body and soul, he did this so that our double nature would be united to him spiritually, like a fiancé to Christ's betrothed, but also physically, like a husband united to his wife indissolubly through the bodily union of a consummated marriage. In his members, the consummation is still awaited, for the bond of mutual love between them and God is not yet so indissoluble that it deserves the name marriage. Now the Christian sighs with longing and must be satisfied with betrothal-gifts. Gradually, husband and wife come to resemble each other. Christ emptied himself to take on human form so that he could, through mutual love, imprint on his beloved his image and likeness. Thus, so to speak, God falls in love with humankind and descends into their nature and life, so that humankind might fall in love with God and advance into God.[353]

And so when he comes to the highest level of love, Godfrey remains the humanist, who celebrates the gifts of nature and grace. Marital love,

---

[351] *Microcosmus*, 224.

[352] By the twelfth century, the idea that the Holy Spirit is the bond of love between Father and Son was traditional. Here, Godfrey seems to suggest that the Holy Spirit binds or connects the soul to Father and Son.

[353] *Microcosmus*, 225.

from the onset of desire to its consummation, is the prime metaphor for love between God and humankind, a love that reached its climax in the Incarnation of the Son. Marital intimacy is a gift from God and the sacrament of the greatest gift of all.

The grace of the Spirit working through charity does not simply transform individuals. Human beings are siblings stemming from one earthly father, Adam.[354] Christ became neighbor to all humans in the flesh and inculcated love of neighbor by his teaching and example. He loved all as friends and tried to turn into friends those who were enemies toward him.[355] Grace brings human beings together in one body under Christ, their Head, animated by the love that is the Holy Spirit.[356] Theologically speaking, the human being is a microcosm when he is worthy to have God dwell in him.[357] In the glory of the final consummation, all men and women together will form a single microcosm, God's eternal kingdom.[358]

COMMONALITIES AND DIFFERENCES AMONG THE VICTORINES AND BEYOND

This concluding section does three things. First, it summarizes the main elements of the Victorine teaching on love, looking for commonalities and differences among them.[359] Secondly, it sketches St Thomas

---

[354] *Microcosmus*, 219.

[355] *Microcosmus*, 216–18.

[356] *Microcosmus*, 239–40.

[357] *Microcosmus*, 225.

[358] *Microcosmus*, 236.

[359] In 1952, Mortimer J. Adler was instrumental in establishing the Institute for Philosophical Research. The purpose of this institute was to take stock of Western thought on key topics of philosophical interest, such as freedom, justice, happiness, and love. The results of the collaborative effort to sort out the issues about love appeared in a book by Robert G. Hazo, *The Idea of Love*, Concepts in Western Thought (New York: Frederick A. Praeger, 1967). In his introduction to the volume, Adler avowed that "of all the ideas so far subjected to dialectical analysis by the Institute, the idea of love proved to be most difficult" (Hazo, xi). "Love" proved to have a very wide variety of meanings, which are not closely connected, and some of the terms needed to analyze love are themselves difficult to define. The participants decided to concentrate on interpersonal love, and not love of God or love of inanimate objects. For that reason, the template Hazo provides is not a perfect fit with the Victorines, for whom God's love for human beings and human beings' love for God are of fundamental importance. Nevertheless, Hazo's framing of the philosophical issues regarding interpersonal love can serve as a useful point of reference for the discussion that follows. Some key issues are the respective roles of tendency and cognition in love, whether love of others is benevolent or acquisitive or both, and how supernatural love interacts with natural love.

Aquinas' teaching on love to highlight particularly what Aquinas' understanding has in common with the Victorines and with St Augustine. Finally, it contrasts what might be called the classical tradition of Christian thought about love (elaborated by Augustine, the Victorines, and Thomas Aquinas) with some ideas that are influential in contemporary culture.

Victorine Understanding of Love

The Victorines would all agree that love is a tendency that is innate and broad. Love focuses on objects that are perceived or judged to be desirable, but the tendency of love precedes awareness of the object. The Victorines do not develop any theory of cosmic love. They would agree that one may love carrots, but it does not seem that they think that carrots love the sun or porous soil.[360]

Love is constitutive of the Trinity. Utterly benevolent love is what moved the Triune God to create the universe and humankind within it. That same benevolent love invites human beings to share in the life of the Trinity. The Father sent the Son into the world out of sheer benevolence, and the Son laid down his life for his friends and for those who considered themselves his enemies but whom he wished to make friends. He in turn sent the Spirit, to whom love is appropriated in the Trinity, to pour out divine love into the hearts of those who welcome him.

Thus, in common with Augustine before them and Aquinas afterwards, the Victorines believe there is a religious experience of love that is humanly impossible without God's grace. For the Victorines, *caritas*, the love poured into the soul by the Spirit, enables one to love God more fully and to love others more compassionately and more universally than one could apart from it. *Caritas* is transformative, expanding and purifying one's capacity and effort to love God and others.

The Victorines see human love as participating in divine love and fulfilled only in an infinite, divine object. Human beings are created in God's image and likeness. God is supreme Love; human beings are inherently lovers. Hugh of St Victor wrote, "The force of love is such that you necessarily are like the object of your love, and by the com-

---

[360]   This summary of Victorine thought on love depends on what has preceded, and so it requires few references.

munity of love you are transformed in some way into the likeness of the beloved."[361] That is, by loving God and guiding others to love God, a human being becomes most perfectly what she is—the image and likeness of God.

One characteristic feature of Victorine teaching on love, particularly manifest in the writings of Achard and Richard, is the interweaving of contemplation and compassion. They think of the Christian life as both ascent and descent. One ascends toward contemplative and nuptial union with God through a disciplined life of reading, meditation, prayer, and virtuous action. Then, transformed into the image of Christ, the Christian—like Him—returns from contemplative union with God to compassionate service and care of others. Christian life is, then, not a ladder with rungs—the bottom one of which is reading and the top is contemplation—but a double spiral staircase set within a many-sided tower, within which continuous ascending to contemplative union and descending to compassionate service are framed and nurtured by reading, meditation, prayer, and disciplined virtue.

Augustine taught that there are four possible objects of love: things beneath us, ourselves, our equals, and God. He recognized the beauty and goodness of the things beneath us, but saw beautiful things as properly directing our attention elsewhere, to uncreated beauty.[362] He saw love of body and self as so natural that they need not be commanded. Hence, Jesus' command is not fourfold, but twofold: to love the supreme Good in which we find beatitude and to love those who can share beatitude with us. One loves God, who is ontological and moral goodness, and one loves good people for the goodness they receive or can receive from God. The earlier Victorines seem to operate within the fourfold Augustinian framework, but Godfrey breaks with it. In the *Microcosm*, Lady Charity corrects Godfrey's endorsement of the Augustinian scheme of four possible objects of love. She tells him that there are six objects that should be loved: God and the God-man, friends and enemies, and one's own soul and body. Particularly striking is her emphasis on loving one's own body, whose relation to the soul he describes in a series of complementary metaphors.

---

[361] *Arrha* 13 (Sicard, 233; tr. Feiss, VTT 2): "Ea vis amoris est, ut talem te esse necesse sit, quale illud est quod amas, et cui per affectum coniungeris, in ipsius similitudinem ipsa quodammodo dilectionis societate transformaris."

[362] Philip Cary, *Outward Signs: The Powerlessness of External Things in Augustine's Thought* (New York: Oxford, 2008), 100–6, states this in a radical way.

Although the Victorines do not often invoke Augustine's *uti/frui* distinction, they do share his eudaemonism: the love that lies at the basis of human seeking is directed toward reaching happiness. To love another is to wish him the same happiness as one wishes for oneself.[363] Paradoxically, loving others in this way is also the way one finds happiness oneself, because one is fulfilling God's command and loving in a way that mirrors God's benevolence.[364] Again, "the soul acquires its own good by loving God above all things. In loving God it loves its own self."[365] Moreover, the Victorines have a strong sense of all the baptized as members of the body of Christ. In loving another, in helping her, in rejoicing in her successes (the greatest of which is that she loves as Christ did), one loves oneself, for in Christ all are one.[366]

In the *Idea of Love*, Robert Hazo writes, "All theories of supernatural love exclude sexual desire as a form of supernatural love."[367] However, there are indications that the Victorines did think that sexual love can be an expression of *caritas*. According to Hugh of St Victor,

[363] Hugh of St Victor, *Sacr.* 2.13.6 (PL 176.528D–529A): "Geminam nobis sacra Scriptura charitatem commendat; Dei videlicet et proximi. Charitatem Dei ut sic ipsum diligamus ut in ipso gaudeamus. Charitatem proximi ut sic ipsum diligamus, non ut in ipso, sed ut cum ipso gaudeamus in Deo. Hoc est, ut Deum diligamus propter se ipsum; proximum autem propter Deum" ("Sacred Scripture commends to us a twofold love, namely of God and of neighbor. Love of God, that we may so love him that we may rejoice in him. Love of neighbor, that we may so love him, not that we may rejoice in him, but that we may rejoice with him in God. That is, that we may love God for God himself, and our neighbor on account of God"). Hugh goes on (530AD) to say that God is to be loved wherever he is found: in God himself, in the neighbor, within and without, above and below, far and near. One loves a honeycomb for the sweet honey that is within it: "Ita dilige Dominum Deum tuum, quia dulcedo est ipse, et bonitas et veritas. Proximum autem tuum dilige, quia receptaculum est dulcedinis, bonitatis et veritatis: et si in eo inveneris quod habere debet dulcedinem et bonitatem et veritatem, dilige in ipso illa et dilige ipsum propter illa. . . . Dilige ergo Deum quia bonitas est. Dilige proximum quia ex bonitate bonus est; vel si bonus non est, ut sit bonus qui bonus esse potest" ("Therefore, love the Lord your God, because he is Sweetness and Goodness and Truth. Love your neighbor because he is a container of sweetness, goodness, and truth; and if you find in him the sweetness and goodness and truth that he ought to have, love those things in him, and love him because of them. . . . Love God because he is Goodness. Love your neighbor because he is good from Goodness or, if he is not good, so that the one who can be good may be good").

[364] As Jennifer A. Herdt observes in *Putting on Virtue: The Legacy of the Splendid Vices* (Chicago: University of Chicago Press, 2008), 12, Augustine perceived "correctly that the pursuit of eudaimonia [happiness or beatitude] need not compete with acting virtuously for its own sake (as also it does not compete with the pursuit of God as our true final end)."

[365] Osborne, Jr., *Love of Self*, 28, summarizing the teaching of Hugh of St Victor.

[366] This is particularly emphasized in Hugh's *On the Betrothal-Gift of the Soul*, 21–28 (Sicard, 238–48). See D. Poirel, "Love of God, Human Love: Hugh of St Victor and the Sacrament of Marriage," *Communio* 24 (Spring 1997): 108–9.

[367] *Idea of Love*, 99.

It is rightly said that "a man leaves his father and his mother and cleaves to his wife, and they become two in one flesh": in the cleaving to one's wife is the sacrament of the invisible community, which ought to develop in spirit between God and the soul; in being two in one flesh is the sacrament of visible participation, which occurs in the flesh between Christ and the Church. "They become one flesh," is therefore a great sacrament, in Christ and the Church, but "they will be two in one heart, in one love" is a greater sacrament, in God and the soul.[368]

More conclusive is Godfrey's assertion in *Mircrocosm*, 225, that the union of the soul with God is best expressed by the analogy of the bride aglow with desire for her husband, for in human affections there is nothing more similar to the union of the soul and God. Earlier in *Microcosm*, 196 and 207, Godfrey says that family bonds can be expressions of charity. Not just life in the cloister or martyrdom, but also an ordinary blameless life is a path to salvation and an adornment of the Church.

It was suggested earlier that Augustine tended to treat friendship as a separate topic and did not discuss it in the context of his theology of love. That may be because the second half of the great commandment to love God and neighbor encompassed all, both friends and enemies, indiscriminately. According to Godfrey, Christ gave his life not just for his friends, but also for those who thought of themselves as his enemies, whom he wanted to change into his friends. However, the Victorines scarcely mention friendship among people or the friendship with God to which Christ invites human beings. This is odd for two reasons. It is clear that at least some of them value friendship, as Hugh's letter

---

[368] *BM Virg.*, Jollès, 208 [PL 176.864AB]: "Recte ergo dicitur: 'Relinquet homo patrem suum et matrem suam et adherebit uxori sue, et erunt duo in carne una' ut, in eo quod adheret uxori sue, sacramentum sit invisibilis societatis que in spiritu facienda est inter Deum et animam; in eo autem quod duo sunt in carne una, sacramentum sit visibilis participationis que in carne facta est inter Christum et Ecclesiam. Magnum igitur sacramentum: 'erunt duo in carne una,' in Christo et Ecclesia. Sed maius sacramentum: 'erunt duo in corde uno, in dilectione una,' in Deo et anima." I owe this citation to Poirel, "Love of God," 104. One might construe "sacrament" here in a completely extrinsic way and so argue that *caritas* is not involved, but if one admits that *caritas* is involved in the union of hearts, then the parallelism suggests that *caritas* is involved in the union of bodies as well. See also Teresa Olsen Pierre, "Marriage, Body, and Sacrament in the Age of Hugh of St Victor," in *Christian Marriage: A Historical Study*, ed. Glenn W. Olsen (New York: Crossroad, 2001), 218–27, who calls attention to *Sacr.*1.8.13 (PL 176.314CD), where Hugh writes that marriage, a sacrament that existed both before and after the Fall, has two dimensions: the marriage itself, which consists in a social covenant, and the act or function of marriage, which consists in sexual intercourse. The marriage covenant is a sacrament of the union between God and the soul, and carnal intercourse is a sacrament of the union between Christ and the Church.

to Ralph de Mauriaco and some of Richard's covering letters make
clear. Secondly, the Victorines from Hugh to Godfrey lived between
1120 and 1180, a period Brian Patrick Maguire has termed "The Age of
Friendship."[369] This is the age that produces Aelred of Rievaulx's *On
Spiritual Friendship*[370] and a flurry of letters of friendship. The only
explanation for the absence of references to friendship in the Victorines
seems to be that they take friendship for granted and focus their attention on love of all neighbors, whether friend, foe, or stranger.[371]

In discussing love, none of the Victorines celebrates love of earthly
things. With Augustine, they agree that all that God has made is good
and beautiful, but reality is hierarchically organized and human beings
should focus their love on what is equal to or greater than themselves.
One counterweight to this is Richard's analysis of six forms of contemplation in *The Mystical Ark* (*Arca Moysis* or *Benjamin major*). These are
laid out in a hierarchical scheme. The first form of contemplation en-
gages the imagination in contemplation of the form and image of visible things: one attends to and is amazed by the number, greatness,
diversity, beauty, and joy of the physical things perceived by the senses.[372] These same perceptible features of the natural world are the subject of Hugh's *On the Three Days*. In the second form of contemplation
described in *The Mystical Ark*, reason focuses on the order, disposition,
causes, and utility of the same physical things. The devotion, wonder,
and joy deriving from both of these forms of contemplation can lead
directly to ecstatic union with God.[373]

This is significant because contemplation and love are closely intertwined in Victorine thought. The fire that illumines the mind to see
also enkindles the will to love. Describing the third of the four degrees
of violent love of God, Richard writes,

> In this state when the mind is alienated from itself, when it is snatched
> up to the secret place of that divine mystery, when it is surrounded on
> all sides by the fire of that divine love, penetrated deep within, and

---

[369]   Brian Patrick McGuire, *Friendship and Community: The Monastic Experience, 350–1250*, CS
       95 (Kalamazoo, MI: Cistercian Publications, 1988).
[370]   Aelred of Rievaulx, *De spiritali amicitia*, ed. A. Hoste, in Aelred of Rievaulx, *Opera ascetica*,
       ed. A. Hoste and C. H. Talbot, CCCM 1 (Turnhout: Brepols, 1971), 281–350; *Spiritual Friend-
       ship*, tr. Lawrence Braceland, ed. Marsha Dutton, CF 5 (Collegeville, MN: Cistercian Publica-
       tions, 2010).
[371]   This was Brian Patrick McGuire's suggestion in a private conversation in May 2010.
[372]   *Arca Moys.* 1.6, 2.1–11 (Aris, 12–13, 22–34; tr. Zinn, 161–62, 174–90).
[373]   *Arca Moys.* 4.22 (Aris, 118–20; tr. Zinn, 302–05).

completely enflamed, it goes completely out of itself, clothes itself in a kind of divine feeling and, configured to the beauty it sees, it passes completely into another glory.[374]

The rapture or ecstatic union with God induced by this passionate love of God is the same as that ecstasy induced by contemplating the number, greatness, diversity, beauty, and joy of physical things. Richard seems to think of them as pathways leading directly to ecstatic love and to awareness of that Beauty in which they participate. If so, they become such pathways by being loved.

Thomas Aquinas

It is remarkable how much Augustine, the Victorines, and St Thomas Aquinas agree on the basic questions regarding love.[375] The major change in the sixty years between the death of Godfrey of St Victor and the first writings of Thomas Aquinas is the availability of the Aristotelian corpus. Aristotle's writings do not lead Thomas Aquinas to a notion of love that fundamentally differs from that of Augustine or the Victorines, but they do provide some new conceptual tools.

---

[374] *Quat. grad.* 38 (Dumeige, 167.4–15; tr. Kraebel, VTT 2:291–92): "In hoc statu dum mens a seipsa alienatur, dum in illud divini arcane secretarium rapitur, dum ab illo divini amoris incendio undique circumdatur, intime penetratur, usquequaque inflammatur, seipsam penitus exuit, divinum quemdam affectum induit et inspecte pulchritudini configurata tota in aliam gloriam transit."

[375] Hazo, 197–204, 224–38. These paragraphs on St Thomas draw on Hazo and a number of authors who give many references to St Thomas' own works. The authors consulted from the vast literature on Aquinas on love and friendship include Thomas Aquinas, *On Love and Charity: Readings from the "Commentary on the Sentences of Peter Lombard,"* tr. Peter A. Kwasniewski, Thomas Bolin, and Joseph Bolin (Washington, DC: Catholic University of America Press, 2008); Rebecca Konyndyk DeYoung, Colleen McCluskey, and Christina Van Dyke, *Aquinas's Ethics: Metaphysical Foundations, Moral Theory, and Theological Context* (Notre Dame, IN: University of Notre Dame Press, 2009); Paul Wadell, *The Primacy of Love: An Introduction to the Ethics of Thomas Aquinas* (New York: Paulist, 1992); Brian Davies, *The Thought of Thomas Aquinas* (Oxford: Clarendon, 1992); Aidan Nichols, *Discovering Aquinas: An Introduction to His Life, Work, and Influence* (Grand Rapids: Eerdmans, 2002); Jean-Pierre Torrell, *Saint Thomas Aquinas,* tr. Robert Royal, 2 vols. (Washington, DC: Catholic University of America Press, 1996–2003); Daniel Schwartz, *Aquinas on Friendship* (Oxford: Clarendon, 2007); James McEvoy, "The other as oneself: friendship and love in the thought of St Thomas Aquinas," in *Thomas Aquinas: Approaches to Truth: The Aquinas Lectures at Maynooth, 1996–2001,* ed. James McEvoy and Michael Dunne (Portland, OR: Four Courts, 2002), 16–37; Servais Pinckaers, "The desire for happiness as a way to God," in McEvoy and Dunne, *Thomas Aquinas,* 53–65).

According to Thomas Aquinas, the perfection of Christian life consists in charity toward God and neighbor.[376] Charity is a participation in God's eternal reality by way of a created habit in the soul.[377] Its efficient cause is the Trinity, and its exemplary cause is the Holy Spirit.[378] Charity is friendship between God and man by which man loves God and God loves man. As a form of friendship, charity is mutual love, communion, and self-transcendence (*ecstasis*).[379] The more one grows in charity, the more servile fear gives way to filial fear;[380] the more *amor* is perfected by *caritas*, the more like God one becomes.[381] Charity is a virtue residing in the will and is the mover, form, and end of all the other virtues.[382] It is possible to have charity not only for God and for others, but also for both oneself and one's body, which too will share in beatitude.[383] Charity consists in following Christ.[384]

Like Augustine and the Victorines, Aquinas teaches that there is a hierarchy of being[385] and he ponders the proper order and measure of charity.[386] One loves God above all, in the manner of a friend loved for his own sake, There is no limit to how much God can be rightly be loved.[387] For the sake of a friend, we love "those belonging to him, be they children, servants, or anyone connected with him at all, even if they hurt or hate us, so much do we love him."[388] Hence, love of God requires that charity extend to enemies as well as friends. Although he shares with Augustine and the Victorines the evangelical conviction that love embraces both friends and enemies, Thomas goes beyond them in carefully considering the order and measure of love towards different categories of people.[389]

---

[376] *Sum. theo.* 2-2.184.3; Torrell, *Saint Thomas Aquinas*, 2:351–66.

[377] Davies, *The Thought of Thomas Aquinas*, 288.

[378] DeYoung, 149, 158–59; *In I Sent.* (Paris), 17.1.1 (tr. Kwasniewski, 13). In taking this position, Aquinas disagrees with Peter Lombard, on whom he is commenting.

[379] *Sum. theo.* 1-2.65.5; Torrell, *Saint Thomas Aquinas*, 2:336–40; McEvoy, "The other as oneself," 22–24.

[380] DeYoung, 158.

[381] Wadell, 63–78, commenting especially on *Sum. theo.* 1-2.65.5; and *Sum. theo.* 2-2.23.1, cited by Nichols, *Discovering Aquinas*, 107.

[382] *In III Sent.* 27.2.1–4 (tr. Kwasniewski, 148); *Sum. theo.* 2-2.23.7–8; Wadell, 125–28; DeYoung, 142–46, 236 note 45.

[383] *In III Sent.* 28.7 (tr. Kwasniewski, 199); DeYoung, 134–37.

[384] Torrell, *Saint Thomas Aquinas*, 2:367–69.

[385] DeYoung, 14–18.

[386] DeYoung, 135.

[387] *Sum. theo.* 2-2.27.6.

[388] *Sum. theo.* 2-2.23.1.

[389] *In III Sent.* 29–30 (tr. Kwasniewski, 202–61).

The Aristotelian notion of final causality leads Thomas to think of love as a cosmic phenomenon. Thomas speaks of three kinds of love: natural (in inanimate beings), sensitive, and rational love.[390] Each thing seeks its own good; human beings seek happiness, which includes the material goods that correspond to the sensitive appetites as well as the perfect Good that can satisfy their deepest longing of mind and will.[391] In a broad sense, Thomas can speak of love in the will as a passion but, strictly speaking, love (*amor*) is a passion when it is an involuntary inclination or feeling. All the other passions—fear, joy, desire, and sadness—are expressions of the basic passion of love; they are specified by particular objects.[392]

Everything in the universe has a natural inclination to seek not just its own good, but also the good of the whole universe, of which its own good is a part. The common good of the whole universe is the Trinity, the origin and end of the whole.[393] In addition to the inclination toward the good of the universe, human beings have—by a general sort of love—an innate inclination toward friendship with all other human beings.[394]

Aquinas' use of the Latin terms *amor* and *dilectio* for natural love and *caritas* for supernatural love resembles the use Augustine and the Victorines made of those terms. In place of the Augustinian division of *amor* into *cupiditas* and *caritas*, Aquinas makes a basic distinction between two kinds of love: the love of concupiscence (*amor concupiscentiae*) and the love of friendship (*amor amicitiae*). Sometimes, he uses the former to refer to acquisitive or self-centered desire and the latter to mean benevolent desire for the good of another. At other times, he uses the love of concupiscence to refer to the means, and the love of friendship to refer to the person (end) for whom a good is sought, whether that person is oneself or another. This latter distinction makes clear, in a way that Augustine's *uti/frui* distinction did not, that human persons are to be loved as ends and not as means.[395]

---

[390] *In III Sent.* 27.1.2 (tr. Kwasniewski, 129–31).
[391] Wadell, 44–62; Pinckaers, "The desire for happiness," 53–65.
[392] *In III Sent.* 27.1.3 (tr. Kwasniewski, 132–37); Wadell, 79–89, 94–105; DeYoung, 182.
[393] Osborne, 69–112.
[394] *Sum. theo.* 2-2.114.1 ad 2: "Omnis homo naturaliter omni homini est amicus quodam generali amore" ("Every human being is naturally a friend to every other human being by a kind of general love"); McEvoy, "The other as oneself," 31.
[395] Hazo, 228–30.

Influential in Thomas' use of the term "love of friendship" is Aristotle's distinction of friendship into three sorts: friendships of virtue, pleasure, and utility. As Aristotle and Aquinas describe them, in the first sort of friendship, which is friendship in the proper sense, one wishes good for a worthy person; in the latter two, self-interest is either the predominant motive or the complete aim.[396] Aquinas distinguishes three acts that characterize friendship of virtue: benevolence, which wills the good of the other; concord, by which friends will and reject the same things; and beneficence, by which someone does good deeds for the person loved and does him no harm.[397]

Doing good for others can bring pleasure and growth in virtue to oneself, and one may anticipate in sharing in the good that one wishes for the other; provided these are concomitants, not causes, in such cases, doing good is benevolent. Similarly, one can hope that the other will reciprocate, even if that is not the purpose for which one acts. Loving others benevolently is an expression of love for God, because such love fulfills the divine law, the ultimate aim of which is to establish people in friendship with God and so bring them to complete happiness.[398]

Sexual desire is a passion of the sensitive appetite; that is, it is an inclination based in the body. When sexual intercourse occurs within marriage for the proper motives it can be an act of virtue. In fact, the friendship between husband and wife can be very great, for they are united not only in the flesh but also in a whole range of shared domestic activity.[399]

Created and recreated in the image of the Trinity, human beings express that image perfectly at the level of action when, with the aid of grace, they come to know God and, from the Word formed in their mind, their love for God bursts forth.[400] Grace brings an experience of God, a taste of the divine sweetness.[401] That taste provokes a desire for full union with God; but once it is experienced, other desires are experienced differently.[402] Only when one reaches perfect union with God

---

[396] Hazo, 206–16.
[397] Schwartz, *Aquinas on Friendship*, 6–10. McEvoy's "'The other as oneself,'" 16–37, contains a fine summary of Aquinas' understanding of friendship; his notes refer to the literature on the subject.
[398] DeYoung, 157; Hazo, 235–38.
[399] Hazo, 231–33.
[400] *Sum. theo.* 1.43.5 ad 2; *Sum. theo.* 1.93.7, discussed in Torrell, *Saint Thomas Aquinas*, 2:90–91.
[401] Torrell, *Saint Thomas Aquinas*, 2: 90–98.
[402] Torrell, *Saint Thomas Aquinas*, 2:325–26.

will "the restlessness of desire cease because of the fulfilling presence of the supreme good."[403] For Thomas, as for the Victorines, love and knowledge are interwoven. In the beatitude of heaven, the One seen is united to the seer so that there is a kind of mutual penetration through love.[404]

In spite of the centuries that separate them and the philosophies upon which they drew, Augustine, the Victorines, and Aquinas give the same answers to most of the important questions about love. That they have so much in common is the result of many things: their shared respect for the Bible, especially for Jesus' teachings and example regarding love; the influence of Augustine on the later writers; and the heritage of Greek and Latin philosophy. More than that, they share a great respect for individual experience and for reasoned analysis, they value piety, and they reverence mystery. However, love looks very different when viewed from the standpoint of scientific reductionism and a hermeneutic of suspicion.

LOVE CONQUERS ALL?

Virgil wrote, "Love conquers all," which Augustine, the Victorines, and Aquinas all believe to be true. The poet went on to say, "and let us yield to *love*."[405] Had he said *caritas* or *dilectio*, they could agree with this second proposition; but he said *amor*, and so they might add a caution: "Let us indeed yield to love, provided it is ordered and measured and leads oneself and the other to the perfect Good."

One strand of the Enlightenment project aimed to torch such quibbles with the flame of Reason, which at times has turned out to be abstract, imperialistic, and reductionist.[406] Where this reductionist rationalism has prevailed, such Reason scorched not only the tradition represented by the Victorines, Augustine, and Aquinas, but also the passion and dreams of Virgil, the love of the *Song of Songs* and, even more, the mystics' dream of union with God. It seems that "the repres-

---

[403] Torrell, Saint Thomas Aquinas, 2:335, citing Thomas' *Compendium theologiae*.
[404] *In I Sent.* 1.1 (tr. Kwasniewski, 3–6); cf. *In III Sent.* 27.1.4 (tr. Kwasniewski, 137–43); DeYoung, 148–49.
[405] Virgil, *Eclogues* 10.69 (*Eclogues; Georgics, Aeneid I–VI*, ed. G. P. Goold [Cambridge: Harvard University Press, 1999], 508.538): "Omnia vincit amor, et nos cedamus amori."
[406] Wendell Berry, *Life Is a Miracle: An Essay against Modern Superstition* (Berkeley: Counterpoint, 2000), 23–91.

sion of divine eros ... leads to the repression of human eros."[407] There may be "sex in the city," but the presence there of love, much less Lady Charity, is less certain. Of course, there are millions of those whom Godfrey of St Victor described as decent, ordinary people, who express active charity in lives of simple goodness and concern for the needy, and provide society and church with fitting adornment. However, in the thoughts and worldview of many among contemporary intellectual and cultural elites—and those influenced by them—love is problematic. "Modern love has become the privileged site for the trope of irony."[408] Lovers are observed with "Oh yeah," or "Just wait," but perhaps underneath that skepticism is a hankering for something lost. One might wish for transcendence and passionate devotion, but there seems to be no going back to the pre-Enlightenment era and, although Marxists think that history is a process of self-transcendence, its current vector seems to be progressing ever further from any sense of transcendent meaning.

At the heart of this modern rationalism is an assumption that "the experience and testimony of the individual mind is to be explained away, excluded from consideration when any rational account is made of the nature of human being and of being altogether."[409] Immediate experience is not to be trusted; the self, its thoughts, and its loves are not what they seem. Such distrust clashes with the Augustinian and Victorine emphasis on self-knowledge and inward experience as a crucial avenue toward God, the source of truth and love.

The Victorines believe that love transcends the realm of the human, and divine *caritas* is expressed by the cross of Christ and poured into human hearts by the Holy Spirit. In modernity, these transcendent bonds connecting human love with the divine *caritas*, the inner life of God, have been severed. Even purely human love in its ecstatic transports is anomalous in a rationalized world, where abstraction, generalization, and quantification are the tools, and utility is the goal. Love has been disenchanted. Reductionist rationalism counts as real only what empirical science is able to verify or falsify. Such rationalism is an extremely influential master narrative today. Within it, love is ex-

---

[407] Edmée Kingsmill, *The Song of Songs and the Eros of God: A Study in Biblical Intertexuality* (Oxford: Oxford University Press, 2010), 27.

[408] Eva Illouz, "Love and Its Discontents: Irony, Reason, Romance," *Hedgehog Review*, 12/1 (Spring 2010): 22. This article has been the stimulus and source for much of what follows.

[409] Marilynn Robinson, *Absence of Mind: The Dispelling of Inwardness from the Modern Myth of the Self* (New Haven: Yale, 2010), 22.

plained in categories such as "the unconscious," "libido," "hormones," "brain chemistry," and "selfish genes."

Psychoanalysis views romantic love as the result of the way people form attachments in early childhood. Thus, for example, one marries a person who resembles the parent with whom one has unresolved issues. Such theories encourage self-scrutiny; one monitors and labels one's emotions. This encourages one to be "suspicious of every impulse and motive that does not express the few but potent urges of the primitive self."[410]

Psychology provides guidance for meeting one's needs and finding wellbeing. Self-sacrifice and self-forgetfulness, longings for communion or for the Eternal are not often considered or, if they are, they are often regarded as dysfunctional. Emotions are to be molded to one's needs and well-being, not to the service of others. Rather than being ordered and measured, emotions are manipulated.

Biology studies the chemical bases of love, and so it tends to see love as merely an epiphenomenon. Richard's madly infatuated lover, sliding down the first three degrees of violent love, has heightened amounts of dopamine and norepinephrine in her brain. That she can think of nothing but the beloved is the effect of serotonin. Fortunately, the elevated levels of these chemicals in the brain tend to decrease after several years.

Evolutionary biologists and psychologists explain that feelings of love and impulses of altruism were selected over time to prompt men and women to stay together long enough to propagate and raise new members for the species or to maintain enough cohesiveness for the group to survive.

These explanations are not without plausibility. Aquinas in particular would be astonished if mental processes did not have physiological concomitants. However, while Augustine tended to see the soul as moving an inert body, these modern scientific explanations tend to see biological processes as moving a puppet consciousness. Someday, we are told, consilience will explain all reality in terms of physics.

For a reductionist theory of love, which maintains that only self-interest motivates human action, the fact that people act altruistically is a problem and a puzzle. Assuming that competition for limited resources is a basic principle of life, then altruism—particularly toward strangers—is difficult to explain. For the reductionist, altruism cannot

---

[410] Robinson, 107.

be what it seems; it must aim at benefit to oneself or to one's clan. If someone thinks she is being altruistic, she does not know herself. Such an assumption means that the twofold commandment to love God and neighbor encourages behaviors that are hypocritical.[411]

The setting—and results—of such a reductionism is a disenchanted world. Mystery has no place; to have a longing for transcendence is to abandon the real world for dreamland. One does not move from contemplation to compassion; one negotiates symmetrical relationships wherein guarantees are provided so that power and satisfactions will be equitably distributed. One does not fall in love; using the Internet, one sifts through potential mates using rational criteria to find the best deal. Such self-interested utilitarianism is not the love that cements human community.

By contrast, the Victorines believe that love in all its forms—love of God and the God-man, love of friends and enemies, love of self and (we can add) love of the physical world—are analogous, interconnected, and fundamental. Human beings are most happy when conscious choice and passion are in harmony with each other, with human nature, and with God—who made human beings in his image and likeness. Each sort of love can be the occasion for wonder, devotion, and joy that draw the self out of a world of empirical fact, abstract analysis, and utility and into something more expansive and more real.

These are two very different answers to the questions, "What is this thing called love?" and "What truly should be loved?" No one has all the answers, and so we dialogue with the past and the present, knowing that "we dare not rest the whole weight of the heart's longing in any finite good,"[412] or in any human wisdom.

[411]   Robinson, 31–75.
[412]   See above, note 1.

HUGH OF ST VICTOR

THE PRAISE OF THE BRIDEGROOM

INTRODUCTION AND TRANSLATION
BY HUGH FEISS OSB

INTRODUCTION

AUTHENTICITY

In his study of the manuscript tradition of Hugh of St Victor's works, Rudolf Goy lists 64 manuscripts that contain *The Praise of the Bridegroom*. Two of those are no longer extant, and several do not contain the work on the pages cited. Of the manuscripts listed by Goy, half attribute it to Hugh. The work is listed in the *Indiculum* of Hugh's works compiled under Abbot Gilduin. There are least twenty more manuscripts not listed by Goy.[1]

THE SCRIPTURAL TEXT

This work is a commentary on the Canticle of Canticles (Song of Songs) 4:6–8.[2] Hugh comments on the Old Latin version of these verses,[3] which came to him through the liturgy at St Victor, where it was used as an antiphon for the office of the Assumption.[4] In the 380s

---

[1] Rudolf Goy, *Die Überlieferung der Werke Hugos von St. Viktor*, Monographien zur Geschichte des Mittelalters 14 (Stuttgart: Anton Hiersemann, 1976), 268–77; H.-M. Rochais, "Enquête sur les sermons divers et les sentences de saint Bernard," *Analecta Sacri Ordinis Cisterciensis* 18 (1962): 141–42. Hence E. Ann Matter's hesitations about Hugh's authorship of the work seem unfounded: E. Ann Matter, *The Voice of My Beloved: The Song of Songs in Western Medieval Christianity* (Philadelphia: University of Pennsylvania Press, 1990), 147 note 40, with reference to her earlier article, "Eulogium sponsi de sponsa: Canons, Monks, and the Song of Songs," *The Thomist* 49 (1985): 560–64.

[2] The first half of this introduction draws upon Brendan M. Dardis, "Eulogium sponsi et sponsae" (MA diss., St Benedict, OR: Mt. Angel Seminary, 1985).

[3] A. Wilmart, "L'ancienne version latine du Cantique I–II," RBen 28 (1911): 11–36; D. de Bruyne, "Les anciennes versions latines du Cantique des cantiques," RBen 38 (1926): 101.

[4] Paris, Bibliothèque nationale, Ms. lat. 14816, f.258v. Cf. Fourier Bonnard, *Histoire de l'abbaye royale et de l'ordre de chanoines réguliers de Saint-Victor de Paris*, 2 vols. (Paris: Arthur Savaète, 1904–7) 1: xxix. In a chapter sermon Godfrey of St Victor quotes Song of Songs 4:6 according to the text of this antiphon: "Sermo in generali capitulo," ed. Helmut Riedlinger, *Die Makellosigkeit der Kirche in den lateinischen Hoheliedkommentaren des Mittelalters*, BGPTMA 38/3 (Münster: Aschendorff, 1958), 188–90. Other medieval liturgical books had the same antiphon. Chrysogonus Waddell (private correspondence) identified it in the *breviarium* of Molesme where it is a third nocturn antiphon for the Feast of the Assumption. It appears as a processional antiphon in the *Antiphonary* of St-Denis (Paris BN Ms. lat. 17296 [R.-J. Hes-

Jerome revised the Old Latin text of the Canticle in the light of Origen's *Hexapla* and, with a few small variations, this is the text Hugh comments on in this work.[5] In the 390s Jerome began a new translation from the Hebrew, which was the one used in the Medieval West. Hugh himself uses this latter version elsewhere in his works, where he cites or interprets almost one third of the Canticle.[6]

THE EXEGETICAL TRADITION

The Canticle was very popular among monastic authors, who produced many commentaries on it.[7] They drew on a rich tradition. Origen interpreted the Canticle dramatically: bride and bridegroom converse, and each has a chorus of followers.[8] The bridegroom and bride symbolize either Christ and the Church, or the Word and the

---

bert, *Corpus Antiphonalium Officii*, Rerum Ecclesiasticarum Documenta, Series Maior, Fontes, 9 (Rome: Herder, 1968), 3:264, no. 3160]), in the *Consuetudines Floriacenses saeculi tertii decimi*, ed. Anselmus Davril, Corpus Consuetudinum Monasticarum 9 (Siegburg: Franciscus Schmitt, 1976), 207, 202, 219, as an antiphon for the third nocturn of the Assumption in a manuscript from Corbie (Amiens B.M. 115, 337v, Cluniac usage), and in a fourteenth-century breviary from Montier-la-Celle (Troyes, B.M. 109, fol. 286v). A version of the same text was put to music by the English composer Leonel Power (d. 1445). Richard of St Victor (*Serm. cent.* 9 [PL 177.918]) begins a sermon with a citation of Song of Songs 4:7 according to the Vulgate text.

5   *Cantici canticorum vetus latina translatio a S. Hieronymo ad graecum textum hexaplarem emendata*, ed. Albertus Vaccari (Rome: Storia e Letteratura, 1959), 24. Jerome seems to cite this translation in *Adv. Jov.* 1.30 (PL 23.264BC). This text survives in Epiphanius' Latin translation of Philo of Carpasia's commentary on the Canticle: Philonis Carpasii, *Commentarium in Canticum canticorum, ex antiqua versione latine Epiphanii Scholastici*, ed. Aldo Ceresa-Gastaldo, Corona Patrum (Turin: Società Editrice Internazionale, 1979). See A. Vaccari, "Latina Cantici canticorum versio a S. Hieronymo ad Graecam Hexaplarem emendata," *Biblica* 36 (1955): 258–60; A. Vaccari, "S. Hieronymi in Canticum," *Gregorianum* 42 (1961): 728–29.

6   See especially "Pro Assumptione Virginis" ("For the Assumption") (*Oeuvre* 2:112–61), "De beatae Mariae virginitate" ("On the Virginity of the Blessed Mary") (*Oeuvre* 2:182–253), and the *Miscellanea* (PL 177.469–590).

7   Jean Leclercq, "Écrits monastiques sur la Bible aux xiᵉ–xiiᵉ siècles," MS 15 (1953): 98–104; André Cabassut and Michel Olphe-Galliard, "Cantique des Cantiques: Histoire de l'interpretation spirituelle," DSp 2 (1953): 86–109; Friedrich Ohly, *Hohelied Studien. Grundzüge einer Geschichte der Hoheliedauslegung des Abendlandes bis um 1200*. Schriften der wissenschaftlichen Gesellschaft an der Johann Wolfgang Goethe Universität, Frankfurt am Main, Geisteswissenschaftliche Reihe 1 (Wiesbaden: Franz Steiner, 1958), 121–276; Rosemarie Herde, "Das Hohelied in der lateinischen Literatur des Mittelalters bis zum 12. Jahrhundert," *Studi Medievali* 8 (1967): 957–1073.

8   Origen, *In Cant. hom.* 1.1 (Baehrens, 28.19–22); *Comm. in Cant.* prol. (Baehrens, 61.11–22); cf. Chrysogonus Waddell, "The Song of Songs in the Stephen Harding Bible," *Liturgy OCSO* 18/2 (1984): 28–32.

soul.[9] Origen related the Canticle to contemplation.[10] Gregory of Elivira's commentary on the Old Latin text of the Canticle introduced an apologetic element into the interpretative tradition that finds an echo in *The Praise of the Bridegroom*.[11] Bede wrote an important commentary; other Carolingian commentaries on the Canticle were not very original.[12]

Twelfth-century authors produced many commentaries on the Canticle. The commentary of Rupert of Deutz (d. 1129) accentuated interior, mystical experience and introduced a consistent Mariological interpretation. The proximity of two early Marian feasts, the Assumption and the Nativity, to the reading of the Canticle in the Divine Office during August helped foster the Mariological interpretation. Although in *The Praise of the Bridegroom* Hugh is commenting on an antiphon for the Feast of the Assumption, he does not give the text a Mariological interpretation as he does elsewhere.[13]

Although Hugh of St Victor's understanding of the Canticle draws on this exegetical tradition, he seldom draws on it for details. The meanings he assigns to names like Sanir, Hermon, and Lebanon were conventional as were the allegorical understandings of lion and leopard.[14] When he goes beyond such commonplaces, Hugh makes his own

9   Origen, *In Cant. hom.* 1.1 (Baehrens, 28.28–29.4); 1.7 (Baehrens, 51.23–28); *Comm. In Cant.* prol. (Baehrens, 61.8–11); 1 (Baehrens, 89.9–13).
10   Origen, *Comm. In Cant.* prol. (Baehrens, 75.2–79.21), where he relates three books attributed to Solomon to three divisions of philosophy: moral (Proverbs), natural (Ecclesiastes), theoretical or contemplative (Canticle). For this, see Jerome, *Epistulae* 107:12 (PL 22:876–77); Hugh of St Victor, *In Eccl.* 1 (PL 175.116BC); *Didasc.* 4.8 (Buttimer, 80–81; tr. Taylor, 109–10); Richard of St Victor, *Apoc.* 2.6 (PL 196.766B); *LE* 2.13.12 (Châtillon, 487.11–13); *LE* 2.12.16 (Châtillon, 440.37–40), quoting the *Glossa ordinaria*; Ps.-Richard of St Victor, *Cant.* prol. (PL 196.409AD). In *Quat. grad.* 25–27 (Dumeige, 152–55), Richard distinguishes psalms, prophets, and the Song of Songs. See also *Quat. grad.* 21–23 (Dumeige, 148–51); Mark Sheridan, "Mapping the Intellectual Genome of Early Christian Monasticism," in *Church, Society and Monasticism*, ed. Eduardo López-Tello García and Benedetta Selene Zorzi, Studia Anselmiana 146 (Sankt Ottilien: EOS, 2009), 330–32.
11   Ohly, *Hohelied*, 30; Hugh of St Victor, *Eulogium*, 19 (PL 176.992D–994A).
12   Bede, *In Cantica canticorum*, ed. D. Hurst, CCL 119B (Turnhout: Brepols, 1983), 165–375; Alcuin, *Compendium in Canticum canticorum* (PL 100.639–64 = PL 83.1119–32); Haimo of Auxerre, *Enarratio in Canticum canticorum* (PL 117.295–358 = PL 70.1055–1106); Angelôme of Luxeuil, *Enarrationes in Cantica canticorum* (PL 115.551–628).
13   Rupert of Deutz, *Commentaria in Canticum canticorum*, ed. Rhaban Haacke, CCCM 26 (Turnhout: Brepols, 1974); Ohly, *Hohelied*, 121–37; Hugh of St Victor, *Assumpt.* (PL 177.1209–22). For Hugh's Mariological thought, see Roger Baron, "La pensée mariale de Hugues de Saint-Victor," *Revue d'ascétique et de mystique* 31 (1955): 249–71; Jollès, *Œuvres* 2.
14   In his *Exposition of the Canticle of Canticles*, which carefully analyzes the Canticle according to the four meanings of Scripture (literal, doctrinal, moral, and anagogical), Honorius

way. He is not writing a commentary; he is using an uncommon translation; and he has originality. Because of that originality it is possible to trace the influence of *The Praise of the Bridegroom* in later commentators like Godfrey of Auxerre and Thomas the Cistercian.[15]

TITLE, METHOD, AND MESSAGE

The manuscripts give several different titles to this work, such as *Praise of the Bridegroom and Bride, The Love of the Bridegroom for Bride, Of the Bridegroom and Bride,* and *Treatise on the Song of Songs.* Some call it a *tractatus* or a *sermo,* but *eulogium* is the description that appears most frequently.[16] Elsewhere Hugh calls Song of Songs 4:7 a "eulogium."[17] A likely scenario is that Hugh preached or taught about the antiphon at the Eucharist, a chapter meeting or in a colloquy or class, then wrote up his notes into a polished work of exegesis.

Hugh is writing a commentary on a section of the Canticle in which Hugh thinks the bridegroom is thinking about what he is going to say to his beloved when he goes to see her. The first part of the speech he formulates is something any man in love might say to his beloved: "You are all beautiful, perfect." Interpreting the rest of the passage requires more ingenuity. Although he does not mention that the Latin text he is commenting on differs from the usual text, he does note a textual variant ("Sanir" for "Seir"), and he makes use of Jerome's explanation of Hebrew names. Hugh enters into the scene as the author of the

---

Augustodunesis also lingers over the allegorical meanings of these geographic names. See Matter, *Voice,* 73.

[15]   Citing Hugh's work, Geoffrey of Auxerre (*Expositio in Cantica canticorum,* ed. Ferruccio Gastaldelli, Temi e Testi 19 [Rome: Storia e Letteratura, 1974], 1:229–31) refers explicitly to Hugh's *The Praise of the Bridegroom*: "A certain great master of our time, Hugh of St Victor, is known to have produced a brief treatise on this short passage. His starting point was a certain antiphon that some sing" ("Magnus quidam nostri temporis magister Hugh de Sancto Victore super hoc capitulo brevem noscitur edidisse tractatum, occasione cuiusdam antiphonae, quae apud aliquos canitur" [Gastaldelli, 1:220.19–22]). Having summarized *The Praise of the Bridegroom,* Geoffrey then inserts an abstract of Hugh's *Sermon on the Assumption* (1:231–34). The commentary attributed to Thomas the Cistercian can be found in PL 206; he cites Hugh extensively at 423A–427D. On the influence of *The Praise of the Bridegroom,* see also Matter, *Voice,* 136–37.

[16]   Goy, *Überlieferung,* 268–77.

[17]   *Assumpt.* prol. (PL 177.1209–10): "Illud eulogium, 'Tota pulchra es, amica mea,' quod in laudem matris et virginis de Canticis canticorum sumptum canit Ecclesia" ("That eulogium, 'You are totally beautiful, my friend,' taken from the Canticle of Canticles," "which the Church sings in praise of the Virgin Mother").

Canticle depicts it, imagining the bridegroom thinking about his bride and what he will say to her. He thinks about the geographic references and the animals: just as words have meanings referring to things, so in the Bible things have spiritual meanings: the allegorical, tropological, and anagogical meanings that refer respectively to matters of doctrine, morality, and contemplative prayer.[18]

Origen related three books ascribed to Solomon to three sorts of philosophy: Proverbs (moral philosophy), Ecclesiastes (physics or natural philosophy), and the Canticle (contemplation). However, Hugh's reading in *The Praise of the Bridegroom* concentrates on the tropological meaning (morality) rather than on contemplation itself. Nevertheless, the Bridegroom's thrice-repeated "Veni (Come!)," is an invitation to the soul to contemplate Him. The dramatic details of the passage, which Hugh closely studies, and the allegorical meanings of the names of geographical features are to help the reader to become "brightened" so that she may be united to the infinite, ineffable beauty of the Light of the Bridegroom in an embrace of love and joy. Meditation points toward contemplation.[19]

Hugh's procedure is very simple: having established the scene (par. 1), he determines that the bridegroom and the bride represent

[18]   Hugh's exegetical theory and practice will be treated at length in the next volume of this series. Hugh lays out his hermeneutical theory in *Didascalicon*, books 5 and 6; *On Sacred Scriptures and Their Authors*; *Homilies on Ecclesiastes*; *On the Sacraments* 1, prol.; and *The Diligent Investigator*. Hugh consistently teaches that one should begin with the letter of the text and search for the historical sense intended by the author. Then as the reader immerses himself in the text and the text penetrates the reader's heart, under the guidance of the Spirit and on the foundation of the Church's creed, there will emerge spiritual meanings. These may be doctrinal, moral, or anagogical (referring to contemplative insight or beatific vision). For Hugh's exegesis, see Beryl Smalley, *The Study of the Bible in the Middle Ages* (Notre Dame, IN: University of Notre Dame Press, 1964), 83–105; Jean Châtillon, "La Bible dans les écoles du XII⁰ siècle," *Le Moyen Âge et la Bible*, ed. Pierre Riché and Guy Lobrichon (Paris: Beauchesne, 1984), 178–83; Henri de Lubac, *Medieval Exegesis: Vol. 3: The Four Senses of Scripture* (Grand Rapids, MI: Eerdmans, 2009), 211–68; Dominique Poirel, *Hugues de Saint-Victor* (Paris: Cerf, 1998), 65–80; Franklin T. Harkins, *Reading and the Work of Restoration: History and Scripture in the Theology of Hugh of St Victor* (Toronto: Pontifical Institute of Mediaeval Studies, 2009).

[19]   Ann W. Astell (*The Song of Songs in the Middle Ages* [Ithaca, NY: Cornell University Press, 1990], 73–89) argues that Victorine commentaries on the Canticle are contemplative in aim and style. Images cohere vertically by leading the reader toward the One, rather than connecting horizontally. This seems to be more true of Adam of St Victor's use of the Canticle and Hugh's *Assumption of the Virgin* than it is of *Praise of the Bridegroom*, which, as Matter (*Voice*, 135) writes with only slight exaggeration, "moves entirely on the tropological level." However, Astell (*Song*, 180) is surely correct about the aim of Hugh in writing *Praise of the Bridegroom*. As the *Glossa ordinaria* said of the author of the Canticle, Hugh's aim is the love of God (Dove, 79 = PL 113.1128): "Finis, dilectio Dei."

God and the soul. Within this literal and allegorical framework, he then proceeds through the text phrase by phrase, and in less than 4,000 words conveys a great deal of information both about the meaning of the words and about his understanding of the Christian life. The work falls into three scenes: the Bridegroom plans a visit to his bride; he makes a speech in praise of her; he calls her to him by a specific road (cf. par. 10).

> *"I will go for myself (Ibo mihi)"* (par. 1–3)

God sometimes comes to the soul with gifts of grace; at other times God seems absent. The bride is dowered with gifts—some general, some specific to her. Through the Spirit she gives birth to virtues. God's apparent absence is to purify and make the heart know its needs.

> *to the mountains of Myrrh and the hills of Lebanon* (par. 4–5)

The Father's power works in the soul through mortification of evil desires, and the Son's wisdom illumines ignorance. In the soul thus purified the Spirit's love enkindles the soul's desire. There is, however, no remedy for willful malice, the sin against the Spirit.

> *And I will speak to my spouse: "You are utterly beautiful, my nearest, and there is no blemish in you"* (par. 6–9)

God speaks to the sinful soul to show her how befouled she is. God speaks words of love to the beautiful soul as to a bride. The soul is beautiful with a beauty derived from her supremely beautiful Bridegroom.

> *Come to Lebanon, my bride, come to Lebanon* (par. 10–11)

God invites the soul to return into—and then to rise above—herself, for God is both immanent within and transcendent. The second invitation is from participated purity to Purity itself.

> *You will come and cross over to the mountain of Seir (or Sanir)* (par. 12–15)

The desire of the flesh for what is outside the soul (Esau) gives way to the desire of the Spirit for what is within (Jacob). Desire for physical things that are not necessary can be trimmed off without harm; desire for physical necessities ought to be satisfied with sufficiency, if not trimmed to the point of austerity.

and Hermon (par. 16–17)

Those who are separated from Christ need to be separated from the devil's domain and become members of Christ. There are three increasing degrees of such separation: by faith, by faith and moral uprightness, and by faith and outstanding virtue.

from the dens of lions and from the mountains of leopards (par. 18–20)

The desires of the flesh are sleeping lions that can be awakened and indulged, which indulgence leads to torment, first through conscience, then through punishment. Panthers symbolize heretics who splotch faith and bring disunity. The soul must move from pride to humility, from fierce craving to endurance, from the many to the One, and from foulness to beauty, to union with the Bridegroom.

Theology of Love

Hugh says that it is pleasant to talk about what it is pleasant to do; we never grow tired of talking about what we want very much (par. 1). Love is something Hugh talks and writes about often. In this instance, Hugh begins with a man deeply in love with a woman to whom he is engaged (or possibly even married). All that the groom can talk about is love (par. 7). Taking this understanding of the literal meaning of the text as his starting point, Hugh accepts the deeply felt love of a man and a woman as a God-given fact of human existence (par. 1). His subsequent cautions against "the desires of the flesh" do not question this initial given. The love that the bridegroom feels is an exclusive love, too intimate to be shared (par. 2). The love of the bridegroom is a longing, a desire, to be present with his bride. He wants to be with her and to be held by her. At the same time, he does not want to be with her so much that their love cools into routine, nor separated so much that it slips toward forgetfulness (par. 1).

Having established that the bridegroom and bride are God and the soul, Hugh develops his spiritual interpretation, which is not so much about ecstatic union with God as it is about the sort of life that leads to such unitive love, a life that involves a rhythm of divine presence and absence, of sweet contemplation and its cessation. The soul is God's bride by a threefold title: (1) the gifts of grace, (2) her love for her Spouse, and (3) the virtues she brings to birth (par. 2). All have received these gifts, some of which are shared by all, while others are unique to the redeemed. Success and failure, peace and anxiety are God's gifts to help people grow in virtue and avoid despair or dissipation. Gratitude for both enables the soul to grow in love of God (par. 3).

Love requires self-discipline and purity of heart, which Cassian taught is the other side of genuine love.[20] Purity of heart enables one to see clearly with the eyes of faith. We are to be big-souled and humble. In conversation with God we receive charity, the opposite of hostility and hard-heartedness (par. 4). Sin is an affront to the Trinity in whose image human beings are made: sins of weakness offend the Father, to whom power is appropriated; sins of ignorance are against the Son; sins of malice offend the Holy Spirit. This last kind of sin is most deserving of punishment. One could conclude from this that failure to learn to love is a serious matter (par. 5).

God speaks words of rebuke to the sinful soul, words of encouragement to the justified. Fear and increased self-awareness bring the former to repentance; praise and interior joy increase the love that the latter has (par. 6). The bride is dear and near, because she is turned toward God, in whose beauty and love she participates (pars. 7–8). By distinguishing distant and most distant—and far, near, and nearest—in relation to perfect Beauty, Hugh acknowledges the gradations in Christian life and loving (par. 8–9). The groom went to his bride, not to stay but to draw her to himself (par. 10). It is not enough for one to exchange a scattered mind for interiority; one must rise above oneself to find one's Spouse (par. 11).

One of the disciplines that foster the growth of genuine love is temperance in the use of earthly goods. Physical necessities must be met, but one can do so indulgently, moderately, or very abstemiously. There is some correlation between limiting physical satisfactions and strengthening the spirit. Under the guise of necessity, self-indulgence in pleasure can find a foothold in the soul (par.12–15). In order to be a living member of Christ, one must separate oneself from communion with the devil (par. 16). Faith is the first step, but then one must

---

[20]   Columba Stewart, OSB, introduction to Harriet Luckman and Linda Kulzer, OSB, eds., *Purity of Heart in Early Ascetic and Monastic Literature* (Collegeville, MN: Liturgical Press, 1999), 2–15. The essays in this volume trace the range of meanings and background of this concept in biblical and early Christian authors, particularly monastics. Note especially Gertrude Gillette, OSB, "Purity of Heart in St Augustine," 175–95. On Cassian, see also Columba Stewart, OSB, *Cassian the Monk*, Oxford Studies in Historical Theology (New York: Oxford University Press, 1998), 41–48.

gradually leave behind the pleasures of the flesh in order to rise to a spiritual way of life, which requires patient endurance (par. 17). However, the alternative is to grow cold in divine love and yield to sin, with the result that one is stricken first in conscience and then in hell (par. 18). Alluring one in this miserable direction are the proud lovers of this world (par. 19). Instead, we are to flee the world in order to approach God, to leave behind multiplicity so that we may be gathered into One (par. 20).

Thus, Hugh's understanding of the Christian life, the life devoted to growing in love, is dramatic. It requires choice and conversion; the love of God admits no rivals. One must choose between love of the world and love of God. And yet it is a beautiful world, a world in which lovers tell each other, "You are utterly beautiful, my nearest and dearest." Utterly beautiful yes, but a created beauty, bright but not Brightness itself. To learn how to love this beautiful world without being scattered and drawn away from Beauty itself requires the disciplines of moderation, self-discipline, patience endurance, and purity of heart. They are difficult, but for love of such a Spouse who calls, "Come, come, come over here to me," they are possible by the inspiration and gifts of the Spirit.

THE TRANSLATION

The *Praise of the Bridegroom* appears in Migne's *Patrologia latina* twice: among the works of Hugh of St Victor, its author, where it is entitled *De amore sponsi ad sponsam* (PL 177.987–94) and again among the sermons of Peter Comestor (PL 198.1784–88). This translation was made from a preliminary collation of forty manuscripts prepared by Christopher Evans.

There is an earlier, slightly condensed, English translation of the Migne's text in Hugh of St Victor, *The Divine Love: The Two Treatises De Laude Caritatis and De Amore Sponsi ad Sponsam*, tr. A Religious of C.S.M.V. [Sr. Penelope Lawson], Fleur de Lys Series 9 (London: Mowbray, 1956), 26–38. There is also a translation of paragraphs 1–17 in Richard A. Norris, Jr., *The Song of Songs: Interpreted by Early Christian and Medieval Commentators*, The Church's Bible (Grand Rapids: Eerdmans, 2003), 167–72.

"I will go for myself to the mountain of Myrrh and to the hills of Lebanon, and I will speak to my bride. 'You are utterly beautiful, my nearest,[1] and there is no blemish in you. Come to[2] Lebanon, my bride, come to Lebanon. You will come and cross to Mount Seir and Hermon from the dens of lions, from the mountains of leopards.'"[3]

1. "I will go for myself to the mountain of Myrrh and to the hills of Lebanon, and I will speak to my bride." A certain bridegroom is speaking here, who has a bride. He promises that he is going to visit her. Notice, therefore, that this bridegroom is not always at home. Maybe, then, he is afraid that his love will grow stale. Because it would become tiresome more quickly if he were always present, sometimes he pulls himself away; sometimes he withdraws for a while, so that when absent he is sought and when present he is more tightly held. And so it happened that he was away when he said these things. However, lest a longer delay would cause some degree of forgetfulness, he was preparing to return and said: "I will go for myself." He is speaking with himself about what he is going to do, because it is pleasant to speak about what it is pleasant to do. I do not know why it is that we never grow tired of talking about what we want very much.

2. "I will go for myself," he says. He goes for himself, because a singular love admits no one to share its secret. He goes for himself, because he who allows no one to share his love does not want a companion on the journey.[4] But you ask, who is this and who is his bride? The Bridegroom is God; the bride is the soul.[5] The bridegroom is home when he fills the mind with interior joy; he goes away when he takes away the sweetness of contemplation. By what likeness is the soul called the bride of God? She is a bride because she is dowered[6] with gifts of graces. She is also a bride because she is united (*sociata*) with him in a chaste love. She is a bride, because[7] by the inspiration (*aspirationem*) of the Holy Spirit she is to be made fruitful with virtues, her offspring.[8]

3. There is no soul who has not received the betrothal-gift (*arram*) of this Bridegroom. But one kind of betrothal-gift is common, another kind is special.[9] It is a common betrothal-gift that we have been born, that we have sensation, that we know, and that we discriminate.[10] It is a special betrothal-gift that we are reborn, that we have attained remis-

sion of sins, that we have received gifts (*carismata*) of virtues.[11] What each one has is his betrothal-gift. For the rich man, his wealth is his betrothal-gift; by it he is supported so that the hardship of poverty may not break him. For the poor man, poverty is his betrothal-gift; he is chastened by it so that he may not be moved by abundance to dissipate into intemperance (*incontinentiam*). For the strong man, strength is his betrothal-gift; he is fortified by it so that he may grow strong for good work. For the weak man, weakness is his betrothal-gift; he is restrained by it from performing evil. For the wise man, wisdom is his betrothal-gift; he is enlightened by it so that he may advance.[12] For the ignorant person, simplicity[13] is his betrothal-gift; he is humbled by it so he will not become proud. And so the loving Creator, in accord with his goodness, dispenses whatever human weakness bears in this life, either to correct evil or to promote virtue. For this reason we ought to give thanks in all things, so that, while we acknowledge his mercy everywhere, we may always advance in love of him.

4. "I will go for myself," he says, "to the mountain of Myrrh, etc." Myrrh, which is bitter to the taste[14] and keeps the bodies of the dead from rotting, signifies the mortification of the flesh. Lebanon, which is interpreted as "brightening," signifies purity of heart.[15] This then is the way by which the bridegroom comes to the bride. He comes by way of the mountain of Myrrh and the hills of Lebanon, because first he kills the craving (*concupiscentia*) of the flesh through abstinence and then wipes away the ignorance of the mind through purity of heart. After that, as though on the third day,[16] he comes to converse with the bride and enflames her soul with desire for him. Hence, it is fitting that he says "mountain of Myrrh," not "hill of Myrrh," and "hills of Lebanon," not "mountains of Lebanon," because we must be steadfast in affliction and humble when we succeed in virtue. The height of a mountain signifies the pre-eminence of magnanimity,[17] and the limited height of the hill stands for the restraint of humility. Likewise, that he put "mountain" in the singular and "hills" in the plural signifies that in the mortification of exterior delight we lose little, while in the enlightening of the mind within we find manifold good. We interpret "on the mountain of Myrrh" as strength against the craving of the flesh; "on the hills of Lebanon" as enlightenment of the mind against ignorance; "the conversation of the bridegroom" as charity opposing ill will and hardness of heart.[18]

5. Power pertains to the Father, wisdom to the Son, and charity to the Holy Spirit.[19] In another context this is said with reference to sin-

ning against the Father and the Son and the Holy Spirit respectively. For when we sin out of weakness, we sin against the Father, as though against power.[20] When we sin out of ignorance, we sin against the Son, as though against wisdom. However, when we sin out of malice, we sin against the Holy Spirit, as though against love. Therefore, sinning against the Father and the Son is forgiven here or in the future. Because someone who sins from weakness or ignorance has some excuse in his fault, he ought also to have some remission in punishment—either in this life so that if he repents he more easily gains forgiveness, or in the next world so that if he perseveres in evil he undergoes a more bearable punishment. However, those who sin out of wickedness have no excuse for their crimes, and therefore they should have no remission in punishment. If they repent in this world, then they must be punished until they give full satisfaction or, if they do not repent, they must be punished with full damnation in the world to come. And so such as these find no remission here or in the world to come, not because pardon (*venia*) is denied penitents, but because full satisfaction is owed for a full-blown sin.

6. "I will speak," he says, "to my bride." God speaks in two ways to a soul: in one way to the prostitute, in another way to the bride; in one way to the sordid, in another to the beautiful; in one way to the sinner, in another to the justified.[21] He rebukes the foulness of the former; he praises the beauty of the latter.[22] By his rebuke he strikes fear into the former; by his praise he enkindles the latter to love (*amorem*). He speaks to the former when he shows her blemishes to her; he speaks to the latter when he reminds her of the gifts which he has granted to her. He enlightens the darkness of the former, so she may recognize what she is and deplore what she has done; he touches the latter with a feeling of interior sweetness, so that she may recall what she has received and not forget him who gave it.

7. "I will speak," he says, "to my bride." "If I am the bridegroom, if I am going to speak to the bride, know that I can speak of nothing but love (*amorem*)." Therefore, after the bridegroom had said this to himself, he immediately undertook a journey; and, coming and seeing the bride, then—as though struck with wonder at her beauty (*specie*)—burst out in these words: "You are utterly beautiful, my nearest, etc." Alternatively, this phrase is joined with the preceding "I will speak to my bride," namely in this way: "You are utterly beautiful, my nearest." But the former reading is more elegant. "You are utterly beautiful, my

nearest."[23] And so,[24] you are utterly beautiful because you are nearest; if you were not nearest, you would not be utterly beautiful.

8. Notice what he said: "You are utterly beautiful, my nearest." Every soul is either turned away from God or turned toward God. Of those turned away, one is distant, another is most distant. Of those turned toward God, one is near, another is nearest.[25] She who is distant is dirty now, but not utterly; she who is most distant is utterly dirty. Likewise, she who is near is beautiful, but still not totally so; she who is nearest is utterly beautiful. "You are utterly beautiful, my nearest."[26]

9. "And there is no blemish in you." He is completely beautiful (*totus speciosus*) in whom no beauty is lacking. He is totally beautiful in whom there is nothing sordid. "I am completely beautiful because everything beautiful is in me. You are utterly beautiful because nothing sordid is in you. 'There is no blemish in you.'"[27]

10. "Come to Lebanon, my bride." Up till now we have heard by what road the bridegroom came to the bride and what he said when he came to her. Next let us hear by what road the bride should come to the bridegroom. He says, "Come to Lebanon." He invites and calls her, because he has come to her not to stay with her but to draw her to himself.

11. "Come to Lebanon, come to Lebanon. You will come." Twice he invites her, saying, "Come." The third time he adds firmly, "You will come." But what is this affirmation, if not a congratulation, by which he rejoices over our good resolution? It is as if he said: "I praise your obedience; I see your resolution; I am not unaware of your devotion. I call and you answer; I invite and you are ready." Therefore, "You will come." But why does he say, "come" twice? He does it so that whoever is outside of himself may first return to himself, and whoever is within himself may ascend above himself.[28] First, he is in us and warns wrongdoers to return to their heart;[29] then he is above us to invite those justified to himself. "Come," he says, "come." From outside come within to yourself. Then, within, come from within above yourself to me. "Come to Lebanon, my bride, come to Lebanon." Come from Lebanon; come to Lebanon.[30] Come from the brightened Lebanon to the Lebanon that is not brightened but bright. Come from the cleansed heart to the Cleanser of hearts, who is not cleansed but clean.[31] You do not reach me, if you remain yourself. Rise above yourself and you will find me.

THE PRAISE OF THE BRIDEGROOM

12. "You will come and cross to the mountain of Seir[32] or Sanir."[33] "Seir" is interpreted as "shaggy" or "hairy."[34] "Sanir" is interpreted to mean "nocturnal bird" or "stench."[35] "Seir" is the same as "Edom," that is, "Esau." Esau and Jacob were two brothers. Esau was born first, but was supplanted by Jacob who was born after him. Esau was a hunter and an avid outdoorsman. Jacob, a simple man, stayed at home.[36] What do these two brothers denote if not two movements in human beings: the craving of the flesh and the craving of the spirit? We know what the Apostle said. It is not the spiritual that is first, but the fleshly;[37] that is, Esau is born first. However, when the craving of the spirit is strengthened, the craving of the flesh grows weaker; that is, Esau is supplanted by Jacob who was born later. Likewise, the craving of the flesh, like Esau the hunter, feeds outside, whereas the craving of the spirit, like Jacob the simple man, finds delight within.[38] Now "Seir" is hairy, the unclean and ugly movement of the flesh. Rightly is it called hairy, because just as hair sinks its roots in the flesh but grows out beyond the flesh, so the movement of the flesh arises from necessity, but by growing beyond it flows into pleasure (*voluptatem*). And just as hair can be cut off without pain but cannot be pulled out without pain, so the desire of the flesh, insofar as it concerns superfluous things outside the feeling of the flesh, is cut off without damage, but insofar as it concerns necessity, that is, insofar as it is, as it were, within the flesh, it is not uprooted without damage.[39]

13. See, then, we have said what "Seir" is; now let us see what "the mountain of Seir" is. This "Seir" has a mountain and it has a valley. Let me say more: it has a mountain; it has a field; it has a valley.[40] But in the valley is what is weak; in the field is what is strong; on the mountain is what is insuperable. "Seir" on the mountain is the appetite of the flesh in necessity; "Seir" in the field is the appetite of the flesh in satiety; "Seir" in the valley is the appetite of the flesh in pleasure. When the flesh accepts only sustenance to live, "Seir" is on the mountain. When it takes nourishment for strength, "Seir" is in the field. When it begs pleasures for wantonness, "Seir" is in the valley.

14. Why therefore is it ["Seir," the craving of the flesh] insuperable on the mountain? It is because the sustenance of the flesh is necessary for those still dwelling in this mortal life. Why is it strong in the field? It is so because fleshly strength is sometimes useful for growth of the soul. Why is it weak in the valley? It is so because fleshly pleasure is always superfluous. It is prohibited in the valley, allowed in the field,

rewarded on the mountain. In the valley it serves, in the field it fights, on the mountain it reigns. In the valley is excess; in the field, temperance; on the mountain, sparseness. In the valley it is easily trampled down with the help of grace; in the field it is overcome with difficulty; on the mountain it cannot be overcome, for our daily needs continually strengthen it. The one who cuts off superfluous things tramples "Seir" in the valley. The one who also reduces necessities somewhat conquers "Seir" in the field. However, the one who grants only the things that are necessary to sustain nature, as "Seir" on the mountain, pays what is owed to one who exacts it (*exactori obsequium reddit*). However, one should note that this "Seir" is conquered without difficulty at the place where it is most dangerous for it to hold sway, but it can be tolerated without danger in the place where it is insuperable.

15. But if one reads "Sanir," which is interpreted as "nocturnal bird" or "stench," that too can fittingly refer to the same carnal movement. Either it is called "nocturnal" because it comes in a hidden way when the allure of pleasure creeps in under the guise of necessity, or because blindness of mind is born through carnal delight. Thus, a "nocturnal bird" is a hidden and unforeseen movement of the flesh. Why the craving of the flesh is called "stench" requires no explanation now.

16. "And Hermon." "Hermon" is interpreted as "anathema of it."[41] Now what is the "of it" if not "of anathema," as if to say, "anathema of anathema"? We should first ask, what is "anathema"? Then, why should "anathema *of anathema*" be added? "Anathema" means "separation"; "anathema of anathema" means "separation of separation." If perhaps to be separated is bad, then to be separated from what is separated is good. Who, however, can better be called "anathema" than the apostate angel? At the beginning he separated himself through pride from the company of that heavenly city, and, when he did not wish to be a member of the true Head, he was cut off from the unity of his body as retribution for his wickedness and became the head of all the wicked. It is clear then that, according to the first birth whereby every human being is conceived in sin and born with sin, he is a member of this head and pertains to this group. But whoever, reborn through the sacraments of faith, is made a member of Christ is separated from the union of the other body. Who, then, is anathema, if not the devil and his members? And who are anathema of anathema, if not those who, separated from the body of the devil, have become members of Christ?[42]

17. We have now said what "Hermon" signifies; now let us see what "Mount Hermon" signifies. What was said above about "Seir" can now be said about "Hermon"—namely, that the mountain of "Hermon," the field of "Hermon," and the valley of "Hermon" are different things. The valley of "Hermon" can stand for those who through faith have now indeed separated from the devil, but still lie prostrate in base pleasure through a carnal life. The field of "Hermon" stands for those faithful who, holding a kind of middle position, are not pushed down to the depths through the pleasure of the flesh, but are not able to be raised to heavenly things through a spiritual way of life. The mount of "Hermon" stands for those who not only are separated from the devil through faith, but also are raised up against the devil through eminent virtue and constancy of mind. To be sure these are the ones whom the ancient enemy loathes (*invidet*) more; he sees (*videt*) that not only are they separated from him, but they are also raised up against him. Therefore, those whom he sees withdrawing from him and standing opposed to him are the ones whom he constantly tries to oppress with persecution. Therefore, to the extent they hold the common enemy of all more inimical to themselves in a singular way (*singulariter*), they sustain heavier tribulations. Therefore, we find no better interpretation for "the mountain of Seir" than the austerity of the saints, and no better interpretation of "the mountain of Hermon" than their patient endurance (*patientiam*).

18. Then there follows: "from the dens of lions." What is understood by "the dens of lions" if not, so to speak, senseless[43] cruelty? And what is senseless cruelty if not the desire of the flesh that now delights certain unwary people through experience, but afterwards tortures them first through their conscience and then through punishment?[44] Notice now how the cruelty of future damnation sleeps in the pleasure of carnal desire. Solomon says, "A dripping honeycomb are the lips of a prostitute and more sleek than oil is her throat, but her end will be as bitter as wormwood and sharper than a two-edged sword."[45] And again: "Who is very small? Let her turn to me and speak foolishness. Secret waters are sweeter, hidden bread tastes better. And he did not know that giants are there and in the depths of the netherworld his companions."[46] And the Lord speaking to Job about the ancient enemy said: "He sleeps in the shade in the secret place of reeds, in damp places."[47] The devil takes his rest in those minds that, cold interiorly—away from the heat of divine love—now rejoice exteriorly in the fleeting delight

of carnal pleasures and do not foresee the bitterness that will follow afterwards. The dens of lions are the allurements of carnal pleasures, which now do seem pleasant (*mollia*) in experience, but afterwards will be felt as cruel in punishment. Now, certainly, the lion is lying down and sleeping, because now through the delight of sin the devil presents himself to carnal minds as charming and does not yet show what he will be like. But then he will begin to wake up, when he holds fast in guilt those who are now freely letting him seduce them with unlawful pleasures, and then he will openly rage at them and drag them against their wills to torments.

19. There follows: "from the mountains of leopards." A leopard[48] is procreated by a lion and a panther. A lion is cruel; a panther is spotted. If a lion because of his cruelty fittingly signifies demons, then the panther because of his variegated coloring signifies heretics, who—because they cut apart the unity of faith with diverse and perverse teachings— bear a body infected as though by certain blemishes. Therefore who are the leopards, if not proud lovers of this world, whom the devil first brings forth to falsehood (*perfidia*) through the teaching of the heretics and then inflames to vices through love of this world. The "mountains of leopards" are the riches and triumphs of this world, in which the perverse take pride. They reproach the life of the elect all the more vehemently, as they behold the elect downcast in this world and themselves exalted.

20. Therefore, well does he say to his bride: "You will come and you will cross to Mount Seir and Hermon from the dens of lions, from the mountains of leopards,"[49] as though to say: "You will cross to Mount Seir from the dens of lions; you will cross to Mount Hermon from the mountains of leopards." But what is it to go from the dens of lions to Mount Seir, if not to go from incontinence to chastity, from pleasure to restraint? And what is it to go "from the mountains of leopards" to Mount Hermon, if not to go from pride to humility, from inflicting pain to bearing it (*de crudelitate ad patientiam*)? And note that he said "from the den*s*," not "from the den," "from the mountain*s*," not "from the mountain," and "to the mountain," not "to the mountain*s*." From the dens to the mountain, from the mountains to the mountain, that is, we advance from many to one, because the more we begin to approach God by fleeing the world, the more we are gathered into one. Amen.

NOTES

1   "proxima": the superlative of "proprior," "near," which may also connote "dearest."

2   Many of the manuscripts read "a Lybano" "from Lebanon," rather than "ad Lybano" which is an ungrammatical way to say "to Lebanon." In paragraph 11, Hugh seems to begin by commenting on a reading that had "Come to Lebanon, come to Lebanon," and then shifts to commenting on the reading "Come from Lebanon, come to Lebanon." Perhaps this represents some sort of textual contamination between the Old Latin and the Vulgate; see the next note.

3   Song of Songs 4:6b–8. Hugh's Latin texts reads: "Ibo michi ad montem Myrre et ad colles Lybani et loquar sponse mee: Tota speciosa es, proxima mea, et macula non est in te. Veni ad Lybano, sponsa, veni ad Lybanum. Venies et transibis ad montem Seyr et Hermon a cubilibus leonum, a montibus leopardorum." The Vulgate version is quite different: "Vadam ad montem murrae et ad collem turis. Tota pulchra es amica mea et macula non est in te. Veni de Libano, sponsa, veni de Libano, veni coronaberis, de capite Aman de vertice Sanir et Hermon de cubilibus leonum de montibus pardorum." Hugh's text goes back to an Old Latin translation that seems on the whole to be a literal rendering of the Septuagint; e.g., in the phrases "Ibo michi" and "proxima mea." In the light of the Greek, "Ibo michi" could be translated as "I will betake myself," but Hugh makes a point of the dative "michi" that requires the translation "I will go for myself." The *Glossa ordinaria* and its Carolingian sources do not betray many traces of the Old Latin version that Hugh quotes. The *Glossa ordinaria (In Canticum canticorum*, ed. Mary Dove, *Glossa ordinaria*, part 22: CCCM 170 [Turnhout: Brepols, 1997], 245) does note that "Lebanon, a mountain in Phoenicia, means 'whiteness' (or 'brightness') in Hebrew," and "frankincense" ("thus" in Greek); hence the Vulgate, "Vadam ad montem murre et ad collem turis." Bede, *In Cant.* 3.4.6 (Hurst, 254) says the latter explains why some codices have "ad collem Libani" ("to the mountain of Lebanon"). In his comments (par. 12), Hugh refers to the reading "Sanir" as an alternative to "Seir." In what follows the repeated references to Song of Songs 4:6–8 will not be footnoted.

4   Hugh of St Victor, *Subst. dilect.* 4 (Baron, 92.127–28 [PL 176.18A]); tr. Butterfield, in this volume.

5   Hugh of St Victor, *In Hier. coel.* 6 (PL 175.1038C); *In Eccl.* 5 (PL 175.157A); *BM Virg.* (Jollès, 194.173–74, 208, 246, 248 [PL 176.860C, 864B, 874D, 875AC]); *Arrha* (Sicard, 234, 256–64, 268 [PL 176.954D, 961D–964A, 965D–966A]); tr. in this volume; *Misc.* 1.91 (PL 177.521–522D); *Sacr.* 2.11.3 (PL 176.481BC, 482CD).

6   "subarrata": This is the past participle of the verb "subarrare," which does not appear in dictionaries of classical Latin (e.g., Lewis and Short; Oxford), but is widely attested in Carolingian authors (J. F. Niermeyer, *Mediae latinitatis lexicon minus* [Leiden: Brill, 1984], 996; Albert Blaise, *Dictionnaire Latin-Français des auteurs chrétiens*, rev. Henri Chirat [Turnhout: Brepols, 1954], 780). It is derived from *arra*, betrothal-gift, or earnest money, which occurs in the title of Hugh's *Soliloquy on the Betrothal-Gift of the Soul*, translated elsewhere in this volume. Cf. *Sacr.* 2.4.15 (PL 176.438BC): "Annulus sacramentum fidei significat, quo sponsa Christi Ecclesia subarrata est" ("The ring signifies the sacrament of faith with which the Church, the Bride of Christ, is dowered"); *Lament* (PL 175.274A).

7   Some early manuscripts insert here the phrase, "per aspirationem Spiritus Sancti" ("through the in-breathing of the Holy Spirit").

8   Apponius, *Explanatio in Canticum canticorum* (PLS 1.906); Hugh of St Victor, *Misc.* 1.148 (PL 177.553C); *Sacr.* 1.6.17 (PL 176.273B–274A; tr. Deferrari, 105–7); 2.2.2 (PL 176.416CD; tr. Deferrari, 224–25); *Libellus* 1 (Sicard, 126 [= PL 176.684D]).

9   In his *Soliloquy on the Betrothal-Gift of the Soul* this two-member distinction is expanded to three: common, special, and singular.

10   The last three verbs are "sentimus," "sapimus," and "discernimus": they could be translated as "we feel," "we savor," and "we discern." See Hugh of St Victor, *Unione* (Piazzoni, 889–87 [PL 177.287D–288A]).

¹¹ *Arrha* 58 (Sicard, 270 [PL 176.966BC]; tr. Feiss, VTT 2:222–23); Hugh of St Victor, *Sacr.* 1. prol. 2 (PL 176.183A–184A); *Script.* 2 (PL 175.11AB); *Archa Noe* 4.3 (Sicard, 92–93 [PL 176.667AC]); *Quid vere* (Baron, 98.56–68; tr. in this volume]; *Sent. QR* (Lottin, pp. 271–72); *Sapientia* (PL 176.854D).

¹² "proficiat": "Proficere" means "to advance oneself" or "to be of service to others." The former meaning is suggested by the use of this same verb at the end of this paragraph.

¹³ *Didasc.* 5.8 (Buttimer, 108.27–28; tr. Taylor, 131): "Simplicitas monachi philosophia eius est" ("The simplicity of the monk is his philosophy").

¹⁴ Jerome, *Heb. nom.* (de Lagarde, 147): "Myrra amara" ("Myrrh = bitter"); Isidore, *Etymologiae* 17.8.4 (PL 82.621AB); Apponius, *In Cant.* 6 (PLS 1.903); Bede, *In Cant.*, 3.4.5–6 (Hurst, 253.344–45); Alcuin, *Compendium in Cantica canticorum Salomonis* (PL 83.1123C); Haimo, *Expositio in Cantica canticorum* (PL 70.1075B); Angelôme of Luxeuil, *Enarrationes in Canticum canticorum.* (PL 115.609); Robert of Tumbalenia, *Super cantica canticorum* (PL 79.509D–510A).

¹⁵ *Glossa Cant.* (Dove, 245): "Libanus mons Phenicis, hebraice interpretatur candidatio, grece thus, unde supra 'vadam at montem myrrae et ad collem thuris'" ("Lebanon is a mountain in Phoenecia which in Hebrew means 'brightening,' and in Greek 'myrrh,' hence the phrase above: 'I will go to the mountain of myrrh and to the hill of frankincense'"); Isidore, *Etymologiae* 14.8.2 (PL 82.521B); Bede, *In Cant.*, 3.4.8 (Hurst, 254.405–8); Alcuin, *In Cant.* (PL 83.1123CD); Hugh of St Victor, *Assumpt.* (PL 177.1222D).

¹⁶ Hugh speaks at length of the significance of "the third day" in his work, *On the Three Days*, translated in the first volume of this series.

¹⁷ According to St Thomas Aquinas, *Sum. theo.* 2-2, q. 129, magnanimity (literally, "largeness of soul") is that part of fortitude that concerns stretching the mind toward great things (art. 1–2). Humility and magnanimity are compatible. Magnanimity makes a person think himself worthy of great things because of God's great gifts to him. Humility makes a person think little of himself in view of his own deficiency and honor others more than himself because of God's gifts to them (art. 3, ad 4). Humility restrains one from desiring to aim for great things against right reason, whereas magnanimity urges the mind to great things in accord with right reason (2-2, q. 161, art. 1, ad 3); humility keeps a person from confiding only in his own powers (2-2. q. 161, art. 2, ad 2).

¹⁸ This might also be translated: "On the mountain of Myrrh we receive strength against carnal desire; on the hills of Lebanon we receive enlightenment of mind against ignorance; in the conversation on the bridegroom we receive love (*caritatem*) against malice and hardness of heart." Hugh's contemporary, Hildegard of Bingen (1098–1179), was fiercely eloquent in her denunciations of hardheartedness (*duritia cordis*), which she contrasts to mercy: *Liber vitae meritorum*, 1.6–8, 70, 107–9, ed. A. Carlevaris, CCCM 90 (Turnhout: Brepols, 1995), 15–16, 41–42, 55–56; tr. Bruce Hozeski, *The Book of the Rewards of Life* (New York: Oxford University Press, 1994), 14–15, 40–41, 53–54; *Scivias*, 3.3.8, ed. A. Führkötter and A. Carlevaris, CCCM 43A (Turnhout: Brepols, 1978), 380–81; tr. Columba Hart, *Scivias* (New York: Paulist, 1990), 348–49; *Ordo virtutum*, ed. P. Dronke, *Opera minora*, CCCM 226 (Turnhout: Brepols, 2007), 513, lines 188–90; tr. Audrey Ekdahl Davidson, *The Ordo Virtutum of Hildegard von Bingen* (Kalamazoo, MI: Medieval Institute Publications, Western Michigan University, 1984), 19.

¹⁹ The attribution of power, wisdom, and charity, to the Father, Son, and Holy Spirit, was a major concern of Hugh's *On the Three Days*, which was translated and discussed in VTT 1:49–102. See, for example, *Sacr.* 1.2.6–13, 22 (PL 176.208B–211C, 216C); 1.3.26–27 (PL 176.227C–230B); *Misc.* 1.63 (PL 177.504D–505A); *Misc.* 1.83 (PL 177.518B); *Sent. QI*, 5 (Lottin, 186).

²⁰ Mark 3:29.

²¹ "justificatos": Hugh uses the word twice in this short work. Except to the theologically attuned, "justified" has a connotation of smugness. In Latin the sense of "having been made right (by God)" is more evident. For the Victorines, one is reformed to be just through Christ, and then brought by him to beatitude in heaven. In inviting the justified person to ascend,

he is calling him to a foretaste and, ultimately, to the full and permanent experience of beatitude.

²² Hugh of St Victor, *Sacr.* 2.13.3–6 (PL 176.527B–531C); *Archa Noe* 3.1 (Sicard, 55–56 [PL
176.647B–648A]); *Septem donis* (Baron, 124).

²³ The distinction Hugh is making is not immediately clear, and several manuscripts show an
effort by a scribe to improve the clarity. Hugh prefers to think of the bridegroom saying to
himself, "I will go for myself to the mountain of Myrrh and to the hills of Lebanon and I will
speak to my bride." Then when he gets there he exclaims, "You are utterly beautiful, my nearest, and there is no blemish in you." The alternative is that the groom said to himself, "I will
go for myself to the mountain of Myrrh and to the hills of Lebanon, and I will say to my bride,
'You are utterly (*tota*) beautiful, my nearest, and there is no blemish in you.'" Then he went
and said: "Come."

²⁴ One could insert here: "in either case."

²⁵ Hugh of St Victor, *Epistola ad canonicos Lucenses*, cited in F. E. Croydon, "Notes on the Life
of Hugh of St Victor," *Journal of Theological Studies* 40 (1939): 251; *Misc.* 2.67 (PL 177.627D).

²⁶ Philip of Harveng, *Commentaria in Cantica canticorum* 4.17 (PL 203.379C–380A).

²⁷ Hugh of St Victor, *Assumpt.* (Jollès, 118 [PL 177.1211C]).

²⁸ Hugh of St Victor, *Archa Noe* 3.2 (Sicard, 56.39–40 [PL 176.648A]): "dum animus ab exterioribus abstractus ad se ipsum colligitur, robustior ad contemplanda eterna sublevatur" ("when
the mind, withdrawn from exterior things, is gathered to itself, it is more solid and is raised up
to the contemplation of eternal things"); *Misc.* 1.55 (PL 177.502A); *Misc.* 1.6 (PL 177.482B).

²⁹ Isa. 46:8.

³⁰ At this point, Hugh speaks for the first time of coming *from* Lebanon to Lebanon. This shift
in prepositions is reflected in the variant readings that the manuscripts give for the citation
from the *Canticle,* as noted above.

³¹ *Misc.* 2.46 (PL 177.611AB).

³² Gen. 25:25; 32:3, 36:8; Deut. 2:4–8.

³³ Deut. 3:8–9; Ezek. 27:5; 1 Chron. 5:23.

³⁴ On the interpretation of "Seir," see Jerome, *Heb. nom.* (de Lagarde, 72 and 84); Ambrose, *De
Isaac vel anima*, 5.47, ed. C. Schenkl, CSEL 32/1 (Vienna: Tempsky, 1897), 671.9; John of Mantua, *In Cantica canticorum*, ed. Bernhard Bischoff and Burkhard Taeger, Spicilegium Friburgense 19 (Fribourg Switzerland: Universitätsverlag, 1973), 3:91.25–28; Anselm of Laon,
Enarrationes in Cantica canticorum (PL 162.1207D).

³⁵ *Glossa Cant.* (Dove, 247): "Sanir fetor, vel nocturna avis quando decipit" ("'Sanir,' stench, or
the nocturnal bird when it deceives").

³⁶ Gen. 25:25–27; 27:36; 32:3.

³⁷ 1 Cor. 15:46.

³⁸ On this entire section see also Isidore, *Etymologiae* 7.6.33–34 (PL 82.277B).

³⁹ Hugh of St Victor, *Unione* (PL 177.288BC).

⁴⁰ Origen, *In Cant. hom.* 2.10 (Baehrens, 56.6–12); Isidore, *Etymologiae* 14.8.1 (PL 82.521A),
14.8.19 (PL 82.523A), 14.8.22 (PL 82.523A), 14.8.23 (PL 82.523B); Richard of St Victor, *XII
patr.* 75 (Châtillon, 306).

⁴¹ Jerome, *Heb. nom.* (de Lagarde, 86.9; 93.5–6; 119.16–17); Apponius, *In Cant.* 7 (PLS 1.908);
Glossa Cant. (Dove, 247): "Hermon anathematizatio"; Philip of Harveng, *Commentaria in
Cantica canticorum* 4.21 (PL 203.385BC).

⁴² Hugh of St Victor, *Misc.* 1.48 (PL 177.496); *Didasc.* 5.4 (Buttimer, 98.1–6, 101.29–102.24; tr.
Taylor, 122–23, 125 ([first and seventh rules of Tyconius]); *Sacr.* 1.8.11 (PL 176.312BC); Roger
Baron, "Textes spirituels inédits de Hugues de Saint-Victor," *Mélanges de science religieuse,*
13 (1956): 163; *Misc.* 2.51 (PL 177.616BC); Bruno of Segni, *Expositio in Cantica canticorum* 4
(PL 164.1258BC).

⁴³ "sopita": from "sopire," "to deprive of feeling or sense, especially by putting or lulling to sleep."
"Sopitus" can mean "dead." To translate it as "senseless" may be a stretch. "Slumbered" would

be more usual and fits with "den" and the "dormi" (sleeps) of the next sentence. The translation by a Religious of the C.S.M.V., *Divine Love*, 36, reads "fierceness asleep."

[44]   *Physiologus* 1, tr. Michael J. Curley (Austin, TX: University of Texas Press, 1979), 4; Ps.-Hugh of St Victor, *De bestiis* 2.1 (PL 177.57BC); Apponius, *In Cant.* 7 (PLS 1.908); Paterius, *Expositio veteris et novi testamenti* 12 (PL 79.911CD).

[45]   Prov. 5:3–4.

[46]   Prov. 9:16–18.

[47]   Job 40:16 (Vulg.); Pseudo-Richard of St Victor, *Cant.* 24 (PL 196.476CD).

[48]   Isidore, *Etymologiae* 12.2.11 (PL 82.435B): "Leopardus ex adulterio leonae et pardi nascitur" ("A leopard is born from the adulterous union of a lioness and a male pard"). A pard was a large spotted cat. The leopard (*Lonza*) that appears in Dante's *Inferno,* Canto 1, lines 31–36 (*The Divine Comedy of Dante Alighieri. Vol. 1: Inferno*, ed. and tr. Robert M. Durling [New York: Oxford, 1996], 28–29, 36 note) and is usually understood to be a symbol of fraudulence fits the usual description of a "pard." The leopard does not appear in bestiaries, though the "pard" and the "panther" do. Richard of St Victor, in *Erud.* 3.11 (PL 196.1358CD), connects the "pard" with fraudulence: "Recte hypocritarum fraudulentia in pardo figuratur qui per totum corpus maculis quibusdam respergitur" ("The fraudulence of hypocrites is rightly symbolized by the 'pard,' whose entire body is speckled with some kind of spots").

[49]   *Glossa Cant.* (Dove, 245): "Leones propter superbiam vel violentiam, pardi propter crudelitatem vel variationem artium malignarum" ("Lions on account of pride or violence, leopards on account of cruelty or the variety of malign arts").

HUGH OF ST VICTOR

ON THE SUBSTANCE OF LOVE

INTRODUCTION BY HUGH FEISS OSB
TRANSLATION BY VANESSA BUTTERFIELD

INTRODUCTION

This short work is found in many important manuscripts of Hugh's works,[1] in the *Indiculum* of Merton College 49, and in the *Patrologia latina* both among Hugh's works (PL 176.15–18, where it is misleadingly made to be chapter 4 of the *Dialogue on the Sacraments*) and among the works of Pseudo-Augustine (PL 40.843–46). It was previously translated in Hugh of Saint-Victor, *Selected Spiritual Works*, tr. a Religious of C.S.M.V. (New York: Harper & Row, 1962), 187–91.

If the ideas in the surprising little work *What Truly Should Be Loved?* are recognizably Hugh's and point toward some of his major works, *On the Substance of Love* does not go far beyond the ideas of St Augustine. Hugh says one might hesitate to write about love, which seems to be the province of love poets who write about it candidly and sometimes scandalously. But his purpose is different: it aims at engendering self-awareness and, thus, an ensuing caution about one's desires (pars. 2–3).

The first paragraph is very carefully crafted. The first verb, *serimus*, can mean either to sow or to sew (weave together). Speaking about love helps assure that it will produce a good crop or a beautiful tapestry. Love is a flame that can consume or purify; it is a stream arising deep in the heart that can simply flow down toward external things, or be directed toward interior things. In the first case, desire draws the heart; in the second, the heart directs desire. From this one source comes everything that is good or bad. It is in us and from it comes everything that is from us. The name of the one source is *amor* or *dilectio*. The names of the two streams are cupidity and charity: cupidity for what is external, charity for what is internal. As Augustine writes:

> There is a foul love, by which the mind runs after things inferior to itself. It is more properly called cupidity. It is the root of all evil. . . . The love of things that should be loved is better called *caritas* or *dilectio*. . . . That by which God and the soul are loved is properly called the purest

---

[1]   Baron, *Six opuscules*, 25.

and consummated *caritas*, provided nothing else is loved; it is also right to call it *dilectio*.[2]

On the unstated premise that every act of the will involves love, all moral good and evil flow from love (pars. 1, 3). Hugh defines love as "the delight of somebody's heart toward something on account of something."[3] It can take two forms: seeking what one does not have, or enjoying what one does have (cf. par. 8). Either of these can be good or bad. In the latter case, what is bad is not the (being of the) lover, the object of the love, or the love itself, but the disordered way in which one loves. It is lack of order that is bad (par. 5). Here Hugh makes a metaphysical assertion that reflects Augustine's philosophy of evil: God made all that is and insofar as something is, and is formed, it is good. Deformation, lack of form, is what is evil. Moral evil is deformation or disorder in the will's act, which is love. Where there is ordered love, there is nothing bad. For that reason, Augustine, followed elsewhere by Hugh of St Victor, could declare: "Love and do what you will."[4]

Hugh sees charity as the chain or rope that connects God and human beings. God created human beings freely, motivated solely by charity. God made them with the force of love within them so that they would search for and find happiness in God. Then, Hugh uses the metaphor of a bee drawing honey from a flower.[5] One can drink happiness

---

[2]   *Div. quaest.83*, 35–36 (PL 40.23–25): "Est enim et [amor] turpis, quo animus se ipso inferiora sectatur, quae magis proprie cupiditas dicitur, omnium scilicet malorum radix. . . . Amor rerum amandarum, charitas vel dilectio melius dicitur. . . . Deus igitur et animus quo amatur, charitas proprie dicitur purgatissima et consummata, si nihil aliud amatur: hanc et dilectionem dici placet."

[3]   "amor est delectatio cordis alicuius ad aliquid propter aliquid" (Baron, 86). A Religious of the C.S.M.V., *Selected Spiritual Writings*, 288, translates: "the attachment of any heart to anything, for any reason."

[4]   For this expression, see Giles Constable, *"Love and Do What You Will": The Medieval History of an Augustinian Precept*, Morton W. Bloomfield Lectures IV (Kalamazoo, MI: Medieval Institute Publications, Western Michigan University, 1999). Both Hugh and Richard of St Victor quote the adage. Constable shows that Hugh of St Victor, *Sacr.* 2.13.12 (PL 176.545D–546D, 548CD; tr. Deferrari, 397, 399); *Sacr.* 2.14.6 (PL 176.561AD, 562BC; tr. Deferrari, 413, 414), and Richard of St Victor, *Adnot. Psalm. 44* (PL 196.322D–323A), *Adnot. Psalm. 118* (PL 196.358D–359A), are emphatic that genuine love will show itself in good deeds, although if the opportunity to do good deeds is lacking a loving good will is enough. As Hugh puts in succinctly: "You cannot have the will without the deed, when you can do the deed" ("Sed voluntatem sine opere habere non potes, quando opera potes" (*Sacr.* 2.14.6 [PL 176.561B]).

[5]   The metaphor of the bee gathering honey was widely used. Herrad of Landsberg, Abbess of Hohenburg, used it to describe her composition of the *Hortus deliciarum*. Fiona Griffiths explores the meaning and background of the metaphor and gives an ample bibliography in

from God as much as one wants. Since God is never lessened, the only limit is one's own desire. Ultimately, one will enjoy the taste of God eternally (pars. 6, 7). Referring back to his earlier hesitations (par. 2), Hugh writes that he does not regret writing about love (par. 7).

Alluding to the twofold commandment to love God and neighbor (Mark 12:30–31), Hugh makes a point that is very important to him: love of God, self, and neighbor are in complete harmony. All who love God are one in the object of their love. Moreover, love unites those who love each other in charity. This has two results: the neighbors, to whom one is united through love, supply one's needs (Hugh strikingly says, "they supply what one cannot obtain in oneself from God to whom all cling"); the good of all is completely the good of each (par. 7). This sense of the oneness of all Christians in charity is an essential element in the logic of love as Hugh sees it.[6]

Finally, Hugh writes about how to order charity, whether love is running in search of its objects—God above, neighbor alongside, the world below—or love is resting in enjoyment of them. His strategy is to say that love as seeking or desire may be from/about/regarding (de), with (cum), or unto (in + accusative). Love of God manifests all three: it receives the capability to love from God; it runs with God when it is aligned with God's will; it runs to God who is the goal of its striving for happiness and rest (pars. 9–10). Desire can run regarding the neighbor by rejoicing about his progress and salvation; it can run with the neighbor on the way to and in arriving at God (par. 11). Love runs from the world when, having seen God's work outside oneself, one turns inwardly to God in ardent wonder and praise. Such is rightly ordered love; all else is disordered desire (par. 13). Desire would be ordered wrongly if it ran with the world—relying on mutable, temporal things for happiness—or if it ran to the world, wanting to rest always in its delights (par. 12).

Hugh's understanding of love as running from the admired exterior world to interior praise of God raises a question. Hugh wrote *On the Three Days* in which he showed the many ways in which God's power, wisdom, and goodness can be known from the things that God has made. He also wrote *On Vanity* and the *Homilies on Ecclesiastes*, which emphasize the mutability and deceptive allurements of the world. *On*

---

her *The Garden of Delights: Reform and Renaissance for Women in the Twelfth Century* (Philadelphia: University of Pennsylvania Press, 2007), 82–107.

[6]   For example, *Arrha* 25–28 (Sicard, 244–48 [PL 176.957D–959]; tr. Feiss, VTT 2:212–14).

the *Three Days* and some of the autobiographical passages in his writings indicate that Hugh sees the world as sacramental; his metaphysics says it is good and beautiful. Yet, for that very reason he fears that the world will lead its admirers astray so that they will rest in it and not in God. In *On the Substance of Love* he writes that one, having seen the outward manifestation of the world, needs to turn inward to God. The question is: Is the world a signpost or a sacramental window? It has been said that John of Damascus envisaged "the soul attaining transcendent reality through the senses, rather than by abandoning the senses."[7] To what extent would Hugh have endorsed this way of running unto God?

Both *substantia* in the title, "*De substantia dilectionis*" ("On the Substance of Love"), and "*natura*," which occurs in paragraph 3, have many philosophical uses and connotations. It seemed best to translate them literally, although Hugh is not using them in a narrowly technical sense. In his French translation (*Six opuscules*, 83, 85) Baron translates them as "realité" and "nature" respectively. The division of this translation into parts and paragraphs is the translator's; Baron divides the work into the same four parts, but gives paragraph numbers only for part IV.

---

[7]   Andrew Louth, *St John of Damascus: Tradition and Originality in Byzantine Theology*, Oxford Early Christian Studies (New York: Oxford, 2002), 45–46.

[I]

1. Daily we sow a sermon about love, lest love should by chance spark in our hearts and become enkindled, making a flame of fire either consuming everything or purifying everything. For from this flame is everything that is good; and everything that is bad is from it. One fountain of love (*dilectionis*) springing from within pours into two streams.[1] One stream is love (*amor*) of the world: desire (*cupiditas*); the other is love (*amor*) of God: charity. In the middle is the human heart, whence the fountain of love (*amoris*) breaks forth. When it cascades down through passion (*affectum*) to exterior things, it is called cupidity (*cupiditas*); but when it directs its desire (*desiderium*) to interior things, it is named charity. Therefore, there are two streams that emanate from the fountain of love: cupidity and charity; the root of everything bad is cupidity, and the root of everything good is charity.[2] Accordingly, from this fountain is everything that is good; from it also is everything bad. Therefore, whatever it is, it is a great thing that is in us, and from it is everything that is from us: this, then, is love.

2. What is love? And how great is love? Or whence is love? The Word of God also speaks about this. Does this business not rather belong to those who are accustomed to dishonor chastity? Look how many there are who willingly accept the mystery of love, how few there are who do not blush to speak words about it openly. Therefore, what are we doing? Perhaps we may have a brow shamed by much wickedness, we who do not feel ashamed to depict the love just mentioned, a love that even unchaste people sometimes cannot put into words without shame. But it is one thing to search out an inclination to sin (*vitium*) so that it may be rooted up; it is another to excite such an inclination so that virtue and truth will not be loved. Therefore, for our part we are searching out and seeking what within us divides our desires in many ways and leads our one heart toward different things. We do so in order that we may know about them and knowing about them we may beware. The unchaste search out the same thing so that they may know it, but that knowing it they may do it.

3. However we find this is nothing other than love, which, although by nature a singular and unique movement of the heart, in

action is divided. When it moves in a disorderly fashion, that is, toward those things to which it should not, it is said to be cupidity; but when it is ordered, it is called charity. Therefore, by which definition will we be able to signify this very movement of the heart, which we call love? It is advantageous for us to look at it more closely lest it be hidden to a certain degree and not known, and so neither avoided when it is bad, nor desired or discovered when it is good. When it is bad, from it such great evils come; and when it is good, such good things come forth!

[II]

4. Therefore, how do we define this love? Let us search into it, let us consider it, because what is sought is hidden, and the deeper it is situated in the heart the more it rules the heart in either direction.

5. Love seems to be—and love is—the delight of somebody's heart toward something on account of something. It is desire in seeking, and delight in thoroughly enjoying; it runs by means of (*per*) desire, it rests by means of delight. O human heart, here is your good and here is your bad: if you are good you are not good in any other way; nor are you otherwise bad if you are bad, but only because you love either well or badly that which is good. Therefore he who loves is not bad, nor is what he loves bad, nor is the love by which he loves bad, but that he loves badly is bad; and this is what every evil is. Therefore, set charity in order and then nothing is bad.

[III]

6. We wish to recommend a great thing,[3] provided we are capable of what we wish. Almighty God lacks nothing, because he himself is the highest and true good, who neither is able to receive from another something by which he could increase since all things are from him, nor is able to lose from himself something by which he could diminish since in him all things stand together firmly immutable. He created a rational spirit, from charity alone, from no necessity, in order to make him a sharer in his own happiness. Further, so that the ra-

tional spirit would be apt to thoroughly enjoy such great happiness, he fashioned love in him—fashioned a taste for things belonging to the spirit, as it were, thereby sensitizing him to the taste of internal sweetness, so that through this same love he would taste the pleasure of his own happiness and would cling to it with untiring desire. Therefore God coupled (*copulavit*) the rational creature to himself through love, so that by always clinging to the very Good by which he was to be made happy, he would suck from it by affection and would drink from it by desire and would possess happiness in it by joy.[4] Suck, O little bee, suck. Suck and drink the indescribable goodness of your sweetness. Plunge in and replenish—for He does not know diminishment—provided you do not begin to grow weary of drinking. Therefore, cling and adhere, take and enjoy. If this taste is eternal, the beatitude will be eternal also.

7. No longer should it cause us regret to have talked about love. It should not cause us to repent where there is such great benefit; it should not cause us shame where there is such integrity. Therefore through love the rational creature has been united to his own maker, and it is the chain of love alone that binds both together,[5] by a bond as happy as it is firm. On account of which, so that there would be both an undivided union and a perfect harmony on both sides, there is a twofold connection in the love of God and neighbor, so that through the love of God all would belong together in one, and through the love of one's neighbor all would become one with each other, so that what each one could not obtain in himself from that One to whom all were clinging, he might more plentifully and more perfectly possess in another through love of his neighbor, and the good of all would become wholly the good of each.

[IV]

8. Therefore, order love.[6] What is it to put charity in order? If love is desire, let it run well; if it is joy, let it rest well. For love is, as was said, the delight of somebody's heart toward something because of something: desire in seeking and delight in enjoying thoroughly; running through desire, and resting through joy; running to it, and resting in it. To what? Or in what? Listen, if perhaps we can explain, where our love should run, and in what it should rest.

9. Indeed there are three things that can be loved well or badly—that is, God, neighbor, and the world. God is above us, our neighbor next to us, and the world is under us. Therefore, order love. If it runs, let it run well. If it rests, let it rest well. Desire runs; joy rests. Because joy has only one form, because it is always in one, it cannot be altered by change. However, desire admits of a change of motion, and for that reason does not confine itself in one thing, but manifests various forms. For its every course is either from (*de*) that, or with that, or in that toward which it is directed. Therefore how should our desire run? There are three things: God, our neighbor, and the world. In the course of our desire, let God have three of these things, our neighbor two of them, the world one of them, and then there is ordered charity in desire.

10. For love can run by (*per*) desire in an ordered way from (*de*) God and with God and unto God. Love runs from (*de*) God, when it receives from (*de*) God himself the wherewithal to love him. It runs with God, when it opposes his will in nothing. It runs unto God when it desires to rest in God himself. These are the three things that pertain to God.

11. There are two things that pertain to love of neighbor. For desire can run from or regarding (*de*) a neighbor and with a neighbor, but it cannot run unto a neighbor. From or regarding (*de*) a neighbor, so that it may rejoice about his salvation and progress. With a neighbor, so that it desires to have him on the way of God both as a companion on the journey and as a partner in arrival. But it cannot run unto a neighbor in order to establish hope and trust in a human being. These are the two things that pertain to a neighbor: from (*de*) him and with him, but not unto him.

12. There is one thing that pertains to love of the world, to run from (*de*) it, not with it or unto it. Desire runs from (*de*) the world, when having seen the work of God outwardly it changes itself (*se convertit*) inwardly through wonder and praise to be more ardent toward him. It would run with the world, if on account of the mutability of temporal things—either by being cast down in adversity or raised up in prosperity—it conformed itself to this age. It would run unto the world if it wanted to rest always in its delights.

13. Therefore, order love, so that it may run by (*per*) desire from (*de*) God, with God, and unto God; from (*de*) a neighbor, with a neighbor, but not unto a neighbor; from (*de*) the world, but not with the world

and not unto the world—so that in God alone love rests through joy. This is ordered love, and outside of this love everything that is done is not ordered love, but disordered desire

NOTES

1   To this point Hugh has used the word "dilectio" for love. He will now use "amor" as a synonym for "dilectio." "Amor," in turn, divides into "cupiditas" and "caritas." "Cupiditas" is uncontrolled passion or feeling (*affectus*) for exterior things; "caritas" is directed desire (*desiderium*) toward interior things.

2   1 Tim. 6:10; Augustine, *Div. quaest. 83*, 35–36 (PL 40.24–25), discussed in the introduction to this translation; *En. Ps.* 90.1.8 (Dekkers and Fraipont, 1260 [PL 37.1154]): "the root of all evils is cupidity, just as the root of all goods is charity" ("radix omnium malorum cupiditas, sic radix omnium bonorum caritas est").

3   Baron (*Six opuscules*, 27) observes that by introducing this paragraph with "magnam rem," Hugh emphasizes its importance.

4   Constable (*Love*, 34) notes that when translating Augustine Brian Stock rendered "affectus" by "disposition." That would work here, where there seems to be a progression: disposition, desire, possession.

5   "in idipsum": literally, "into the selfsame." See the discussion of this expression in note 5 for *What Truly Should Be Loved?* elsewhere in this volume. For the command to love God and neighbor, see Mark 12:30–31.

6   Song of Songs 2:4.

HUGH OF ST VICTOR

ON THE PRAISE OF CHARITY

INTRODUCTION AND TRANSLATION
BY FRANKLIN T. HARKINS

INTRODUCTION

In the *indiculum*, the index of the earliest edition of the works of Hugh of St Victor that Abbot Gilduin compiled in 1141, *On the Praise of Charity* (*De laude caritatis*) appears in the second volume among various sermons and spiritual works. More specifically, *On the Praise of Charity* is found between two other short works on love with which it frequently circulated in medieval manuscripts, namely the *Soliloquy on the Betrothal-Gift of the Soul* (*Soliloquium de arrha animae*) and *On the Substance of Love* (*De substantia dilectionis*).[1] The work—a beautiful, passionate, wide-ranging, and theologically profound encomium for charity—enjoyed a wide distribution and significant influence throughout the High and Late Middle Ages, as attested by the more than 100 manuscripts that have been identified.[2]

DATE

Damien van den Eynde dates *On the Praise of Charity* prior to *On the Substance of Love* on the basis of the particular phrase with which Hugh begins this treatise proper: "It is known that so many have already been inclined to praise charity that if I begin (*cepero* or *coepero*) to speak in praise of it, it may seem more like presumption perhaps than piety" (sec. 2). Van den Eynde reads *cepero* here as Hugh's affirmation of a reluctance to "begin," on the heels of many before him, singing charity's praises in several separate works. Thus, this word reveals, for Van den Eynde, the temporal primacy of *On the Praise of Charity* vis-

---

[1]   Joseph de Ghellinck, "La table des matières de la première édition des oeuvres de Hugues de Saint-Victor," *Recherches de science religieuse* 1 (1910): 270–89, 385–96, here 279–82. On manuscripts containing *De laude caritatis* in tandem with *De arrha animae* and *De substantia dilectionis* found at St Victor, see Gilbert Ouy, *Les manuscrits de l'abbaye de Saint-Victor: catalogue établi sur la base du répertoire de Claude de Grandrue (1514)* (Turnhout: Brepols, 1999): 2:256–57, 261–62.
      I would like to thank Angela Kim Harkins and Frans van Liere for their helpful suggestions on this introduction and the translation that follows.
[2]   See Dominique Poirel, introduction to *Oeuvre* 1, 180.

à-vis other works in which Hugh treats love under the various terms *amor, dilectio,* and *caritas*.[3]

Dominique Poirel has contested Van den Eynde's reading of Hugh's *cepero* and the dating based on it.[4] Noting that charity (*caritas*) for Hugh is the highest among several forms of love, Poirel maintains that *On the Praise of Charity* and *On the Substance of Love* neither treat exactly the same subject[5] nor treat their respective subjects in the same way. Poirel understands Hugh, then, as beginning *On the Praise of Charity* not with the aim of placing this work within a larger literary corpus on love, a corpus having been penned by his predecessors and/ or to be penned by himself. Rather, Poirel sees the Victorine as simply placing himself within sacred history and his own praises of charity among those more noble ones—both spoken and lived—of the saints from the beginning of the world.[6] Assuming that Poirel is correct about Hugh's intent regarding *cepero*, we must conclude that the exact date of *On the Praise of Charity* is unknown.

LITERARY STRUCTURE

The work may be properly divided into six major parts as follows (numbers in parentheses indicate section numbers provided in Patrice Sicard's edition[7] and retained in the present translation):

1. Prologue (sec. 1)
2. The Praise of the Saints (secs. 2–4)
3. Charity as Guide on the Road to God (secs. 5–8)
4. Charity as the Very Road or Way (*uia*) to God (secs. 9–12)
5. Charity as God Himself (secs. 13–15)
6. Conclusion (sec. 16)

Following a prologue addressed to a certain Peter, presumably a priest and friend, Hugh begins *On the Praise of Charity* by explaining that from the beginning of the world saints have commended charity

---

[3] Damien van den Eynde, *Essai sur la succession et la date des écrits de Hugues de Saint-Victor* (Rome: Pontificium Athenaeum Antonianum, 1960), 165.
[4] *Oeuvre* 1:176–77.
[5] In this claim, Poirel follows Roger Baron, "Note sur la succession et la date des écrits de Hugues de Saint-Victor," *Revue d'histoire ecclésiastique* 57 (1962), 88–118, here 105.
[6] *Oeuvre* 1:176–77.
[7] *Oeuvre* 1:182–207.

either by word or deed. He highlights the ancient martyrs in particular, who forsook the goods of this life—even life itself—for the sake of God (and the eternal things of God) on account of charity. Reflecting on the great treasure that is charity, Hugh proceeds to explain (in a way reminiscent of Augustine's two cities) how our lives are determined by the choices we make, choices that are determined by what we love. As such, charity serves as our guide (*dux*) on the road to God, the end toward which our lives should be directed. Hugh goes on to explain that charity is not merely our guide on the road to God, it is also itself the very road to God. Charity is, in fact, the most excellent of roads "which alone knows the traffic of our salvation" (sec. 10). It is the road whereby God Himself, in the Person of the Son, descended to humankind in order that humankind might ascend to God. Hugh's laudation reaches its rhetorical height as charity is identified with God Himself. Invoking such scriptural passages as 1 John 4:16, the Victorine explains that the Holy Spirit is the gift of divine love who is consubstantial and coeternal with Him by whom the Spirit is given. God dwells in and with those to whom He has given the gift of charity, which roots out vices and plants the virtues in the human soul. Having praised charity to the best of his ability, Hugh realizes the utter inadequacy of his words. He ends, then, with a prayer inviting charity into his own and his reader's heart so that they might receive God as their guest and inhabitant.

The detailed enumeration of the signs whereby charity manifests itself in the human person (sec. 15) provides a fitting complement to Hugh's initial treatment of *caritas* among the ancient saints and martyrs (secs. 2–4). Sections 2–4 and section 15 serve, then, as bookends to his treatise, forming an *inclusio* between which the reader is not only invited to join voice with Hugh's in praise of charity, but also exhorted to join his or her life with those of the righteous throughout the centuries who have experienced "how sweet is the love of God and how bitter and foul is the love of this world" (sec. 15). For Hugh, after all, both humans and God best express the praise of charity in deed more than in word.

MAJOR THEMES AND AUGUSTINIAN INFLUENCE

A central and recurring theme of *On the Praise of Charity* is the power of charity to compel beings, both divine and human, to act with justice or righteousness. Hugh teaches that, from the beginning of time, charity alone has driven the servants of God to forsake the enticements of this world in favor of the eternal things of God (sec. 2). Abel, Abraham, St Paul, and especially the martyrs conspicuously manifest the persuasive power of charity (secs. 2–4). Indeed, they demonstrate that love is—as the bridegroom of the Song of Songs 8:6 affirms—"strong as death" and "fierce as hell" (sec. 3). Christ's Incarnation, passion, and death demonstrate charity's power to compel, even overcome, God himself. Hugh invites his reader to realize the profound strength of charity by contemplating "God having been born of a woman, as an infant, swaddled with cloths, crying in a cradle, sucking the breasts," and later "seized, bound, wounded with scourges, crowned with thorns, spattered with spittle, pierced, fixed [to a cross] with nails, and given gall and vinegar to drink" (sec. 11). Charity's purpose in drawing God down from heaven and obliging Him to suffer and die was, according to Hugh, not only to enable the human sinner to ascend to God along the same road of righteousness but to incite him or her to do so (sec. 11).

The influence of Augustine's understanding of love on Hugh's presentation is unmistakable. Indeed, although Hugh nowhere cites Augustine directly, *On the Praise of Charity* provides ample confirmation of the Victorine's traditional status as "a second Augustine" (*secundus Augustinus*).[8] The basic bifurcation—within which Hugh treats love, not only here but also throughout his corpus—is between charity and cupidity (sec. 4),[9] a central Augustinian distinction. According to Augustine, a keen scriptural exegete in his own right, charity is the very love of God Himself, which God gives to humans in order that they might come to enjoy God as their ultimate end; cupidity, by contrast, is the prideful love of self (and, by extension, of other creatures), which precludes one from loving God rightly. For Augustine, these two kinds of love determine how each human lives in this world—each type of love constituting one of the two metaphorical cities—as well as how he or she lives in the world to come.[10] The question of what one finally

---

8   On the title *secundus Augustinus*, see Roger Baron, "Rapports entre saint Augustin et Hugues de Saint-Victor. Trois opuscules de Hugues de Saint-Victor," *Revue des études augustiniennes* 5 (1959): 391–429; Joseph de Ghellinck, *Le mouvement théologique du XIIᵉ siècle*, 2nd ed. (Bruges: Editions "De Tempel," 1948), 185; and Franklin T. Harkins, *Reading and the Work of Restoration: History and Scripture in the Theology of Hugh of St Victor* (Toronto: Pontifical Institute of Mediaeval Studies, 2009), 6, 41, 108 with nn. 130, 136, 198, 202, and 297.

9   See Dominique Poirel, *Hugues de Saint-Victor* (Paris: Cerf, 1998), 114–23.

10   In *The Literal Meaning of Genesis*, for example, Augustine writes: "These two loves—of which one is holy, the other unclean, one social, the other private, one taking thought for the com-

chooses to love, whether God and the eternal things of God or the transitory pleasures and rewards of this world, is central to Hugh's aim in *On the Praise of Charity*. That this is so, and indeed the very way in which Hugh formulates this fundamental question, reveals the decisive influence of Augustine. Furthermore, for both Augustine and Hugh, how one loves what one loves is also crucial. The former distinguishes between *uti* (a relative love according to which the lover loves the object of love as a means to loving something else) and *frui* (an absolute love according to which the lover loves the object of love as an end in itself). This same distinction determines the way Hugh represents charity here.[11] Employing the verb *fruor*, the Victorine adopts the Augustinian teaching that among all beings God alone should be loved with the love of enjoyment (secs. 6, 8). And for Hugh, as for Augustine before him,

mon good because of the companionship in the upper regions, the other putting even what is common at its own personal disposal because of its lordly arrogance; one of them God's subject, the other his rival; one of them calm, the other turbulent; one peaceable, the other rebellious; one of them setting more store by the truth than by the praises of those who stray from it, the other greedy for praise by whatever means; one friendly, the other jealous; one of them wanting for its neighbor what it wants for itself, the other wanting to subject its neighbor to itself; one of them exercising authority over its neighbor for its neighbor's good, the other for its own—these two loves were first manifested in the angels, one in the good, the other in the bad, and then distinguished in the two cities, one of the just, the other of the wicked, founded in the human race under the wonderful and inexpressible providence of God as he administers and directs everything he has created. These two cities are mixed up together in the world while time runs its course, until they are sorted out by the last judgment, and one of them, joined to the good angels, attains eternal life in its king, while the other, joined to the bad angels, is dispatched with its king into the eternal fire" (11.15.20; *Saint Augustine On Genesis*, The Works of Saint Augustine, pt. 1, vol. 13, ed. John E. Rotelle, OSA, tr. Edmund Hill, OP, and Matthew O'Connell [Hyde Park, NY: New City Press, 2002], 439–40); "Hi duo amores—quorum alter sanctus est, alter immundus, alter socialis, alter privatus, alter communi utilitati consulens propter supernam societatem, alter etiam rem communem in potestatem propriam redigens propter adrogantem dominationem, alter subditus, alter aemulus deo, alter tranquillus, alter turbulentus, alter pacificus, alter seditiosus, alter veritatem laudibus errantium praeferens, alter quoque modo laudis avidus, alter amicalis, alter invidus, alter hoc volens proximo quod sibi, alter subicere proximum sibi, alter propter proximi utiliatatem regens proximum, alter propter suam—praecesserunt in angelis, alter in bonis, alter in malis, et distinxerunt conditas in genere humano civitates duas sub admirabili et ineffabili providentia dei cuncta, quae creat, administrantis et ordinantis, alteram iustorum, alteram iniquorum, quarum etiam quadam temporali conmixtione peragitur saeculum, donec ultimo iudicio separentur, et altera coniuncta angelis bonis in rege suo vitam consequatur aeternam, altera coniuncta angelis malis in ignem cum rege suo mittatur aeternum" (*De genesi ad litteram* [Zycha, 347–48]).

[11]   On Augustine's distinction between things to be used and things to be enjoyed, see *Doc. Chr.* 1.3.3–1.5.5 (Martin, 8–9). For a general consideration, see Raymond Canning, "*Uti/frui*" in *Augustine through the Ages: An Encyclopedia*, ed. Allan D. Fitzgerald, OSA (Grand Rapids, MI: Eerdmans, 1999), 859–61.

it is charity that enables the human to choose to enjoy God rather than the world (sec. 6).

Hugh's image of charity as the road (*uia*) of salvation that leads God down to humankind and humankind up to God also finds its roots in Augustine. In *De doctrina Christiana I*, Augustine envisions this present life as a "road of the affections" (*uia affectuum*) along which the post-lapsarian person journeys back to his or her heavenly homeland (*patria*).[12] For Augustine, all the visible things of this life are to be used (*uti*) as vehicles by which to arrive at the enjoyment (*fruitio*) of the Triune God.[13] In Augustine's view, the single most important *visibile* that reveals God's great love and that, in turn, both enabled and encouraged the fallen human to love God rightly, is the Incarnation of the divine Word.[14] And it is by His crucifixion, in particular, that the Incarnate Word tears away the "thorny hedge" that sin erects between a human being and God.[15] Such Augustinian teachings provide the theological fodder and the rhetorical inspiration for Hugh's acclamation of charity as the road that directs God Himself down to earth and that orders fallen human beings to their divine end. For Hugh, the Incarnation and crucifixion, as we have seen, serve as prime examples of charity's compelling power, a power worthy of unutterable praise.

EDITIONS AND TRANSLATIONS

The Latin edition from which the following translation was made is that of Patrice Sicard found in *Oeuvre* 1, pp. 182–200. A Latin edition is also found in the *Patrologia Latina* (PL 176:969–76). In addition to the French translation of Sicard in *Oeuvre* 1, *De laude caritatis* has been previously translated into French and Italian and twice into English:

H.-D. Simonin, "Hugues de Saint-Victor. A la gloire de la charité, Présentation et traduction," in *La vie spirituelle* (Supplément, 1930): 29–36, 70–75, 129–30.

Vincenzo Liccaro, Ugo di San Vittore. *Didascalicon, I doni della promessa divina, L'essenza dell'amore, Discorso in lode del divino amore* (Milano: Rusconi, 1987), pp. 273–86.

---

[12]   *Doc. Chr.* 1.17.16 (Martin, 15); 1.4.4 (Martin, 8).
[13]   *Doc. Chr.* 1.3.3 (Martin, 8); 1.5.5 (Martin, 8–9).
[14]   *Doc. Chr.* 1.10.10–11.11 (Martin, 12).
[15]   *Doc. Chr.* 1.17.16 (Martin, 15).

The Divine Love: The two treatises De Laude Caritatis *and* De Amore Sponsi ad Sponsam *by Hugh of St Victor*, tr. A Religious of C.S.M.V. [Sr. Penelope Lawson] (London: A. R. Mowbray & Co., 1956), pp. 9–24.

Hugo's Praise of Love, tr. Joseph McSorley (Patterson, NJ: St Anthony Guild Press, 1941). First printed in *Catholic World* 72 (1901): 727–37.

In the following translation, I have aimed to preserve Hugh's distinction between *caritas* and other words falling under the general rubric of "love" (e.g., *dilectio* and *amor*) by consistently rendering *caritas* as "charity" and by supplying Hugh's Latin in parentheses in cases where I thought it might prove helpful for clarification. In the introduction to his translation of select readings on love from Thomas Aquinas's *Scriptum on the Sentences*, Peter Kwasniewski explains well the justification for this choice:

> For a translator wishing to be clear, *caritas* presents no difficulty: it must be translated "charity." The fact that for some people "charity" has come to mean nothing other than tossing a coin into a beggar's cup is no reason to throw it out of theology where it occupies the queenliest of places; like many other beautiful but endangered species in the English language, it rather needs to be rescued and bred in captivity. For the scholastics, charity means nothing less than the very love that is God's essence, the love that Christ manifested in his death on the cross. The reductionism that makes "charity" equivalent to almsgiving or other works of mercy—which are really charity's *effects*—must be resisted in the name of both sound English and sound theology.[16]

It is precisely this burgeoning scholastic theology of charity that Hugh sets forth with acclamatory eloquence here in *On the Praise of Charity*.

---

[16]   St Thomas Aquinas, *On Love and Charity: Readings from the "Commentary on the Sentences of Peter Lombard,"* Thomas Aquinas in Translation, tr. Peter A. Kwasniewski, Thomas Bolin, and Joseph Bolin (Washington, DC: Catholic University of America Press, 2008), xxii. For further discussion of Aquinas' vocabulary on love see the online *Supplement to On Love and Charity* (Washington, DC: Catholic University of America Press, 2008) 22–24 (cuapress.cua. edu/Books).

1. Hugh to Peter, the servant of Christ: *Taste and see that the Lord is sweet.*[1]

When I was considering, dearest brother, how I might arouse your love (*dilectionem*) to thoughts of me, it first occurred to me that I, who ask of you nothing other than the gift of love itself, should write to you concerning that very love. Insofar as I have been able, therefore, I have commended charity (*caritatem*) with [all] the words at my command so that when you read of its praise you might understand how ardently I both love it in you and desire it from you. Nor should your own charity be angry at me if I, myself tepid, conduct the meager breeze of my words near to its fire, already burning brightly, not so that that [fire] rages more [intensely] but rather so that your charity might recognize the effort of my own desire for it. Read, therefore, and love; and what you read on account of love, this read so that you might love. It is all because of love: love sends, love receives; it is love that is given, love that is repaid.

The Prologue ends, the treatise begins.

2. It is known that so many have already been inclined to praise charity that if I begin to speak in praise of it, it may seem more like presumption perhaps than piety. For from the beginning of the world, who among the saints appeared who did not commend charity to us either by word or by deed? Charity made Abel a martyr,[2] [and] charity led Abraham out of [his own] land[3]: for the former through charity innocently suffered death, and the latter through charity willingly forsook his native soil; and both through charity exchanged earth for heaven. It is charity alone which from the beginning has persuaded the servants of God to flee the allurements of this world, to trample pleasures under foot, to curb carnal concupiscence, to subdue desires, to despise honors, [and] finally to reject all the delights of this present life and even, on account of the desire for eternal life, not to fear death itself

3. Paul had experienced this power of love (*uim dilectionis*) when he said: "Who will separate us from the charity (*caritate*) of Christ? Tribulation, or difficulty, or persecution, or famine, or nakedness, or

peril, or the sword? For I hope that neither death, nor life, nor angels, nor principalities, nor powers, nor things present, nor things to come, nor might, nor height, nor depth, nor any other creature will be able to separate us from the charity (*caritate*) of God which is in Christ Jesus our Lord."[4]

Hence the bridegroom in the Song of Songs admonishes the bride concerning the virtue of love: "Set me as a seal upon your heart, set me as a seal upon your arm; for love is strong as death, desire (*emulatio*) is fierce as hell."[5] Indeed, death destroys the living, but hell spares not the dead. Therefore "love is strong as death," for just as death annihilates the flesh's faculty of sense perception, so does love annihilate the desire of carnal concupiscence. "Desire is fierce as hell," for it compels those whom it inwardly draws toward the longing for eternal things not only to spurn external pleasures but also to endure adverse and violent things in order to attain that which they love.

4. Let us consider how many torments the martyrs endured to reach the kingdom of heaven. What great power of love, we believe, burned in those who did not spare themselves for the sake of God! Let us consider what they renounced, what they sought after, [and] what they endured. What they renounced we see; what they sought after we do not see, but believe; [and] what they endured we have heard. They renounced temporal goods, they sought after eternal goods, and they endured torments. Come now and let us see if our heart is willing to abandon all the things of this world; to love neither glory, nor honor, nor wealth; not to take pleasure in favorable things; to not delight in flattery; to not rejoice in luxurious things. "Lord, your eyes have seen my imperfection."[6]

How far I seem to be from this, I will not say perfection, but even from the beginning of perfection! And certainly it was not enough for the friends of God to despise the things [of this world] and trample them underfoot for the sake of the love of eternal things. Rather, having cast all those things aside, they could not be deterred either by threats or by torments as they ran eagerly to fulfill their solemn vow. Charity drew them, and therefore neither did cupidity draw them back nor did adversity deter them. So they ran: they left the world behind them and had God in front of them. But torments were introduced in order to examine them [so as to determine] with what kind of desire they were seeking God or with what steadfastness they were scorning the world. Truth was examined, charity was proved, injustice was confounded. Fearlessly they approached the punishments, and their flesh was despising its wounds exteriorly to the same degree that love had wounded their minds interiorly. They approached and endured; and by dying they confessed the desire with which they ran while alive. O charity, how did you taste to them? How sweet were you to those whom you compelled to endure such great things for your sake? By what bonds did you draw to you those whom—despite the world drawing them back with its delights and driving them away with its torments—you could have never lost? They ran because you drew them, they endured because you supported them, they arrived because you received them. How unquenchably you burned in their breasts, for you could be snuffed out neither by insults, nor by rewards, nor by punishments! These things flooded them like rivers, but many rivers and many waters were not able to extinguish charity.[7]

5. O charity, what shall I say about you? How shall I praise you? If I could taste you, I could estimate your value; if I could know your worth, I could pay a price for you. But as it turns out you exceed my paltry means, and in my power I am unable to meet your price. Nevertheless, I will give what I have, and I will even give all that I have. I will exchange all the wealth of my household for you: all that is in the dwelling place of my body, all that is in the dwelling place of my heart I will give for you, and when I have given everything I will account it as nothing. I will gladly give up all the pleasures of my flesh and all the delights of my heart for you, so that I might be enabled to have and to enjoy you alone. You alone are dearer to me [than all these things], you alone are more advantageous, you alone are sweeter, you alone are more delightful; pleasing more, satisfying more abundantly, saving more securely, preserving more successfully.

6. I will also speak of you to others. Tell me, O human heart, which would you rather choose: to rejoice always with this world, or to be with God forever? You choose what you love more. Listen, then, so that you might set your love aright and not delay your choice. If this world is beautiful, what kind of beauty do you think exists where the Creator of the world is? Love, then, so that you might choose; love better so that you might choose more beneficially; love God so that you might choose to be with God. Therefore, choose according to love (*per dilectionem*). But the more you love, the sooner you desire to arrive at [the object of your love] and the more quickly you hurry in order to take hold of it. Therefore, run by means of love and take hold by means of love (*per dilectionem*).

Similarly, the more you love, the more ardently you embrace [what you love]. Therefore, enjoy according to love. See how love is everything to you: it is your choice, it is your running, it is your arrival, it is your dwelling place, it is your beatitude. Therefore, love God, choose God, run, take hold, possess, enjoy.

7. "I have already chosen," you say. "By what road (*uia*) should I run in order to arrive?" One runs to God on the road of God. "I cannot run alone on an untried road," you say. "Give me companions so that I might not stray." Run on the road of God with those who are already running on it. You cannot have better companions on this road than those who have already been running on it for some time and who, on account of their considerable running experience and their familiarity with strenuous exercise, are not afraid of taking a wrong turn or of falling short.

"What, then, is the road (*uia*) of God," you ask, "and who are the runners on it?" "The ways (*uie*) of the Lord are right, and the righteous walk in them."[8] Righteousness, then, is the road and the righteous are those who run on it. And lest it bother you that I speak here of walkers and there of runners, [know that] walking quickly is the same as running, which he was doing who said, "I ran the road of your commandments,"[9] and elsewhere, "Blessed are the undefiled on the road, who walk in the law of the Lord."[10] He wrote these two lines not with the intention of declaring himself more blessed than the blessed—by describing them as walking and himself as running—but rather so that you would understand that walking and running are the same. Now you have the way, you have companions on the way, you have an inheritance in your native land (*patriam*); you have that by which you should proceed, those with whom you should go, that at which you should arrive [and] where you should rest. That by which you should proceed is righteousness; those with whom you should go are those who love and continually run after righteousness; that at which you should arrive and in whom you should rest is the Author of righteousness and the Fountain of life. No road is straighter than righteousness, no fellowship is better than that of the righteous, no rest is more tranquil than God. Proceed safely and quickly so that you might arrive soon and rest happily. To proceed with speed is to love ardently.

8. See, therefore, how your whole good depends on charity: by means of charity (*per caritatem*) you choose the road, by means of charity you run on the road, [and] by means of charity you arrive at your native land (*patriam*). Do you wish to know why you choose the road of righteousness by means of charity alone? "Whoever loves me," says the Lord, "will keep my word."[11] Of this same word it is said else-

where: "your word is truth."[12] And concerning truth the psalmist says, "I have chosen the way (*uiam*) of truth, I have not forgotten your judgments."[13] Therefore, if the word of the Lord is truth, the way (*uia*) of truth is certainly chosen by means of that charity whereby the word of the Lord is fulfilled. Consequently, charity chooses the road (*uiam*) of righteousness. But is it possible for the road of righteousness to be chosen and run without charity? Listen to the very same testimony of the psalmist that I called to mind above: "I ran the road of your commandments when you enlarged my heart."[14] But what is an enlarged heart except a heart inflamed with love (*amore feruens*), a heart filled with charity (*caritate impletum*)? By means of charity (*per caritatem*), then, the heart is enlarged and, the heart having been enlarged, the road of righteousness is run. And so you choose by means of charity, you run by means of charity, you take hold and you enjoy by means of charity. "God is charity," says John the apostle, "and whoever abides in charity abides in God and God in him."[15] He who has charity, therefore, has God, possesses God, [and] abides in God. O bountiful charity by means of which we love God, choose God, run to God, arrive at God, [and] possess God!

9. What more shall I say about you, charity? I have declared you our guide on the road of God; what if I also call you the very road of God itself? Certainly, charity, you are such a road, but you are a road unlike other roads. When the apostle Paul said, "Still I will show you a more excellent way (*uiam*),"[16] he indeed spoke of you, O charity. For you are the most excellent and most preeminent road which makes crooked roads straight (*uias distortas dirigens*) and makes straight roads known. You are the source of all straight roads: all straight roads go forth from you and come back into you. For the commandments of God, all of which hang on you and exist in you, are His roads. You are the fullness of righteousness, the perfection of the law, the consummation of virtue, the recognition of truth.

Therefore, you are a road, O charity. What kind of road are you? The most excellent one, which carries, directs (*dirigens*), and leads [the human] through [to God]. Whose road are you? You are the road of the human to God and the road of God to the human.

10. O happy road, which alone knows the traffic of our salvation! You lead God down to the human, [and] you direct (*dirigis*) the human to God. God descends when He comes to us; we ascend when we go to God. Yet neither God nor we are able to go to the other except through you. You are the mediator, uniting opposites, associating the

disconnected, and leveling in a certain way dissimilar things. You bring God low and lift us high. You draw God down to the lowest things and lift us up to the highest. And yet you do so in such a way that His descent is not abject (*abiecta*) but rather holy (*pia*), and our elevation is not proud but rather glorious. Therefore, you have great power, O charity, for you alone were able to draw God down from heaven to earth. O how powerful is your bond, whereby both God could be bound and the human, having been bound, broke the bonds of iniquity! I do not know if I am able to say anything greater in your praise than that you draw God down from heaven and elevate the human from earth to heaven. Your great virtue is that by means of you God is brought all the way down to earth and the human is exalted all the way up to heaven.

11. Contemplate God having been born of a woman, as an infant, swaddled with cloths, crying in a cradle, sucking the breasts. I see Him later seized, bound, wounded with scourges, crowned with thorns, spattered with spittle, pierced, fixed [to a cross] with nails, and given gall and vinegar to drink. First He suffered indignities, then dreadful things. And yet, if we look for the reason why He deigned to undergo those [indignities] and suffer those [dreadful things], we find none but charity alone. O charity, how much you are able to do! If you were so powerful where God was concerned, how much more powerful are you where the human is concerned? If God suffered such great things for the sake of the human, what will the human refuse to endure for the sake of God? But perhaps you conquer God more easily than the human. You are able to prevail over God more readily than over the human because the more blessed He is, the more obliged God is to be overcome by you. You knew this very well, which is why you first overcame God whom you could conquer more easily. Even after you compelled Him out of obedience to you to descend from the throne of His Father's majesty all the way down to take upon Himself the weaknesses of our own mortal state, you still had to contend with us rebels. You compelled Him, bound by your chains and wounded by your arrows, so that the human would be more ashamed to resist you when he saw how you had triumphed even over God. You wounded the Impassible One, you bound the Invincible One, you drew the Immutable One, you made the Eternal One mortal. You did all these things in order to soften our hard hearts and prick our insensitive affections so that they might shake off their own sluggishness and your arrows might more readily penetrate them.

12. Nor did you do this in vain, for many have been overcome in such a way by you. Many have already given you their hands. Many already bear your arrows driven into their breasts and long for them to be thrust in more deeply still. For they have been wounded delightfully and sweetly, and they are neither grieved by nor ashamed of having received your wounds. O charity, how great is your victory! First you wounded the One, and through Him subsequently you have overcome all.

13. O charity, I have praised you as much as I can, but I seriously wonder whether something more excellent still might be said in praise of you. For I do not know whether it is a greater thing to say that you are God or that you have overcome God. If the former is greater, then I will gladly and boldly declare concerning you: "God is charity, and whoever abides in charity abides in God and God in him."[17] Listen, O human, lest you still imagine that possessing charity is a very small thing: listen, because "God is charity." Can it be a small thing to have God abiding within you? It is such a great thing to possess charity, for God is charity. Charity alone has the distinct privilege that God is called it and is it: God cannot be so identified with any other [virtue]. For "God is humility" or "God is patience" is not said in the same way that "God is charity" is said. This is so because, although every virtue is the gift of God, only charity can be called not only the gift of God, but also God. Charity is the gift of God because the Holy Spirit is given by God to the faithful. On the other hand, charity is also God because the same Spirit is consubstantial and coeternal in the same divine nature with Him by whom He is given. God, therefore, grants the other gifts of grace even to those whom He condemns (reprobat). But He saves charity alone, as if it were He Himself, as the reward for those whom He loves (diligit) very much.

14. Charity, therefore, is the special fountain from which the stranger does not receive because, as we said, even those who are estranged from God on account of their wicked lives sometimes lay hold of the other gifts of grace, but an evil human cannot possess charity. On the other hand, whoever has charity is no longer a stranger to God, but he abides in God and God in him.[18] Charity is so intimately related to God that God refuses to make His dwelling where there is no charity. "If anyone loves me, [Jesus] says, he will keep my word and my Father will love him, and we will come to him and make our dwelling with him."[19] If, then, charity is with you, God comes to you and abides with you; [but] if you depart from charity, God also departs from you and does not

remain with you. If you have never had charity, God has never come to you nor dwelt with you. If you have abandoned the charity that you initially possessed, God has departed from you; [but] if you have remained in this initial charity, God is with you and remains with you.

15. Charity cures every weakness of the soul. Charity pulls up all vices by the roots. Charity is the source of all the virtues. Charity illumines the mind, purifies the conscience, delights the soul, [and] reveals God. Pride does not puff up the soul in which charity dwells, hatred does not ravage it, anger does not shatter it, unforeseen sadness does not shake it, greed does not blind it, gluttony does not inflame it, [and] luxury does not pollute it. It is always pure; it is always chaste, always calm, always happy, always conciliatory, always kind, always moderate, untroubled in adversity, restrained in prosperity, despising the world, loving God, producing its own advantages by loving the good works of all, gladly bestowing its own advantages on all, not fearing scarcity, not greatly desiring abundance. He in whom the charity of God dwells is always contemplating when he might arrive at God, when he might leave the world behind, when he might avoid temptation, [and] when he might find true peace. His heart is always lifted up and his desire is always elevated to heavenly things. Whatever he is doing—whether he is walking or sitting or working or resting—his heart does not depart from God. When he is silent, he is contemplating God; when he is speaking, he wishes to talk about nothing but God and what pertains to the love of God. By exhorting others to charity, he kindles himself and commends charity to all. He reveals to all, not only with his voice but also with his actions, how sweet is the love of God and how bitter and foul is the love of this world. He derides the glory of this world, denounces anxiety, and shows how foolish it is to have faith in things that pass away. He marvels at the blindness of men who love these things; he marvels that they did not long ago despise all these transitory and futile things. He thinks that what tastes sweet to him is sweet to all, that what he loves is pleasing to all, [and] that what he knows is obvious to all.

By these signs charity makes itself known and distinguishes those in whom it dwells, not only inwardly in the will but also outwardly in their behavior.

16. So much has already been said about charity, and yet still more could be said. But so much of what should be said cannot be said. What then, O good charity, beloved charity—what shall I say that is worthy of your merits? After the many great proclamations of your praise made

by our ancestors, my own insignificance certainly would not have dared to say anything about you if one had ever been able to speak sufficiently about you.

Flow into us, therefore, O sweet and pleasant charity. Enlarge our heart, expand our desire, unfold the inmost part of our mind, [and] amplify the dwelling place of our heart so that it can receive God as its guest and inhabitant. May our only Redeemer and Savior Jesus Christ the Son of God pour and lavishly distribute you in our hearts through His Holy Spirit so that He Himself with the Father might deign to come to us and make a dwelling in us, [Christ the Son] who with the same Father and the Holy Spirit lives and reigns, [one] God forever and ever. Amen.

NOTES

1   Ps. 33:9 (Vulg).
2   Gen. 4:2–8.
3   Gen. 12:1–4.
4   Rom. 8:35, 38–39.
5   Song of Songs 8:6.
6   Ps. 138:16 (Vulg).
7   Cf. Song of Songs 8:7.
8   Hos. 14:10 (Vulg).
9   Ps. 118:32 (Vulg).
10   Ps. 118:1 (Vulg).
11   John 14:23.
12   John 17:17.
13   Ps. 118:30 (Vulg).
14   Ps. 118:32 (Vulg).
15   1 John 4:16.
16   1 Cor. 12:31.
17   1 John 4:16.
18   Cf. 1 John 4:16.
19   John 14:23.

HUGH OF ST VICTOR

WHAT TRULY SHOULD BE LOVED?

INTRODUCTION BY HUGH FEISS OSB
TRANSLATION BY VANESSA BUTTERFIELD

INTRODUCTION

What Truly Should Be Loved? is a very brief, but intriguing summary of Hugh's understanding of love, and indeed of the human condition generally. This introduction will be divided into the same three parts into which the translation—following Roger Baron's Latin-French edition—is divided. References are to paragraph numbers.

1

Hugh begins by summarizing his teaching on love. In effect, he spells out the reasoning and longing that led Augustine to exclaim, "Our heart is restless until it rests in Thee!"[1] The logic of Hugh's argument in 1–2 is this:

(i)   A human being cannot help but love: she will love either herself or something outside herself.
(ii)   Happiness, the heart in possession of its deepest desire, will be found only in loving the perfect good.[2]
(iii)   The self is not a perfect good, nor is any created thing or combination of created things.
(iv)   God is the perfect good.
(v)   Therefore, the human being finds peace only in God.

This replicates the opening argument of *The Betrothal Gift*, announced in the question: "Tell me, please, my soul, what is it that you love above all things. I know love is your life and I know that you cannot be without love."[3]

Hugh says that the human heart and mind (*mens*) are made for love. In the second section (6), Hugh intimates the close interconnection

---

[1]   *Conf.* 1.1.1 (O'Donnell, 3): "fecisti nos ad te et inquietum est cor nostrum donec requiescat in te." For the restlessness of the human heart, see the articles in *Communio* 34:2 (2007).
[2]   Hugh seems to take it as given that there is only one perfect good.
[3]   *Arrha* 5 (Sicard, 227–28; tr. Feiss, VTT 2:205).

between faith and love; faith steers love toward the heart's delight. (One is reminded of "Self," an interlocutor in *The Betrothal Gift of the Soul*.) Hugh is not doing technical analysis of the makeup of the human person, but speaking about the deepest longings and relations of the self, using two words that are vague enough to encompass all its dimensions, though "mind" refers more directly to thought and "heart" more to will and affectivity.

Although in this life the human mind finds itself unable to be completely at peace in the love of God, it should become more practiced in focusing on God's wondrous works and so less unstable, until finally by God's grace it will become perfectly stable in heaven (3). This is an interesting prescription for stability of heart: practice focusing on "the works of God and his wonders," while restraining vain thoughts. Hugh's *On the Three Days* is an example of how to do that. Viewed as God's wondrous works, things are symbols, windows even, leading to God in whom true rest lies.

2

Hugh then illustrates striving for greater stability by a brief allegory (*exemplum*). We are to think of ourselves in a stormy sea, where the tide pulls us here and there. This is a theme frequently sounded in Hugh's writings. For example, Book One of Hugh's *On Vanity* contains a series of vignettes describing various forms of earthly happiness, e.g., marriage, a school, a rich man's house, each of which is followed by a sketch of what happens when that source of happiness becomes a source of misery. In the first of these vignettes, Hugh describes some sailors guiding their ship across a serene, sunlit sea. They banquet amid music; even the fish gather to rejoice. Then the picture fades, replaced by a scene of storm and shipwreck.[4] The sailors become food for those same fish.

The dialogue between teacher and inquirer (or reason and the soul) in Book Two of *On Vanity* begins by comparing time to a great stream that leads downward to death and asks, Where now are all the earthly

---

4   *Vanitate* 1 (PL 176.705C–706B).

goods of times past?[5] Later, the inquirer says the teacher has impressed him with three new ideas. The first is that

> this whole world with all the things in it is flowing past like cascading waters, whose flood and changing currents we may compare either to a flood sweeping all before it or to a great sea—reality is very much like that.[6]

Faith provides a boat, in which we can try to focus on things above, while we avoid being dragged down by earthly things, turning to the things of the world only to meet our needs (4). The notion of things that meet our needs is important in Hugh's theology. Sin has left humankind ignorant, sinful, and needy. Divine revelation taught and received in faith counters ignorance, the discipline of virtue corrects the sinful will, and the mechanical or useful arts supply human needs.[7] We can think of three possible situations in which human beings may find themselves. One person does not believe in eternal things and desires only passing things; he is like a man overboard in the roaring sea. Another believes in eternal goods, but loves transitory things; he is on the ship but is headed for shipwreck. A third person believes in eternal goods and focuses his love on them. He is secure on the ship, like the solid land, and firmly set in the stormy sea (5). Thus, our faith builds a ship and our love dwells in it. In a mutual indwelling, the law of God dwells in our hearts by faith, while by love we dwell in God's law (6). Again, this echoes *On Vanity*, when it continues with the second new thing the inquirer has learned from the teacher:

> The second is that the human heart, lifting itself from these passing and changeable things, and gradually collecting itself into one so that where it is closest to mutable things it seems like that part of the ark that is borne by the flood from below, but where it approaches closer

---

5   "Where are they?" ("Ubi sunt?") is a widely used convention or topos for the transitory character and vanity of earthly goods and pleasures; for example, the medieval student song *Gaudeamus igitur*: "Where are those who were before us in the world?" ("Ubi sunt qui ante nos in mundo fuere?")

6   "universus mundus iste cum omnibus que in eo sunt in modum decurrentium aquarum praeterfluens, cujus inundationes et motus mutabilitatis sive diluvio omnia occupanti sive mari magno comparemus res ipsa simillima" (PL 176.714AB). All translations are the author's. For an alternative (and generally excellent) translation of much of *On Vanity*, Books I and II, see Hugh of Saint-Victor, *Selected Spiritual Writings*, tr. A Religious of C.S.M.V. (New York: Harper & Row, 1962), 157–82.

7   See, for example, *Didasc.* 1.5 (Buttimer, 12; tr. Taylor, 51–52); *Didasc.* 2.1 (Buttimer, 24–25; tr. Taylor, 62).

to eternal and immutable things it appears in some way to be united and collected into one.[8]

3

Hugh concludes by giving guidance about how to build the ship or ark in the heart. He says one should consider God's two great works of creation and restoration. The first brought the universe into existence in six days; the second, centered on Christ, provides the medicines that save us. The theme of the two works of God is central to Hugh's theology. It is sounded at the beginning of his *On the Sacraments*:

> For there are two works which contain everything that is made. The first is the work of creation. The second is the work of restoration. The work of creation is that by which it happens that things that were not came to be. The work of restoration is that by which it comes about that the things that had perished are made better. For the work of creation (*opus conditionis*) is the creation (*creatio*) of the world with all its elements. The work of restoration is the Incarnation of the Word with all his sacraments; either those that preceded from the beginning of the world, or those that follow until the end of the world.[9]

So, to build an ark of faith in one's heart, one should study the two works of God or, perhaps, Hugh's thought about them.

A second interesting aspect of Hugh's directives for building the ark of faith is the parallel he draws between the six days of creation and the six ages of the world. Augustine developed the notion that the history of the world is divided into six ages: from Adam to Noah, from Noah

---

[8]   "Secundum est cor humanum ab his transitoriis et mutabilibus se erigens et paulatim colligens se in unum ut ubi mutabilibus proximum est, ibi quasi arca deorsum in fundo latum appareat, coadunantur autem et quodammodo in unum colligatur, ubi magis aeternis et immutabilibus appropinquat" (PL 176.714B).

[9]   *Sacr.* 1, prol. 1: "Duo enim sunt opera in quibus universa continentur quae facta sunt. Primum est opus conditionis. Secundum est opus restaurationis. Opus conditionis est quo factum est ut essent quae non erant. Opus restaurationis est quo factum est ut melius essent quae perierant. Ergo opus conditionis est creatio mundi cum omnibus elementis suis. Opus restaurationis est incarnatio Verbi cum omnibus sacramentis suis, sive iis que praecesserunt ab initio saeculi sive iis que subsequuntur usque ad finem mundi" (PL 176.183AB). For an alternate translation see Hugh of St Victor, *On the Sacraments of the Christian Faith (De sacramentis)*, tr. Roy J. Deferrari (Cambridge, MA: Mediaeval Academy of America, 1951). See also, *Vanitate* 2 (PL 176.716C); *Archa Noe* 4.3 (Sicard, 92–94).

to Abraham, from Abraham to David, from David to the Babylonian Captivity, from the Babylonian Captivity to the First Coming of Christ, from the First Coming of Christ to his Second Coming.[10] Hugh follows this division.[11]

Adding a different twist to the various distinctions he makes in his treatise *On the Ark of Noah*, but echoing a passage in *On Vanity*, Hugh says that the three decks of the ark symbolize how God did some of these works without intermediaries, some through angels, and some through the works of human beings.

Then he concludes by saying that the supreme *cubitus* is God, the author of all things. The obvious reference of *cubitus* is to the top of the mast that Hugh places on Noah's ark in his depiction of it. The drawing of the top of the mast is the first thing Hugh describes in his *Little Book*. Christ is at the very center of the ark as Alpha and Omega of all salvation and salvation history.[12] Hugh is making an unmistakable, if indirect, reference to his book on Noah's ark[13] However, here he alters the symbolism of the cubit: instead of standing for Christ, it stands for God, the supreme author of all things. This is in keeping with the theocentric (and not even explicitly Trinitarian) focus of most of *What Truly Should Be Loved?*

Unlike the ark treatises, in which the individual Christian is given a rich ecclesial and sacramental template on which to chart his growth in Christ, in *What Truly Should Be Loved?* the individual reader is set

---

[10] *De catechizandis rudibus* 22.39 (Combès and Farges, 116–17); *Civ. Dei* 22.30 (Dombart and Kalb, 865); Augustine, *Div. quaest. 83*, 58.2 (PL 40.43). The idea of the six ages of the world was often used after Augustine; e.g., Isidore, *Etym.* 1.5.38 (Lindsay [Oxford: Oxford University Press, 1911], online version: LacusCurtius, http://penelope.uchicago.edu/Thayer/e/roman/texts/isidore/home.html.

[11] *Libellus* 2 (Sicard, 131, 126–32, 138); *Script.* 17 (PL 175.24AB); *Sacr.* 2.6.8 (PL 176.454D–455D); *Misc.* 1.82 (PL 177.517C), where Hugh brings the six ages of the world into relationship with the six ages of a human being ("infantia," "pueritia," "adolescentia," "juventus," "virilis aetas," "senectus"). On these six ages of the world and of human life, see Joachim Ehlers, *Hugo von St. Viktor: Studien zum Geschichtsdenken und Geschichtsschreibung des 12. Jahrhunderts*, Frankfurter historische Abhandlungen 7 (Wiesbaden: Steiner, 1973), 140–51. On the six days of creation, see also *Sent. div.* prol. (Piazzoni, 920; tr. Evans, VTT 1:120); 3 (Piazzoni, 932–36; tr. Evans, VTT 1:133–36).

[12] *Libellus* 1 (Sicard, 121–23).

[13] Baron, in Hugues de Saint-Victor, *Six opuscules*, 30, 99, transltes "cubitus" as "siège," "seat" or "headquarters." There are two similar Latin words: (1) the second declension noun "cubitus" (m.) or cubitum (n.) meaning "cubit," and (2) the fourth declension noun, "cubitus," meaning "lying down" or "couch." It seems much more likely that here "cubitus" means "cubit." Baron may have been misled by a passage in *Vanitate* 2 (PL 176.719D–720A), where at the end of a thorough tour of the house (ark) one reaches the throne of the king ("solium regis").

in relation to God rather than to his fellow Christians. He finds stability in the ark of faith, not explicitly in the ark of the sacramental Church and its mysteries. However, by referring to the second work of God, the work of restoration, Hugh does point in the direction of Christ and the mysteries that flow from him. For the most part, though, Hugh speaks here of love and its disciplines with reference to the individual's relation to God.

Hugh's message in the final section dovetails with the third new lesson that the inquirer in *On Vanity* drew from the teacher's instruction:

> Then you place God on the third and highest place, so that God like a steersman directs, and like an anchor holds fast, and like a harbor receives the ark of the human heart, resting on the fluctuating sea beneath it. So I saw these three: at the bottom, this world like a flood; in the middle, the human heart like an ark; and at the top, God like a steersman.[14]

CONCLUSION

In this little work—*What Truly Should Be Loved?*—there are no quotations from the Bible, and the only allegory is that connected with the ark. Augustine's influence is pervasive, in particular the need to love something, the search for happiness, the three levels of reality,[15] the distinction between transitory and eternal goods, and the use of *in idipsum*. In less than 1000 words, Hugh manages to allude to and even briefly summarize his *On Vanity, On the Sacraments, The Ark of Noah, The Little Book on Forming the Ark,* his other treatises on love, and perhaps even *On the Three Days.*

The most intriguing questions are, why did Hugh write this little work and for whom? Various possibilities come to mind. Hugh may

---

[14]   *Vanitate* 2: "Deinde in supremo et tertio loco Deum constituis, ut arcam cordis humani deorsum huic fluctuanti salo insidentem, et quasi gubernator dirigat, et quasi anchora teneat, et quasi portus excipiat. Video itaque haec tria imo quasi diluvium quoddam mundum istum, in medio quasi arcam quamdam cor humanum, in supremo quasi gubernatorem Deum" (PL 176.714BC).

[15]   On these themes, see the references in Vernon Bourke, ed., *The Essential Augustine* (New York: Mentor, 1964) and Etienne Gilson, *The Christian Philosophy of St Augustine* (New York: Random House, 1960): the need to love something (Gilson, 135), the search for happiness (Bourke, 151–53; Gilson, 3–10), the three levels of reality (Bourke, 43–65).

have written it as a present for his students, as a memento of when he had discussed with them the contents of his writings. Or perhaps he had to give a sermon or brief talk on short notice, so he scribbled some quick notes, drawing ideas from books that he had written or was writing or re-writing, or was planning to write, and then later shaped those notes into an essay. Again, maybe toward the end of his life he was reminiscing and wrote this little meditation incorporating the ideas that shaped and animated his teaching and writing.

Whatever the occasion for its composition, this brief text, more essay than sermon, is a unique summary of some of Hugh's central ideas that structure the writings that he has left us. His life and his writings offer an answer to the question, "What Truly Should Be Loved?"

A Note on Chronology

In *On Vanity* (PL 176.717D) Hugh mentions an earlier work he had written, *On the Ark*. In his *Little Book on Forming the Ark* (ed. Sicard, 143, lines 115–16), Hugh writes that he has produced a book called *On the Three Days*. Using these references and the arguments on chronology developed by Sicard,[16] we can form a relative chronology of some of Hugh's works and assign some dates, though the individual elements of this reconstruction have varying degrees of probability:

1120/25	*On the Three Days* (*De tribus diebus*)[17]
1126–27	*On the Ark of Noah* (*De archa Noe*)
1127	*Sentences on Divinity* (*Sententie de divinitate*)
	On Sacred Scriptures and Their Authors (*De scripturis et scriptoribus sacris*)
1128–29	First redaction of the *Little Book on the Formation of the Ark* (*Libellus*)
	Dialogue on the Sacraments of the Natural Law (*Dialogus de sacramentis naturalis legis*)
	On the Vanity of the World (*De vanitate mundi*)

---

[16] Patrice Sicard, *Diagrammes médiévaux et exégèse visuelle: Le Libellus de formatione arche de Hugues de Saint-Victor*. Bibliotheca Victorina 4 (Turnhout: Brepols, 1993) 119–38.

[17] The first date is the early one proposed by Poirel; see the introduction to *On the Three Days* in volume one of this series. Sicard places the date for *On the Three Days* as after 1123, about 1125.

The work that bears the closest resemblance to *What Truly Should Be Loved?* is *On Vanity*. So close are the two works that it seems probable, though by no means certain, that *On Vanity* was written before or contemporaneously with *What Truly Should Be Loved?* That would place the date of composition of the latter somewhere close to 1130.

TITLE

"Quid vere diligendum est" ("What Truly Should be Loved") is the title that Baron gives the work in Hugues de Saint-Victor, *Six opuscules spirituels*, SC 155 (Paris: Cerf, 1969), 94–99. There Baron edits it from two manuscripts: Vatican, Reg. lat. 167 and Laon, BM 173. The text appears twice in Migne's *Patrologia latina*: PL 177.563D–565A (*Misc.* 1.171), and, conflated with *De substantia amoris,* among the works of [Pseudo-] Augustine, PL 40.846–48, where it is missing the last sentence. In the manuscripts it is given various titles, such as "De vere [*sic*] amore et quod sine amore cor vivere non possit" (Paris BN 2530, fol. 105ra, cited by Baron, *Six opuscules*, 29). Hitherto, the title has been translated in the indicative: "[This is] What Truly Should Be Loved." Grammatically and rhetorically, it seems better to translate it as a question: "What Truly Should Be Loved?"

[1]

1. The life of the heart is love, and for that reason it is utterly impossible for the heart that desires to live to be without love. Consider what follows from this. If, then, the human mind[1] is not able to be without love, it is necessary either that it loves itself or certainly that it loves something else. Because it does not find perfect good in itself, if it loves itself only, its love cannot be happy.[2] Therefore, it is necessary that if it desires to love happily, it should seek something other than itself to love.

2. If, however, it begins to love an imperfect thing outside of itself, it stirs up its own love, but does not drive away misery. Therefore, it does not love happily until it turns itself (*se convertit*)[3] toward the true and highest good through the desire of love. Because the highest and true good is God, he alone loves happily who loves God, and the more he loves the happier he is.[4] Therefore, this is the repose of our heart: when it is made firm in love of God through desire and does not hunger after something further, but rejoices with a certain happy security in that to which it clings. Because its appetite does not extend beyond it and fear does not drive it back, it rests, as it were, in the very reality (*in idipsum*)[5] of pleasure without vexation.

3. Because of its weakness, the human mind cannot always, but only infrequently, be fixed on that sweetness of divine contemplation. Meanwhile, through a certain effort, it will become accustomed to that stability to which it is not yet able to attain; that is, if we cannot always think about God, let us at least—by restraining our heart from illicit and vain thoughts—continue to consider the works of God and his wonders so that, while we are trying to be always less unstable, finally—at sometime, by God's grace—we can become truly stable.

[2]

4. However, let me furnish an example of this advancing for you. This whole world is, so to speak, a kind of flood, because—by fluctuat-

ing with uncertain results—all the things that are in this world cascade down like water. However, true faith, which does not promise transitory things but eternal things, lifts the mind (*animum*) from desire of this world to desire of heavenly things, as though from a kind of storm. The waters can, to be sure, carry it; but it cannot be totally immersed because it uses this world according to necessity, but it is not entangled through affection by the desires of the world.

5. Therefore, the force of the running water drags with it, as though in the storm without a ship, whoever does not believe in eternal things, but only desires the things that are passing. But he who believes in eternal things and loves transitory things, this person takes the ship into a shipwreck.[6] However he who both believes in eternal goods and loves them goes safely through the waves of the fluctuating sea in a ship. And since, because of his faith's desire, he does not leave the ship, he already represents, as it were, the stability of the earth in the midst of storms.

6. Therefore if we want to cross this great sea unharmed, let us first build a ship so that we may have sound faith; then we must inhabit the ship of faith through love, so that we may both believe what we ought to love and love what we believe. Thus, the law of God will be in our heart through knowledge of upright faith, and our heart will be in the law of God through love.

[3]

7. But so that you may more easily know how and from what you ought to build this ship or ark in your heart—through which, after having been led from the shipwreck of this flood, you may arrive at a quiet harbor—consider the two works of God, namely the work of creation and the work of restoration. The work of creation is the creation of heaven and earth and of all that they contain. They were made in six days. But the work of restoration is the Incarnation of the Word and all things that, from the beginning of the world up to the end, either preceded to foretell it, or will follow to confirm it. All of these occurred in six ages.[7] But the works of restoration are more pertinent to the Catholic faith. For that reason the saints love them more, because they recognize in them the medicines of their salvation.

8. However, God is producing these things in part through human beings, in part through angels, and in part through himself—so that in

the spiritual ark the lowest deck[8] is the works of human beings, the second is the works of the angels, the third is the works of God,[9] and the supreme cubit is God, the creator of the universe.[10]

NOTES

1   Although Hugh began by writing of the human heart ("cor"), "mens" (a feminine noun) is the subject for most of the first section, until Hugh changes the subject to "we" and "heart" near the end of par. 3. "Mens" is a very broad term; it can be translated as mind, heart, disposition, conscience, reason, intention, and so on; it can even be translated as "person" in the non-technical sense of the term as used in contemporary speech. Here it is translated as "mind" and referred to as "it."

2   For the next few sentences, Hugh uses some closely related words for happiness ("felicitas"): "feliciter," "felicius," and "felix." He may be deliberately avoiding "beatitudo" and "beatus," which suggest the full and eternal beatitude of heaven.

3   The notion of conversion toward the good has roots both in the biblical teaching about conversion of heart and in the Neoplatonic idea that each stage in the emanation from the One turns back toward the One by contemplating the stage above it.

4   Hugh is here adopting the Augustinian idea that the human being occupies a middle place below God above and above the world below. See, for example, the texts from the writings of St Augustine assembled in Vernon J. Burke, ed., *The Essential Augustine* (New York: Mentor, 1964), 43–62; Hugh of St Victor, *Vanitate* 2 (PL 176.713C–714D); *Arca* 4.2 (Sicard, 90.28–31).

5   "in idipsum": "in(to) the selfsame." The phrase occurs in a number of places in the Latin Bible. In some of those passages, notably in Ps. 4:9 (Vulg.), it can be taken to refer to God: "in pace in id ipsum dormiam et requiescam" ("I will sleep and rest on peace unto it itself"). This verse was set to music by several Renaissance composers (e.g., John Sheppard [1515–58] and Thomas Tallis [1505–85]). However, the most important occurrence is Ps. 121:3 (Vulg.): "Ierusalem quae aedificatur ut civitas. Cuius participatio eius in idipsum" The Douai-Rheims translation renders this, "Jerusalem, which is built as a city which is compact together." Augustine commented on this verse in his *Enarratio* on Ps. 121:3 (Dekkers and Fraipont, 1805): "What is '*idipsum*'? What is always the same; what is not now one thing and now another? It is what is eternal, for what is always one-way-and-another is not [truly in being] because it does not stay the same. It is not completely non-existing, but it does not exist supremely. And what is it that [fully] is, if not he who when he sent Moses, said to him: 'I am who I am'? . . . Hold fast to the flesh of Christ . . . So that you may be made a sharer '*in idipsum*,' as he earlier became a sharer in you, that is, the Word became flesh" ("Quid est 'idipsum'? Quod semper eodem modo est; quod non modo aliud, et modo aliud est? Quod aeternum est. Nam quod semper atque aliter aliter est, non est, quia non manet; non omnino non est, sed non summe est. Et quid est quod est, nisi ille qui quando mittebat Moysen, dixit illi: 'Ego sum qui sum'? . . . Retine carnem Christi . . . Ut autem efficiaris tu particeps in idipsum, factus est ipse prior particeps tui, et Verbum caro factum est").

6   In *Vanitate* 2 (PL 176.713BC), Hugh writes: "Think, then, that those who love this world are like shipwrecked sailors who are plunged into the depths of the sea and pulled down under" ("Deinde cogita amatores hujus mundi quasi quosdam naufragos qui mersi in hujus salis profundo deorsum rapiuntur"). Cf. *Archa Noe* 2.1 (Sicard, 34.48–49).

7   See the introduction to this work.

8   "mansio": in Roman times, an official stopping point for those traveling on a road. More generally it meant a dwelling or house. Although there is no warrant for it in standard Latin dictionaries (Lewis and Short; Niemyer; Blaise), it is here translated as "deck." *Selected Spiritual Writings* translates it as "storey." "First" (*prima*) is rendered as "lowest," because that is clearly what Hugh intended.

9   *Archa Noe* 4.9 (Sicard, 115.103–8); cf. *Tribus rerum* (Buttimer, 134.4–5; 135.5–7).

10   *Arca Noe* 1.5 (Sicard, 24.27–30); *Libellus* 1 (Sicard, 121–36).

HUGH OF ST VICTOR

SOLILOQUY ON THE BETROTHAL-GIFT OF THE SOUL

INTRODUCTION AND TRANSLATION
BY HUGH FEISS OSB

INTRODUCTION

THE COVERING LETTER: DATE AND RECIPIENTS

The *Soliloquy on the Betrothal-Gift of the Soul* (*Soliloquium de arrha animae*) is addressed to Brother G. and the other brothers of Hamersleben.[1] St Pancraz at Hamersleben was a monastery of canons regular originally founded in 1108 by the reforming bishop Reinhard of Halberstadt (1107–1123), who took office after a period of unrest and decline following the death of the vigorous bishop Burchard II (1059–88). Bishop Reinhard wanted the monastery to serve as a catalyst to improve the quality of his clergy. The monastery was originally located at Osterwieck, about 17 miles northeast of Halberstadt. Because the peace of the cloister was disturbed by the noise of the neighboring market, the monastery was soon moved to Hamersleben, 13 miles north of Halberstadt, where it remained until it was suppressed in 1804. At Hamersleben, as at Osterwieck, the canons were responsible for the pastoral care of the parish church. The noble lady Thietburg and her daughter Matilda endowed the community with a rich gift of land. The monastery became an important institution in its rural setting and in turn founded several other monasteries.[2]

By at least 1112, the provost of the community was Thietmar. During his long term of office, he tried unsuccessfully to create a congregation of canons regular in the region. Thietmar died while visiting Rome late in 1138. There is no reference to the next abbot, Siegfrid, until 1140. It has been conjectured that the "beloved brother, G.," was Günther, who

---

[1]   This covering letter has been analyzed by Ludwig Ott, *Untersuchungen zur theologische Brief-literatur der Frühscholastik unter besonderer Berücksichtigung des viktoriner Kreises*, BG-PTMA 34 (Münster: Aschendorff, 1937), 348–538; F. E. Croydon, "Notes on the Life of Hugh of St Victor," *JTS* 46 (1939): 234; Jerome Taylor, *The Origin and Early Life of Hugh of St Victor: An Evaluation of the Tradition*, Texts and Studies in the History of Mediaeval Education, 5 (Notre Dame, IN: University of Notre Dame Press, 1957): 54–57; Roger Baron, "Notes bi-ographiques sur Hugues de Saint-Victor," *Revue d'histoire ecclésiastique* 51 (1956): 920–34.

[2]   Karlotto Bogumil, *Das Bistum Halberstadt im 12. Jahrhundert*, Mitteldeutsche Forschungen 69 (Cologne: Böhlau, 1972): 107–13, 196–98.

had traveled to Rome with Thietmar and may have served as interim superior of the monastery until a new abbot was elected.[3] Most scholars now agree that Hugh was a native of Saxony, whose uncle, also named Hugh, accompanied the young Hugh to France and on the way secured relics of St Victor at Marseilles. These relics he donated to the Parisian abbey with a large sum of money, when he and his nephew joined the community.[4] This occurred a year or two

[3]   Sicard, *Oeuvre* 2:214–15, 284, n. 1, who cites E. Böhmer, "Hugo de Sancto Victore," *Damaris* (Stettin, 1864) 222–64. According to Croydon, "Notes," 234, Thietmar, as provost, with two priests, Günther and Adelbert, witnessed a charter for a monastery at Halberstadt in AD 1133. A newly discovered manuscript of Hugh's *Soliloquy* names the recipient as Gunterus: see Paul Rorem, *Hugh of St Victor* (New York: Oxford University Press, 2009), 209 note 1.

[4]   On the much discussed question of Hugh of St Victor's nationality and origins, see the summaries Sicard, *Hugues de Saint-Victor et son école* (Turnhout: Brepols, 1991), 13–17, and Dominique Poirel, "*Hugo Saxo*. Les origins germaniques de la pensée d'Hugues de Saint-Victor," *Francia. Forschungen zur westeuropäischen Geschichte* 33/1 (2006): 163–69, where the relevant sources are cited. Among the most important of the earlier studies are Croydon, "Notes," 232–53; Taylor, *Origin*, and Jürgen Miethke, "Zur Herkunft Hugos von St. Viktor," *Archiv für Kulturgeschichte* 54 (1972): 241–61. Evidence for Hugh's Saxon origins and his uncle's association with St Victor is provided by two entries in the necrology of St Victor, cited by Taylor, *Origin*, 59–60 from Bonnard, 1:95 (for the first of them, see also PL 175.clxiii): February 11: "Anniversarium solemne pie memorie magistri Hugonis, a primario iuventutis sue flore in hac domo nostra servitio Dei seipsum tradens celestis sapientie donum celitus sibi datum tam excellenter accepit ut in tota latina ecclesia nullus ei in sapientia posit comparabilis inveniri. . . . De quo et illud specialiter memorie tradere volumus quod beati Victoris reliquias multo labore quesitas multa difficultate impetratas ab urbe Massilia ad nos detulit" ("The solemn anniversary of Master Hugh of loving memory, who dedicated himself from the first flowering of his youth to the service of God in this our house. He received so excellently the gift of heavenly wisdom given him from on high that in the whole Latin Church no one could be found comparable to him in wisdom. . . . We would like especially to recall that he brought to us from the city of Marseilles the relics of Blessed Victor sought with much labor and received after much entreating"). May 5: "Anniversarium solemne bone memorie Hugonis sacerdotis, Halberstadensis ecclesie archidiaconi, qui de Saxonia ad nos venit, magistrum Hugonem nepotem suum sequutus, ecclesie nostre canonicum; quique habitum regularem in nostra ecclesia suscipiens, in ea laudabilem vitam consummavit. Hic rebus suis magnifice satis locum nostrum ampliavit in auro et argento et vestibus pretiosis, tapetibus et cortinis, et alia supellectili varia. De quo hoc specialiter commendare et memorie tradere volumus quod eius sumptibus et impensis huius ecclesie nostre edificum factum et constructum est" ("Solemn anniversary of the happy memory of Hugh, a priest, archdeacon of the church of Halberstadt, who came to us from Saxony, following his nephew, Master Hugh, a canon of our church; receiving the regular habit in our church, he completed his praiseworthy life in it. Here with his goods he endowed our monastery magnificently with gold, silver, precious vestments, tapestries, carpets, and various other coverings. We wish especially to commend and remember that the building of our church was constructed at his expense"). See Adam of St Victor's sequence for the liturgical feast commemorating the reception of St Victor's relics at the abbey, "Ex radice caritatis," 26.7–9 (Grosfillier, 357): "Pars istius nobis data / per fideles est allata / ab urbe Massilia" ("A part of the saint has been given to us; / it was brought by the faithful / from the city of Marseilles").

after 1113, the year when, five years after the founding of St Victor of Paris, William of Champeaux left it to become bishop of Châlons-en-Champagne.

If, as seems probable, Hugh received his early education at Hamersleben, he was personally acquainted with some of the members of the community. Although twelfth-century letters could be quite effusive,[5] the tone of personal affection in the covering letter for the *Soliloquy* seems to be more than literary convention.[6] Hence, it is reasonable to think that Hugh wrote the covering letter to the community at St Pancraz at Hamersleben when the community was adjusting to the death of its long-time leader. If all this is so, and the letter and *Soliloquy* were written at the same time,[7] they are among Hugh's last writ-

---

[5]   See the discussion of "letters of friendship" in Jean Leclercq, *Love of Learning and the Desire for God*, tr. Catharine Misrahi (New York: Fordham University Press, 1974), pp. 226–28. Examples would include the letters Anselm wrote from Bec and much of Pierre de Celle's correspondence. For salutation forms in particular, see Carol Dana Lanham, *Salutation Formulas in Latin Letters to 1200*, Münchener Beiträge zur Mediävistik und Renaissance-Forschung 22 (Munich: Arbeo, 1975).

[6]   Just before the final termination of the letter, Hugh adds a common disclaimer: he does not wish to stir up the recipients with rhetorical flourishes. Nevertheless, the *Soliloquy* is Hugh's most perfectly crafted literary work, and he is not unaware of this. Authors who have studied Hugh's style include L. Negri, "Lettura stilistica di Ugo di San Vittore, 'De arrha animae,'" *Convivium* 24 (1956): 129–40; R. Baron, *Études sur Hugues de Saint-Victor* (N.p.: Desclée de Brouwer, 1967); V. Liccaro, *Studi sulla visione del mondo di Ugo di S. Vittore*, Università degli Studi di Trieste, Facoltà di magistero, 12 (Udine: Del Bianco, 1969), 79–84. Hugh tells why the style and emotion of the letter are so striking: "I could not hide my feeling of devotion toward you." *Devotio* toward God is for Hugh the heart of prayer: a turning to God with sentiments of love and humility (*Virtute orandi* [PL 176.979B]). For those who nourished one's first steps in religious life and in learning, a feeling of devotion, of love and humility, would be most appropriate. Hugh concludes the letter:
      Greet Brother B. and Brother A., and all the others, all of whose names I hope are written in the book of life, even if I am not able to enumerate them one by one in the present [letter].
It may well be that in the quarter century that intervened between Hugh's departure from Hamersleben and the writing of the *Soliloquy* all but three of the canons he had known in the Saxon community had died or moved elsewhere. The community at Hamersleben was founded only in 1108. Membership of a religious community was likely to be both small and unstable in its early years.

[7]   One can at least conclude that the letter was carefully designed to echo the contents of the *Soliloquy*. Having specified the title, "I have sent Your Charity a soliloquy of love, entitled *On the Betrothal-Gift of the Soul*," Hugh indicates that the purpose of the work is that "you may learn where you should seek true love and how you should arouse your hearts to heavenly joys by zealous spiritual meditations." Then he anticipates one of the central contentions of the *Soliloquy*, that singular love for one is compatible with singular love for all: "Dearest brother, I ask this of you, that you receive this with the rest in memory of me, not that what is specially sent to you excludes the rest, nor that what is commonly given to all diminishes the prerogative of the gift." The phrase "in memory of me" echoes Christ's words at the in-

ing, since he died in 1141. It certainly seems very likely that the *Soliloquy* was written after the *Praise of the Bridegroom*, whose distinction between common and special gifts the *Soliloquy* expands to include the third category of singular gifts.[8]

MANUSCRIPTS

The *Soliloquy on the Betrothal-Gift of the Soul* was Hugh's most popular spiritual work. There are extant over 500 Latin manuscripts. That over 125 of these manuscripts date from the fifteenth century and over 75 from the fourteenth is testimony to Hugh's continuing popularity in the later Middle Ages.[9]

TRANSLATIONS

The *Soliloquy* was often translated into the vernacular during the Middle Ages. An Old Norse translation,[10] fourteenth-century Spanish and Italian translations, and fifteenth-century Catalan and French translations have been published. The published French translation, begun by Pierre Crapillet (d. 1460) and completed by a less qualified successor after Crapillet's death, was preceded by three French translations of the fourteenth century and two fifteenth-century abridgments. The only one of these that is complete, that of Pierre de Hangest (d. 1349), survives in eight manuscripts. Crapillet's translation was also

---

stitution of the Eucharist at the Last Supper (1 Cor. 11:24; "First Eucharistic Prayer," Roman Canon). If this letter and gift are Hugh's last farewell, he may know that his days on earth are coming to a close and wish to leave a final token of his love for the community where he spent his early years as a student and a religious.

[8] Damien van den Eynde, *Essai sur la succession et la date des écrits de Hugues de Saint-Victor*, Spicilegium Pontificium Athenaeum Antonianum 13 (Rome: Pontificium Athenaeum Antonianum, 1960), 106–8; Roger Baron, *Études sur Hugues de Saint-Victor*, 84–85, 87. Van den Eynde, compares *Praise of the Bridegroom* 3 (PL 176.987CD) with *Soliloquy* 36–37 (PL 176.961AB), 54–55 (PL 176.965AB), and 59–60 (PL 176.966BC).

[9] Goy, *Überlieferung der Werke Hugos von St. Viktor*, 278–328, lists 327 manuscripts. Christopher Evans' research indicates that there are at least 500 Latin manuscripts of the work.

[10] Gunnar Hardarson, *Littérature et spiritualité en Scandinavie médiévale: La traduction norroise du De arrha animae de Hugues de Saint-Victor*, Bibliotheca Victorina 5 (Turnhout: Brepols, 1995). His edition is based on three Old Norse manuscripts.

followed by two further fifteenth-century abridgments. There was a medieval German translation as well.[11]

EDITIONS

The *Soliloquium de arrha animae* was first printed separately[12] in 1473.[13] The *Soliloquium* appeared in Clichtove's edition of Hugh's *opuscula* (*Opera*, Paris: H. Stephanus, 1506) and in the collections of Hugh's *Opera omnia* edited by J. Borderius, 3 vols. (Paris: Jodocus Badius Ascensius and Joannes Parvus, 1526), Thomas Garzoni de Bagnacaballo, 3 vols. (Venice: J. B. Somaschum, 1588), J. Volmari, revision of Garzoni de Bagnacaballo's edition, 3 vols. in one (Mainz: A. Hierat, 1617), and the 1648 edition of Rouen (Rothomagi: J. Berthelin, 1648), which was used by Migne in the *Patrologia latina*. Karl Müller published an edition in 1913, based on a very small manuscript base.[14] Patrice Sicard

---

[11]   For some manuscripts of the Italian, French, and German translations, see Goy, *Überlieferung der Werke Hugos von St. Viktor*, 501–4. According to Vincenzo Liccaro, *Studi sulla visione*, 80 note 83, the Italian translation was published as *Soliloquio* (Florence, 1919) from Florence, B.M. codex Pal. 161. The Spanish translation was edited by Luis Getino, *Dialogo de las arras del alma. Traducción del siglo XIV códice de Santo Domingo el Real de Madrid*, Biblioteca clásica Dominicana 16 (Salamanca: Fides, 1925). The Catalan translation by Antoni Canals (d. 1419) was edited by Martí de Riquer, *Scipió e Anibal; De providència (de Sèneca). De arrha de ànima (d'Hug de Sant-Víctor)*, Els nostres clàssics: obres completes dels excriptors catalans medievals, colecció A, 49 (Barcelona: Barcino, 1935). For the French translations, see Robert Bultot and Geneviève Hasenoehr, eds., *Pierre Crapillet, Le 'Cur Deus homo' d'Anselme de Canterbury et le 'De arrha animae' d'Hugues de Saint-Victor*, Université catholique de Louvain, Publications de l'Institut d'études médiévales 2/6 (Louvain-la-Neuve, 1984), 88–89, and Robert Lerner, "New Light on the Mirror of Simple Souls," *Speculum* 85 (2010): 9.

[12]   I derived my information on these early editions from the printed catalogues of the national libraries of England and France, the *National Union Catalogue* of libraries of the United States, and from bibliographies of incunabula: Ludwig Hain, *Repertorium bibliographicum . . . usque ad MC*, 2 vols. in 4 (repr. Milan: Görlich, 1948); Walter A. Copinger, *Supplement to Hain's Repertorium* (repr. Milan: Görlich, 1950); Dietrich Reichling, *Appendices ad Hainii-Copingeri Repertorium*, 7 vols. in 2 (Munich: I. Rosenthal, 1905–11); Robert Proctor, *An Index to the Early Printed Books in the British Museum*, 4 vols. (London: Charing Cross, 1898).

[13]   *Soliloquium in modum dialogi* (Strassburg: C. W. Civis Argentinensis, 1473). There may have been several versions of this edition. Hain (no. 9028) lists another edition of the same year: *Soliloquium in modum dialogi*, with the interesting, if rather ungrammatical, incipit: "Soliloquium hugonis in modum dyalogi ad animam suam eandem instruens multivarie et pulchrae quatenus super omnia ex multis causis qnas [*sic*] demonstrat diligat deum." Copinger adds the bibliographical information: Nuremberg: A. Koburger, 1473.

[14]   Karl Müller, ed., *Soliloquium de arrha animae und De vanitate mundi*, Kleine Texte für Vorlesungen und Übungen, 128 (Bonn: A. Marcus and E. Weber, 1913), pp. 3–25, 49. Müller corrects the text of the PL, using primarily two manuscripts: BNF lat 5317 and Stuttgart Landesbibliothek, Cod. theol. et phil. 205. In his estimation neither manuscript is very good.

edited the text from Paris, BN lat. 2566, correcting it with a few readings drawn from Müller's edition.[15]

The *Soliloquy* was translated into French and published at Paris around AD 1600 by John of St Victor. More recently Hugh's work has been translated in modern French and annotated by Michael Ledrus and most recently by Dominique Poirel and Patrice Sicard.[16] There are two modern English translations: F. Sherwood Taylor, *The Soul's Betrothal-Gift* (Westminster, England: Dacre Press, 1945); Kevin Herbert, *Soliloquy on the Earnest Money of the Soul*, Medieval Philosophical Texts in Translation 9 (Milwaukee: Marquette University Press, 1956).

The Title

According to the manuscript tradition, the title of Hugh's work is *Soliloquium de arrha animae* (*Soliloquy on the Betrothal-Gift of the Soul*). Each of the nouns in this title is important for understanding the nature of the work.

Soliloquium. This word was coined by St Augustine to serve as the title of an early work of his that was structured as a dialogue between "Augustinus" and "Ratio." Near the end of his *Soliloquia* Augustine acknowledged that the title was a new and rather rough-sounding word but, he said, at least it described the nature of the work. Probably as a manifestation of the growing emphasis on interiority that accompanied the twelfth-century renaissance, *Soliloquia* were a popular form of religious writing in the twelfth and thirteenth centuries; for example, Adam Scot, *Soliloquium de instructione animae*; Ps.-Bernard, *Soliloquium*; Ps.-Augustine, *Soliloquia*; Bonaventure, *Soliloquium*. The genre continued to be popular during the era of the Devotio Moderna and beyond.[17]

He used as well the *editio princeps* and the edition of Rouen (1648). There is an online version of the Latin text: http://www.thelatinlibrary.com/hugo/hugo.solo.html.
[15]   *Oeuvre* 1:226–82.
[16]   Michael Ledrus, *Le gage des divines fiançailles*, Museum Lessianum, section ascètique et mystique 12 (Bruges: C. Beyaert, 1923); Sicard and Poirel, *Oeuvre* 1:227–83.
[17]   Augustine, *Soliloquia*, 2.7, ed. Pierre de Labriolle, *Oeuvres de saint Augustin* 1/5 (Paris: Desclée de Brouwer, 1948), 112; tr. Thomas F. Gilligan, St Augustine, *Works 1*, FOC 5 (New York: CIMA, 1948), 397. Jerome cites the title in a letter to Augustine, *Ep.* 105.5, ed. Isidorus Hilberg, CSEL 55 (Vienna: Tempsky, 1912): 246:6–10.
Adam Scot's *Soliloquium de instructione animae* (PL 198.843–72) is a dialogue between "Ratio" and "Anima" on the nature of the religious life of a Premonstratensian canon. In it, "Ratio" instructs "Anima" with confidential questionings ("secretis interrogationibus").

Although it is not a *soliloquium* itself, the Victorine *De contempla-tione et ejus speciebus* (*On Contemplation and Its Kinds*) gives a defini-tion of the term. The unknown author envisages successive stages of the spiritual life: "meditatio," "soliloquium," "circumspectio" and "as-censio." "Soliloquium" is

Hugh of St Victor's *De vanitate* seems also to be a dialogue between Ratio and Anima, al-though in the PL the participants in the first two books are "docens" and "interrogans." The first two books of this work have been edited by Karl Müller with his edition of the *Solilo-quium de arrha animae*, pp. 26–48, where he gives the participants as "Ratio" and "Anima." Hugh also uses the dialogue form in *Epitome Dindimi in philosophiam* and *Dialogus de sacramentis*.

Ps.-Bernard, *Soliloquium* (PL 184.1157B–1168B) draws on Augustine and may echo Hugh's *Soliloquium*. In it, the author addresses his heart. There are several references to the relation-ship between Christ and his spouse.

Ps.-Augustine, *Soliloquia* (PL 40.863–98) is a monologue addressed to God; a brief discussion of the work with a bibliography may be found in Robert S. Sturges, "A Middle English Version of the Pseudo-Augustinian *Soliloquies*," *Manuscripta* 29 (1985): 73–79. The work is inspired by Augustine's *Soliloquies* and Hugh of St Victor's *Soliloquium*.

Bonaventure, *Soliloquium*, ed. A. C. Peltier, *Opera omnia* (Paris: Vivès, 1868), 12:85–131, is a dialogue between "anima" and "homo" by which "anima" is helped to deeper self-knowledge. This work draws on both Ps.-Bernard, *Meditationes* (PL 184.485–508) and Hugh's *Soliloquium*. Thomas à Kempis' *Opera omnia*, ed. Henricus Sommalius, rev. Eusebius Amort, 3 vols. (Co-logne: Krakamp, 1759), 2:1–59, contains a *Soliloquium* in which the author collected various devout thoughts he wished to keep in his heart. He apologized for the rhetorical quality of the work, in which he says he varied the form: "nunc loquens, nunc disputans, nunc orans, nunc colloquens; nunc in propria persona, nunc in peregrina [p. 1]" ("now speaking, now disputing, now praying, now conversing, now in his own person, now in another's person"). The speaker addresses now God, now his soul. One passage sounds like a summary of Hugh's *Soliloquium*: "Ecce iste dulcissimus Sponsus et dilectissimus amicus meus, Dominus meus Iesus Christus, amator animarum sanctarum, ex amore cessare non valens, attraxit me miseram ad se. Et cum non essem, dedit mihi esse, vivere, sapere, et communi hac frui luce contulit et renasci per gratiam baptismi. . . . De hinc, cum multis peccatis me deformassem, non aspexit ad meam foeditatem" ("Behold this most sweet Bridegroom, my beloved Friend, my Lord Jesus Christ, the lover of holy souls, unable to cease from love, drew me, a wretch, to himself. And when I was not, he gave me being, life, knowledge, and he granted me to enjoy this common light and to be reborn through the grace of baptism. . . . Hence, although I had deformed myself with many sins, he did not look at my sordidness"; c. 15, p. 28). The conclusion Thomas à Kempis draws is the same as Hugh's: "Dulcissime Domine, Tu solus unicus, et singularis dilectus meus" ("Most sweet Lord, You [are] my sole, unique, and sin-gular beloved"; c. 17.7, p. 37).

Poirel and Sicard, *Oeuvre* 1:212–13, give other examples and editions. Regarding one later form of the genre, see Thomas O. Sloan, "Rhetoric and Meditation: Three Case Studies," *Journal of Medieval and Renaissance Studies* 1 (1971): 45–58.

The Devotio Moderna was a religious movement of earnest, interior, practical Christianity that flourished in the fourteenth and fifteenth centuries, especially in the Lowlands. See John Van Engen, *Devotio Moderna*, Classics of Western Spirituality (Mawhah, NJ. Paulist, 1988), and *Sisters and Brothers of the Common Life: The Devotio Moderna and the World of the Later Middle Ages* (Philadelphia: University of Pennsylvania Press, 2008).

discourse which someone holds with himself and about himself, giving birth to contempt of himself. It is called *soliloquium* because a man addresses himself alone; that is, when the interior man is not disturbed by the exterior, but probes the secrets of his heart, considers and looks into his mind and conscience for the sake of contempt of himself.[18]

It is noteworthy that although in his *Soliloquy* Hugh considers the soul's self-inflicted disfigurements, his aim is not to foster contempt of self, but recognition of the gifts received from God.

Arrha. "Arrha" ("arra," "arrabo") is a word whose classical meaning was "earnest money." This sense of *arrha* is brought out clearly by St Augustine who distinguishes it (more sharply than ordinary usage often did) from *pignus*:

> A "pledge" (*pignus*) is such that when the thing itself is given the pledge is returned. However, "earnest money" (*arrha*) is given from the thing which is promised by this giving; when the thing itself is given, what was given is completed, not changed.[19]

Today, one gives a pledge to a pawnbroker; the pledge is returned when the loan is paid off. One gives earnest money to a real estate agent; when the purchase is finalized, the earnest money is applied toward the price of the house.

The term "arrha" was early associated with betrothal and marriage gifts.[20] The word has passed into Spanish ("arra," "arras"), where it has both the wider significance of a pledge in a contract and specific applications to marriage customs.[21] Influenced partly by 2 Cor. 5:5 ("God has given us the Spirit as a pledge"), Christians incorporated "arrha"

[18]   Roger Baron, ed., *La contemplation et ses espèces*, Monumenta Christiana Selecta 2 (Tournai: Desclée, 1955): 428: "Soliloquium sequitur: quod est alicuius ad se et de se solum eloquium, ipsius generans contemptum. Soliloquium dicitur quia vir se solum alloquitur, id est, quando homo interior ab exteriori non turbatur, sed cordis secreta rimatur, mentem et conscientiam, ob sui contemptum considerat et speculatur."

[19]   Augustine, *Sermo* 156.15.16 (*De verbo apost.* [Rom 8.12–17] PL 38.858): "Pignus enim quando ponitur, cum fuerit res ipsa reddita, pignus aufertur. Arrha autem de ipsa re datur, quae danda promittitur, ut res quando redditur, impleatur quod datum est, non mutetur." For Augustine's use of the term "arra," see also *Jo. ev. tr.*, 13.13 (Willems, 138;) 13.16 (Willems, 139); 32.5, (Willems, 302); *En. Ps.* 84.2 (Dekkers and Fraipont, 1162); 122.5 (Dekkers and Fraipont, 1818); 127.8 (Dekkers and Fraipont, 1872); 148.8 (Dekkers and Fraipont, 2170); *Sermo* 378 (PL 39.1673–74); *In 1 Jo.* 2.11 (Agaësse, 174); 9.11 (Agaësse, 404); *Confessiones* 7.21.27 (Knöll, 168.2–6).

[20]   See, for example, Peter Chrysologus, *Sermo* 140 (PL 52.575A); Gregory of Tours, *Historia Francorum*, ed. W. Arndt and Br. Krusch, MGH SS Rerum Merov. 1 (Hanover: Hahn, 1885), 1.47 (54:1–3); 4.46 (181:3–7); 10.16 (428:11–12); *Liber vitae* 20 (741:16–18).

[21]   Real Academia Española, *Diccionario de la lengua española*, 20th ed. (Madrid: Real Academia Española, 1984), 1:127–28.

into their vocabulary; because of its connection with marriage, "arrha" was particularly apt to describe the espousal of the soul with God or more specifically with Christ.[22]

Anima. Hugh's use of "anima" ("soul") reflects the very wide usage of the term in earlier Christian tradition. According to Hugh, the nature of a human being consists of two substances: the soul, and the body or flesh. Only when these two are present does one have a complete human being.[23] "The flesh lives from the soul, and the soul from the flesh; both live, but the flesh has all that it has from the soul, whereas the soul does not have its life totally from the flesh."[24] By its union with the soul, the body shares in the soul's immortality.[25] The soul, as the active principle in a human being, operates through a threefold power: vegetative, sensory, and rational. However, the soul is not divided; it is fully present in each of its powers.[26] The same soul gives life to the body and lives in itself through understanding. In this latter capacity it is called spirit.[27] Human beings are restlessly in search of perfect beauty and goodness in which they can find peace, for such is the dignity of human beings that nothing less will satisfy them.[28] The activities of the rational soul are two: knowledge of the truth and love of virtue.[29] By knowledge the soul is God's image, by love it is God's likeness. Hence the soul is like a mirror in which God can be known.[30] God has implanted in human beings an innate affection for their bodies, which should be loved for their beauty and perfection, but not preferred to the soul.[31]

---

[22] 2 Cor 5:5 (Vulg.): "qui dedit nobis pignus [Greek: 'arrabona'] Spiritus." The Old Latin seems to have had exactly the same text as the Vulgate: *Bibliorum Sacrorum Latinae Versiones Antiquae seu Vetus Italica,* ed. Petrus Sabatier, 3 vols. in 6 (Paris: Franciscus Didot, 1751) 3/2:738.

[23] *Misc.* 1.122 (PL 177.546–47); cf. *Sacr.* 2.1.11 (PL 176.403B, 409BC); 1.6.1 (PL 176.263–64).

[24] *In Eccl.* 1 (PL 175.123D): "Vivit autem et caro ex anima, et anima ex carne, et utrunque vivit, sed caro ex anima totum quod habet, anima in carne non totum habet quod vivit." Cf. *Misc.* 1.16 (PL 177.485C); 1.47 (PL 177.495CD); *Sacr.* 2.2.4 (PL 176.418A).

[25] *In Eccl.* 18 (Jollès, 40–47 [PL 175.249B]).

[26] *Didasc.* 1.3; 2.4 (Buttimer, 7–10, 27–29; tr. Taylor, 48–50, 64–66).

[27] *Cant. BM* (Jollès, 40–47 [PL 175.418C–420C]).

[28] *Sacr.* 1.6.6 (PL 176.268A); *Misc.* 1.7 (PL 177.482D); *Quid vere* (Baron, 94 = *Misc.* 1.171 [PL 177.563D]; tr. Feiss, VTT 2:179). The restlessness of the human heart is a fundamental theme of Hugh's *Ark of Noah* and *Vanity.*

[29] *In Eccl.* 2 (PL 175.141BC). This distinction, "cognitio veritatis/dilectio virtutis," pervades the *Misc.*; e.g., 1.13 (PL 177.485A); 1.17 (PL 177.485D–486C); 1.23 (PL 177.490C).

[30] *Adnot. in Pent. Gen.* 1 (PL 175.37C); *Sacr.* 1.6.2 (PL 176.264CD); *Archa Noe* 3.7, (Sicard, 64 [PL 176.651D–652A]); *Didasc.* 1.8 (Buttimer, 15–16; tr. Taylor, 54–55).

[31] *Sacr. dial.* (PL 176.25D); *Sacr.* 1.7.19 (PL 176.295); 2.13.7 (PL 176.531D–532A).

The image of God in the soul, its capacity for knowing and loving, has been damaged by sin, so that what God originally created good needs to be restored and reformed to its pristine beauty.[32] Sin has disordered human loves so that human beings tend to love the wrong things or the right things in the wrong measure. The aim of Hugh's *Soliloquy* is to teach and to inspire the reader to love rightly.

OUTLINE AND THEMES

Hugh's *Soliloquy* is designed like a fresco portraying seven vivid scenes, or, more accurately, a sound recording of a conversation divided into seven sections: (1) *Self* and *Soul* agree to have a confidential discussion. (2) The dilemma of *Soul* is that nothing that she can perceive satisfies her desire for a perfect love, but she cannot love what she cannot see. (3) *Self* explains that though *Soul* cannot see the Lover she seeks, she can deduce his goodness and his love for her from the perceptible gifts of being and life she shares in common with all other created things, the gifts of grace she shares with other baptized believers, and the unique gifts that God has given to her alone; her squandering of her gifts through sin; and the greater gift of restoration through Christ. (4) An allegory based on the biblical book Esther helps *Soul* see her true situation. (5) In what seems to be an autobiographical passage,[33] Hugh's *Self* turns to God and prays a *confessio* of thanksgiving. (6) *Soul* turns to her vices and disavows them. (7) *Soul* describes the visit and touch of the Spouse and her longing for Him.

Continuity among these seven scenes is assured by their temporal sequence, the narrative line, and by thirteen motifs that are woven into them. These motifs are (1) in charity what is common to many is singular to each; (2) now/then, journey/arrival; (3) other or alien; (4) fear and shame; (5) experience (especially of beauty); (6) sight, sound, and touch; (7) beauty of face and the ugliness of the prostituted soul; (8) mirror; (9) image and likeness; (10) sacraments; (11) questions and reasons; (12) memory; (13) newness.

---

[32] *Sacr.* 1.7.26–27 (PL 176.298AD); 1.7.16 (PL 176.294BC). For the distinction "opus conditionis/ opus restaurationis" see, for example, *Sacr.* 1 prol. 2–3 (PL 176.184B–185B); 1.1.28 (PL 176.204B); *Vanitate* 2 (Müller, 42:31–43:31).

[33] See Rorem, *Hugh of St Victor*, 162–63.

Sources

The primary source of the *Soliloquy* is the biblical tradition that from the time of the prophets saw the relationship between God and his people as a marriage. In Hosea God says, "I will allure her, and bring her into the wilderness, and speak tenderly to her. . . . And in that day, says the Lord, you will call me 'My husband'" (Hos. 2:14, 16). Other prophets sounded this theme. Like Hosea, they looked back with nostalgia to the days of the exodus, when God and Israel were newly wed and very much in love (Jer. 2:2). After that time, Israel had been seduced by the surrounding nations and their gods. Hosea voiced the antithetical theme of Israel's adultery and harlotry: "plead—for she is not my wife, and I am not her husband—that she put away her harlotry from her face, and her adultery from her breasts" (Hos. 2:3). "You have a harlot's brow, you refuse to be ashamed" (Jer. 3:3). These themes received extended development in two powerful chapters of the book of Ezekiel (16 and 23).

If Israel was unfaithful to the Lord, he remained faithful to her: "Return, faithless Israel, says the Lord. I will not look on you in anger, for I am merciful" (Jer. 3:12). "For a brief moment I forsook you, but with great compassion I will gather you. In overflowing wrath for a moment I hid my face from you, but with everlasting love I will have compassion on you" (Isa. 54:7–9). "As the bridegroom rejoices over the bride, so shall your God rejoice over you" (Isa. 62:5).

These ideas were incorporated into the New Testament and thence into Christian tradition. Jesus is the groom who presides at a wedding feast (Mark 2:19–20; Matt. 9:15; 22:1–14; 25:1–13; Apoc.19:6–8; 21:2; 22:17). The union of Christ and the church is "a great mystery" of marital love: "Christ loved the church, gave himself up for her, that he might sanctify her, having cleansed her by the washing of water with the word, that he might present the church to himself in splendor, without spot or wrinkle or any such thing, that she might be holy and without blemish." (Eph. 5:32, 25–27; cf. 2 Cor. 11:2; Gal. 2:20).[34]

As was noted in the introduction to *The Praise of the Bridegroom*, the marriage of Christ and the church received extensive development in patristic and medieval commentaries on the *Song of Songs*.[35] In the

---

[34]   Pierre Andrès, "Marriage et vie chrétienne," *DS* (1980) 10:361–64.

[35]   In addition to the sources cited in the introduction to *The Praise of the Bridegroom*, see also Pierre Andrès, "Marriage spirituel," *DS* (1980) 10:389–93.

third century Origen extended the figure of Christ's marriage to the
church to the relationship of the Word to the individual Christian soul.
As he did in *The Praise of the Bridegroom*, in his *Soliloquy* Hugh prefers
to apply the imagery of the *Song* to the marriage of God and the soul,
rather than to Mary or to the union of Christ and the church. However,
for Hugh as for St Augustine, the individual Christian and the church
are inseparable. How Hugh embellishes this rich image of the marriage
of God and his people may be illustrated by one example. The beauty
of *Soul*, which reflects the unsurpassable beauty of God himself, has
been obscured by her sins. In a telling sentence at the end of paragraph
41, Hugh describes the harlot-soul. There were unkind descriptions of
old women and harlots in Roman and Christian satirists, with some of
which Hugh may have been familiar. However, his description seems
to be of his own devising. In par. 41, Hugh describes *Soul* as deformed
and debased in the parts of her body which correspond to the body
parts of the bride (and to a lesser extent of her beloved) praised in the
Song of Songs: "because of your uncontrolled fornications your breasts
have hung loose. Your brow is wrinkled, your cheeks shrunken, your
eyes tired and dull, your lips pallid, your skin dried, your strength
broken, and you are hateful even to your lovers."[36]

> *Arrha* 41: prae nimiis fornicationibus tuis laxata sunt ubera tua . . .
> Because of your habitual fornication your breasts have hung loose . . .
> *Song of Songs* 4:5; cf. 1:1; 4:10, 12; 7:3, 7–8: duo ubera tua sicut duo hinuli
> capreae gemelli. Your two breasts are the twin fawns of a gazelle
>
> *Arrha* 41: rugosa effecta est frons tua . . . your forehead is wrinkled
> *Song of Songs* 2:14: facies tua decora . . . your forehead is beautiful
>
> *Arrha* 41: genae tuae marcidae . . . your cheeks are shrunken
> *Song of Songs* 1:9; 4:3; 5:6; cf. 5:13: pulchrae sunt genae tuae turturis /
> fragmen mali punici . . . your cheeks are like a dove's / like a slice of a
> pomegranate
>
> *Arrha* 41: languentes et stupentes oculi . . . your eyes are languishing
> and stupified

[36] The texts of the *Song* are from *Biblia sacra iuxta Vulgatam versionem*, ed. Robert Weber, et al., 4th ed. (Stuttgart: Deutsche Bibelgesellschaftt, 1994). For parallels in one classical text, see Juvenal, *Satirae*, ed. C. F. Hermann (Leipzig: Teubner, 1883), 6:121, 142–44. A similar contrast is drawn in the Spanish life of St Mary of Egypt, *St Mary of Egypt: Three Medieval Lives in Verse*, tr. Hugh Feiss and Ronald Pepin, Cistercian Studies 209 (Kalamazoo, MI: Cistercian Publications, 2005): compare section VI (pp. 123–24) with section XV (pp. 138–39).

Song of Songs 4:1; 7:4; (cf. 5:12) tu pulchra oculi tui columbarum + 5:8: quia amore langueo . . . you are beautiful, your eyes like those of doves / I am languishing for love

Arrha 41: labia pallore obducta . . . your lips are pale
Song of Songs 4:3, 11; cf. 5:3 sicut vitta coccinea / favus distillans labia tua . . . like a scarlet headband / a dripping honeycomb are your lips

Arrha 41: exsiccata cutis . . . [your] skin is dried out
Song of Songs 1:4; nigra sum sed formosa (cf. 5:10: dilectus meus candidus et rubicundus; 7:6) . . . I am black but beautiful (my beloved is white and ruddy)

Arrha 41: virtus infracta, ipsis quoque amatoribus tuis odiosa . . . your strength is broken, you are hateful even to your lovers
Song of Songs 1:4: Ecce, tu pulchra es amica mea (1:13: amica mea speciosa mea) . . . Behold, you are my beautiful friend (my gorgeous friend)

A second source for the *Soliloquy* seems to be some sermons in Augustine's *Sermons (Tractatus) on the First Epistle of John*. In his mature works (with the exception of the last books of *On the Sacraments*) Hugh seldom quotes other authors.[37] He uses others' ideas, but refashions them in his own way. In the *Soliloquy* he makes reference to no other work except the Bible, but if there is any single work which may have inspired Hugh's work it is these sermons of the bishop of Hippo.

There are differences of emphasis which arise from methodological causes: (1) Augustine's *tractatus* were public sermons; Hugh's *Soliloquy* is addressed to the individual reader. (2) Augustine had pastoral concerns about the unity of the church and orthodoxy in faith, which were not on Hugh's mind when he wrote the *Soliloquy*. (3) Augustine was giving a continuous commentary on a book of Scripture, so he had to follow the epistle's line of thought; Hugh was crafting a devotional work.

There are also different theological emphases in the two works: (1) Augustine is more explicitly Christological. (2) Augustine does not celebrate the gifts common to all creation; his sacramentalism is more narrowly ecclesial;[38] he acknowledges the beauty of the world, but

[37]   H. Weisweiler, "Die Arbeitsmethode Hugos von St. Viktor: Ein Beitrag zum Entstehen seines Hauptwerkes *De sacramentis*," *Scholastik* 20–24 (1949): 59–87, 232–67; Ludwig Ott, "Hugo von St. Viktor und die Kirchenväter," *Divus Thomas* (Fribourg) 27 (1949): 180–200; 293–332.

[38]   Augustine, *In 1 Jo.* 1.1–2 (Agaësse, 112–16); 3.5 (Agaësse, 194); 3.12 (Agaësse, 208); 5.6 (Agaësse, 258); 6.11 (Agaësse, 302); 7.6, Agaësse (322–24).

seems to see it more as a temptation and a distraction[39] than as an *arrha* of love, a term which for him is confined to the gift of the Holy Spirit. (3) Augustine's eschatology is more insistent; the contrast between then and now is more sharply drawn.[40] (4) In his sermons on 1 John, Augustine locates the human being's resemblance to God in charity, whereas for Hugh it includes the whole life of the soul.[41]

Apart from these differences of method and theology the parallels between the two works are striking; ideas presented in Books Nine and Ten of *On 1 John* are especially close to Hugh's ideas. The affinity of the two works will be clear from a brief, three-part summary of the parallel ideas in Augustine's work.

Augustine addresses his audience as Hugh addressed Brother G.: "Your Charity."[42] Every human being is searching for the proper object of her love.[43] The ultimate alienation is not to love God.[44] Some people do not believe in the last judgment; others fear its punishments. Some of the latter become troubled in their conscience. This unrest is a positive step, because it prods them to good works.[45] Once the chaste soul has begun to grow in good works, she begins to desire Christ. She renounces her adultery not out of fear, but out of a desire for the embraces of her spouse.[46]

Secondly, to love is a grace. What enables Christians to love their spouse? Christ loved them first. He found them ugly and unclean. By loving them he made them beautiful. God, who is unchangingly beautiful, loved those who were corrupt and depraved and made them beautiful.[47] Thereafter, as their love grows, they become more beautiful. Even if Christ shows them that some corruption remains in them, they

---

[39]   *In 1 Jo.* 2.11 (Agaësse, 172).
[40]   *In 1 Jo.* 1.5 (Agaësse, 124); 2.10 (Agaësse, 170); 4.7 (Agaësse, 232–34); 5.7 (Agaësse, 262); 7.1 (Agaësse, 314–16); 8.13 (Agaësse, 366–68); 10.5 (Agaësse, 420); 10.6 (Agaësse, 424).
[41]   *In 1 Jo.* 4.9 (Agaësse, 238); 8.6, (Agaësse, 350–52).
[42]   *In 1 Jo.* 9.1 (Agaësse, 374).
[43]   Cf. *In 1 Jo.* 4.6, (Agaësse, 230): "Tota vita Christiani boni sanctum desiderium est" ("All the life of the good Christian is holy desire of the good").
[44]   *In 1 Jo.* 7.6 (Agaësse, 322).
[45]   *In 1 Jo.* 9.4 (Agaësse, 384).
[46]   *In 1 Jo.* 9.2 (Agaësse, 378–80; tr. Rettig, 249): As she mortifies "members which are on the earth" (Col. 3:5) and grows in good works, "the chaste soul begins to desire Christ. She desires the embrace of the spouse; she renounces adultery. . . . With perfect and sincere charity she does not fear" ("coeperit desiderare Christum casta anima, que desiderat amplexus sponsi, renuntiat adulterio . . . non trepidat in caritate perfecta atque sincera"). Cf. 9.11 (Agaësse, 404); 9.5–6 (Agaësse, 388–90).
[47]   *In 1 Jo.* 9.9 (Agaësse, 396).

are not so much ashamed as displeased, because they are anxious to please their beloved. Their love is focused on God; they love not the pilgrimage, but the goal.[48]

Finally, Augustine emphasizes the closeness of the bond which unites all in Christ. United with Christ, each Christian is joined in an intimate way with all the other children of God, who are also united with Him. "Whoever loves the sons of God, loves the Son of God. . . . By loving he becomes one of Christ's members; by love he is embodied in Christ; and there will be one Christ loving himself."[49] "As a result of this intimate union, whenever one member suffers, all do; whenever one glories, all do. Love then is indivisible: to love a brother is to love Christ; to love Christ is to love the Father."[50] One cannot love the head and trample on the feet.[51]

In the absence of direct quotations, it is possible that the ideas in Hugh's *Soliloquy* that correspond remarkably with Augustine's *Commentary on 1 John* do not reflect direct borrowing. There are, however, four passages where the similarity of language increases the probability that in writing the *Soliloquy* Hugh was influenced by Augustine's work:

> (1) *Augustine* (9.9, Agaësse, 396): Amavit nos . . . foedos et deformes, . . . et ex deformibus pulchros faceret / He loved us who were . . . foul and deformed and from being deformed made us beautiful.
> *Hugh* (par. 44): cum foeda esses, dilexit te, ut pulchram faceret / When you were foul, he loved you so that he made you beautiful.

> (2) *Augustine* (7.10, Agaësse, 332): tenete eam [caritatem], amplectimini eam; dulcius illa nihil est / Cling to love; embrace it; nothing is sweeter than it is.
> *Hugh* (par. 68): quasi quiddam amplexibus amoris intus teneo . . . nihil amplius quaerens / I hold something within me with embraces of love, . . . seeking nothing else.

> (3) *Augustine* (1.4, Agaësse, 120): non *erubescas* de illa, si quando tibi *foedam* ostenderit, *displiceat* tibi foeditas tua, ut percipias pulchritudinem illius / Don't be ashamed of it, if sometimes he shows you to be foul. Let your foulness displease you, so that you perceive his beauty.

---

[48]   *In 1 Jo.* 9.10 (Agaësse, 400–2); 1.4 (Agaësse, 120).
[49]   *In 1 Jo.* 10.3 (Agaësse, 414): "filii Dei corpus sunt unici Filii Dei; et cum ille caput, nos membra, unus est Filius Dei. Ergo qui diligit filios Dei, Filium Dei diligit. . . . Et diligendo fit et ipse membrum, et fit per dilectionem in compage corporis Christi; et erit unus Christus amans se."
[50]   *In 1 Jo.* 10.3 (Agaësse, 414–16, quoting 1 Cor. 12:26–27).
[51]   *In 1 Jo.* 10.8 (Agaësse, 430–32).

Hugh (par. 66): multa sunt in me de quibus coram oculis eius *erubesco*,
et pro quibus iam magis illi *displicere* timeo, . . . o maculae *foedae* . . .
(Cf. par. 67: diligit tamen hoc ipsum, quod tu quoque ea in temetipsa
iam odisse coepisti, quae illi *displicent*). / There are many things in me
about which I blush before his gaze and on account of which I fear
I now displease him greatly . . . O foul spots . . . (He loves this very
thing, that you also have begun to hate in yourself the things that displease him).

(4) *Augustine* (2.11, Agaësse, 172–74): si . . . illa acceptum anulum plus
diligeret quam sponsum . . . nonne in ipso dono sponsi adultera anima
deprehenderetur? . . . Ad hoc utique arrham dat sponsus, ut in arrha
sua ipse ametur / If . . . she loved the ring she received more than her
spouse . . . would not the soul in that very gift be caught out as an
adulterer? . . . For the bridegroom gives the betrothal gift so that in the
betrothal gift he will be loved.
Hugh (par. 18): Cave . . . ne . . . non sponsa sed meretrix dicaris, si mu-
nera dantis plus quam amantis affectum diligis. . . . Dilige in donis illius
quod data sunt ab illo / Be careful . . . lest . . . you be called not a bride
but a whore, if you love the gifts of the giver more than the affection of
the lover. . . . Love in his gifts the fact that they are given by him.

The second chapter of the biblical book of *Esther* is a third source
of Hugh's *Soliloquy*. In paragraphs 53–55, Hugh presents a moral or
tropological interpretation of this chapter of the Bible. Esther was one
of the least commented books of the Old Testament. The most widely
disseminated interpretation was that of Rhabanus Maurus, which was
largely taken over by the *Glossa ordinaria*.[52] That interpretation was a
rather static, doctrinal interpretation:

    Ahasuerus = Christ
    Mordecai = the Church
    Esther = the Church or Mary
    Vashti and Haman = proud Jews
    young virgins = the different people called to Christ and put under the
       care of
    Hegai = the pastoral and teaching care of the church, which leads to
       the

---

[52]   Rhabanus Maurus, *Expositio in librum Esther* (PL 109.635–50); *Biblia sacra cum glossa interlineari, ordinaria* . . . (Venice: 1588), fols. 305–8; Richard of St Victor, *Serm. cent.* 91–93 (PL
177.1183B–1191A); See Kimberly Vrudny, "Medieval Treatment of the Queen: Austrian Manuscripts and the Quest for Esther," *ARTS* 8/1 (1995), 14–21; Vrudny, "Medieval Fascination
with the Queen: Esther as Queen of Heaven and Host of the Messianic Banquet," *ARTS* 11/2
(1999), 36–43.

bridal chamber = heaven for those with true faith and pure
consciences

By contrast, in Hugh's *Soliloquy*, the passage is presented as a coher-
ent narrative with a personal point: Christ (Ahasuerus) came into the
world to find himself a bride uniquely worthy of a royal marriage. Since
the Jewish people (Vashti) would not accept him in his mortal form,
he sent out messengers (apostles) to gather into the hall of the royal
women (the present Church) young virgins (souls), who give birth to
royal children rather than slaves (they serve God out of love, not fear).
The many young virgins who are called to the Church are anointed,
treated, and adorned, but only a few will be chosen to reign as the king's
spouse and to enter his bedroom (the heavenly Jerusalem). Those
whom the king loved were dirty and foul, but his gifts transformed
them (they are washed in baptism, anointed with chrism, fed with the
Eucharist, clothed in good works, perfumed in virtues, able to see their
faces in the mirror of Scripture, and renewed and washed again with
tears of compunction).

Love of God and Contempt of the World

Robert Bultot thought that Hugh of St Victor's theology of love—
like the theology of other clerics and monks of his time—was distorted
by Augustine's Neoplatonism so that Hugh undervalued time, entertained a dualistic view of human nature, and held the world, the body,
and human feeling in contempt. In Bultot's judgment, for Hugh and
the Augustinian tradition, if earthly realities are valued, then either
they are valued apart from God in sin, or they are absorbed by the
supernatural. Thus the knowledge of botany is virtuously valued by the
devout Christian because it helps her understand the Bible or love God
more; it is sinfully valued by the worldly person, whom it distracts with
useless curiosity or covetousness (*vana curiositas* and *cupiditas*) from
knowledge and love of God. In Augustine's theory of ordered love, only
God can be loved for his own sake, only God can be enjoyed (*frui*);
other things are to be loved for God's sake and used (*uti*). Hugh does
not make room for love and enjoyment of other people. Bultot quotes
a passage in Hugh's *Soliloquy* that he says reflects Augustine's ideas:

If one loves [creatures], . . . it is necessary to love them not in place of
God, nor with him, but [to love] them for him and him through them,

[and] him above them all [par. 17] . . . for love is not perfected if one cherishes another at the same time as the well-beloved or if one cherishes only a being which is not sovereignly lovable [par. 21].

Bultot comments:

It would be difficult to be clearer. The love which Hugh permits one to have for creatures is the Augustinian pseudo-love which takes as its objects not what they are in themselves, but the symbol of the divine attributes that one sees in them and the spiritual message one takes from them.[53]

It is not clear that Professor Bultot's criticism of the *Soliloquy* is justified. The primary theme of the *Soliloquy* is that human beings should have a unique love for God, just as spouses have a unique love for each other. God's gifts are the tokens of his love for each human being. Although it is the soul, the inner self, who receives these gifts, they include the material world, her own bodily endowments, and her fellow human beings, as well as her intellect and virtues. These gifts are to be esteemed and loved, but not more than their giver.

Self says the *Soul* can have only one spouse, who is the object of a unique love. That spouse is God. However, God is not remote or merely present as a provident observer and generous provider: God so loved the world and each individual in it that he sent his only Son, who by humbling himself restored each person's beauty. He so united each and all Christians to himself that what is given to each is given to all; love of each is love of all. Hence, although each can only love one Spouse, or commit adultery, her unique love of her Spouse is compatible with—in fact, implies—love of other people and of all her Spouse's gifts to her and to them. The only possible response to these gifts is love and gratitude. *Self* never urges *Soul* to join a monastery or adopt any other voca-

---

53   Robert Bultot, "A propos du 'contemptus mundi' dans l'école de Saint-Victor," *Revue de sciences philosophiques et théologiques* 51 (1967): 20. Bultot is quoting the French translation of Ledrus, pp. 71, 73. Bultot's article is a critique of F. Lazzari, *Il "contemptus mundi" nella scuola di S. Vittore* (Naples: Istituto Italiano per gli Studi Storici, 1965). In this instance I have translated the quotation from Hugh's *Soliloquy* from Bultot's French. The Latin is "nec ista pro illo nec ista cum illo, sed ista propter illum et per ista illum et supra ista illum diligas (par. 17) . . . laudabilis amor non sit, si uel alter cum solo diligitur, uel, qui summe diligendus non est, solus amatur" (par. 21). Bultot's comment is as follows: "Il est difficile d'être plus net. L'amour qu'Hugues admet pour les creatures est le pseudo-amour augustinien, qui prend pour objet non ce qu'elles sont en elles mêmes, mais le symbole qu'on y voit de attributes divins et le message spirituel qu'on leur prête."

tion; he asks her to love her unique spouse in a unique—but not exclusive—way.

Moreover, there are several ways in which Hugh's *Soliloquy* seems to overcome some of the limitations of the metaphor of "ordered charity," which implies that on each level of reality, one's love should be proportioned to the inherent worth of the object. First, Hugh insists that God's love is not ordered to the inherent worth of pre-existing objects. God's love makes things have whatever goodness and beauty is in them; and God loves sinners when they do not deserve to be loved. Secondly, one need not and ought not choose between love of the One and love of the many. God's love for each embraces all; human beings' love for each other embraces all with one and one with all. Thirdly, love is deeply personal: the soul's highest good is the supremely beautiful spouse. *Soul* insists that if she is to love her unseen spouse in a singular fashion then he should love her singularly also. By saying this, she puts the whole discussion in the realm of personal relations, not of discrete objects. Things are to be loved as subjects or servants, but also as gifts, betrothal gifts of One who is Friend, Spouse, and Lord. This does not mean that things are not to be loved for themselves "within the love of God."[54]

If in his *Soliloquy*, a work of his maturity, Hugh overcomes some of the antinomies in Augustine's formal, theological formulas, it may be because Hugh learned from pseudo-Dionysius that whatever participates in Good-Beauty is good and beautiful by this very fact, so it is not necessary to turn inward to the self in order to reach upward toward the Good; physical objects are themselves sacraments of the divine, invitations to ecstatic love of God. On the other hand, perhaps it was not pseudo-Dionysius who taught Hugh this, but the school of his

---

[54] The phrase is from Bultot, "A propos," 18: "Aimer le monde pour lui-même en dehors de Dieu, c'est pécher. Mais il est parfaitement possible d'aimer un être pour lui-même a l'intérieur de l'amour de Dieu: c'est en cela que consiste l'authentique humanisme Chrétien; or cette attitude Hugues la condamne." Two other works from that decade treat the same issues: Heinz-Robert Schlette, *Die Nicthigkeit der Welt: Der philosophische Horizont des Hugos von St. Viktor* (Munich: Kösel, 1961); Enzo Liccaro, *Studi sulla visione*. The question is genuine: To what extent did the Neoplatonism of St Augustine and the Victorines devalue human embodiment and the material world with negative impact on Christian spirituality and theology? It may well be that Augustinian and Victorine theology contained unresolved tensions between appreciation and contempt ("Bejahung und Verneinung"—Schlette) for God's material creation, human embodiment, marriage, and human work in the world. Hugh's *Homilies on Ecclesiastes* and his work *On the Vanity of the World* are certainly not optimistic about earthly goods and activities. The absence of friendship from Hugh's thinking on love is also puzzling. However, Hugh's *Soliloquy*, taken by itself, does not seem to deserve Bultot's criticism.

own experience. He had always loved learning and the beauty of the world. Now, at the end of his life, he was no longer tempted by that same fragile beauty to forget God. As he was about to leave it behind, he composed a *confessio gratiae* that embraced all God's gifts.

We have an account of his last days from Osbert, the infirmarian at St Victor who attended him as he was dying. The day before Hugh died, Osbert visited him after saying Mass. Hugh asked him to breathe on his face in the form of a cross so that he might receive the Holy Spirit. After Osbert had done so, Hugh declared:

> Now I am secure; now I walk in truth and purity, now I am based upon a solid rock and I cannot be moved again. Now, although the whole world with its pleasures should come before me, I would reckon it as nothing and not for all of it would I do anything against God. Now especially I recognize God's mercy towards me, so that of all the things which God has done for me in all my life to this day, none can be so pleasing, gentle, and acceptable to me as what God has deigned to do with me at the present moment. Blessed is the Lord my God forever.[55]

The "nothing" of the world appears in the context of Hugh's vivid sense of the presence of God, the Holy Spirit. It is not a statement of ontological worth, but of comparison between the finite and the infinite. As the world seemed to Benedict and Gregory the Great and will seem to Julian of Norwich, to Hugh—who like them sees the world in the light of God—it seems small as a hazelnut, almost nothing.[56]

---

[55] PL 175.clxi: "Modo," inquit, "securus sum, nunc in veritate et puritate ambulo, modo fundatus sum supra firmam petram et non possum moveri amplius: nunc licet totus mundus cum delectationibus suis veniret coram me, quasi pro nihil ipsum reputarem, nec pro ipso toto aliquid contra Deum facere. Modo praecipue cognosco misericordiam Dei circa me, ita ut de omnibus quae fecit mihi Deus in tota vita mea usque ad diem hanc, nihil horum tam gratum, tam suave, tam acceptum mihi esse potest, quam hoc, quod in praesenti mecum facere Deus dignatus est. Benedictus Dominus Deus meus [Ps. 143:1 (Vulg.)] in aeternum."

[56] Hugh Feiss, "Julian of Norwich: *Dilation*: God and the World in the Visions of Benedict and Julian of Norwich," *American Benedictine Review* 55 (2004): 55–73.

1. To G., a beloved brother, and the rest of the servants of Christ dwelling in Hamersleben. Hugh, a servant in every way of your holiness, [wishes that you] walk in one peace and reach the one rest.[1]

2. I have sent to your charity (*caritati*) a soliloquy of love (*dilectionis*),[2] which is entitled *On the Betrothal-Gift of the Soul*, that you may learn where you should seek true love (*amorem*) and how you should stir your hearts toward heavenly joys by devoting yourselves to spiritual meditations.[3] I ask, dearest brother, that you with the others accept this in memory of me. What is sent to you specially does not exclude the rest, neither does giving it jointly to all threaten the prerogative of the gift to you.[4] My aim here is not to rouse you with rhetorical flourish, but I have not been able to hide my affectionate devotion (*affectum devotionis*) toward you.

3. Greet brother B. and brother A., and all the others, whose names, although I am not able to list them here singly, I hope are all written in the book of life. Farewell.[5]

SOLILOQUY ON THE BETROTHAL-GIFT OF THE SOUL

4. *Self*.[6] I will speak secretly to my soul, and what I desire to know I will require of her in friendly conversation. No outsider will be admitted, but alone by ourselves we will talk together with open hearts (*aperta conscientia*). In that way I will not be afraid to ask about her secrets, and she will not be embarrassed to respond truthfully.

5. Tell me, please, my soul, what is it that you love above all things? I know that love is your life, and I know that you cannot be without love. But I would like you to confess to me without embarrassment: what among all things have you decided you will love?

6. Let me say more, so that you may understand more clearly what I am asking you. Look at the world and everything in it. You see many beautiful and alluring sights that attract human affections and that, according to the various pleasures that come from using them, en-

kindle desires to enjoy them.[7] Gold and precious stones have their brilliance; physical beauty has its splendor; embroidered tapestries and dyed clothing have color. There are countless things like these, but why list them for you? See how you know them all, you have seen almost all of them, and you have experienced most of them. You remember even now that you have seen many, and you still see many in which you can experience and verify what I am saying. So, I beg you, tell me: Among all of these, what have you made uniquely your own? What do you wish to embrace in a unique way and to enjoy always? For I am certain that you love one of these things which are seen, or if you have now set all of them aside, you have something else that you love more than all of these.

7. *Soul.* Just as I cannot love what I have never seen, so there is nothing among all of these visible things that I have not been able to love till now. Yet I have not found among all these something that should be loved more than all the rest. By many experiences, I have learned that the love of this world is false and fleeting. I am always forced either to lose my love when what I have chosen for myself perishes, or to change it when something that is more pleasing comes along. I thus remain uncertain, carried on the tide of my desires, since I can neither be without love nor find true love.

8. *Self.* I am glad that at least you are not stuck in the love of temporal things, but I am sad that you are not yet at rest in the love of eternal things. You would be more unhappy if you made exile your home. Now, however, because you are wandering in exile, you need to be called back to the way. You would make exile your home if you wanted to have an eternal love in this passing life. But now you wander in exile because, while you are drawn by desire (*concupiscentiam*) of temporal things, you do not find love of eternal things. However, that you have learned to change your love for the better can be a great starting point of salvation for you. If a greater beauty is shown you that you find more pleasing to embrace, you will be able to tear yourself away from all love of temporal things.

9. *Soul.* How can what cannot be seen be shown? And how can what cannot be seen be loved? Certainly, there is no true and lasting love in things that are temporal and visible; nevertheless what cannot be seen cannot be loved. Eternal misery always follows a being who lives forever, if everlasting love is never found. For no one can be happy without love, because in this alone misery lies: not to love what one is.[8] Indeed, who would call someone happy or even human who, forgetful of his

humanity and spurning the peace of community, loved himself alone with a solitary and miserable love? It is necessary, therefore, that you either approve the love of the things that are seen or, if you take that away, show other things that may be loved more wholesomely and more joyfully.

10. *Self.* If you think you must love those temporal and visible things because you behold in them a certain beauty that belongs to their kind, why do you not love (*diligis*) yourself instead because by your seemliness you surpass the comeliness and beauty of all visible things.[9] O, if you would look at yourself! O, if you could see your face, you would certainly recognize how blameworthy you were when you thought something outside of you was worthy of your love!

11. *Soul.* The eye sees all things; it does not see itself. By the light with which we detect other things we do not see our own face, in which the light is placed.[10] Human beings learn about their faces from others' indications; more often they know their own faces (*facies*) and the appearance (*species*) of their countenance (*vultus*) by hearing rather than by seeing. Perchance you bring me some other kind of mirror in which I can know and love the face of my heart, as if anyone would not very rightly call a fool someone who, to feed his love, ceaselessly pondered the likeness of his countenance in a mirror.[11] Because I cannot contemplate my face and what my countenance looks like, I very easily direct my impulse of love toward things outside that seem wonderful. This is especially so because love can never bear being alone. It would in some fashion cease to be love if it did not pour out the force of its love on another companion equal to itself.

12. *Self.* Anyone to whom God is present is not solitary, nor, therefore, is the force of love extinguished if its desire is restrained from low and vile things. Someone who loves dishonorable things or admits things unworthy of his love into the company of his love does great injury to himself. First of all, then, it is necessary that each one consider himself and, when he has recognized his dignity, not love things beneath himself lest he do injury to his love. For even things that considered in themselves are beautiful fade in comparison with more beautiful things. And just as it is improper to connect deformed things with beautiful ones, so it is completely unbecoming to equate with what is most beautiful something that has only a weak impress of beauty.[12]

13. My soul, you do not wish to have a solitary love, so do not have a prostituted one either. You seek a unique love; seek also for one uniquely chosen. You know that love is a fire, and that fire seeks kin-

dling so that it may blaze. Be careful not to throw on it what causes it
to smoke and stink instead. The force of love is such that it is necessary
for you to be like the object of your love. The association of love will
somehow transform you into the likeness of the one to whom you are
conjoined by affection. Therefore, my soul, pay attention to your beauty
and you will understand what sort of beauty you should love. Your face
is not invisible to you. Your eye sees nothing well if it does not see itself.
For when it is clear-sighted in contemplating itself, no external, passing
likeness or shadowy image of the truth can deceive it. But if it happens
that your internal vision is obscured by negligence, and you are unable
to contemplate yourself as is fitting and expedient, why do you not at
least ponder how you should value yourself based on another's
judgment?

14. You have a spouse, but you do not know him. He is the most
beautiful of all, but you have not seen his face. He has seen you—because
unless he had seen you, he would not love you. Until now he did not
want to show himself to you, but he has sent gifts—he has given a betrothal-gift, a pledge of love (*pignus amoris*[13]), a sign of affection (*signum
dilectionis*). If you could know him, if you could see his appearance, you
would no longer be uncertain about your beauty. For then you would
know that someone so beautiful, so handsome, so elegant and unique
would not have been captivated by the sight of you if a singular beauty,
wondrous beyond that of others, had not drawn him.

15. Therefore, what are you going to do? You cannot see him now
because he is absent. And so you are not afraid or ashamed to do him
harm, because you disdain his singular love and prostitute yourself
basely and shamelessly to alien lust.[14] Do not act this way! If you cannot
yet know what he who loves you is like, at least consider the betrothal-
gift that he has given. Perhaps you could recognize in his gift, which is
in your possession, with what affection you should love him and with
what zeal and diligence you should save yourself for him. His betrothal-
gift is remarkable; his gift is noble, because neither would it suit someone great to give small things, nor would a wise person have given great
things for something small. Therefore, what he has given you is great,
but greater yet is what he loves in you. So, what he has given is great.
What has your spouse given you, O my soul? Perhaps you are waiting,
and you do not know what I am going to say. You are wondering from
whom you have received something great, and you do not find that you
possess or have received anything in which you can glory. Therefore,
I will tell you so that you may know what your spouse has given you.

16. Look at the entire world and consider if there is anything in it that does not serve you. All of nature directs it course to this end, that it may serve you and be useful to you; it serves your pleasures and needs alike with an inexhaustible abundance. Heaven, earth, air, and sea— with all that are in them—do not cease to fulfill this task. This task the circuit of seasons serves with unending sustenance by annual renewals and recurrent rebirths, renewing what is ancient, reforming what is collapsed, and restoring what is worn out. Who do you think arranged this? Who commanded nature to serve you thus with one accord? You receive a benefit, and you do not recognize its source. The gift is obvious; the giver is hidden. Nevertheless, reason itself does not let you doubt that this is not your due, but another's favor. Therefore, whoever he is, he has given you much. Whoever gave you all this, which is so great, is to be loved much. The one who could give so much, and wished to give so much, loved much. He is shown by his gift to be so loving and so deserving of love that it is as stupid not to desire (*concupiscere*) further the love (*amorem*) of someone so powerful as it is irreverent and perverse not to love (*amare*) someone so loving.

17. Look, therefore, O heedless and rash soul, see what you are doing, while in this world you long to be loved and to love. The whole world is subject to you, and you do not disdain to admit to the fellowship of your love not, I say, the whole world, but almost any tiny part of the world that is not even outstanding by its beautiful appearance, needed utility, great quantity, or highest goodness. If you love these things, at least love them as subjects, love them as servants, and love them as gifts, as the betrothal-gift of a spouse, as the presents of a friend, as the favors of your lord. Thus, that you may always remember what you owe him, do not love these things instead of him or alongside him, but love them for his sake; love him through them and beyond them.

18. Take care, my soul, that you are called not a bride but a whore, if you love the gifts of the giver more than the affection of the lover. You cause his love greater injury if you accept his gifts and do not respond by loving in return.[15] Either refuse his gifts, if you can, or if you cannot refuse his gifts, respond with a return of love. Love him; love yourself on his account; love his gifts on his account. Love him so that you may enjoy him; love yourself, because you are loved by him; love in his gifts the fact that they are given by him. Love him for yourself and love yourself for him; love his gifts from him to you for you. This is pure and chaste love, containing nothing sordid, nothing bitter, noth-

ing passing, beautiful in its chastity, joyful in its sweetness, stable in its eternity.

19. *Soul.* Your words have enflamed me. I have conceived ardor and I am on fire inside. Although I have not yet seen him, who you assure me is so lovable, you are, I confess, enkindling my love of him by the very sweetness of your words and the gentleness of your urging. I am driven by your arguments to love above all things the one from whom I see that I have received all things as a pledge of love. However, one thing still remains that seriously threatens in me the happiness of this love, if the hand of your consolation does not wipe it away, as it has the other things.

20. *Self.* I promise you faithfully that there is nothing in this love that rightly ought to displease you. Still, lest I seem to deceive your readiness to believe rather than to bear witness to the truth, I want you to lay open what bothers you so that strengthened again by my arguments you may grow stronger in your desire of him.

21. *Soul.* I want you to remember—what I guess has not been forgotten—that a little while ago, when you were commending an acceptable and wholesome love, you said that love must be not only unique but uniquely chosen, that is, a love fixed on one who alone is loved and to be loved. For that reason love is not perfectly praiseworthy if either someone else is loved along with one's beloved, or if the one loved ought not to be loved supremely. Suppose that I love someone uniquely chosen and uniquely loved. However, I suffer this injury to my love: loving only one, I am not the only one loved. For you yourself recognize how many people and certainly what sorts of people have in common with me the betrothal-gift of his love that you place before me.[16] How can I then glory in the privilege of singular love, when I have received this privilege, which you claim is so great, in common with bestial people,[17] even I would say, with wild beasts? What does the light of the sun do for me more than it does for the reptiles and worms of the earth? All alike live, all breathe; there is the same food and the same drink for all. Why is this so great? Why is this so singular? You certainly see how it is. Therefore, you are not giving satisfactory proof that he is to be loved in a singular way, if you do not show that he also has loved in some singular fashion. I admit that these privileges would be great and worthy of a singular love, if they had been given to me singly.

22. *Self.* This diligence of yours cannot displease me. It shows that you desire to love perfectly, since you are inquiring so diligently about the cause of perfect love. So I am glad to address what needs to be

discussed with you so that I may defend the love of the best from the accusation of wrongdoing that you bring against it and at the same time reassure you completely, so you will not waver because of doubts about love of him.[18] There are three things in which you may find what bothers you. Distinguish what gifts you have received from your spouse. Some are given commonly, some specially, and others singularly. The ones given commonly serve all together with you and on your account. The ones given specially are not granted to all, but to many together with you and on your account. The ones given singularly are given to you alone.

23. What, then? Does he love you less because he granted certain gifts to all together with you? Would he have made you happier, if he had given the world to you alone? Imagine that human beings have not been created upon the earth, and there are no wild animals. You alone possess the riches of the world. Where, then, is that pleasing and useful community of shared human life (*societas humane conversationis*)? Where are the comforts and delights that you now enjoy? See, therefore, that he gave much to you when he created these things with you for your consolation. If the world serves them and all these things serve you, how are all of them not made also for your service? Does the head of a household eat his bread alone? Does he drink his cup alone? Does he dress alone? Is he alone warmed by his fire? Does he dwell alone in his house? Nevertheless, all that is possessed by those who serve him— either through love or subjection—is rightly said to be his. Therefore, both the things that serve you and also the things necessary for those who serve you—all these are given to you and are subject to you.

24. *Soul.* You have cut down rather than uprooted what was bothering me. What concerned me was this: I—who love uniquely—am not uniquely loved, because I see that the pledge of love to me has been granted equally to others. Your arguments have persuaded me to believe that those things that I see given in common for the use of those serving me are also given to me singly. I confess that in this you have spoken fittingly enough, but you have not spoken adequately regarding what was bothering me. By your arguments I am informed that all the things that foster the life of irrational things are to be assigned rather to my account, because the things that are nurtured by them are also destined for my use. However, that does not establish the privilege of a singular love because it is clear that these are subjected not to me alone, but to all people as much as to me—and to many even more so.[19] With regard to all these things that have been granted in common for

people's use, even if some unjustly claim something more for themselves, those err when they ascribe something singly to their account.
Therefore, there is a special love of the Creator for human beings in
which they have a reason to glory more than other creatures, but not
in relation to each other. When you argue for a singular love, you say
that among other things the community of my fellow human beings
has been given to me. I cannot find anything singular in this, since my
company is granted to them just as theirs is granted to me. In that community I suffer not only the loss of the glory of uniqueness, but also
the slight of their participation. For how many unbelievers, how many
criminals, how many unclean are there, who can likewise glory in that
community?

25. *Self.* Do not be upset that participation in the use of temporal
things is the same for the good and the wicked. Nor should you think,
because you see that they share similarly with you in all these things,
that God loves them in the same way. Just as wild beasts are not created
for themselves but for humankind, so wicked people live not for themselves but for the good. As their lives serve the utility of the good, so
there is no doubt that all that nurtures their lives ought to be credited
to the account of the good. The wicked are permitted to live among the
good so that their society may provide a challenge in the lives of the
good. By their happiness (*felicitatem*) they admonish good people to
seek the greater goods in which the wicked cannot participate, while
by their wickedness they push the good to love virtue more ardently.
Finally, when the good see them devoid of divine grace, rushing headlong down every slope of vice, they learn what great thanks they should
return to their Creator for their salvation. Therefore, for the increase
of our salvation and as a pattern of glorification, the divine plan requires that just as we learn in the life of the wild animals that supreme
happiness does not lie in using them, so also in the lives of wicked men
we learn that the highest happiness does not lie in dominating them.
So, these things must be granted indifferently to the good and the
wicked, for the good would not believe that greater things are kept for
them if they did not see that these things are common to both the
wicked and the good. So do not worry any more about the society and
happiness of the wicked. Nor should you think that, because you have
them as companions in the use and dominion of passing things, they
are to be assigned the privilege of singular love along with you. Even
in this, as we said already, they advance your salvation because with
you they are able not only to use but also to rule over those things.

26. But what shall I say about the company of the good? The only thing that remains now is for you to consider whether, because he does not love you without the company of the good this a reason why you cannot glory in a singular love of your spouse. Therefore, I want you to remember the position I asserted earlier, which then you judged as unsuitable to prove what was being discussed then and is still being discussed. I repeat it now so that I may discuss more carefully in your presence whether or not its truth can contribute something for us toward what we are trying to demonstrate. I said that the Creator grants the company of other people to you as a gift so that from it you may gain support for your life and not be wasted away by a lonely and idle life. And so just as the life of the wicked is a challenge for you, so the life of the good is a support. The good are such that you ought not disdain to have them as sharers in your happiness and your love. For if you love those who are truly good, the charity, which is in you, will rejoice over whatever benefit is extended to them, not as another's, but as your own.

27. Therefore, although it would be blessed to enjoy that love even alone, it is much more blessed to delight in it with the shared joy of many good people. When the sentiment of love (*dilectionis*) is expanded also to co-sharers, the pleasing joy of charity (*caritatis*) is increased. For spiritual love (*amor*) then becomes better in a singular way to each when it is common to all. It is not lessened by the participation of many; one same fruit of it is found wholly in each. The company of the good is not an obstacle to the privilege of your singular love, because your spouse loves you in all those whom he loves on your account. Through this he also loves you singularly, because he loves nothing without you. You should not worry that his mind is drawn away into the love of many as though by affection and so is less toward each, because it seems to be partitioned in some way or divided among all. He is present in each just as he is in all, because he would not extend a different or a greater affection of love to each if he loved each without the participation of all.

28. Because another besides this one is not to be loved by all uniquely, nor can another besides this one love all uniquely, therefore let all love one uniquely so that all may be loved by one uniquely. In one let all love themselves (*se*) as one so that they become one by the love of one. That love is unique, but not private; single, but not solitary; participated, but not divided; common and singular, singular for all and complete for each; not decreasing through participation, nor wearing

out through use, nor aging through time; ancient and new[20]; desirable
to feeling, sweet to experience; eternally fruitful, full of happiness; re-
freshing and satisfying and never causing weariness.

29. *Soul.* Your assertions are pleasing enough to me, and I confess
that because of them I am now beginning to desire love of this one
more ardently on the same grounds that earlier I had begun to loathe
it more. There is just one thing I still desire, and if I can gain it from
you, I will have no doubt that I have been completely satisfied. This is
it: Is it somehow possible to show how this chaste spouse is present
affectively and effectively to each of those whom he loves, just as he is
present to all? I could not doubt his affection if I knew this were true
in fact.[21]

30. *Self.* O my soul, if you persist for so long in what you began and
judge yourself dissatisfied, and if you do not fully recognize the singular
benefit which your spouse has extended to you, I will also gladly accede
to your request in this as well. For I know that your insistence is born
of devotion rather than from stubbornness. For in this also your most
excellent lover has provided for you, so that you would have something
in which you could glory in him singularly.

31. Just as he has given common and special gifts, so he has also
granted singular ones. Those that occur for the use of all are common,
like the light of the sun and air for breathing. Special gifts, by contrast,
are those that are granted not to all but, as it were, to a specific community, like faith, wisdom, and discipline. Singular ones are those that
are imparted to each individual as his own, like primacy (*principatus*)
among the apostles to Peter, the apostolate to the gentiles to Paul, and
the privilege of love to John.[22]

32. Consider, therefore, my soul, the gifts you have received: the
ones that are common to all, the ones special to some, and the singular
ones you alone have received. In all these gifts he loved you, whether
he granted them to all in common with you, or especially to some, or
singly to you alone. Moreover, he loved you with all these with whom
he associated you in participation in his gift. Beyond all these, he loved
you by preferring you to them in the gift of his singular grace. In every
creature, you are loved; with all good people, you are loved; beyond all
evil people, you are loved. And if it does not seem much to you that
you are loved beyond all wicked people, how many good people are
there who have received less than you? However, because I see that,
from a desire for a singular love, you are instead pressing forward toward the things that are given singly, I want what has already been said

to suffice even though there are many things that could still be said about those in whom and with whom you are loved. I do not wish you to think it of little account to be loved in so many gifts and with such people, where you have both all the good as comrades and the wicked and all created things as subjects.

33. O my soul, you have now seen how great are the gifts in which you are loved; you have seen with what sort of people you are loved; now, to the extent you are able, consider those in preference to whom you are loved. I am speaking to you, my soul. You know what you have received and you need to know that better still, so that you do not begin either to presume regarding what you have not received or fail to give thanks for those things that you have received. Would that I could remember them in a way that would profit you and please the one who gave them to you! For he gave you these things so that you may always keep them in mind and never, through forgetfulness, grow cold in his love.

34. My soul, first ponder that once you were not, and your coming to be was his gift. So it was his gift that you came into being. But had you given him anything before you came to be, so that he would repay you by your coming to be? Surely not! You had given nothing, and you could have given nothing before you came to be. You received gratis from him your coming to be. To whom were you preferred when you were made? Who could receive less than the one who received coming to be? Nevertheless, unless to receive being were to receive something,[23] one who was not could not begin to be; and unless to be was better than not to be, he who is would have received nothing more than he who is not. Why therefore, my God, did you make me, if not because you wanted me to be rather than not to be?[24] And you loved me more than all those who did not merit to receive being from you. When, therefore, my God, you gave me being, you gave me a good, a great good—a good, your beautiful good;[25] and when you gave this to me, you preferred me to all those to whom you did not choose to give this great good of yours.

35. O my soul, do we say something when we say this to our God, to our God by whom we were made—made, who were not, and who have received more than all who were not? Yes, certainly, yes, we do say something, and we say much when we say this. We should always be saying this, so that we never forget him from whom we received so great a good.

36. Even if he had given nothing more,[26] yet for this we should always praise and love him. Now, however, he has given more, because

he gave not only being, but beautiful being, fair being, which exceeds being-merely-something by its form[27] as much as it exceeds nothing by its existence. In this, that-it-is is very pleasing, but that it-is-such is still more delightful. In this, my soul, notice that you are preferred to all whom you see have not received such, and so excellent, a good of existing.

37. But this could not be the end of the most excellent giver's generosity. He still gave something more and drew us more toward his likeness. He wished to draw toward himself through likeness what he was drawing toward himself through love. He gave us being and beautiful being; he also gave us life, so that we excel by being those which are not, by form those which are disordered or unconnected, and by life those which are inanimate. You have incurred a great debt, my soul; you have received much, and you have had nothing from yourself. For all these gifts you have nothing to give in return, except only that you love. What has been given through love cannot be better or more fittingly requited than through love. You have received all this through love. God was able to give life also to other creatures, but in this gift he loved you more. To be sure, he did not love you more because he found more to be loved in you, but, because out of free graciousness he loved you more, he made you such that now he can love you more deservedly.

38. *Soul.* The more I hear, the more I want to hear. Go on please, and tell me what follows next.

39. *Self.* After being, after beautiful being, and after life, sentience and discernment were also given through the same love. Unless that love had preceded, the generous giver would have given nothing, and the needy recipient would have received nothing. How sublime and how beautiful have you been made, my soul! At what did this adornment of such quantity and quality aim, if not that the same one who clothed you was preparing you as a bride for his bridal chamber. He knew for what work he created you; he knew what kind of adornment suited that work. Therefore he gave what was suitable, indeed so greatly suitable that he who gave it loved it. He adorned you outwardly with senses and illumined you inwardly with wisdom, giving the senses as exterior adornment, and wisdom as interior raiment; giving the senses, as though attaching shining jewels exteriorly, and giving wisdom, as though decorating the appearance of your countenance interiorly with natural beauty. Look how your adornment exceeds the beauty of all jewels; see how your face surpasses the beauty of all forms. It was fitting that she who was to be led into the bedchamber of the Heavenly King[28]

be so adorned. How greatly are you loved, beyond how many others, when you are made thus! How singular the gift, a gift not granted to all, but destined only for those loved and to be loved!

40. You were able to glory a great deal, and you needed to be well guarded, so you would not lose such a gift, sully such adornment, corrupt such great beauty, or become more wretched by its loss or diminishment than you would have been if you had not received it or not received it so perfectly. You needed to be on guard lest, injured by the loss of that beauty, you would suffer disfiguring ugliness and, having been cast down, you would have become viler than if you had not received it. You should have guarded the former and feared the latter so that, guarded, the gift would endure, and its loss, guarded against, would not happen.

41. But see what you have done, my soul. You left your Spouse and prostituted your love with strangers. You corrupted your integrity, soiled your beauty, scattered your adornment. You became so vile, so sullied, and so unclean that you were no longer worthy of the embraces of such a Spouse. Your forgot your Spouse, and you have not given the thanks that such great gifts deserved. You have become a whore, and because of your uncontrolled fornications your breasts have hung loose. Your brow is wrinkled, your cheeks shrunken, your eyes tired and dull, your lips pallid, your skin dried, your strength broken, and you are hateful even to your lovers.[29]

42. *Soul.* I was hoping that so many laudatory pronouncements were heading in another direction, but, as I see, you have spoken these things to increase my embarrassment. By proving that I was ungrateful for the many gifts that I received and did not protect, you showed even more clearly that I deserve contempt. I would like it if what you told me had not happened or at least that what happened had not been told, so that forgetfulness would have blocked out my shame, even if my presumption had not avoided guilt.[30]

43. *Self.* These things were said not for your shame but for your instruction, so that you may become more humble[31] before him who both made you when you were not and redeemed you when you had perished. This too I mentioned in proof of his love so that, taking the opportunity it provides, I will now begin to tell how much that Spouse of yours, who showed himself so lofty when he created you, deigned to humble himself when he restored you. There he was so sublime, and here so humble, but no less lovable here than there, because no less wonderful here than there. There, he mightily established great things

for you; here, he mercifully sustained harsh things for you. In order to raise you from where you had fallen, he deigned to come down here where you were lying. To return justly to you what you had lost, he deigned to suffer lovingly what you endured. He came down, he assumed, he suffered, he conquered, and he restored: he came down to mortals, he assumed mortality, he suffered the passion, he conquered death, and he restored humankind.

44. Look, my soul, stand amazed at such wonders, such benefits shown on your behalf. Think how much the one who deigned to do such great things on your account loves you. You had been made beautiful by his gift; you were made sordid by your wickedness. But once again you have been cleansed and made alluring by his kindness; in both, his charity has been at work. Formerly, when you were not, he loved you and so he made you. Afterwards, when you were sordid, he loved you and so made you beautiful. In order to show you how much he loved you,[32] he did not want to free you from death except by dying, so that he not only imparted the benefit of his kindness, but also manifested the affection of his charity. Now he loves you with as sincere a charity as if you had always remained with him. He does not scold you for your guilt, nor reproach you about his gift. And if hereafter you choose to stay with him faithfully, love him as you ought, and keep your love for him blameless, he promises that he is going to give you things even greater than what have gone before.

45. *Soul.* Now, somehow, I am beginning to love my fault, because, as I see, having done wrong profited me not a little. Because of it what I wanted to know with all my desires has become clearer than the light. O happy fault[33] of mine, since he is drawn by love to wash it away. His very love, which I desired and longed for with all my heart, has appeared. I never would have recognized his love so well, if I had not experienced it in the middle of such great dangers. O how happily did I fall, since I arose happier after my fall. There is no greater love (*dilectio*), no more sincere love (*amor*), no holier love (*caritas*), no more ardent affection (*affectus*). He who was innocent died for me, though he found in me nothing to love. What, then, Lord, did you love in me and love so much that you died for me? What sort of thing did you find in me that for me you wished to undergo things so harsh?

46. *Self.* O my soul, accuse yourself before the Lord that up till now you have been ungrateful for his great gifts and have not wanted to know his many mercies. However, so that you can understand still better how much you owe him, I wish you to pay careful attention to

me as I proceed with the rest of his gifts following in the order we have already laid down.

47. *Soul.* I want to listen always to what is so sweet to me, so I would like you to repeat the same thing endlessly, if I were not hurrying on to the other things that remain to be heard.

48. *Self.* So, then, you had wandered off and had perished. Because you had been sold off in your sins, he came after you to buy you back. He loved you so much that he paid the price of his blood for you, and by that covenant[34] both led you back from exile and redeemed you from servitude.

49. *Soul.* I did not know that God loved me so much. No longer should I consider myself vile, for I pleased God so much that he chose to die for me so he would not lose me.

50. *Self.* And what if you began to ponder the number and kind of people who have been castoffs in comparison to you because they could not acquire this grace that was given to you? Certainly you have heard how many generations of people have died from the beginning till now. Without the knowledge of God and the price of their redemption, all of them have fallen into eternal death. Your Redeemer and Lover preferred you to all of these when he granted you this grace that none of them merited to receive. And what will you say? Why do you think you have been preferred to all of them? Were you stronger, wiser, nobler, and richer than all of them so that instead of them you merited to obtain this special grace? How many strong, wise, noble, and rich people were there among them, but nevertheless all of them, abandoned and cast off, perished. In preference to all of them you alone were taken up; and you can find no reason why this happened to you except the freely given charity of your Savior. Your Spouse, your Lover, your Redeemer, your God, chose and preferred you.[35] He chose you among all and took you up from all and loved you in preference to all. He called you by his own name, so that you would always remember it. He wished you to be a sharer in his name, a sharer in truth of the name. He anointed you with the oil of gladness with which he himself was anointed, so that whoever is called "Christian" from "Christ"[36] is anointed by the Anointed.[37]

51. *Soul.* I confess that much has been given to me, but I ask you: If, as you assert, I have already been taken up, why am I still put off so I cannot yet come to the embraces of the Spouse?

52. *Self.* You do not know, my soul, you just do not know how filthy you were before, how polluted, how deformed and dirty, torn and scat-

tered, full of every horror and distortion. So how do you expect to be led into that bridal chamber of modesty and chastity so quickly, if you are not first brought back to your earlier beauty by being refined with some care and effort? This is the reason that you are now waiting, this is why your Spouse still withdraws his presence from you and does not yet admit you in mutual embraces and sweet kisses: she who is unclean ought not to touch him who is clean, and it is not fitting that a vile person see someone beautiful. However, when you have been prepared and decently adorned, you will finally enter that bedchamber of the heavenly Spouse and remain there without any embarrassment. Then you will not be ashamed of your earlier foulness, you will have nothing foul, nothing to be ashamed of. So first strive to take care of your appearance (*formam*), to adorn your face, arrange your clothes, wipe away your blemishes, restore your cleanness, correct your behavior, keep discipline, and, when everything has finally been changed for the better, present yourself as a worthy bride for a worthy Spouse.

53. I want to say something else to make you more cautious, lest, because you hear that you are elected, pride may swell you up or negligence make you careless. Have you heard what King Ahasuerus did, when he repudiated Queen Vasthi because of her arrogance? It is a striking deed, a useful example, a grave danger. She was cast down because of her pride. The king issued a command that from his entire realm beautiful, young virgins should be gathered and led to the city of Susa and entrusted to the house of the women under the care of Hegai, the eunuch, who was the provost and guardian of the royal women. There they were to receive female accoutrement and other things they needed to use. So, with everything furnished abundantly according to the royal favor, they were to be cultivated[38] and adorned. For six months they were to be anointed with oil of myrtle, and for another six months they were to use certain cosmetics. And so prepared and adorned, they would pass from the dining hall[39] of the women to the bedchamber of the king, so that the one from among all of them who had most pleased the eyes of the king would sit on the royal throne in place of Vashti. See how many were selected so that the one who seemed most alluring and adorned in the eyes of the king could be chosen. The ministers of the king select many for refinement, but the king himself chooses one for his nuptial chamber. The first choice of many is made according to the command of the king; the second choice of one is made according to the will of the king.

54. Let us consider if, perchance, this example can be adapted to the subject we are presently considering. The King, the Son of the supreme King,[40] came into this world, which he had created, to espouse to himself a chosen wife, a unique wife, a wife worthy of the royal nuptials. But because Judea disdained to receive him when he appeared in humble form, she was cast down. The ministers of the King, namely the apostles, were sent throughout the whole world to gather souls and lead them to the city of the King, that is, to the holy Church. In it is the house and dwelling place of the royal women, that is, holy souls, who are made fruitful and bring forth children not for servitude but for the realm. Because they serve God not out of fear but out of love, they give birth to good works in freedom. Many of those called enter the Church through faith and there receive the sacraments of Christ as ointments and antidotes prepared for the restoration and adornment of souls. But because the voice of truth says, "Many are called, few are chosen," not all who are admitted to this cultivation are to be selected for the realm, but only those who strive to cleanse and cultivate themselves through those sacraments, so that, when they are led into the presence of the King, they may be found such as he wishes to choose rather than repudiate.

55. Therefore, see where you are placed, and you will understand what you need to do. Your spouse placed you in the dining hall, where the women are adorned. He also gave various cosmetics and different adornments (*species*), and ordered that you be served royal foods from his table. He granted whatever could promote health and provide refreshment, whatever could restore appearance (*speciem*), whatever could increase beauty (*decorem*). Take care, then, not to neglect to cultivate yourself, lest on your last day, when you are presented again in the sight of this Spouse, you may be found—God forbid!—unworthy of his company. Prepare yourself as befits the bride of the King, and the bride of the heavenly King, the bride of the immortal Spouse.

56. *Soul.* Again, you have struck me with bitter sorrow and great fear. So far as I can understand your words, I have a new perspective (*propositum*), but I have not escaped the danger. I have changed my perspective, because I have converted from the wandering and unstable love (*amorem*), which used to drag me around, to a unique love (*dilectionem*). I have not escaped the danger, because as you assert, unless I strive to show myself worthy in every way, I do not attain the fruit of this love. Therefore it now remains for you to explain more fully to me about the dining room in which the royal women are fed, about the

royal food that is given to them, about the ointments with which they are anointed, and about all the other things that are furnished for their cultivation or beauty. I am, then, moved by his love to devote myself hereafter to those things without which I see that I cannot reach the outcome of that love. Would that I may deserve to be the one whose beauty and adornment the king will praise! How happy will be the one whose efforts lead to that end; she will be more elect than the elect. If I could direct my effort to that goal, then how insignificant I would think all that labor was. I ask, therefore, that you not be slow to lay out for me, one by one, what are the remedies by which I ought to reform my appearance to have this beauty. I passionately desire to please him, whose charity toward me I recognize is so very kind and whose love I know is so pleasant.

57. *Self.* Yes, it is really necessary that you do it. I am praying that he, who has already granted you the will to do this, will also grant you the strength to perfect it. You ask what the dining hall is and also what the king's bedchamber is. Set these two rooms before your mind, because you need to consider them. There is the dining hall; there is the king's bedroom. In the dining hall the brides are prepared for the wedding, but in the bedroom the wedding is celebrated.[41] The present Church is, so to speak, the dining hall, in which the brides of God are now prepared for the future wedding, whereas the heavenly Jerusalem is, so to speak, the king's bedchamber in which the wedding itself is celebrated. After the times of adornment, they pass from the dining hall to the bedchamber of the king, because after the times of acting well they come to receive the fruit of their good work. The present Church is rightly called the dining hall because of the three categories (*ordines*) of believers: the married, the continent, and pastors (*rectores*) or virgins.[42]

58. Let us see next what are the ointments and kinds of cosmetics, what are the foods, and what are the clothes prepared for the cultivation of the brides. No one should fail to note that just as the spouse, as a free gift, first loved those who were stained and filthy in some way, so he also freely granted them every beauty aid. Unless they receive it from him, they have nothing from themselves with which to please him. So know also that whatever you have with which to adorn yourself also pertains to his love, since you have nothing from yourself unless you have received it from him. The first thing provided here is the font of baptism and bath of rebirth, in which you wash away the stains of past sins. Then chrism and oil are provided, by which you are anointed with

the Holy Spirit. After you have been anointed and imbued with the oil of gladness, you come to the table and receive there the food of the body and blood of Christ. By it, you are nurtured and refreshed interiorly and drive off that harmful leanness of earlier fasts, and so you are rejuvenated again with your former fullness and restored strength. Then you put on the clothes of good works and are groomed with the fruit of alms, fasts, prayers, holy vigils, and other works of devotion as if by a varied adornment. Finally, there follow the perfumes of the virtues, whose sweet odor diffuses and puts to flight that stench of old filths in such a way that you seem completely changed and transformed into someone else. You are made happier, more eager, and healthier. You also receive a mirror, the Holy Scriptures, in order to see your face, so that the way you are groomed may have nothing less or otherwise than is fitting.

59. So, what do you say, my soul? Do you know whether you have as yet received any of these? Surely you have been washed in the font; surely you have received the anointing with chrism; surely you have eaten the same food and drunk the same drink from the table of the King. If perchance you have become soiled again, you have tears by which you can again wash yourself clean. If the anointing has dried up on you, you may anoint yourself again through good and loving devotion. If you are again emaciated by long fasting, washed by tears, and renewed by the anointing of devout contrition, you may return again to your refreshment.

60. See how a loving arrangement brings everything together for you. What you did not have was given to you. What you lost was restored to you. You were never abandoned, so you know how much you are loved by the one who loves you. He does not want to lose you, and so he waits with such great patience and lovingly grants again and again what you have lost so often through negligence, provided that you wish to recover it. O, how many have already perished who had received these things with you, but having lost them did not merit receiving them again with you. You have been loved more than all of them, because he so kindly returned to you what you lost, whereas he so strictly denied to them what was lost. Has no grace for acting well been given you? On the contrary, by his largesse good will has not been denied you. If you do great works, you are mercifully exalted. If you do not do great works, perhaps being humbled saves you. He knows better than you what will help you. For this reason, if you want to think rightly about him, understand that all that he does for you is done well. For

example, maybe you do not have the grace of virtues, but when you are struck by an unwholesome impulse (*vitiorum impulsu*) you are better strengthened in humility. The scent of humble weakness pleases God more than proud virtue. Do not dare to judge rashly anything in his ordering of things, but always pray to him with fear and reverence, that he may support you in the way that he knows how. If anything wicked still remains in you, let him lovingly wash it away; if you have begun anything good, let him bring it to completion, and let him lead you to himself by the way that he has chosen.

61. What more can I say to you? Is there anything more that we can say to manifest his love?[43] I am speaking to you, my soul, is there anything? What will you say? If you talk about what pertains to you, you cannot speak about what concerns others. If you speak of what concerns others and you, then you cannot speak of all. For who could speak of all? And nevertheless we know that love (*caritas*) is the origin of everything. Behold two people are born: they share the same noble lineage, and they are born in the same hour. One is left in poverty; the other is buoyed up by riches. Love is at work in both cases, because it humbles the first through poverty and consoles the latter with abundance. One is weak, and the other strong. One is restrained from doing evil; the other grows strong for good work. Love proves both; it reproves neither. One is illumined through wisdom, the other is left in his simple understanding; the latter to look down on himself, the former to strive to acknowledge his Creator; but love wishes to be present to both. Such is the love of God in us; insofar as it lies in his goodness, human weakness does not suffer anything that he does not arrange for our good.

Confession

62. I confess[44] to you your mercies, Lord, my God, because you, the sweetness of my life and the light of my eyes,[45] have not abandoned me. "What will I give to you in return for all that you have returned to me?"[46] You want me to love you, and how will I love you? How much will I love you? Who am I to love you? And nevertheless, "I love you, Lord, my Strength, my Ground, my Refuge, my Liberator, my God, my Helper, my Protector, the Horn of my salvation, my Support."[47] What else may I say? You are the Lord, my God. O my soul, what will we do for the Lord, our God, from whom we have received so many and such

great good things? He was not content to give us the same goods that he gave to the rest. Even in the bad things in our lives we recognize him as loving us in a singular way, so that we may love him in a singular way for both the good things and the bad things of our lives.

63. Lord, you have given me to recognize you and to understand more than many others what has been revealed of your secrets. You have left some of my contemporaries in the darkness of ignorance and poured the light of your wisdom in me rather than in them. You have given me to know you more truly, to love you more purely, to believe in you more sincerely, and to follow you more ardently.[48] You have given me keen awareness (*sensum capacem*), an agile mind, a tenacious memory, a ready tongue, pleasing speech, convincing teaching, effectiveness in work, graceful demeanor (*gratiam in conversatione*), progress in studies, results in undertakings, consolation in adversities, caution when things go well. Wherever I have turned, there your grace and mercy preceded me. And often when I seemed to myself to be exhausted, you suddenly delivered me; when I was wandering, you brought me back; when I was ignorant, you taught me; when I was sinning, you corrected me; when I was sad, you consoled me; when I was despairing, you comforted me; when I fell, you lifted me up; when I stood, you held me; when I went, you led me; when I came back, you received me. You did all these things for me, Lord, my God, and many other things. It will always be pleasant (*dulce*) to think and speak and to give thanks about things, so that I may praise you and love you for all your gifts, Lord, my God.

64. See, then, my soul, you have your betrothal-gift, and in your betrothal-gift you know your spouse. Keep yourself untouched for him, keep yourself unsullied, keep yourself untainted, and keep yourself unblemished. If you were once a whore, now you have become a virgin;[49] in one way or another his love has regularly restored purity to the corrupted and preserved the chastity of the pure. Therefore, always think about how much mercy he has shown you and, in the process, ponder how much he loves you, because you know that his beneficence has never failed you.

65. *Soul.* I confess that this love is rightly called singular, for although it is poured out on many, it embraces each one uniquely: a truly beautiful and wondrous good that is common to all and wholly for each. It guards all, fills each, is present everywhere, takes care of all, and provides for each just as it does for all.[50] When I consider his mercies toward me, it

certainly seems to me that, if it is all right to say so, God does nothing else except provide for my salvation, and he seems to me so completely occupied with guarding me that he forgets all others and chooses to be occupied with me alone. He shows himself always present; he offers himself always prepared. Wherever I turn, he does not desert me; wherever I am, he does not draw back; whatever I do, he is equally present to help. Finally, he shows clearly by the very outcome of his working that he is perpetually looking at all my actions and thoughts, and, insofar as it pertains to his goodness, assisting them as an ever-present (*individuus*) helper. From this it is evident that although we still cannot see his face, nevertheless his presence can never be evaded.

66. I confess, however, that as I think about this more attentively, I am struck at the same time with fear and shame, because I see that he, whom I want so much to please, is everywhere present to me and sees all my secrets.[51] O how many things there are in me that cause me to blush before his eyes! Now I am more afraid of displeasing him by these things than I am confident of pleasing him by the things which are praiseworthy in me, if there are any. O would that for a little while I could hide from his eyes, until I washed away all those blemishes and finally appeared before his gaze unsullied and without a blemish! For how will I be able to please him in this deformity, when I myself am so strongly displeased by it? O old stains, O disgusting and vile stains, why do you hang on so long? Go away, leave, and no longer presume to offend the eyes of my Beloved! Do not deceive yourselves. By his help you are not going to stay with me forever, although to this point, while I have been procrastinating, it has not been possible to exterminate you. I pronounce an oath over you: I will neither keep nor love you any more, because I utterly detest and completely abhor your filth. In fact, now I would not want to be infected with you even if I could not be seen. How much more is this so now, because I am visible to him and to offend him saddens me more certainly than even my foulness does. So go away! In vain do you still cling to me because, even if you remain with me, you are not mine. I declare that you are foreign to my lot, and henceforward I wish to have no communion with you. I have another model (*exemplar*) to which I wish to be conformed. I constantly refer to it and, as much as I can, I draw my likeness from it more and more. From this, then, I have also learned that I must exterminate you and now I recognize how I may do this.

67. *Self.* Something wonderful is transpiring with us, which perhaps does not arouse your wonder, because you do not yet understand what

I wish to say. Notice how from the beginning of our conversation (*sermonis*) you brought forward many things that seemed to militate against love, and by them the power of love was never weakened but rather more fully established. You said that love cannot be singular and at the same time common, but then love was proven to be more wonderful, because it was shown to be both common and singular. Again, you said that you were not perfectly loved, because you had heard that you were chosen for grooming, but still you did not see yourself taken up to the bridal chamber. Once again his love toward you is shown to be even greater, as great as his patience that awaits your perfection.

68. Finally, now, you began to doubt whether he can love you in your deformity, which you suffer, be it unwillingly. But when you entertained this doubt, you forgot that formerly you were completely vile yet still loved. If therefore you were deemed worthy of love then, when you were completely corrupt and had as yet no beauty, how much more will he love you now, when you have begun to be made beautiful and to put aside the earlier filth. For this, too, belongs to the praise of his love, that he deigns to love someone imperfect. Although he still sees in you certain things that do not please him, he loves how you also have begun to hate in yourself those things that displease him. He pays more attention to your resolve than to your state; he notices not what you are but what you wish to be, provided you try as hard as you can to merit being what you still have not begun to be.

69. *Soul.* I have one last question to ask you, which I hope you will receive kindly. What is that sweet something that sometimes touches me when I remember him and affects me so strongly and pleasantly? Then, somehow, I begin to be completely alienated from myself and drawn away in some way. Suddenly I am renewed and completely changed, and I begin to experience a wellbeing that is beyond what I can describe. My conscience is joyful, all memory of the misery of past sorrows is forgotten, my mind exults, my understanding grows clear, my heart is illumined, and my desires are joyful. Then I see myself to be elsewhere, I do not know where. Interiorly, it seems as though I have hold of something in the embraces of love. I do not know what that is, and nevertheless I work with all my might to keep it always and never lose it. My mind struggles in some kind of delight so that it will not slip away from what it desires to embrace always. As if it has found in it the object of all its desires, it exults deeply and ineffably, seeking nothing else, desiring nothing more, and always wanting to be thus. Is this my

beloved? I ask, tell me, so that I may know if it is he, so that if he comes to me again, I may beg him not to leave but to remain forever.

70. *Self.* It truly is your Beloved who visits you, but he comes invisibly, in a hidden way, and incomprehensibly. He comes to touch you, not to be seen by you; he comes to move you, not to be grasped by you; he comes not to pour himself completely into you, but to offer you a taste; not to fulfill your desire, but to elicit your affection (*affectum*). He is extending to you certain first fruits of his love; he does not offer full and perfect union. This is the core of his betrothal-gift to you: he, who in the future will give himself to you to see and to possess unendingly, now sometimes offers himself to you as a foretaste so that you may recognize how sweet he is. At the same time, you are consoled meanwhile for his absence, when you are unceasingly refreshed by his visitation so you will not grow faint.

71. My soul, we have said many things; I ask you after all these: recognize One, love One, follow One, lay hold of One, and possess One.

72. *Soul.* This I choose, this I desire, and for this I long with all my heart.

NOTES

1. The paragraph numbers have been inserted by the translator. They differ somewhat from the paragraph numbers in earlier translations.
2. What Hugh is sending is a "soliloquium dilectionis" in several senses: it is a soliloquy whose topic is love; it is a soliloquy expressing Hugh's love for the canons of Hamersleben and also his own love of Christ.
3. In this sentence, Hugh uses three words for love. "Caritas," here used as a title of respect, signifies the love (*agape*) that Jesus asked of his disciples: sincere love of God and unselfish care of one's neighbor. "Caritas" is "amor" that is ordered and measured by reason and faith. "Amor" which is disordered or immoderate is "cupiditas." "Dilectio" adds to the notion of love an element of choice. At the end of this paragraph Hugh speaks of "affectus," which means feeling, affect, or affection. All of these words for love, except "cupiditas," occur in par. 45.
4. Throughout the work that follows, Hugh is going to distinguish what God gives to all in common (*communiter*), what he gives specially (*specialiter*) to many, and what he gives uniquely, or singly (*singulariter*), to an individual. In the translation I have tried to render these words consistently as "in common," "specially," and "singly." "Singly" is somewhat jarring, but "individually" has too many individualistic connotations and it does not emphasize difference enough, whereas "uniquely" seems to stress difference too much.
5. The references to love and manifestations of love extended in common, specially, and singly evoke a central theme of the work to follow. This can be seen as an indication that the work and the letter were written at the same time.
6. The earliest manuscripts have "H." or "Hugo" or "Homo"; pending the completion of the critical edition, we have chosen the reading "homo." "Homo" means "human being," but to translate it that way would be too impersonal. Our contemporary use of "self" is burdened with the last four hundred years of Cartesian, Romantic, and Freudian understandings of and preoccupations with the individual self, as well as the last fifty years of post-Enlightenment efforts to dissolve that self. However, as Hugh's soliloquy makes clear, in the twelfth century interest in and awareness of the self and its desires were intense. So, "self" seems the best translation. Sicard, *Oeuvre* 2:285 note 14, notes that most preceding editions have opted as we have for "homo" and "anima," but he prefers "Hugo," especially since the *Confessio* near the end of the work seems to refer to Hugh personally. This raises questions about the distance between the authorial "H" and Hugh of St Victor, the person. Perhaps in the *Confessio* the two coincide more closely than they do elsewhere in the treatise.
7. The contrast between "uti/use" and "frui/enjoy" is a key element in the Augustinian notion of love; see above, 54–60.
8. "... quod non diligit quod est." Sicard (*Oeuvre* 2:231) translates this as "not to love what one is" ("qu'il n'aime pas ce qu'il est"). He cites (*Oeuvre* 2:298 note 32) in support of this translation a parallel passage in *On the Three Days*: "Beatus autem quomodo esse potest, cui idipsum non placet quod est? Quisquis igitur beatus est et se ipsum diligit *et id quod ipse est diligit*" ("How can someone be blessed, who is not pleased by what he is? Whoever is blessed loves both himself and what he is"). Nevertheless, I am tempted to translate, "not to love what is."
9. Latin is well supplied with words for "beauty." In this sentence three of them appear in this order: "decus," "species," "decus," and "pulchritudo." In classical Latin "decus" (genitive: decoris, related to the Greek word doxa) means anything that adorns or honors; "species" is a very flexible word signifying sight, outward appearance, spectacle, semblance, pretext, ornament; "pulchritudo" means beauty. By the twelfth century, the three words could be used almost interchangeably. Hugh of St Victor, like his confreres Achard and Richard, had a deep appreciation of beauty. When, as in this passage, he mentions beauty often, he varies his vocabulary to achieve rhetorical beauty. Most of this paragraph and part of paragraph 13 are quoted in the anonymous Middle Dutch *Dedulinghe op Cantica Canticorum*; see Rik van

Nieuwenhove, Robert Faesen and Helen Rolfson, *Late Medieval Mysticism of the Low Countries*, Classics of Western Spirituality (New York: Paulist, 2008), 100.

[10] This sentence states the simple fact that our eyes are so positioned on our face that we cannot see it or them. Two further things should be kept in mind: (1) the medieval theory of vision held that the human eye (analogous to a modern sonar) sends out rays that reflect back off objects to make them visible; (2) medieval mirrors gave very poor images of the person looking into them.

[11] This seems to be an allusion to the myth of Narcissus. For a twelfth-century summary of the story, see the account of "The First Vatican Mythographer," in *The Vatican Mythographers*, tr. Ronald E. Pepin (New York: Fordham University Press, 2008), 78–79.

[12] "infimam quandam et imaginariam pulchritudinem": a weak beauty expressible in sensory images.

[13] Virgil, *Aeneid*, 5:538 (*Eclogues, Georgics, Aeneid I–VI*, ed. G. P. Goold [Cambridge, MA: Harvard University Press, 1999], 94.69).

[14] "aliene libidinis": either "another's lust" (objective or subjective genitive) or "a different lust."

[15] From here to the end of the paragraph "love" translates "diligere" and "dilectio."

[16] "obicis": this could be translated as "with which you reproach me" instead of "that you place before me." See Taylor, *Soul's Betrothal-Gift*, 14.

[17] "bestialibus": this might mean "cattle" instead of "bestial people."

[18] "ab illius dilectione": could also be translated "his love."

[19] "multis vero amplius": Taylor, *Soul's Betrothal-Gift*, 16, translates, "who are moreover very numerous indeed."

[20] Augustine, *Conf.* 10, 27 (O'Donnell, 134): ""Sero te amavi, pulchritudo tam antiqua et tam nova, sero te amavi!" ("Late have I loved you, beauty so ancient and so new, late have I loved you!").

[21] The word play "affectus/effectus" (affect/effect or feeling/fact) occurs elsewhere in Hugh's writings: e.g., Hugh of St Victor, *Sacr.* 1.7.11 (PL 176.291D–292A); *Potestate* (PL 176.839C–840B). In par. 69, "Soul" describes her experience of the presence of her Beloved.

[22] Hugh of St Victor, *Misc.* 1.98 (PL 177.528–29); Arno of Reichersberg, *Scutum canonicorum regularium* (PL 194.1521AB), where John is seen as emblematic of monks and Peter of the canons regular: "Solus Joannes inter apostolos Christi hoc privilegium amoris obtinuit, ut dilectus Domini vocaretur. De Martha autem et Maria ipse scribit Joannes, quia diligebat Jesus Martham, et sororem ejus Mariam et Lazarum. Ipse idem Apostolus, qui ex privilegio, ut dictum est, amoris, se unum a Domino dilectum esse commemorat, hoc ipso privilegio, quod nulli aliorum ascripsit Apostolorum, feminas insignivit. In quo etiam honore, etsi fratrem earum ipsis aggregaret, eas tamen illi praeposuit, quas in amore praecellere credidit" ("Among the apostles of Christ only John obtained this privilege of love, to be called the Lord's beloved. Referring to Martha and Mary, this same John wrote that Jesus loved Martha, her sister Mary, and Lazarus. This same apostle, who by what is termed the privilege of love relates that he was the one beloved by the Lord, bestowed that same privilege, which he ascribed to none of the other apostles, on these women. He also included their brother with them in this honor, but he put them before him, because he believed they were superior in love"). Cf. J. Châtillon, "La spiritualité de l'ordre canonial," in the collection of his writings edited by Patrice Sicard, *Le mouvement canonial au moyen âge: reform de l'église, spiritualité et culture*, Bibliotheca Victorina 3 (Turnhout: Brepols, 1992), 143–44.

[23] "Et tamen nisi hoc esset aliquid accipere": Kevin Herbert, *Soliloquy on the Earnest Money of the Soul*, Medieval Philosophical Texts in Translation 9 (Milwaukee: Marquette University Press, 1956), 23, translates: "And yet, unless something were there to receive existence . . ." However, Hugh's point seems to be that existence itself is a gift that takes one from non-being to being and so confers something.

[24] Here for the first time, *Self* addresses God directly. This shift from one interlocutor to another is reminiscent of many of the Psalms and anticipates the *confessio* of paragraphs 62–63.

²⁵ "bonum et magnum *bonum*, bonum et pulchrum bonum tuum michi dedisti." Some early manuscripts omit the italicized "bonum" so that the translation then would read: ". . . you gave me your good, good and great, good and beautiful."

²⁶ One is reminded of the refrain sung at Seder meals: "*Dahyenu*, it would have been enough."

²⁷ See, for example, *Sacr.* 1.1.13 (PL 176.188–89).

²⁸ By this point the Spouse is clearly identified with God and so nouns referring to him will be capitalized.

²⁹ Ezek. 23:29. See the introduction for contrasts with the description of the bride of the Song of Songs.

³⁰ Herbert, 25, notes that Soul has been brought to compunction. She recognizes her misery (*miseria*) and in devotion she will embrace the mercy of God (*misericordia*). Cf. Hugh of St Victor, *Virtute orandi* 1–4 (PL 176.977–79; tr. Feiss, VTT 4); *Sacr.* 1.1.12 (PL 176.195C–196A).

³¹ "obnoxia": Herbert, 25, translates, "more vividly aware of your obligations."

³² Sicard, *Oeuvre* 2:258, puts this clause with the preceding sentence.

³³ Hugh cites this expression, "O felix culpa," from the *Exultet*, the Easter Proclamation ("Praeconium Paschale") sung by the deacon at the Easter Vigil. This proclamation seems to date back at least to the sixth century.

³⁴ "quo pacto": This could mean generally "by that means," but I take it to connote specifically the covenant in Christ's blood. Taylor, *Soul's Betrothal-Gift*, 26, translates: "by such a bargain."

³⁵ "elegit ergo et preelegit": "eligere" = to choose, pick out; "praeeligere": to choose rather, to prefer. Sicard, *Oeuvre* 2:263, hints at the divine foreknowledge and predestination, a connotation not entirely lacking: "Tu as donc été élue, *choisie a l'avance*" ("Thus you have been selected, chosen in advance").

³⁶ This could also be translated, "by Christ."

³⁷ Cf. *Sacr.* 2.7.1 (PL 176.459). *Christos* is the Greek translation of Messiah, the Hebrew word for "anointed." Cf. Ambrose of Milan, *De Spiritu sancto* 1.3.44, Faller, CSEL 79, 32: "He who has named one has signified the Trinity. If you name Christ, then you designate the Father, by whom the Son was anointed, and the Son himself, who was anointed, and the Spirit, with whom the Son was anointed."

³⁸ "exolorentur": Taylor, *Soul's Betrothal-Gift*, 28, translates, "decked out."

³⁹ "triclinium": In Roman times, an eating couch which surrounded a dining table on three sides, and hence, a dining room. Hugh seems to be thinking of the hall of a medieval manor (or monastery guest facility), where most of the household ate, slept, and conducted business. Only a few were given access to the lord's private chamber.

⁴⁰ *Sacr.* 1 prol. 2 (PL 176.183B–184A), where Hugh develops the metaphor of Christ the King: "Verbum enim incarnatum rex noster est" ("The incarnate Word is our King").

⁴¹ "nuptiae celebrantur": Herbert, 30, translates: "The bonds are consummated."

⁴² The threefold division of the faithful became traditional with Gregory the Great; see, for example, *Mor.* 1.14 (20) (Adriaen, 34); 32.20 (35), (Adriaen, 1656). The third category varies in different authors and contexts between virgins or pastors. For references and a helpful discussion of the variety of influences on and forms of this tripartite schema see Louis-Marie Gantier, "Le pape et l'évêque dans l'ecclésiologie monastique d'Abbon de Fleury (vers 950–1004)," in *Church, Society and Monasticism*, ed. E. López-Tello García and B. S. Zorzi, Studia Anselmiana 146, Analecta Monastica 9 (Rome: Pontificio Ateneo S. Anselmo, 2009): 143–46.

⁴³ "dilectionem": In the rest of the paragraph "love" translates "caritas," except in the last sentence, where Hugh uses "amor."

⁴⁴ As in St Augustine's *Confessions*, "confessio" here has three meanings: confession of faith; confession of sins; confession of praise. On "confessio" see Michele Pellegrino, *Le Confessioni di Sant' Agostino*, Cultura 15 (Rome: Editrice Studium, 1972): 9–14. In this confession, the "self 's" deep faith in God is basic, but implicit; he confesses his sins and weaknesses in order to exalt God's grace shown in God's many gifts to him. He also acknowledges that he is gifted,

and that acknowledgment seems to be autobiographical. If so, it is an example of the truth of the adage, "Humility is truth." Hugh realizes that he is exceptionally and literally gifted; his aim in that acknowledgment is to praise the Giver.

45 These terms of endearment would be at home in a troubadour's love poem. They have biblical antecedents: Prov. 16:24: "dulcedo animae" (the words of the wise are "sweetness to the soul") and Tob. 10:4 (Vulg.); Ps. 37:11 (Vulg.); Bar. 3:14: "lumen oculorum" ("the light of the eyes").

46 The verbs in this sentence are forms of "retribuere," and so the emphasis is not on the gift of creation, but on the gifts of redemption.

47 Here Hugh condenses Ps. 17:2–3 (Vulg.), leaving out the words in brackets: "Diligam te Domine fortitudo mea [Dominus] firmamentum meum [et] refugium meum [et] liberator meus Deus meus adiutor meus [et sperabo in eum] protector meus [et] cornu salutis meae et susceptor meus."

48 It is hard not to see the presence of these phrases in a prayer attributed to St Richard Wych (1197–1262), who served as chancellor of Oxford University and Bishop of Chichester: "Thanks be to you, my Lord Jesus Christ, for all the benefits you have given me, for all the pains and insults you have borne for me. O most merciful Redeemer, friend and brother, may I know you more clearly, love you more dearly, follow you more nearly." The prayer was the basis for the song "Day by Day" in the musical "Godspell."

49 Hugh customarily puts great emphasis on interior intention. From that perspective, virginity is a matter of intention more than it is a physical state. Sicard, *Oeuvre* 2:298 note 115, points out that in his *Letter to Eustochium*, 22.5, ed. F. A. Wright, St Jerome, *Select Letters* (Cambridge: Harvard, 1975), 62–63, Jerome said that virginity once lost could not be regained, and Peter Damian, in his *Letter on the Omnipotence of God,* ed. A. Cantin, *Lettre sur la toute-puissance divine*, SC 191 (Paris: Cerf, 1972): 116 [PL 145:600B–601B], said it could be regained.

50 Three of the verbs (in Latin, participles) in this clause speak of providence, which was an important idea in Hugh's theology. Hugh has argued that God loves each person singly, just as he loves all of humankind collectively. Here he applies this same idea to divine providence. On this divine embrace of the whole and of the indivdual, see *Tribus diebus* 15 (ed. Poirel, 33, 526–28; tr. Feiss, VTT 1, 75): "All beings have been made as if they had been made one by one, in such a way that in observing the totality you admire each."

51 Heb. 4:13.

ADAM OF ST VICTOR

SEQUENCES ON LOVE

INTRODUCTION AND TRANSLATION
BY JULIET MOUSSEAU

INTRODUCTION

Several of Adam of St Victor's sequences allude to a theology of Christian love.[1] The sequences *Gratulemur ad festivum* and *Simplex in essentia* illustrate Adam's concept of Christian love, though many others contribute to a fuller understanding of Adam's thought on this subject. *Gratulemur ad festivum* celebrates the feast of St John the Evangelist, and *Simplex in essentia* was sung during the octave of Pentecost. The first demonstrates the love of Christ for John and treats John as an exemplar of Christian love. The second sequence shows the contrast between the law of fear in the Old Testament and the law of love that rules Christian history, while also emphasizing the role of the Holy Spirit, who inspires Christians to loving action.

Gratulemur ad festivum celebrates the life of St John the Evangelist, alluding both to Scripture and to stories in the hagiographical tradition.[2] Referring to the Gospel of John, Adam calls John the "more beloved" of Christ (v. 3). He is the disciple to whom Jesus commits the care of his pure and precious Mother (v. 4). John's loving-kindness goes hand in hand with his purity of heart and body (v. 5).

John's purity of heart is the source of a number of miraculous events: the sequence alludes to several stories that must be filled out by the hagiographical tradition. John emerges from a vat of hot oil due to his purity; he restores shattered gemstones to wholeness; he is not harmed by the poison he is forced to drink; and he brings several people back to life. A number of John's miracles are noteworthy as acts of kindness: he provides for the needs of the poor and aids those who have lost beloved family. Additionally, the miracles offer opportunities for

---

[1]   Adam of St Victor and his sequences are introduced in *Trinity and Creation*, VTT 1:181–84.

[2]   In this section, Jacobus de Voragine's *Golden Legend*, tr. William Granger Ryan, 2 vols. (Princeton: Princeton University Press, 1993) will be cited as an accessible source for the hagiography surrounding John the Evangelist. However, Adam of St Victor predates this compilation of hagiographical texts. It is likely that he utilized the apocryphal works *Acta Iohannis* and *Virtutes Iohannis* (Eric Junod and Jean-Daniel Kaestli, Corpus Christianorum Series Apocryphorum, 1–2 [Turnhout: Brepols, 1983]). For details about these sources and Adam's use of them, see Jean Grosfillier, *Les séquences d'Adam de Saint-Victor: étude littéraire (poétique et rhétorique), textes et traductions, commentaries*, Bibliotheca Victorina, 20 (Turnhout: Brepols, 2008), 773–84.

preaching the Gospel and winning converts to Christianity, thereby granting them the possibility of salvation in Christ—another significant demonstration of Christian love.

The loving character of the Holy Spirit is central to Adam's sequences for the feast of Pentecost. For example, the sequence *Qui procedis ab utroque*, published in the first volume of this series, describes the Holy Spirit as the love of the Father and the Son, emphasizing his position as equal to both. In that sequence, it is clearly seen that the Holy Spirit's role in human life involves moving the heart to love and easing the heart's troubles. Such care of the human heart inspires the recipient to treat others with love and good works.

The same theme emerges in the sequence *Simplex in essentia*. The light of the Holy Spirit purifies the human heart (v. 2). Once ruled by the Spirit, the Christian is then freed from sinfulness and given full liberty. In the final verse, "May the law of love free us," Adam seeks that freedom from the bonds of sinfulness, which here might be understood as a lack of love. For Adam, then, a life of loving action is the life of true freedom.

More strikingly, the sequence *Simplex in essentia* contrasts the law of the old covenant with the law of the New Testament. Using colorful language, Adam describes the law given to Moses on Mount Sinai as a law wrapped in fear and trembling. This law strikes terror while the law of love, given to the disciples in the person of the Holy Spirit at Pentecost, enriches them with grace and gives them power over sin and sickness. Here again, Christ's law requires love such that a lack of love is the equivalent of lawlessness and sinfulness. The apostles, like John, demonstrate their love through their miraculous actions on behalf of the sick and suffering.

In these examples, Adam of St Victor's theology of Christian love centers on the activity of the Holy Spirit in the heart of the Christian, and on the Christian's loving action on behalf of others. Thus, love and purity of life confound fear and sinfulness and bring freedom.[3]

---

[3]   Many other sequences provide further examples of Adam's concept of Christian love. Most notable are his sequences for the Blessed Virgin Mary. Using beautiful imagery, he describes her loving actions and her purity of heart. Here and elsewhere, Adam is careful to pair the love of spiritual goods with contempt of earthly things, a concept which supports his exaltation of the purity of heart realized in the celibacy of both John the Evangelist and the Mother of God.

GRATULEMUR AD FESTIVUM

SEQUENCE FOR THE FEAST OF ST JOHN THE EVANGELIST

1.
Let us rejoice
for the feast;
let us be glad
for John's
votive celebration.

2.
Thus let our praise be recited
out loud,
that our heart
is not cheated of the savor
by which it tastes joy.

3.
This is one particularly beloved of Christ,
who, reclining on his breast,[1]
drew wisdom from him.[2]

4.
Christ on the cross
commended to him his mother—this virgin
protected the one who did not know man.[3]

5.
He burns inside with charity,
and shines outside with purity,
by his signs and eloquence.

6.
Just as he escaped wicked passion,
so, immune to the punishment,
he escaped from the vat.[4]

7.
He overcame the power of poison
he ruled over death, disease
and even demons.[5]

8.
But the man of such power
was not a man of less loving-kindness
toward those troubled.

9.
When he made solid the broken pieces
of gems, he distributed these
pieces to the poor.[6]

10.
He carries inexhaustible treasure,[7]
who from twigs made gold,
gems from stones.[8]

11.
He was invited by a friend
to celebrate—I say it was Christ,
seen with his disciples—

12.
from the tomb into which he descended,
alive he ascends
to enjoy the highest feast.[9]

13.
You have a crowd of eyewitnesses,
indeed, if you are willing, you may see
with your own sight,
that at his tomb manna springs forth,
food from Christ's banquet.[10]

14.
Writing the Gospel
he bears the character of an eagle,
gazing at the ray of the sun,[11]
namely the beginning,
the Word in the beginning.

15.
By his signs the gentiles,
an evil people, all of Asia
is converted.

16.
By his writings the unity of the church
is enlightened, and enlightened,
it is strengthened.

17.
Hail, vessel of sound purity,
vessel filled with heavenly dew,
clean inside, clear outside,
noble throughout.

18.
Make us follow your holiness.
cause us, through purity of mind,
to contemplate the Trinity,
one in substance.

SIMPLEX IN ESSENTIA

SEQUENCE FOR THE OCTAVE OF PENTECOST

1.
May the Spirit,
simple in essence, sevenfold in graces,
reform us.

2.
May light sent from heaven purify
the hiding places of the heart
and the charms of the flesh.

3.
The law, penal law,[12] obscure law,
preceded in figure[13]
the light of the Gospel.[14]

4.
May the spiritual understanding,[15]
covered with the foliage of the letter[16]
spring forth into the open.

5.
Law from the mountain[17] is given to the people,
new grace is given[18] to the few
in the upper room.[19]

6.
The circumstances of the locations teach us
what is the excellence of the precepts
and the gifts.

7.
The fire, the sound of the trumpet,
the crash of the storm,
the flash of lightning,

8.
strike terror[20]
and do not nourish love,
which anointing pours forth.[21]

9.
Thus on Mount Sinai
the divine law
is imposed on sinners,[22]

10.
the law of fear,
not of love,
punishing unlawful acts.

11.
Behold, the chosen fathers,[23]
recently made god-like,[24]
they loose the bonds of error,

12.
rain down words, resound with threats.[25]
Their miracles harmonize
with new tongues and doctrines.[26]

13.
Showing a cure to the sick,[27]
they condemn disease, not nature.
Pursuing wicked deeds,

14.
they pursue and castigate sinners;
sometimes they loose, sometimes they bind,[28]
with their free power.

15.
That day bears
the type of the Jubilee—if
you seek the mysteries of the day—

16.
in which the Church
blossoms with three thousand
running to the faith.[29]

17.
It is called a Jubilee[30]

either releasing or changing,
calling the alienated things
free to their prior state.[31]

18.
May the law of love free us,[32]
scattered under sins, and by its action
make us worthy
of the gift of perfect liberty.

NOTES

1   Cf. John 13:23.
2   Cf. Col. 2:3; Prov. 3:13–18; Isa. 12:3.
3   Cf. John 19:26–27; Luke 1:34.
4   Ryan, *Golden Legend*, 1:51. John was summoned to Rome by the emperor Domitian, and then thrown into a pot of boiling oil. The legend suggests that he escaped due to his purity.
5   This stanza refers to several stories from the hagiographical tradition. It is told that John drank a cup of poison and was not harmed, and that he raised from the dead a woman named Drusiana, a man named Satheus, and others. See Ryan, *Golden Legend*, 1:53.
6   According to the hagiographical tradition, a philosopher showed a crowd how they should despise the world by having two young men smash their gems to bits. John, following a discussion of the meaning of contempt of riches, reconstituted the gems. The philosopher and the young men then gave the profit the poor. Cf. Ryan, *Golden Legend*, 1:51.
7   Luke 12:21, 33. Adam's sequences contain a great many allusions to the words and ideas of the Scriptures. The compact form of the sequence does not allow for direct quotations. Hence the biblical references given here are not to quotations but to allusions and echoes.
8   Again the saint offers a lesson on earthly riches. Two other young men had renounced their wealth but began to regret it. John gave them twigs and pebbles turned to gold. The situation provided John an opportunity to lecture against the dangers of wealth. Cf. Ryan, *Golden Legend*, 1:52.
9   Cf. Luke 22:30. Tradition holds that John had his own grave dug when he foresaw that he would die. Cf. Ryan, *Golden Legend*, 1:55.
10   Ryan, *Golden Legend*, 1:55.
11   Ezek. 1:10; Rev. 4:7.
12   Rom. 4:13–15.
13   Heb. 10:1–15.
14   2 Tim. 1:10.
15   Col. 1:9.
16   2 Cor. 3:6; Rom. 2:29.
17   Exod. 24:12, 31:18.
18   John 1:17.
19   Acts 1:13.
20   Exod. 19:16–19, 20:18–21.
21   John 14:21, 15:17, 16:27; 1 John 5:2–3; 1 Cor. 16:22.
22   Exod. 19–23.
23   Cf. Hugh of St Victor, *Libellus* 2 (Sicard, 128.51, 129.72).
24   Cf. Gen. 3:5; Ps. 81:6 (Vulg.); John 10:34–36; Acts 14:10.
25   Cf. Richard of St Victor, *LE* 2.10.7.11–18 (Châtillon, 389–90).
26   Acts 2.
27   Acts 5:12.
28   Matt. 16:19.
29   Acts 2:41.
30   Lev. 25:8–55; Num. 36:4.
31   Lev. 25:10–13; Isa. 61:1–2.
32   Rom. 7:6, 8:2; 2 Cor. 3:17.

ACHARD OF ST VICTOR

SERMON FIVE: ON THE SUNDAY OF THE PALM BRANCHES

INTRODUCTION AND TRANSLATION
BY HUGH FEISS OSB

INTRODUCTION

In the general introduction to this volume, it was suggested that though Achard did not write any treatise on love, love is so woven into his thought that it would lose its coherence without it. In showing the truth of that contention, the introduction took as its starting point and framework Achard's *Sermon 5*, which more than any other speaks explicitly about love. Here the goal will be a close analysis of this one sermon in order to understand how Achard thought about love.[1]

Sermon 5 comments on two verses of the Gospel reading for the blessing of the Palms on Palm Sunday.[2] These verses recount that when they came "unto Mount Olivet, then Jesus sent two disciples, saying to them: Go into the village [or: stronghold] that is over against you, and immediately you shall find an ass tied, and a colt with her: loose them and bring them to me."[3] Achard then explicates this citation almost word by word in five paragraphs.

1. *Mount.* In his first paragraph Achard begins from the word "mount." He says that Jesus is a mountain, and so this one mountain is coming to another. To explain the significance of these two mountains, Achard cites Isaiah 2:2: "In the last days a mountain will be prepared, the house of the Lord on the summit of the mountains." On the mountain to which Jesus arrives is the house of the Lord, a city upon a hill. In a puzzling aside, Achard says that the "city" signifies the distinction

---

[1] This sermon has been translated afresh for this volume from the Latin text in Achard de Saint-Victor, *Sermons inédits*, ed. Jean Châtillon, TPMA 17 (Paris: Vrin, 1970): 67–72. For an earlier translation, see Achard of St Victor, *Works*, tr. Hugh Feiss, CS 165 (Kalamazoo: Cistercian Publications, 2001): 140–46.

[2] Palm Sunday is the Sunday before Easter. By Achard's time, a procession and other rituals augmented the celebration of Palm Sunday. Two gospels were and are read. The first of these was read at the beginning of the service before the blessing of the palms and the procession. It told the story of obtaining the donkey and how Jesus, mounted upon it, entered Jerusalem. (See Joseph Pascher, *Das liturgische Jahr* [Munich: Max Hueber, 1963], 115–22.) This is the gospel that Achard comments on.

[3] Matt. 21:1b–2. The English text given here is a slightly altered version of the Douai-Rheims version. Here is the Latin of the two verses: "Et cum adpropinquassent Hierosolymis et venissent Bethfage ad montem Oliveti tunc Iesus misit duos discipulos dicens eis ite in castellum quod contra vos est et statim invenietis asinam alligatam et pullum cum ea solvite et adducite mihi."

between merits and rewards, whereas "house" refers to the unity of two sorts of love (*caritas* and *dilectio*).

The citation enables Achard to introduce a Christological topic dear to his heart: If Christ is the mountain that God prepared, that signifies that he was predestined to be "the Son of God in power" (Rom. 1:4). This power (*virtus*), to which Christ was predestined, is the power, wisdom, and goodness that the Word shares with the Father and the Holy Spirit.[4] This leads Achard to the principle he wishes to endorse: "the humanity assumed has no less by grace than the Word who assumed it has by nature."[5] Achard buttresses this principle with yet another Scriptural authority: "In whom dwelt all the fullness of divinity bodily" (Col. 2:9). Achard interprets this text word by word: "all" refers to all positive attributes, such as power, wisdom, and goodness, but not such negative (*remotive*) attributes as immeasurability and immortality. "Fullness" means the totality of each attribute. "Bodily" means that these attributes are those of the incarnate Christ. At this point Achard returns to the quotation from Isaiah, noting that "on the summit of the mountain" means that the Father gave Christ as the head of the Church. His name is a name that will last forever. That is, his name and dignity are not only connected with his ministry on earth, like the names of angelic ministries such as "archangel" and "principality," but his name will be exalted forever, like the non-ministerial names of angels such as "thrones" and "ardent love" (seraphim) that will last forever. However, Christ's dignity will completely surpass theirs, since he will be exalted to equality with the Father.

Christ is a mountain who comes to the mountain. "Christ" designates a human nature assumed by the Word and sharing by grace in the positive attributes that belong to the Word by nature. Christ is the head of the Church. When the world ends, Christ will remain, exalted above the angels to equality with his Father. In establishing this, Achard has twice mentioned love. "*Dilectio*," the love enjoined by Christ on his

---

4   The place in Victorine thought of these three essential attributes and their appropriation to the three Persons of the Trinity was discussed in VTT 1:55–58.

5   In *Sermo* 5.1, Achard states the principle this way: "Non enim minus habet homo assumptus per gratiam quam Verbum assumens per naturam" ("The humanity assumed has through grace no less than what the Word assuming has by [the divine] nature." The principle is enunciated against the background of a Christology centered on the idea of "homo assumptus." This is not an easy phrase to translate. "Homo" means both "a human being" (it is not gender specific) and "humankind." The Word assumes a human nature and human nature generally. The principle leads its adherents to attribute to Christ very great knowledge and power.

disciples, is identical with "*caritas*," the love that is God.[6] "Rest," "knowledge," and "love," the non-ministerial names of angels, have a special excellence that transcends time.

2. Mount *of Olives*. Having established that Christ is a mountain, Achard says that Christ, who can be called a mountain by all that is in him, is called "of Olives" only with reference to the love (*caritas*) which filled him as he came to the Mount of Olives. Playing on the ambiguity of two words in a scriptural description of a mountain, Achard says Christ is a "stout" (or "rich in fat, oil") mountain, a "many-peaked" (or "coagulated") mountain in/on which God will reside without end or measure (Ps. 67:16–17). On the historical Mount of Olives there were and perhaps still are olive trees, the oil from which floats above all other oils. It stands for love (*caritas*), the preeminent virtue; without it every other virtue is tasteless, unfruitful, and lacking merit. Like oil pressed out of olives, Christ's love (*dilectio*) was ex-pressed or pressed out in the blood that he sweat in the garden on the Mount of Olives and which flowed from his hands, feet, and side while he was on the Cross. What he ex-pressed was the "oil of gladness" by which he was anointed before all his fellows, since he received the Spirit without measure. His very name signifies anointing with oil. All others received grace by sharing in his fullness; hence, his name is rightly called "oil poured out." The grace that made him Christ (so that his humanity had by grace all that the Word had by nature) makes us Christians.

Thus, what brought Christ to the Mount of Olives was charity. He expressed the depths of his charity by pouring out his blood. He was anointed with the Spirit of charity without measure, the charity without which all other virtues are fruitless. Christians are anointed with that same Spirit of love by sharing in Christ's unbounded fullness of grace.

3. *Bethany*,[7] according to Jerome, means "house of obedience."[8] At the Father's bidding, the Son came into the world by his own will. This was a great act of filial devotion (*pietas*) and love (*dilectio*). He left

---

[6] A scriptural passage that may have prompted Achard's mention of this is 1 John 4:7–21, in particular, "diligamus invicem quoniam caritas ex Deo est . . . Deus caritas est . . . nos ergo diligamus quoniam Deus prior dilexit nos" ("Let us love one another because charity is from God . . . God is charity . . . Let us love because God has first loved us").

[7] In paragraph one, Achard cited Matt. 21:1, which has "Bethphage" ("house of figs"). Here Achard uses the more familiar name, "Bethany," which is found in the parallel passages of Mark 11:1 and Luke 19:29 who also refer, to the place as "Bethphage".

[8] Jerome, *Heb. nom.* (de Lagarde, 135 [PL 23.839–40]).

equality with the Father's majesty to descend to the form of a servant; he put on our form in order to redeem us. Having experienced hunger, thirst, and fatigue, he accepted the horrible death of crucifixion. It seems to us, wrongly, that the love (*caritas*) of the suffering Son is greater than that of the Father who ordered it.

And so the human sufferings of Christ, undertaken for our redemption at the Father's command, are a stunning proof of Christ's filial devotion and love.

4. *Go into the stronghold which is ahead of* (*contra*) *you.* The stronghold is the human race which we have caused to be fortified against (*contra*) us. Through sin, our nature has been inhabited by what is alien to us. In us, who are in God's image and likeness, reason should have informed and ruled the will. But now the she-ass of reason is bound by ignorance and error. No longer does humankind enjoy the contemplation of God; it has tumbled down the ladder of knowledge from understanding to reason, to faith, to opinion, to doubt, and finally to error. Its front legs are bound by ignorance of self and ignorance of neighbor, and its back legs by ignorance of the world and ignorance of hell. The colt's head, our will, is bound by idolatry (*im-pietas*) the very opposite of the filial devotion (*pietas*) that brought Christ to us. The allure of the flesh and wickedness of heart bind its front legs; insatiable concupiscence and evil security bind its back legs. These are interconnected: from ignorance of self arises the allure of the flesh, and wickedness of heart comes from ignorance of neighbor; from ignorance of the world comes insatiable desire for it, and from ignorance of hell arises a false and wicked sense of security.

To counter these two dimensions of wickedness, Jesus sends two disciples exteriorly, one teaching what is to be done and another urging that it be done; interiorly he sends the illumination of the truth and the inspiration of goodness. They replace the error and ignorance that bound the she-ass with faith and devotion. They free her from the fourfold ignorance that bound her feet and substitute a fourfold knowledge of self, neighbor, world, and hell. They replace the impiety which bound the head of the colt with its opposite, true worship of God, and replace the bonds on its feet with continence, love of neighbor, contempt of the world, and fear of the Lord.

So, sin clouds reason and makes it subject to the whims of desire; sin hobbles the moral life with ignorance and concupiscence. These are not truly human, but subhuman defects or inclinations introduced by sin. Sin also leads to impiety toward God, the opposite of the piety that led Christ to manifest divine love in the world.

5. *They led them to Jesus and put their vestments on them* (Matt. 21:7). The two disciples leading the she-ass and her colt signify that one comes to Jesus by knowledge of the truth and love of virtue. Their vestments signify examples of virtues. That Jesus sat on the she-ass signifies that when someone is truly perfect, he no longer needs the teaching and exhortation of another. Jesus brings her his own ropes: knowledge of the works of creation, the sacraments of the incarnation of the Word, and the contemplation of heavenly things. Thus he leads her to Jerusalem, which means the true vision of peace.

The loss of knowledge, goodness, and contemplation of God described earlier is remedied by knowledge of truth and love of virtue, which are fostered by virtuous examples. This restoration sets a person on the way to a time when he will no longer rely of external teaching and exhortation but, taught interiorly by Christ, will advance toward the heavenly Jerusalem.

Achard's sermon is a striking example of spiritual exegesis, lightly anchored in a brief historical moment in the life of Christ. It begins with a string of quotations which lead Achard to explain how Christ, who came to the Mount of Olives, is himself a mountain which has come down from heaven because of filial obedience and devotion toward the Father and because of his own love of humankind. In two asides in the first paragraph, Achard equates two words for love, "*dilectio*" and "*caritas*," and at the same time establishes the inseparability of knowledge, love, and rest, which he will again connect in the final paragraph of the sermon. The love that brought Christ to earth is a manifestation of the goodness of God, which is God, but is attributed in a special way to the Spirit, who endowed Christ with the fullness of charity, from which all virtues draw life. Christians draw grace and anointing from Christ, the Anointed, who by the fullness of grace has in his humanity what his divinity has by nature.

Leaving behind equality with the Father's majesty, Christ put on human nature, assuming its hunger, thirst, and fatigue. God's love is ex-pressed as completely as possible in the outflowing of Christ's blood from the olive presses of the Mount of Olives and the Cross.

He came to restore humanity to the image and likeness of God. In restored humanity, knowledge and exhortation received from human teachers combines with Christ's internal enlightenment and inspiring goodness to instill knowledge of truth and love of virtue. These vanquish ignorance and error regarding self, neighbor, the world, and hell and instill piety toward and fear of God, ordered love of neighbor, and contempt of the world, as the Christian moves toward eternal rest.

Whereas Adam of St Victor's sequences do not show clear evidence of the influence of Hugh of St Victor's thought and language, Achard's *Sermon 5* is clearly influenced by Hugh of St Victor: e.g., the pairing of knowledge of virtue and love of virtue, the distinction between external teaching and internal enlightenment, the distinction between the work of creation and the work of restoration, the description of the effects of sin, the centrality of Christ, and the "assumptus homo" Christology. Like Hugh, Achard roots love in the goodness of God, identical with the divine essence. The love that moved Christ to put on and assume human nature is manifest above all in his acceptance of human suffering and death. The grace that Christ the Head had in its fullness is shared by the members of his body, who receive the Spirit of love. Unlike Hugh, Achard grants no merit to virtuous life not inspired by divine charity, which animates all the virtues.

1. Jesus came to the "Mount of Olives" and said to his disciples, "Go into the stronghold, which is in front of you, and you will find a she-ass and the colt of a she-ass" tied up. "Untie them and lead them to me."[1] The disciples, sent by Lord, obeyed him. They untied "the she-ass and the colt" of a she-ass "and led" them to Jesus. "They placed their garments upon them, and made Jesus sit upon them"[2]; Jesus, sitting upon them, came into Jerusalem. The mount came to the mount, the spiritual to the material, truth to the symbol (*figuram*). Regarding the mount it was said: "And in the last days a mountain will be prepared, the house of the Lord on the summit of the mountains."[3] "The house of the Lord" is the city of God that cannot be hidden because it is situated upon this mountain.[4] It is called a city because of the distinction between merits and rewards, but it is called a house because of the unity of charity (*caritatis*) and love (*dilectionis*). He says, "a mountain prepared," that is, predestined, to be the Son of God in power (*virtute*)[5]—namely, the same great power (*potentie*), wisdom, and goodness—which belongs to the Word to whom it is united personally. For the humanity assumed has no less by grace than the Word assuming has by nature.[6] Whence the Apostle says, "In whom dwells all the fullness of divinity bodily."[7] "All" here includes all those things that posit something in God such as power, wisdom, goodness, and the like. For certain things are said of God to rule out something (*remotive*), such as eternal, immense, immortal.[8] By "fullness" is meant the totality of each thing. But so that no one will apply this to the Word, he adds "bodily," that is, in the body of Christ. "On the summit of the mountains," that is, so that he would be the topmost peak of the mountains, not only holy, but the holy of holies.[9] God the Father made him the head of the Church,[10] giving him the "name that is above every name"[11] "that is named" here and "in the future."[12]

There are certain names of angels which pertain to the present state of things such as Angels, Archangels, Virtues, Powers, Principalities, and Dominions, which are given with reference to their ministries on our behalf. Thus, "there are ministering spirits sent on account of those who will receive the inheritance"[13] whose ministries will be eliminated when Christ "hands over the kingdom to his God and Father."[14] Christ himself, "passing" from his humanity to his divinity, "will minister to them,"[15] so that the saints going out and entering will find pasture.[16] However, there are other names that pertain to their future state such as Thrones, Cherubim, and Seraphim. Certain angels are called Thrones, not with reference to their relation to us but because of God's relation to them, for God sits and rests on them,[17] or better, according to the relation they have to God in whom they rest. Cherubim, too, which is interpreted to mean "fullness of knowledge,"[18] and Seraphim, which means "ardent,"[19] are named from the excellence of this knowledge and love. These three will not be eliminated in the future, and perhaps even something will be added to their rest, love, and knowledge in the revelation "of the sons of God,"[20] so that they will not be consummated without us.[21] The dignity of Christ is exalted above these dignities because "his going out is from the highest heavens, and his setting is all the way to its summit,"[22] that is, Christ is exalted to equality with the Father.[23] His is the dignity of all dignity, which can be said of no angel.

2. He came, it says, "to the Mount of Olives."[24] The Son of God, although he can be called a "mount" in regard to all the things that are in him, is not called the Mount of Olives with regard to each of them, but only with regard to the love (*caritatem*) that filled him as he came to the Mount of Olives—for he is the "stout (*pinguis*) mountain, the many-peaked (*coagulatus*) mountain, the mountain on which God is pleased to dwell. Indeed, God will dwell there unto the end,"[25] that is, without limit, without measure. On other mountains he dwells, but not "unto the end," because to them the Spirit is given within measure.[26] The Mount of Olives was formerly and perhaps still is planted with olive trees from which is pressed oil that flows over all other oils. So does love (*caritas*) surpass all other virtues; it rules over them all. Every other virtue is insipid without love (*caritate*), unfruitful, and without any merit.[27] Hanging on the cross, Christ ex-pressed this love (*dilectionem*) for us in his hands, feet, and side, and he did the same on the mountain—when he was in agony—by praying at length, and drops of blood flowed out of his most holy body.[28] I say, "Christ ex-pressed,"[29] as it were, the oil of gladness with which he was anointed more than all his companions,[30] for to him was given the Spirit without measure. It is written regarding this oil: "Your name is oil poured out."[31] To the saints, grace is given in accord with the measure of their participation in the complete fullness of Christ, for which reason his name is said to be "oil poured out." By this grace he is Christ, and we are Christians.

3. He came, it says, from Bethany,[32] which is interpreted to mean "house of obedience."[33] Obedient to the Father, he went out from the

Father and came into the world not by force, but by his own free will. Please note with discernment how great was the filial affection (*pietas*) and how great his love (*dilectio*), which caused him to descend from equality with the Father's majesty in order to receive the form of a slave.[34] He inclined the heavens and descended[35] and put on our form in order to redeem us. In doing so, he experienced fatigue, hunger, and thirst,[36] and bore the other penalties of our weakness, and finally he came to the gibbet of the cross, "having become obedient" to God the Father "even unto death."[37] What death? Death on a cross, a most foul death, a most disgraceful death. O filial love (*pietas*) of Christ! O great proof of love (*dilectionis*)! Even though it really is not greater, the love (*caritas*) of the suffering Son does seem greater than the love of the Father who commands.

4. There follows: he said to his disciples, "Go into the stronghold, which is ahead of you."[38] This stronghold is the human race, which is fortified from out of us against us. But what does it mean that in this stronghold of the human race a she-ass with a colt is found, something that is in human beings but not of human beings? Before sin, as long as "humankind" (*homo*) was "in honor," there was nothing in human-kind that was not of humankind. However, by sinning humankind became "comparable to the beasts and," what is worse, "became like them"[39] by passing over into a kind of beastliness. As Scripture says, in the beginning "God created humankind in his image and likeness; male and female he created them."[40] How is male to be understood if not as reason (*sensus interior*),[41] and female if not as the will? The will ought to walk at the side of reason and be informed and ruled according to it. Reason is changed into a she-ass and the will into the colt of a she-ass by acquiring similar habits. And so there is a switch in sexes, the male is transmuted into the female and female into the male. The head of the she-ass, reason, is tied—that is, what is on top in her, namely the mind—by two ropes, ignorance and error; by ignorance because she does not know the truth, and by error because she believes falsehood. Before humankind sinned, it had God present through intelligence (*intelligentiam*) and enjoyed contemplation of him.[42] Then through its fault it fell from that summit of divine intelligence to reason, from reason into faith, from faith into opinion, from opinion into doubt, from doubt into ignorance, from ignorance into error. This change is of the right hand, not of the Most High,[43] but of the devil. The she-ass has her front feet bound by ignorance of self and ignorance of neigh-bor; her back legs are bound by ignorance of the world and ignorance

of hell. Thus, these four bonds tie up the four feet of the she-ass. The head of the colt is bound by impiety (*impietate*), which is idolatry and worship of demons. His two front feet are bound by the allure of the flesh and wickedness of heart; the other two by insatiable concupiscence and pestilential security. One should not fail to say how the bonds of the colt are produced from the bonds of the she-ass. The allure of the flesh is produced from ignorance of self; wickedness of heart from ignorance of one's neighbor; insatiable concupiscence of the world from ignorance of that same world; wicked security from ignorance of hell. Therefore, to untie these, Jesus sent two of his disciples, whom we understand as teaching and exhortation. Just because we know through teaching what is to be done, we do not immediately do it; therefore it is necessary that exhortation follow.

Alternatively, we can understand these two disciples to stand for the enlightenment of truth and the inspiration of goodness, namely, a right spirit and a good spirit. These two disciples untie the head of the she-ass from error and ignorance; on her head they place their own bonds, namely, faith and devotion. They untie her feet from various kinds of ignorance, namely of self, neighbor, world, and hell. Instead they bind them with their opposites: knowledge of oneself and one's neighbor, and knowledge of the world and hell. They untie the head of the colt from its impiety, replacing it with true worship of God. They untie its feet and bind them with what is opposite—changing the allurements of the flesh into continence, wickedness of heart into love of neighbor, concupiscence of the world into contempt of the world, and wicked security into fear of the Lord.

5. And they lead them to Jesus and put their garments on them.[44] One comes to Jesus through knowledge of the truth and love (*amore*) of virtue, as though led by his disciples. "And" they put on them "their garments,"[45] namely, examples of virtue. "And they had Jesus sit upon them."[46] Those who are so perfect that Jesus sits upon them no longer need the teaching and assistance of another. With Paul they can say, "Be imitators of me, as I am of Christ."[47] Jesus, sitting on top, imposes his bonds, namely, knowledge of the works of the Creator and the sacraments of the Incarnation of the Word,[48] and contemplation of heavenly things. And thus he leads them "into Jerusalem,"[49] into the true vision of peace,[50] to which may Christ, who is our peace, deign to lead us. Amen.

NOTES

1 Matt. 21:1–2.
2 Matt. 21:7.
3 Isa. 2:2.
4 See Matt. 5:14.
5 Rom. 1:4.
6 For this adage (*auctoritas*) see Achard, *Sermon* 4.5 (Châtillon, 60); *Sermon* 14.3 (Châtillon, 175); *Sermon* 15.26 (Châtillon, 230); *Unitate* 1.14 (Martineau, 84; tr. Feiss, 390); Hugh of St Victor, *Sacr.* 2.1.6 (PL 176.383D); *Sapientia* (PL 176.854D–855A); E. Poppenberg, *Die Christologie des Hugo von St. Viktor* (Hiltrup, 1937), 90–103; Richard of St Victor, *Arca Moys.* 4.18 (Aris, 112 [PL 196.159]; tr. Zinn, 294); Peter Lombard, *Sent.* 3.14.1 (Quaracchi, 609); Ps.-Hugh of St Victor, *Quaest. in epist. Pauli* (PL 175.436B); Châtillon, *Théologie*, 200–2, and "*Quidquid convenit Filio Dei per naturam convenit Filio hominis per gratiam*," *Divinitas* 11 (1967): 715–28 (=*Miscellanea André Combes*, [Rome, 1967] 2:319–31), reprinted in Jean Châtillon, *D'Isidore de Séville à saint Thomas d'Aquin: Études d'histoire et de théologie* (London: Variorum, 1985), chapter XI.
7 Col. 2:9; cf. Achard, *Sermon* 1.5 (Châtillon, 31–34).
8 See Achard, *Sermon* 4.5 (Châtillon, 59–60).
9 See Dan. 9:24.
10 See Eph. 5:23.
11 Phil. 2:9.
12 Eph. 1:21.
13 Heb. 1:14; Gregory the Great, *Hom. ev.* 34.12 (PL 76.1254B).
14 1 Cor. 15:24.
15 Luke 12:37.
16 John 10:9.
17 Gregory the Great, *Hom. ev.* 34.10 (PL 76.1252A; 34.14 (PL 76.1255B).
18 Jerome, *Heb. nom.* (de Lagarde, 63 [PL 23.776, 787]); Gregory the Great, *Hom. ev.* 9.18 (PL 76.1054B); 17.12 (PL 76.1144D); 25.3 (PL 76.1191C); 34.10 (PL 76.1252A).
19 Jerome, *Heb. nom.* (de Lagarde, 121–22 [PL 23.830)]; Gregory the Great, *Hom. ev.* 34.10 (PL 76.1252B); 34.14 (PL 76.1255C).
20 Rom. 8:19.
21 Heb. 11:40.
22 Ps. 18:7 (Vulg.): "His going out is from the end of heaven, And his circuit even to the end thereof" (Douai-Rheims).
23 See Phil. 2:6, 9.
24 Matt. 21:1.
25 Ps. 67:16–17 (Vulg.).
26 John 3:34; Achard, *Sermon* 4.5 (Châtillon, 59, where in a note Châtillon observes that this text was often invoked by those who held that as a man Christ had by grace what as God he had by nature [see above, note 6]).
27 Châtillon, *Sermons*, 69 note 26, referring to A. Landgraf, *Dogmengeschichte*, 1/1 pp. 161–201: Achard believed that human nature, deprived of grace, which informs the matter of human nature, is unable to perform the acts of knowledge, love, and joy to which it is ordained. Hence, if unformed by divine love (charity), the virtues are powerless. In this, Achard seems to be harsher than Hugh of St Victor, who admitted the possibility of virtuous activities that were not meritorious in the order of grace, but were still worthy of recompense; see *Sacr.* 1.6.17 (PL 176.273–75) and 2.13.11 (PL 176.539). In the first of these passages, Hugh says that "virtue is nothing else than an inclination/feeling of the mind ordered by reason" (PL 176.273BC: "Virtus namque nihil aliud est quam affectus mentis secundum rationem ordinatur"). Virtues are multiple, but they all originate in the will (*voluntas*). Although natural

acts of virtue, not enabled and aided by grace, do not merit grace for grace, Hugh does not think it fitting to say they are without merit (PL 176.274AB): "Nihil tamen mereri etiam hujusmodi virtutes non mihi convenienter dici posse videtur, quamvis extra bona haec quae propter naturam condita sunt nihil mereantur, quae ex sola sunt natura" ("Therefore it does not seem to me that it can be fittingly said that even virtues of this kind merit nothing, although the things which are from nature alone merit nothing besides these goods which were created on account of nature"). As the introduction noted, Godfrey of St Victor agrees with Hugh.

28 Luke 22:44.

29 Achard is making a play on words: the Latin verb "exprimere" can mean either "to express" in words or "to press out" oil from olives or other berries.

30 Ps. 44:8 (Vulg.).

31 Song of Songs 1:2.

32 Mark 11:1; Luke 19:29.

33 Jerome, *Heb. nom.* (de Lagarde, 135 [PL 23.884]).

34 Phil. 2:7.

35 Ps. 17:10 (Vulg.).

36 John 4:6; Matt. 21:18; John 19:28. Cf. Achard, *Sermon* 1.6 (Châtillon, 34): "secundum carnem esurivit, sitivit, fatigatus est" ("according to the flesh he was hungry, thirsty, and tired"); *Sermon* 3.3 (Châtillon, 50).

37 Phil. 2:8.

38 Matt. 21:2. Châtillon, *Sermons*, 70 note 39, finds a precedent for Achard's development of the word "castellum" in Ambrose, *De Isaac vel anima*, 8.69 (CSEL 32/1, 691 [=PL 14.529A]), and *Ep.* 18/2 (CSEL 82.142 =*Ep.* 81 [PL 16.1241D]). Cf. Achard, *Sermon* 6.3 (Châtillon, 77): "tam tenebrosum et horrendum carcerem captivus ducor" ("I am led captive into such a dark and horrible prison").

39 Ps. 48:13 (Vulg.): "et homo cum in honore esset non intellexit; conparatus est iumentis insipientibus et similis factus est illis" ("And man when he was in honor did not understand; he has been compared to senseless beasts and made like them"). This passage brings Achard close to the theme of "regio dissimilitudinis" that he develops in *Sermon* 9.4 (Châtillon, 105–7) and alludes to in *Sermon* 15.1 (Châtillon, 200). It is also found in a sermon fragment, which may be Achard's, published by Châtillon in *Sermons*, 257: "Quid est terra longinqua, nisi regio a Deo peregrina? Peregrina vero regio Dei peregrina?" ("What is this distant land, if not the region distant from God? This region foreign to God is unlikeness"). This topos derives from Plato, *Statesman* (273d) and Augustine, *Conf.* 7.10.16 (O'Donnell, 82): "Et inveni longe me esse a te in regione dissimilitudinis" ("And I found myself far from you in a region of unlikeness"). It was used at St Victor and elsewhere in a response for the Feast of St Augustine. For further references and secondary literature see Châtillon, *Sermons*, 99–100, notes 3–6.

40 Gen. 1:26–27.

41 "sensus interior": here means "reason" (= "sensus rationis" of *Sermon* 13.7 [Châtillon, 141]). Reason should direct the will and the feelings but, with the coming of sin, willfulness trumps reason and the powers of the soul are at war (*Sermon* 2.2 [Châtillon, 38–39]).

42 Hugh of St Victor, *Sacr.* 1.6.14 (PL 176.271C): "Cognovit ergo homo [ante peccatum] creatorem suum, non ea cognitione quae foris ex auditu solo percipitur, sed ea quae potius intus per inspirationem ministratur; non ea quidem qua Deus modo a credentibus absens fide quaeritur, sed ea qua tunc per praesentiam contemplationis scienti manifestius cernebatur" ("Before sin, humankind knew its creator, not by that knowledge which is received from outside by hearing alone, but rather by that which is provided interiorly through inspiration; not by that by which God, absent from believers, is sought by faith, but by that by which then he was clearly seen by the knower through the presence of contemplation").

43 Ps. 76:11 (Vulg.).

44   Matt. 21:7.
45   Matt. 21:7.
46   Matt. 21:7.
47   1 Cor. 4:16.
48   Here Achard refers to the two works of God that Hugh of St Victor distinguished and ex-
     plained in the two parts of his theological synthesis, *On the Sacraments*. To them Achard
     adds contemplation of heavenly things (*anagogia*), which is permanent in heaven, but at most
     fleeting on earth. His threefold division corresponds to the states of nature, grace, and glory.
     The Victorines use both schemas frequently.
49   Matt. 21:10.
50   Jerome, *Heb. nom.* (de Lagarde, 121 [PL 23.873–74]); Augustine, *En. Ps.* 9.12 (Dekkers and
     Fraipont, 64 [PL 36.122]); Gregory the Great, *Mor.* 35.16.40 (Adriaen, 1800 [PL 76.771D]).

RICHARD OF ST VICTOR

*ON THE FOUR DEGREES
OF VIOLENT LOVE*

INTRODUCTION AND TRANSLATION
BY ANDREW B. KRAEBEL

INTRODUCTION

Richard of St Victor's *On the Four Degrees of Violent Love*, composed about 1170,[1] recounts the loving relationship between God and humanity, the latter taken both as a whole from the beginning of time and as represented by each individual soul. The work thus ranges widely, describing how humanity's ability to love God was affected by the Fall and Redemption, as well as the perils of post-lapsarian love, the ideal love contained within marriage, and, especially, the progress of the soul's love of God. This last category of love is the focus of Richard's tract, culminating finally with the description of a transformative visionary experience, wherein the contemplative is united to God in heaven, and his relationships with other human beings are thereafter forever transformed.

Richard organizes this expansive subject matter within a framework original to him, i.e., the four degrees of violent love.[2] As he first defines them, using metaphors that continue to govern all of his subsequent descriptions, the four degrees are wounding love, binding love, languishing love, and weakening love. In the first degree, once the subject has been pierced by love's darts, he is "ablaze with desire" and "seethes with feeling," yearning to obtain the object of his desire. In the second degree, he thinks about the object of his love constantly, and he is thus, as it were, bound or imprisoned by his love. In the third degree, the amorous subject not only thinks of the object of his love constantly, but he thinks only of that object—or, as Richard clarifies, he can only think of other things *in terms of* the object of his desire. Finally, in the fourth degree, even obtaining his desire does not satisfy the lover, and he constantly seeks new ways to achieve his desire, never being sated.

---

[1]   For the dating of this text relative to Richard's other works, see Pierluigi Cacciapuoti, *Deus Existentia Amoris: Teologia della Carità e Teologia della Trinità negli Scritti di Ricardo di San Vittore (d. 1173)* (Turnhout: Brepols, 1998), 94–95.

[2]   Richard's title, *De quatuor gradibus violentae caritatis*, is a challenge for translators. "Violent love" is jarring in English, even suggesting rape or abuse. Alternatives for "violent" would be "vehement" or "passionate." For a different reason, Richard's title was probably meant to be jarring for Latin readers, because he chose to use the same word, "caritas," to describe obsessive erotic love for another human being and the love between human beings and God.

While these general definitions apply to all of the scenarios that Richard describes, the valence of each one varies according to the particular relationship under consideration, e.g., the first degree of love is different with regard to, on the one hand, one's love for another human being and, on the other hand, one's love for God. One of Richard's primary interests in *On the Four Degrees of Violent Love* is to explore how these degrees can vary and actively be developed in particular directions by his readers.[3]

I

Though Richard explores different kinds of loving relationships in his treatise, he structures his work with a particular end in mind. Intended for his fellow canons regular at St Victor, *On the Four Degrees of Violent Love* charts the contemplative's progress, as he abandons the world (and worldly love) for life in the cloister, as he begins to develop his love of God through prayer and meditation, and, finally, as his love eventually may be fulfilled in this life through contemplative rapture and an experience of union with God. The details of this progress are slowly resolved as Richard cycles through descriptions of the four degrees over and over again.[4]

After the encomium of love and the initial definition of the four degrees that begin the work (Section I, par. 1–4), Richard provides an account of the Fall and Redemption (beginning Section II, 5). In our pre-lapsarian state, before the introduction of sin, we loved God as we ought, and this initial ability to love was in fact a gift from God. Since loving God is the final fulfillment of human potential, to begin by po-

3   Jean Châtillon, "Les quatres degrés de la charité d'après Richard de Saint-Victor," *Revue ascétique et de mystique* 20 (1939): 237–64, provides an account of each of Richard's degrees of love, but he does not recognize the various ways in which Richard reshapes the degrees as his discussion progresses. Such is also the case with the account in Gervais Dumeige, *Richard de Saint-Victor et l'idée chrétienne de l'amour* (Paris: Presses Universitaires de France, 1952), 133–52.

4   The idea that Richard's treatise is in some way mimetic, representing the process of loving God that it seeks to describe, has been explored by Ineke van 't Spijker, "Learning by Experience: Twelfth-Century Monastic Ideas," in *Centres of Learning: Learning and Location in Pre-Modern Europe and the Near East*, ed. J. W. Drijvers and A. A. MacDonald (Leiden: Brill, 1995), 197–206; "Exegesis and Emotions: Richard of St Victor's *De Quatuor Gradibus Violentae Caritatis*," *Sacris Erudiri* 36 (1996): 147–60; *Fictions of the Inner Life: Religious Literature and the Formation of the Self in the Eleventh and Twelfth Centuries* (Turnhout: Brepols, 2004), 129–84.

sitioning us thus bespeaks God's great love for us. Yet, of course, Adam's sin broke the bonds that held us in this particular relationship with God, and our love of God is thereafter obstructed. Though we have the possibility of loving God properly—thanks to the Crucifixion and Redemption, by which God "continued to multiply his chains of love about us"[5]—in our lives as post-lapsarian people we now need to work to ensure that our love is directed properly (par. 5).

Following this account of our current condition as fallen human beings and would-be lovers of God, Richard goes on to describe each of the four degrees in detail (6–17). Yet it is not clear at this point in his text what sort of object Richard's imagined lover desires, whether it be divine or carnal, whether Richard is describing fallen human love for another created thing, or the proper love for God. In fact, in this cycle through the four degrees, Richard is attempting to talk about both possibilities though, as he later notes (see 18), the quality of the degrees is very different when the object of love is carnal and when it is divine. Richard states that, though the first degree of love *can* be good when the object of one's love is another human being, nevertheless, when he desires another person or some material object, the second degree is then necessarily detrimental to the lover, and the final two degrees are progressively worse. At the same time, each successive degree of love is better when the object of one's love is God. Writing simultaneously about both of these scenarios, then, Richard creates a tension in his initial detailed discussion of the four degrees. He moves from celebrating a particular stage of love to describing how one can avoid it, and he both praises and in almost the same breath condemns the successive degrees, as when he describes the fourth degree as "marvelous, nay rather pitiable" (14). By constantly shifting the object of love in this section, Richard attempts to recreate the condition of men and women outside of the cloister: sometimes they may direct their love appropriately toward God, while at other times they desire a variety of carnal things. Richard then concludes this initial discussion with an account of marital love as the pinnacle of extra-claustral life, wherein the first degree of love "tightens the chains of peace between those who are pledged to one another, and it renders that indissoluble and perpetual union [i.e., marriage] pleasing and delightful" (19).

---

[5]   On this metaphor, see A. B. Kraebel, "*Grammatica* and the Authenticity of the Psalms-commentary attributed to Bruno the Carthusian," *Mediaeval Studies* 71 (2009), 81–82 note 48.

Noting that the degrees of love are progressively better when the object of one's love is God, Richard moves his imagined lover into the cloister, as it were, and offers a succession of cycles through the four degrees that demonstrates to the reader how to focus his love on God (Section III, 21–27). His treatment of this topic is only at times explicit, e.g., in his discussion of the four degrees in terms of Deut. 6:5: "In spiritual things, to love something out of deliberation is always prior to doing so on account of emotion. For we never love spiritual things desirously unless we first inflame our mind toward the pursuit of [them]" (24). More frequently, though, Richard does not explain, but rather models, how one ought to focus one's love on God, indicating both the texts one ought to read and how one ought to read them. Most of this section consists of movements through the four degrees wherein each degree is associated with a particular biblical verse, and Richard thereby recommends careful, repetitive study of Scripture, *lectio divina*, as the proper method for directing one's desires entirely toward God.[6]

Though Richard surely expected such biblical study to persist throughout the lives of his audience of canons, his primary interest in *On the Four Degrees of Violent Love* is finally an atypical, perhaps even singular experience: the culmination of one's love for God in an inward flight to heaven and union with the divine (Section IV, 28 ff.). Richard describes how this experience may come about in his final, fullest, and most discursive movement through each of the four degrees (30–46). He begins by noting what appear to be the necessary preconditions for such an experience: one's love must be directed entirely toward God. In this case, finally, each of the four degrees may be described exclusively in relation to God. "In the first degree, the soul thirsts for God. In the second, it thirsts toward God. In the third, the soul thirsts into God. In the fourth, it thirsts in accordance with God." (28)

Richard's description of the four degrees is thereafter focused entirely on loving God, with his account of each degree supported with quotations from Scripture. In this scenario, wounding love consists in the contemplative's gaining a series of tastes of the divine (perhaps a eucharistic reference), though God remains hidden from sight (30–33). Yet such teasing tastes lead the contemplative to desire all the more,

---

6   The classic study of *lectio divina* remains Jean Leclercq, *The Love of Learning and the Desire for God*, 3rd ed., tr. C. Misrahi (New York: Fordham University Press, 1982); see also Mary Carruthers, *The Book of Memory: A Study of Memory in Medieval Culture*, 2nd ed. (Cambridge: Cambridge University Press, 2008) and *The Craft of Thought: Meditation, Rhetoric, and the Making of Images, 400–1200* (Cambridge: Cambridge University Press, 1998).

and as much as possible to reform and properly order his way of life, so that God might find him worthy of further experiences. The soul may then enter the second degree, flight to heaven. Yet, following a delineation of the three heavens common in Latin exegesis of the Pauline Epistles, Richard specifies that this journey is only to the second heaven (34–37).[7] From here, the contemplative may indeed gaze up and behold God, but this experience of God's presence is not complete. Associated with the visions of such prophets as Isaiah and, in the New Testament, John the Divine, the second heaven, as medieval commentators described it, consisted in seeing images representative of truths (such as the vision of the divine throne in Isa. 6) but, because of this imagistic quality, such experiences were still necessarily mediated.[8] Richard's contemplative therefore desires God all the more ardently, seeking to be able to say, along with Paul,[9] that he was snatched up into the third heaven, where he might experience God without any mediation whatsoever.

Richard's third degree of contemplative ascent consists in experiencing unmediated union with God (38–43). The contemplative's soul is "snatched away into the abyss of divine light [and] passes entirely into its God" (38).[10] The predominant metaphor Richard uses to describe this state is of melting iron. The soul, previously solid, is now liquefied by the flame of divine love.[11] The earlier, general metaphor of the third degree, that of languid love, thus comes into play in this final account as well: utterly malleable (since it is "languid" or "liquefied"), the soul can now only desire or will that which the divine impels it to

<hr>

[7] For the three heavens and the ways of seeing associated with each, see the introduction to *The Sermons of William of Newburgh*, ed. A. B. Kraebel (Toronto: Pontifical Institute of Mediaeval Studies for the Centre for Medieval Studies, 2010), 12–14. Richard's account of heaven here may be put in the context of his other writings by consulting Hugh B. Feiss, "Heaven in the Theology of Hugh, Achard, and Richard of St Victor," in *Imagining Heaven in the Middle Ages: A Book of Essays*, ed. J. S. Emerson and H. B. Feiss (New York: Garland, 2000), 145–63.

[8] See also Richard's description of the modes of prophetic sight in *Apoc.* 1.1 (PL 196.686B–687A).

[9] See 2 Cor. 12:2.

[10] Richard's account of the second and third degrees is scrutinized by Csaba Németh, "*Videre sine speculo*: The Immediate Vision of God in the Works of Richard of St Victor," *Annual of Medieval Studies at the Central European University* 8 (2002): 123–37. See also Bernard McGinn, "The Abyss of Love," in *The Joy of Learning and the Love of God: Essays in Honor of Jean Leclercq*, ed. R. Elder (Kalamazoo: Cistercian Publications, 1995), 95–120; McGinn, "Visio Dei: Seeing God in Medieval Theology and Mysticism," in *Envisaging Heaven in the Middle Ages*, ed. C. Muessig and A. Putter (London: Routledge, 2007), 15–33.

[11] On this metaphor, see Robert E. Lerner, "The Image of Mixed Liquids in Late Medieval Mystical Thought," *Church History* 40 (1971): 397–411.

desire or will. Such discussions lead Richard into his final account of the fourth degree (44–46)—for the experience of union with God enjoyed in the third degree can only be fleeting,[12] and the contemplative thereafter returns to his community as a transformed human being. His absolute conformation to the will of God makes the contemplative Christ-like. No longer interested in achieving temporary experiences of vision or union, he is now intent only upon seeing to the salvation of his fellow human beings (or, we might suppose, specifically the other canons regular in his abbey).[13] Thus, again, the insatiability of the general metaphor for the fourth degree returns here, as the contemplative is relentless in seeking new ways to achieve his desired ends.

II

Though in some ways Richard's treatise conforms to general trends in twelfth-century monastic literature, in others it is original and strikingly unique.[14] Perhaps most noteworthy is Richard's optimism concerning the potential experiences a contemplative can achieve in this life. Whilst other writers defer the complete experience of the presence of God to the next life, i.e., the beatific vision of the saints, Richard's interests are confined almost entirely to the present—with the important exception, of course, of the contemplative's concerns for the ultimate salvation of others in the fourth degree. This focus leads Richard to part ways with earlier writers.

Richard appears to signal his optimism regarding the possibilities for contemplative experience at the outset of *On the Four Degrees of Violent Love*. The verse from the Song of Songs 2:5 with which Richard's treatise begins, "I have been wounded by love,"[15] also appears in the

---

[12]   See Richard's quotation of Apoc. 8:1 in par. 38.

[13]   This final emphasis on one's responsibility for the salvation of others supports the self-understanding of the "mixed" life of canons identified by Caroline Walker Bynum, "The Spirituality of Canons Regular in the Twelfth Century," *Jesus as Mother: Studies in the Spirituality of the High Middle Ages* (Berkeley: University of California Press, 1982), 22–58.

[14]   *On the Four Degrees of Violent Love* may be seen, for example, as part of a trend of spiritual "ladder literature" composed throughout the twelfth century. Other prominent examples include Bernard of Clairvaux, *De gradibus superbiae et humilitatis* (SBO 3:13–59; tr. M. B. Pennington, *The Steps of Humility and Pride* [Kalamazoo: Cistercian Publications, 1989]) and Guigo II, ninth prior of the Grande Chartreuse, *Scala claustralium* (ed. Edmund Colledge and James Walsh, SC 163 [Paris: Cerf, 1970] [PL 184.475–84]; tr. Colledge and Walsh, *The Ladder of Monks and Twelve Meditations* [Kalamazoo: Cistercian Publications, 1981]).

[15]   Song of Songs 2:5 in the Old Latin translation.

writings of other medieval authors concerned with similar topics. In his widely disseminated meditations, for example, John of Fécamp (d. 1079) begs Christ to "wound this sinful soul, for which you were even willing to die! Wound it with the fiery and most powerful spear of your abundant love! . . . Transfix my heart with the spear of your love, so that my soul might say to you, 'I have been wounded by your love.'"[16] John thus establishes the wounding love of God to be the pinnacle of the contemplative's desire: he longs to be able to say the words of Song of Songs 2:5. Yet John immediately notes that, while the contemplative might desire this wounding, he will not achieve it until the next life: ". . . that I might wail day and night, accepting no consolation in the present life, until I might deserve to see you in the heavenly marriage chamber."[17]

In contrast to writers like John, Richard begins his treatise with the words of Song of Songs 2:5, and he then quickly goes on to associate the experience they describe with the very earliest stages of contemplative ascent: wounding is but the first of Richard's four degrees. Further, beginning his work with this quotation associates Richard's readers, presumably canons regular, with the words of the Song of Songs. As we have seen, the structure of Richard's treatise is suggestive of a movement from extra-claustral life to life within the cloister, and finally to the contemplative experience that was to be the aim of such a life. This initial quotation from the Song of Songs, taken together with the structure of Richard's writing, suggests that he envisioned his audience of canons, even if they were new to this way of life, as having already reached the first degree of love, having already been pierced by the wounding love for God.

A similarly striking contrast emerges when one compares the use of bridal images in Bernard of Clairvaux's *Sermons on the Song of Songs* and Richard's treatise. Famously, Bernard (d. 1153) interpreted the first verse of the Song of Songs, "Let him kiss me with the kiss of his mouth," as pertaining to the contemplative monk's progressing relationship with God. The monk yearns to kiss the figure of Christ with three

---

[16]   PL 40.935: "Vulnera hanc animam peccatricem, pro qua etiam mori dignatus es; vulnera eam igneo et potentissimo telo tuae nimiae charitatis. . . . Confige cor meum jaculo tui amoris: ut dicat tibi anima mea, 'Caritate tua vulnerata sum.'"

[17]   PL 40.936: "Ut lugeam nocte ac die, nullam in praesenti vita recipiens consolationem, donec te in coelesti thalamo merear videre."

kisses, Bernard writes, the kiss of the feet, the hands, and the mouth.[18] The first of these kisses represents the monk's initial expression of penitence, his admission of his sinfulness and his abasement of himself before God, while the second represents adherence to the monastic rule: "the beauty of temperance and the fruits that befit repentance, the works of piety."[19] The final kiss appears to have something of the quality of mystical union to it, but Bernard never explains this kiss fully: with a coy rhetorical move, Bernard states that he must leave off from his account, since guests have arrived at the monastery.[20] Yet even if this final kiss is meant to represent some form of the experience of God's presence attainable in this life, Bernard is still consciously putting something off: though the soul as bride may thus kiss Christ her bridegroom, she is not yet in this life invited into the marriage bed. The soul remains a virgin wife.[21]

To this Bernardine metaphor we might fruitfully compare Richard's own nuptial imagery (par. 26–27). Richard articulates the first degree as a betrothal, the second as a wedding, the third as the experience of sexual union that Bernard defers, and the fourth as childbirth. The priority Richard gives to the perfected active life in the fourth degree, working toward the salvation of one's brethren, appears to have led him to go beyond Bernard's account: not only is such a full experience of God's presence possible in this life, according to Richard, it does not even constitute the end of the story. Richard's focus on both the active and contemplative lives, therefore, results in an understanding of contemplative potential that is indeed optimistic when compared to the writing of other, earlier authors.

---

[18] Bernard of Clairvaux, SCC 2–4 (SBO 1:8–21; tr. K. Walsh, *On the Song of Songs* [Kalamazoo: Cistercian Publication, 1971–83], 1:16–24).

[19] Bernard, SCC 3.4 (SBO 1:16.21–22; tr. Walsh, 1:19): "Decor continentiae et digne paenitentiae fructus, quae sunt opera pietatis."

[20] Bernard, SCC 3.6 (SBO 1:17.23–26. tr. Walsh, 1:20).

[21] Note that Bernard says that those to whom it is given to utter these words [i.e., Song of Songs 1:1] are comparatively few: SCC 3:1 (SBO 1:14.10–11; tr. Walsh, 1:16): " 'Oscultur me osculo oris sui.' Non est enim cuiusvis hominum ex affectu hoc dicere" (" 'Let him kiss me with the kiss of his mouth.' It is not given to just anyone to say this in a heartfelt way"). For a further discussion of this motif, see E. Ann Matter, *The Voice of My Beloved: The Song of Songs in Western Medieval Christianity* (Philadelphia: University of Pennsylvania Press, 1990), 123–27. On the later development of such motifs, see Amy Hollywood, *The Soul as Virgin Wife: Mechthild of Magdeburg, Marguerite Porete, and Meister Eckhart* (Notre Dame: University of Notre Dame Press, 1995).

Richard's optimism, however, introduces into *On the Four Degrees of Violent Love* certain tensions that need never have troubled earlier writers like John of Fécamp and Bernard. As long as the full experience of God's presence is necessarily delayed until the next life, John and Bernard are able to focus their attention entirely on the contemplative's longing for God. Their instructions (often given in the form of tropological exegesis of selected biblical verses) can be clear and, however rigorous the meditation they recommend, it can always be envisioned as within the ability of the monastic reader to achieve. Richard continues to use language that places the impetus for action on the part of the contemplative, as, for example, when he adapts Matt. 7:8 to describe the movement from the first to the second degrees: "[We must] beg burningly, seek diligently, knock strongly, and press on tenaciously through all of these acts" (33). Yet Richard also makes it clear that God is no passive love object, and progress through each of the degrees also requires the action of God upon the contemplative (see, most fantastically, his description in par. 38).

Richard's account indicates that, as one progresses through the degrees, one's own agency becomes less important, while God's agency becomes ever more so. For example, the proper ordering of one's life in the first degree, described as the soul's own quitting of Egypt and journey through the Red Sea (31), gives way to the soul passively being "snatched away into the abyss of divine love" (38). By this point, Richard suggests, the will of the contemplative and the will of God become the same thing, and so the question of agency becomes redundant. Yet Richard never explicitly comments on the balancing act that goes on between human agency and divine agency prior to this point, and so ultimately, it seems, the would-be contemplative should simply content himself with the first degree of love and the *lectio divina* represented in Section III. If he can do this, further, more advanced experiences of God's love may await him.

III

Perhaps owing in part to what I have called Richard's optimism, *On the Four Degrees of Violent Love* enjoyed considerable popularity throughout the later Middle Ages, exerting influence on a variety of writers in Latin and the vernacular. Rudolph Goy identified no fewer than seventy-eight medieval manuscripts of Richard's tract that survive today.[22] While most of the twelfth-century witnesses are of French provenance, the number of such early manuscripts is dwarfed by the number of later medieval copies, mostly from the fourteenth and fifteenth centuries, originating from all over Europe. This diffusion of manuscripts of Richard's work is reflected in the ever-increasing influence the four degrees exerted over religious writers in the later Middle Ages.[23]

Richard's four degrees of love were taken up in a particularly elaborate fashion in the writing of the English hermit Richard Rolle (1290–1349), and Rolle's subsequent popularity throughout the remainder of the fourteenth century and into the fifteenth century appears to be responsible in part for the four degrees reaching other authors of Middle English devotional prose. As Nicholas Watson has described in detail, Rolle attempted to chart his own experiences of God's presence onto Richard's four degrees.[24] Yet this was not always an easy fit: whereas Richard's final two degrees shift from a focus on solitary experience to life in monastic community, Rolle believed that his experience of the third degree, once achieved, represented a continuous state of being. While it may have been Richard's optimism that drew Rolle to the four degrees, it seems that Richard's schema was not quite optimistic enough for the later writer.

Composed sometime between ca. 1375 and ca. 1425, the devotional guide *Fervor Amoris* presents another example of a Middle English adaptation of Richard's four degrees of violent love, in this case mediated by Rolle's text.[25] Written with a decidedly pastoral purpose in mind, the *Fervor Amoris* abandons Rolle's focus on authority-granting

---

[22] Rudolph Goy, *Die handschriftliche Überlieferung der Werke Richards von St. Viktor im Mittelalter*, Bibliotheca Victorina 18 (Turnhout: Brepols, 2005), 325–38.

[23] For the influence of Richard's text among female writers on the Continent, see Barbara Newman, *From Virile Woman to WomanChrist: Studies in Medieval Religion and Literature* (Philadelphia: University of Pennsylvania Press, 1995), 158–64. Newman also provides an illuminating reading of the *On the Four Degrees* itself in the context of the later-twelfth-century tradition of courtly love. For the influence of Richard's four degrees on Johannes Tauler and Heinrich Suso, see Hugh B. Feiss, "The Grace of Passion and the Compassion of God: Soundings in the Christian Tradition," *American Benedictine Review* 41 (1990): 141–56.

[24] Nicholas Watson, *Richard Rolle and the Invention of Authority* (Cambridge: Cambridge University Press, 1992); "Conceptions of the Word: The Mother Tongue and the Incarnation of God," *New Medieval Literatures* 1 (1997): 85–124, at pp. 103–4.

[25] *Contemplations of the Dread and Love of God*, ed. M. Connolly, Early English Text Society, Original Series, 303 (Oxford: Oxford University Press, 1993). On the title of this text, see Nicole Rice, *Lay Piety and Religious Discipline in Medieval English Literature* (Cambridge: Cambridge University Press, 2008), 29.

solitary experience and, as Nicole Rice has recently described it, "offers literary forms that carefully shape lay devotion according to disciplines holding recognized place within 'ecclesiastical institutions.' "[26] The anonymous author of the *Fervor* therefore restores the focus on the active life that Rolle had de-emphasized in his own articulation of the four degrees.[27]

Richard's treatment by Rolle and Rolle's anonymous adapter is in many ways representative of the later-medieval reception of the four degrees more generally. In most such cases, it seems that Richard's affective language and, especially, his optimism concerning the potential experience of the presence of God in this life, attracted later religious writers to the model presented in *On the Four Degrees of Violent Love*. At the same time, however, each writer had to negotiate anew the complexities and tensions inherent in such a model.

IV

The present translation is based on the critical edition of *On the Four Degrees of Violent Love* by Gervais Dumeige.[28] This is the first complete rendering of the text into English, though an abridged translation was published by Clare Kirchberger in 1957.[29] For the sake of convenience in citations, I have maintained both Dumeige's division of the text into paragraphs and his enumeration of those paragraphs. Based on my own reading of Richard's text, I have additionally divided the translation into larger sections, noted above. Finally, one should bear in mind that Richard uses many words for "love," though the most frequent is "caritas." When I have translated as "love" a word other than "caritas" (e.g., *amor, dilectio, emulatio*), the Latin is provided in parentheses.

---

[26] Rice, *Discipline*, 30.

[27] Rice, *Discipline*, 31–39.

[28] Ives: *Épître a Séverin sur la charité, Richard de Saint-Victor: Les quatres degrés de la violente charité*, ed. G. Dumeige (Paris: J. Vrin, 1955), 126–77.

[29] In *Richard of St Victor: Selected Writings on Contemplation* (London: Faber and Faber, 1957), 213–33. Earlier printings of the text and its translation into languages other than English are detailed by Dumeige, *Richard de Saint-Victor et l'idée*, 171–73.

[I]

1. "I have been wounded by love."[1] Love urges me to speak about love, and I willingly devote myself to its service. Indeed, it is sweet and altogether enjoyable to speak about love (*dilectione*)—a pleasant matter and quite rich, and one that cannot in any way produce tedium in the writer or disgust in the reader. For that which is seasoned with love is flavorful beyond measure on the palate of the heart. "If a man were to give the entire wealth of his house for his love (*dilectione*), he would think it nothing."[2]

2. Great is the power of love (*dilectionis*); the virtue of love is marvelous. There are many degrees in it, and there is a great difference among them. Who is capable of distinguishing them suitably or even so much as enumerating them? Of course among these are the feelings of kindness, of friendship, of marriage and familial relationships, of fraternity, and in this manner many others. Yet beyond all of these degrees of love (*dilectionis*) is that burning and seething love (*amor*), which penetrates the heart and enkindles emotion, piercing through the soul itself to the very marrow of the bones, so that the soul may say, "I have been wounded by love."[3]

3. Let us consider, therefore, what "that complete eminence of the love of Christ"[4] may be, which excels the love (*dilectionem*) of parents and the love (*amorem*) of a child, transcends or extinguishes the feelings of a wife, and even turns the soul into something hated.[5] Oh, vehemence of love (*dilectionis*), oh, violence of love! Oh, the superiority, oh, the utter eminence of the love of Christ! It is this love, brothers, toward which we strain; it is concerning such a thing that we wish to speak: on the vehemence of love, on the total eminence of perfect jealous love (*emulationis*). You know well enough that it is one thing to speak about love and another about its perfection; one thing to speak about love itself and another about the violence of it.

4. I attend to the works of violent love and discover the vehemence of perfect jealous love (*emulationis*). Behold, I see some people wounded, others bound, others languid, others growing faint—and all from love. Love wounds, love binds, love makes one languish, love leads to weakness. Which of these is not powerful? Which of these is not vio-

lent? These are the four degrees of fiery love, to which we will now give our attention. Follow my words in your mind, brothers; attend to what you eagerly desire. Hear about it, and pant for what you strive with such force to attain. Do you wish to hear about wounding love? "You have wounded my heart, my sister, wife, with one look and with one of the locks on your neck."[6] Do you wish to hear about binding love? "I will draw them with the cords of Adam, with the chains of love."[7] Do you wish to hear about languid love? "Oh, daughters of Jerusalem, if you discover my beloved, tell him I am languishing in love (*amore*)."[8] Do you wish to hear about fainting love and love that leads to weakness? "My soul has grown faint," he says, "for your salvation, and in your word have I trusted above all else."[9] And so love makes one weak; it leads to languor. Love has chains; love inflicts wounds.

[II]

5. But what are these cords of Adam, our first father, if not the gifts of God? What, I ask, are these chains of love if not the benefits of God, blessings of nature, grace, and glory? With these chains of kindness God conferred on Adam a responsibility and indebted him to that kindness. He created nature; he conferred grace; he promised glory. Behold "the triple cord"[10]: the gifts of creation, the blessings of justification, and the rewards of glorification.[11] And we know that "the triple cord is difficult to break,"[12] and yet it has been broken, "for from all eternity man has shattered his yoke, he has broken the chains."[13] Yet God has continued to multiply the chains of his love about us "with a strong hand,"[14] so that he has bound us more tightly to himself and entangled us more completely. He conferred his blessings upon us and endured our evils for us, so that in both ways he could restore the guilty to himself—by both the blessings conferred upon us and the evils that he endured for us. In this way, with the cords of love, "he led captivity captive,"[15] liberally giving gifts to men and freely bearing evils on their behalf. Oh, how wickedly strong is he whom such great chains of love cannot hold! Oh, how wickedly free is he who does not become entangled in the laws of this captivity!

6. But, behold, let us return to that degree of love (*amoris*) that we placed in the first position and called wounding. Do you not think that the heart appears to be pierced when that fiery sting of love (*amoris*) penetrates one's mind to the core of his being and transfixes his feelings,

so much so that he is completely incapable of containing or concealing the boiling of his desire? He is ablaze with desire; he seethes with feeling. He boils and pants, groaning deeply and drawing long, deep breaths. These may be for you the sure signs of a wounded soul: the groans and the deep breaths, a face growing pale and pining. Yet this degree sometimes allows a break and yields to the cares and anxieties of pressing work. Such is the habit of those who are tossed about with this type of fever: sometimes they are burned more sharply, while at other times they are revived somewhat by the opportunity of their occupations. But again, after a short break, the boiling fire returns more intensely, and it enkindles the already-shattered mind more sharply and burns it more vehemently. And so often receding and always returning greater than it had been, little by little this fire softens the mind. It smashes and drains bodily strength, until it fully subjugates the soul to itself and prostrates it. It occupies the mind with the constant memory of itself, hems the mind in entirely, binds it entirely, so that the mind cannot pull itself away from that fire or think of anything else— and now from the first degree it crosses to the second.

7. We have said that the first degree wounds and the second binds. Is it not indeed true and beyond any contradiction that the mind is bound when it is unable to forget this one thing or to meditate on anything else? Whatever the mind may do, whatever it may say, this one thing is always tossed back at the mind and returns continually to the memory. Sleeping, a man dreams of it; awake, he considers it anew every hour. From here it is easy, I think, to assess carefully the way in which this second degree goes beyond the first, for it does not permit the mind of a man to be at peace, not even for an hour. Therefore, it has rightly been said that the degree that wounds comes first, while that which binds is second. For it is often less of a concern to be wounded than to be bound. As everyone surely knows, it often happens that a soldier struck and wounded in the clash of battle flees from the hand of his attacker, and, though wounded, he nevertheless escapes and is free. But later, in the contest of battle, that soldier, struck, is made to fall. Fallen, he is caught; caught, he is led away; led away, he is imprisoned; imprisoned, he is chained and bound, now held a captive in every respect. Which of these things, I ask, is more serious or which more troublesome? Is it not more bearable to flee, though wounded, and still remain free, than to be held captive, captured and bound?

8. This degree, unlike the earlier one, does not allow any break, but in the manner of a sharp fever it burns the mind with ceaseless fire and

enkindles it with the continuous boiling of its desire. Neither by day nor by night does it allow the soul to be at peace. And so, just as one who is sick in bed or restrained by chains cannot get away from the place where he is bound, so too one who is in the grip of this second degree of violent love cannot cut free from that one, internal, pre-occupying concern, no matter what he does or where he turns. There-fore, we ought to repel the impetus of the first degree in regard to perverse desires not so much by resisting it as by avoiding it, not so much by struggling against it as by fleeing from it. And we are able to do so if, always alert, we with a provident mind take refuge in useful and honest occupations or meditations, and we fulfill what has been written: "Flee fornication."[16]

9. And so the violence of the first degree can be avoided but not overcome, while the vehemence of the second degree can be neither overcome by resistance nor avoided by flight. Hear the captive moaning and abandoning hope of flight: "Flight has died for me, and there is no one who has regard for my soul."[17] But often, as we see, those who can-not flee can nevertheless redeem themselves. Therefore, when we are unable to repel temptation with virtue or avoid it with prudence, we ought to redeem ourselves with works of mercy and obedience, and rescue ourselves from the yoke of slavery. For these are the true and particular riches concerning which it was written: "The redemption of a man's soul is his particular wealth."[18] But when love (*amor*) has out-grown this second degree of vehemence, where, I ask, might it spread itself further? What could be more vehement than this vehemence, if it cannot be overcome, if it cannot be avoided? If it is altogether un-conquerable, if it is altogether inseparable, what can be more vehement than this vehemence? If it cannot be overcome by any feelings, it is the highest, and if it clings inseparably, it is perpetual. And what violence can be more violent than its violence, if it is the highest and perpetual? But it is one thing to be the highest and another to be unique, just as it is one thing always to be present and another not to admit any com-panion at all. For we are able to be present and to have many compan-ions, and yet we still may hold a higher place before all of them. Therefore, you see how much further the vastness of this utter preemi-nence may yet grow from this point, so that, although it is already the highest, it can also be unique.

10. And so love (*amor*) ascends toward the third degree of violence when it excludes all other emotion, when it loves nothing besides the one or on account of the one. Therefore, in this third degree of violent

love nothing besides the one can satisfy the mind, just as it cannot know anything but on account of the one. The mind loves one, it singles one out, it thirsts for one, and it craves one. For it alone the mind pants, for it alone the mind sighs, because of it alone the mind is enkindled, and in it alone does the mind find peace. There is only one thing in which the mind is restored, one thing by which it is satiated. Nothing is sweet, nothing has any taste unless it is spiced with this one alone. Whatever offers itself besides this one, whatever may perchance come to mind, is quickly driven back and immediately trampled underfoot; it does not fight on the side of the mind's feelings or devote itself to this desire. But who may worthily describe the tyranny of this emotion: in the way it eschews every desire, shuts out every other pursuit, and violently suppresses every exercise that it does not foresee as serving its own cravings? Whatever one may attempt, whatever may happen seems useless, nay, rather, insufferable, unless it coincides with and is to the advantage of the singular end of the mind's desire. When a man is able to enjoy what he loves, he believes himself to have all things simultaneously. Without it, all things are horrible, all things are soiled.[19] For if he cannot enjoy it, his body grows weak and his heart pines. He does not accept counsel, he does not acquiesce to reason, and he accepts no consolation at all.

11. In the second degree a man can still be occupied by outside business in his actions, but not in his thoughts, since he cannot forget what he loves. In this third degree, however, his mind is weak and faint with the excess of his love (*amoris*). Just as he is unable to meditate upon other things, he is likewise unable to perform any other tasks. The second degree envelops his thoughts; this third one dissolves his actions as well. That one binds a man in his thinking; this one enervates him in his action. In the second degree we still move our hands and feet freely, and we can reach out and grasp here and there like a feverish person, since we are still both able and obligated to stretch forth our limbs at discretion's judgment and to exercise them in good works. However, in this third degree the excess of love (*amoris*) is similar to languor: it enervates the hands and feet such that thereafter the mind may not attempt anything at all through its own will. And so in this state, the mind remains as if it were immobile, and it cannot move itself anywhere through thought or action unless its desire draws it there or its emotion impels it.

12. In the first degree, as has already been said, a man is still able to flee his crooked desires through zealous circumspection. However, in

the second degree, when no hiding place remains, he can still redeem himself through good works. But what can help men in the third degree? What kind of remedy can exist, when one can no longer plan for the necessities of life or perform useful tasks? Hear a man who is languishing in his heart and his body—body emaciated and heart tossed about in confusion: "My heart has been disquieted within me; my strength has abandoned me."[20] In this extreme need, I find no other kind of remedy than to gaze at the divine clemency and implore its mercy. If you are altogether languid, if you cannot move your hands and feet freely, you certainly still have a tongue and the ability to move your lips. Therefore, if there remains no opportunity to escape by your own effort, cry out to him who can do all things.

13. I think you now see how much that strength of love (*amoris*) has already increased when, still growing, it climbs toward the vehemence of this third degree, and it is surprising that any means remain by which it can ascend further. In the first degree it pierces affection, in the second it binds thought, and in the third it dissolves action. And so feelings are taken captive in the first degree, thought in the second, and action in the third. The entirety of a man consists in these things, and so what can he have beyond them? If, therefore, everything that there is to a man has been taken captive, what more can be done to him? If that strength of love (*amoris*) is master of everything, if the magnitude of love (*amoris*) swallows up everything, in what way, I ask, can it extend itself further? For if it holds everything fast, then there is nothing further that it can claim. But what do we say if it holds everything fast, and everything is not enough for it? What, I ask, can we say, if everything is under its rule, yet everything still cannot satisfy its desire? Certainly there are incomparably more things that a man cannot do than those that he can. And yet both can be desired: what a man can do and what he cannot do. Therefore, see how boundless is the space into which desire can extend itself even after it has come through the third degree.

14. And so the fourth degree of violent love exists when nothing at all can satisfy the desire of the boiling mind any longer. This degree, unlike the others, knows no limit to its growth, for it has exceeded the limits of human possibility and it always finds something else that it can desire ardently. Whatever it attempts, whatever happens, nothing satiates the desire of the burning soul. The soul is thirsty and it drinks, yet drinking does not quench its thirst.[21] Rather, the more the soul drinks, the more it thirsts. For the thirst or hunger of the greedy, nay,

insatiable soul is not allayed but rather exacerbated when it enjoys at will what it has desired. In this state "the eye is not satiated with what it sees, nor is the ear filled with what it hears,"[22] whether it speaks to one who is absent or looks at one who is present. But who can explain the violence of this highest degree? Who is capable of pondering worthily the utter preeminence of this degree? What, I ask, exists that penetrates the heart of a man more deeply, crucifies him more harshly, stirs him up more vehemently? What, I ask, is more troublesome or what more bitter, when the heart cannot temper its thirst by resisting or extinguish it by drinking? Marvelous, nay, rather pitiable is the gluttony which is neither driven out by any effort nor allayed with any satisfaction. An irredeemable and utterly incurable sickness, for which a remedy is forever sought and nowhere found, nay, everything that is looked to as a saving remedy turns into sustenance for the fury.

15. This is that degree, as we have said, which leads to weakness and makes a man despair of a remedy. And, like an invalid beyond hope, this man lies down with half-dead limbs: now he can do nothing more, nor should he hope for anyone else to do anything for him. Now every care of the physicians is withdrawn from him, and he is left entirely to himself. Alone, he gasps with his breath, and every hour he appears to draw near to his end. Now he takes in his last breath, and he neither notices nor heeds what is going on around him or what is happening to him. And such is the case with the man who pants under the flame of this sort of boiling desire: whatever happens to him, it cannot offer a remedy or provide any consolation. Therefore, whatever consolation is offered, it does not touch his mind. It is as if he were near death and does not at all sense those things that are occurring around him.[23]

16. While the human mind is violently drawn toward this state amid crooked desires, nothing else remains to be done but that other men pray for this man, on the chance that the Lord, considering the faith of these men and restoring him to life, "may return that man to his mother."[24] The Lord is "powerful enough even to raise up sons of Abraham out of stones"[25] and, as often as he wants, leads down to hell and leads back out.[26] In this state love (*amor*) is often turned into something like insanity, unless its impetus is checked with marvelous prudence and equal steadiness. In this state tempers often flare among lovers; they often engage in noisy quarrels, and when genuine causes of enmity are not at hand, they devise false and utterly implausible ones. In this state love (*amor*) often turns into hate, while nothing can satisfy their mutual desire. What we have often seen in certain people then takes

place: the more ardently they formerly appeared to love one another, the more they now attack one another with fierce hatred.[27] Still more amazingly, often at the same time, they hate one another though they never cease to boil with desire, and they love one another though they continue to attack one another as if out of hatred. And so in loving they hate and in hating they love, and all in a marvelous manner—nay, rather miserably, for their hate grows out of their desire and their desire out of their hate. And "fire and hail mixed together are brought forth,"[28] since the boiling of their desire cannot melt the frost of their hate, nor can the hail of their detestation extinguish the fire of their burning concupiscence. But beyond measure, nay, also beyond nature, this fire thrives in water, since the fire of love (*amoris*) boils up more vigorously out of these contraries than it ever could increase from mutual peace.

17. Behold, we now have the four degrees of violence in fiery love (*dilectione*), concerning which we earlier proposed to write. Therefore, the first degree of violence exists when the mind cannot resist its desire, while the second degree exists when that desire cannot be forgotten. Truly, the third degree exists when the mind can know nothing but its desire, while the fourth, which is also the last, exists when not even the very thing the mind desires is able to satisfy it. And so in the first degree love (*amor*) is unconquerable; in the second it is inseparable; in the third it is singular; and in the fourth it is insatiable. That which does not submit to other emotions is unconquerable; that which never retreats from memory is inseparable; that which does not take a companion is singular;[29] when it cannot be satisfied, it is insatiable. And although several elements may be observed in each of the degrees, one should note in particular the excellence of love (*amoris*) in the first degree, in the second its vehemence, in the third its violence, and in the fourth its absolute preeminence. For how great is the excellence of a love (*amoris*) that exceeds all other feelings! How great, I beg, is the vehemence of a love (*dilectionis*) that does not permit the mind to be at peace! How great, I implore, is the violence of a love that violently expels all other emotion! How great is the utter preeminence of a jealous love (*emulationis*) that is never sufficient! Oh, excellence of love (*amoris*)! Oh, vehemence of love (*dilectionis*)! Oh, violence of love! Oh, total preeminence of jealous love (*emulationis*)!

18. These four degrees of love (*amoris*) exist in one way with regard to godly feelings and in another with regard to human feelings—two altogether different ways with regard to spiritual desires and fleshly desires. With spiritual desires the extent to which the number of the

degree is higher is also the extent to which the degree itself is better; in fleshly desires the extent to which it is higher is the extent to which it is worse. In godly feelings the degree that is highest is likewise best. In human feelings the degree that is highest is itself also worst. Truly, in human emotions the first degree can be good, but the second without doubt is bad; the third is worse, while the fourth is the worst.

19. We know that in human emotions marital love (*amor*) ought to hold the first place, and, therefore, in the marriage bed that degree of love (*amoris*) that is accustomed to being master over all other feelings can be good. For in fact the shared feeling of intimate love (*amoris*) tightens the chains of peace between those who are pledged to one another, and it renders that indissoluble and perpetual union pleasing and delightful. Therefore, the first degree in human feelings, as has been said, can be good, while on the other hand the second without doubt is bad. For when it has bound the mind indissolubly, when the mind is not allowed to tend to any other concern, this desire often steals both care for those things that should be provided and provision of those things that should be put in order. However, that third degree of love (*amoris*), which excludes all other emotion, is not only bad, but it also actually begins to be bitter, since it is not always possible to enjoy at will what one wishes, and one cannot draw consolation from any other thing. Yet the fourth degree, as we have said, is the worst of all. What can be found that is worse than what not only disfigures the soul but also makes it miserable? What is more miserable than always being wearied by the desire for a thing, the enjoyment of which can never satisfy you? Above we showed how the mind is burnt in this degree with constant boiling and frost, while hatred is not extinguished because of desire nor desire because of hatred. And what does this condition appear to be, other than a sure model of future damnation, where one always passes from the heat of the fires to the cold of the snows and from the cold of the snows to the heat of the fires?

20. And so this last degree of love (*amoris*) is the worst of all among human desires, while, as has been said, it is the best of all among godly feelings. For in the former whatever is done for the human mind cannot satisfy it, while in the latter whatever one does for his God cannot satisfy his desire. In the former, the mind is always troubled by what is done to it, not what the mind itself is doing. In the latter, the mind experiences greater anxiety for what it might do, rather than because of what is done to it. And so in heavenly desires the greater the emotion and the higher the degree, so much more is it truly better and more

precious. Oh, how precious is that first degree of love (*dilectionis*) in the love (*amore*) of God, when it is unconquerable! More precious by far is the second, when burning emotion begins to be inseparable. Yet still better by far, when one can only find delight on account of God. However, the highest and most precious degree of love exists when nothing is able to satisfy one's desire.

[III]

21. Now, in the first degree "many waters cannot extinguish love, nor will the rivers flood over it,"[30] because it is unconquerable. In the second degree the soul "sets its beloved as a seal over its heart,"[31] because the soul is altogether unable to forget it. In the third degree "if a man were to give the entire wealth of his home for his love (*dilectione*), he would think it nothing,"[32] because he is unable to delight in anything else. However, in the fourth degree "love (*dilectio*) is as strong as death, jealous love (*emulatio*) as cruel as Hell,"[33] because it is a small matter for him to be able to do or undergo anything for his God's sake. In the first degree unconquerable love (*amor*) says, "I will love you, O Lord, my strength."[34] In the second inseparable love (*amor*) says, "May my tongue cling to the roof of my mouth if I do not remember you."[35] In the third degree singular love (*amor*) says, "My soul refuses to be consoled; I was mindful of God and I have been delighted."[36] In the fourth degree insatiable love (*amor*) says: "What might I render to the Lord for all that he has rendered to me?"[37]

22. A man in the first degree is unconquerable and says, "What will separate us from the love of Christ: tribulation, or difficulties, or persecution, or hunger, or nakedness, or danger, or the sword?"[38] In the second "love never fails,"[39] because it is inseparable, and he therefore says, "My soul clings tightly to you,"[40] because it may not be wrenched away from him. In the third a man "judges all things as excrement so that he might gain Christ."[41] In the fourth for him "to live is Christ and to die is gain,"[42] because he desires "to be dissolved and to be with Christ."[43]

23. In the first degree God is loved "with the heart, with the soul, and with the mind."[44] Yet none of these is done in its entirety. In the second God is loved with the entire heart. In the third he is loved with the entire soul. In the fourth, however, he is loved with all of one's strength. Love (*dilectio*) from the heart is love (*dilectio*) that comes

from deliberate consideration. However, to love with the soul is to love with emotion. Counsel pertains to the heart; desire, however, pertains to the soul. But do you wish to learn what counsel we ought to bring to the heart? "Ephraim," it is said, "is a dove led astray, not having a heart."[45] What is it for a people not to have a heart, if not to be without counsel? What is it, I ask, for a people to be a dove led astray and lacking a heart, if not what is said elsewhere: "They are a people without counsel and lacking prudence"?[46] And so to be without a heart is nothing other than to lack counsel and prudence. But now, as has been said, just as counsel pertains to the heart, so too does desire pertain to the soul. "Whoever has lost his life in this world," it is said, "keeps it for eternal life."[47] What is losing one's soul in this world, if not, as has been taught elsewhere, "not to follow one's concupiscence?"[48] For the more a man subdues his desires in this world because of God, the more indeed he increases them in an eternal abundance. And so to love with the heart is to love with counsel and deliberation. To love with the soul is to love with desire and feeling— the former from studious effort and the latter in accordance with one's wishes. To love with the entire heart, with the entire soul, and with all of one's strength is to expend one's every effort, every desire, every exercise on this one thing.

24. Often we are drawn toward loving something by our feelings, and yet we are restrained by our reason. And often we love many things by deliberate choice, though we do not strive after them desirously. And so in fleshly desires loving from the soul is often prior to loving from the heart. However, in spiritual things to love something out of deliberation is always prior to doing so on account of emotion. For we never love spiritual things desirously unless we first inflame our mind toward the pursuit of those things with great effort. Therefore, if we desire to love God with our entire soul, first we endeavor to love him with our entire heart. Let all our thoughts aim toward this end, toward this end be all our deliberation, and about this end be all our meditation, if we wish to love with our every desire. But just as we may never love with our entire soul, unless we first love with our entire heart, so too may we never love with all of our strength, unless we first love with our entire soul. For if we have affection for something that we do not love because of God, surely that adulterous emotion shatters the constancy of the highest love and diminishes its strength, to the extent that it draws or impels the mind toward different desires. Therefore, in the first degree, as has been said, a man loves God with his heart, in the

second he loves with his entire heart, while in the third with his entire soul, and in the fourth with all of his strength.

25. Perhaps till this point David was in the first degree, but now he anticipated the second, when, singing, he said, "I will acknowledge you, O Lord, with my whole heart."[49] He who is in the second degree is able to sing the psalm confidently: "With my whole heart I have searched you out."[50] He who reaches the third degree surely now is able to speak of it in this manner: "My soul eagerly desires your justification, O Lord, at all times."[51] He who ascends to the fourth degree and loves God with all of his strength is surely able to say, "I do not fear what a man may do to me,"[52] "for his heart is ready to hope in the Lord; his heart has been strengthened, and he will not be moved for all eternity, until he looks down upon his enemies."[53]

26. In the first degree a betrothal is made, in the second a marriage, in the third sexual union, and in the fourth childbirth. In the first degree a man says to his beloved, "I will betroth you to myself for all eternity, and I will betroth you to myself in justice and judgment and in mercy and in pity, and I will betroth you to myself in faith."[54] The marriage in Cana of Galilee takes place in the second degree and now it is said to her, "Behold I am your husband and you will not cease to walk after me."[55] Concerning the third degree it is said, "He who clings to the Lord is one spirit."[56] Concerning the fourth it is said, "We have conceived, and we have been, as it were, in labor, and we have given birth to spirit."[57] And so in the first degree the beloved is visited frequently, in the second she is married, in the third she couples with her beloved, and in the fourth she is pregnant.

27. The beloved is therefore always anxious in the first degree. She cries for the return of her beloved and says, "Come, O my beloved, be like the roe deer and the fawn of the stags on the mountains of Bethel."[58] In the second she is invited to come, and these words are therefore said to her: "Come from Lebanon, my sister, my betrothed, come from Lebanon."[59] In the third degree union is fulfilled with her beloved, and she says, "His left hand is under my head and with his right hand he will embrace me."[60] In the fourth degree she glories in her pregnancy and says, "O my little sons, I am in labor with you a second time until Christ may be formed in you."[61] And he therefore says to her, "Your two breasts are like two fawns of roe deer, which are grazing among the lilies."[62]

[IV]

28. Let us go deeper still, and let us speak more plainly. In the first degree the soul thirsts for God. In the second it thirsts toward God. In the third the soul thirsts into God. In the fourth it thirsts in accordance with God.[63] The soul that thirsts for God says, "My soul desired you in the night, but I will also keep watch for you with my spirit in my breast from the early morning."[64] The soul that thirsts toward God says, "My soul thirsted toward God, the fountain of living water: when will I come and appear before the face of the Lord?"[65] The soul that thirsts into God says, "My soul has thirsted into you, my flesh for you in so many ways."[66] The soul that thirsts in accordance with God says, "My soul has eagerly desired your justifications, O Lord, at all times."[67] The soul thirsts for God when it desires to experience what that internal sweetness might be that often intoxicates the mind, when one begins to "taste and see how sweet the Lord is."[68] The soul thirsts toward God when it desires to be lifted up above itself through the grace of contemplation and desires to see "the king in his beauty,"[69] so that it may be truly bold and say, "I have seen the Lord face to face and my soul has been saved."[70] Then the soul thirsts into God when, through ecstasy of the mind, it eagerly desires to cross entirely into God. Thus thoroughly forgetful of itself, the soul can truly say, "Whether in the body or outside of the body I do not know; God knows."[71] The soul thirsts in accordance with God when concerning its own will—not just in fleshly things, but also indeed in spiritual things—the mind relinquishes everything from its own judgment and commits itself wholly to the Lord, never thinking "of things that are its own, but of the things of Jesus Christ,"[72] so that the soul itself may also be able to say, "I did not come to do my will, but the will of my Father who is in heaven."[73]

29. And so in the first degree God enters into the mind, and the mind retreats into itself.[74] In the second degree the mind ascends above itself and is lifted up to God. In the third degree the mind lifted up to God passes into him completely. In the fourth degree the mind goes out on account of God and descends beneath itself. In the first the mind enters into itself; in the second it transcends itself. In the first it proceeds into itself; in the third it proceeds into God. In the first the mind enters for its own sake; in the fourth it goes out for the sake of its neighbor. It enters into the first through meditation; it ascends into the second through contemplation; in the third it is introduced into jubilation; and in the fourth it goes forth out of compassion.

30. And so in the first degree the spirit that is sweeter than honey enters into the soul and intoxicates it with sweetness, so much so that it has "honey and milk beneath its tongue," and they become "the honeycomb dripping on its lips."[75] Men of this sort "will publish the memory of that abundant sweetness,"[76] for "the mouth speaks from an abundance of the heart."[77] This act is the first consolation for those renouncing the world: first it removes them, and often solidifies them in their good resolution. This spirit is "that heavenly food"[78] that often restored those going out from Egypt and fed them through the wilderness. It is that "hidden manna, which no one knows unless he receives it."[79] It is that spiritual and inward sweetness that always nourishes them and gives them milk "as if they were newborn infants,"[80] and little by little it leads them toward mature strength.

31. In this state the soul is led by the Lord "in the wilderness,"[81] and there it is given milk so that it may be intoxicated with inward sweetness. Hear what is said concerning this state when the Lord speaks through his prophet: "Therefore," he says, "behold, I will give milk to her and lead her out into the wilderness, and I will speak to her heart."[82] But first it is necessary to desert Egypt, first it is necessary to cross the Red Sea,[83] first it is necessary that the Egyptians perish in the waters, and first it is necessary that the foods of Egypt fail; only then may we perceive this spiritual nourishment and heavenly food. May he who desires the heavenly foods of the wilderness leave Egypt not only with his body but also with his heart, and may he completely lay aside his love (amorem) of the world. May he who desires to be sated with inward sweetness cross the Red Sea; may he strive to expel every grief and bitterness from his heart. First let the Egyptians be plunged under and perverse habits be destroyed, lest "the angelic citizens"[84] scornfully refuse so base a guest. First it is necessary that the foods of Egypt fail and carnal pleasures become an abomination: only then may one experience those pleasures that are the aforementioned internal and eternal delights. Without doubt, the more the love (amor) of God conquers completely any other feeling, the more often and the more fully it restores the mind with an inward joy. And so in this state the mind sucks "honey from the rock and oil from the hardest stone."[85] In this state, "the mountains will drip sweetness, and the hills will flow with milk and honey."[86] In this state the Lord often visits the starving and parched soul; he often satisfies it with internal sweetness and intoxicates it with the sweetness of his spirit. In this state the Lord often descends from the heavens; he often visits "the one sitting in darkness and the shadow

of death,"[87] and often "the glory of the Lord fills the tabernacle of the covenant."[88]

32. Thus far the Lord exhibits his presence, though he does not at all reveal his face. He pours in his sweetness, but he does not reveal his beauty.[89] He pours in his sweetness, but he does not reveal his appearance. And so, his charm may be perceived, but his true beauty cannot be discerned. Till now "clouds and mist encircled him."[90] Till now "his throne had been in a pillar of cloud."[91] Certainly what is perceived is both gentle and exceedingly alluring, but what is actually discerned is altogether cloudy, since it has not yet appeared in the light. And although he may appear in fire, this fire inflames more than it illumines. The Lord indeed kindles emotion, but he does not yet illumine the intellect. He inflames desire, but he does not yet illumine the intelligence. And so in this state, the soul is able to perceive its beloved, but, as has been said, it is not able to see him. And if the soul sees him at all, it sees him as if in the night, it sees him as though he were under a cloud, and it sees him, finally, "through a mirror in obscurity, but not yet face to face."[92] And therefore the soul says, "Illumine your face over your servant."[93]

33. In the first degree the mind is often visited, often restored, often intoxicated, and sometimes provoked to dare all the more. Therefore, before too long it begins to presume greater things and to demand loftier things, so much so that it may dare to say, "If I have found grace in your eyes, reveal your very self to me."[94] Nevertheless, the mind does not yet gain the end for which it is begging through its prayer, although it may demand it with its most intimate desire. Truly, if we wish to obtain our chosen end, it is necessary "to beg burningly, to seek diligently, to knock strongly,"[95] and to press on tenaciously through all of these acts. Does the Psalmist not seem to you to have labored daily at many tasks—such that, at this very moment, he is about to fail and to have lost hope—when he says, "How long, O Lord? Will you forget me to the end? How long will you turn your face from me?"[96] But knowing that "everyone who asks, receives; everyone who seeks, finds; and to the one who knocks will the door be open,"[97] again and again his confidence is bolstered, and he recovers his strength and says, "My face has sought you out: your face, O Lord, will I seek."[98]

34. Therefore, when the mind reaches the grace of divine contemplation with great striving and burning desire, it is then as if it reaches the second degree of love (*amoris*). The mind then deserves to look through revelation upon "that which the eye has not seen, nor the ear

heard, nor has it ascended into the heart of a man,"[99] so that it is more truly able to say, "God, however, has revealed to us through his Spirit."[100] Did he not appear to receive this grace, who merited to see "angels ascending and descending, and the Lord resting upon the ladder"?[101] Hence he also says, "I have seen the Lord face to face, and my soul has been saved."[102] He had received this grace and returned often as though accustomed to it, and said, "Send out your light and your truth, they themselves have led me and pulled me to your holy mountain and to your tabernacle."[103] They had received this grace and flew with the wing of contemplation, at whom the prophet, marveling, gazed and, gazing, marveled. "Who are these," he asked, "who fly like the clouds and like doves to their windows?"[104] And so in this degree some beg to be given wings like doves, others receive wings like eagles. "Who," he said, "will give to me wings as if of a dove, so that I might fly and be at peace?"[105] And elsewhere the prophet writes, "Those who trust in the Lord will renew their strength. They will obtain wings as if of an eagle: they will fly and they will not fail."[106]

35. In this degree of contemplation, the wings of the soul raise it high above the clouds. In this degree, souls fly up with these sorts of wings all the way to heaven—not only to the first, but even all the way to the second heaven—so that they are able to speak about that which remains: "Our way of life is in heaven."[107] Above this double heaven is still the "third heaven,"[108] which is called the heaven of heavens. Yet even those who have reached the second degree of love are altogether unable to ascend to this third heaven. What the earth is to the first heaven and what the first heaven is to the second, so the second heaven is to the heaven of heavens. And so you may consider the second heaven the earth or, if you wish, heaven, or indeed the heaven of heavens. But it is the heaven of heavens to the first heaven, while to the heaven of heavens it is earth.[109]

36. I believe that the prophet wished to refer to this earth when he said: "My portion is in the land of the living."[110] And so this earth has its heaven; it also has its sun. Nor do I believe this sun to be other than what the Lord promised through the prophet: "Your sun will never set again and your moon will not be diminished, since the Lord will be a perpetual light for you."[111] If, therefore, you are in this heaven or on this earth, you may see the sun, beneath which those angelic spirits boil and burn who have been called the Seraphim, that is, the "burning."[112] On account of this burning, they merit their name "for there is none among them who can hide from his heat."[113] And so you can see the sun

of justice if you are on this earth and you have reached the second degree of love. You are told, "No longer will the sun shine for you through the day nor the splendor of the moon illumine you, but the Lord will be your perpetual light, and your God will be your glory."[114] And so in this state one may experience the truth of this sentence: "How sweet is the light and how delightful for the eyes to see the sun."[115] In this state the soul, thoroughly taught by the instruction of experience, sings this verse of the Psalm: "For one day in your courts is better than a thousand."[116]

37. Who can worthily express the great joy of this vision? Certainly once this joy has been experienced, once it has been tasted, just as when present it cannot be disdained, so too when absent it cannot be forgotten. For when the mind descends from that light and falls back into itself, it brings with it certain vestiges of those thoughts. The mind refreshes itself with those thoughts, nay, it celebrates a feast day, to which the scripture refers, when it says, "And the vestiges of the thoughts will make a feast day for him."[117] Therefore, think of how great the solemnity must be in that abundance of vision, if a feast is celebrated from the vestiges of thought. What kind of joy will there be in the vision itself, if there is so much delight in its recollection? And so in this state the revelation of divine light and the wonder of revelation, together with the recollection and perpetual memory thereof, bind the mind indissolubly, so that it cannot forget the joy it has experienced. And just as the sweetness of the prior degree, once tasted, satiated the soul and transfixed its feelings, so too in this degree the brightness, once beheld, binds thought, so that the soul cannot forget that brightness or think of anything else. And so in the second degree, as has been said, the heaven of heavens and the inaccessible light may be seen, but they may not be approached. Otherwise, if it could be reached, it would not be inaccessible. "Blessed," says the Apostle, "and alone powerful is the king of kings and Lord of lords who alone has immortality and inhabits inaccessible light."[118] And so one cannot approach that which is inaccessible. But finally the Apostle boasts that he has been snatched away to that region of eternal light. "I know," he says, "a man in Christ, whether in the body or outside the body I do not know, God knows, snatched away in this manner all the way to the third heaven."[119]

38. And so the third degree of love exists when the mind of a man is snatched away into that abyss of divine light, so that in this state, the human mind, forgetful of all external things,[120] forgets even itself and passes entirely into its God. That which is written then takes place: "For

those who do not believe may also dwell with the Lord God."[121] And so in this state the mind is fully restrained, the uproar of its carnal desires is put into a deep sleep, and "silence is kept in heaven as it were for half an hour."[122] And whatever trouble is in the mind, it is swallowed up into glory. In this state when the mind is alienated from itself,[123] when it is snatched into that hiding place of divine mystery,[124] when it is completely surrounded by that fire of divine love, the mind is penetrated deeply, it is inflamed wholly, it casts itself off thoroughly, it dresses itself in a sort of god-like feeling, and, conformed entirely to the beauty it has beheld, it passes into a different glory.

39. Consider what difference may exist between iron and iron: between cold iron and glowing hot iron. This difference also exists between mind and mind: between the tepid mind and the mind inflamed with divine fire. For when iron is cast into fire, without a doubt it first appears as black as it is cold. But after it has spent some time amid the flames, little by little it becomes hot, and little by little it lays aside its blackness. Gradually glowing, little by little the iron draws into itself the likeness of the fire, until at last it liquefies entirely: it departs fully from itself and takes on a completely different nature. And so having in this manner been swallowed up on the pyre of divine flame and into the fire of inmost love (*amoris*), having been completely surrounded by the mass of eternal desires, the soul first grows hot, then it glows, and finally it liquefies entirely and passes away from its prior state completely.[125]

40. Do you wish to hear of those who are now growing hot in this sort of fire and are becoming enflamed with the burning of internal desires? "Was our heart not burning within us when he spoke to us along the way and opened the scriptures to us?"[126] And are these men not becoming red hot and conformed to the divine light by the flame of divinity surrounding them and by the glory they beheld, so it is as if they pass into a new glory? "Watching the glory of the Lord with an unveiled face, they are transformed into the same image from brightness into brightness, as if by the spirit of the Lord."[127] Do you still wish to hear of the soul being liquefied by the fire of the divine word? "My soul was liquefied when my beloved spoke."[128] Accordingly, when the soul is admitted into that internal hiding place of divine mystery, because of the magnitude of its wonder and the abundance of its joy in itself, the soul is entirely and immediately dissolved into the one who is speaking; the soul then begins to hear "those hidden words which a man may not speak,"[129] and it understands "the uncertain and hidden

things of divine wisdom made visible to it."[130] And so in this state "the spirit scrutinizes all things, even the depths of God."[131] In this state "he who clings to the Lord is one spirit with him."[132]

41. In this state, as has been said, the soul is liquefied entirely into the one whom it loves and "it becomes completely languid"[133] in its very self, whence it also says: "Prop me up upon flowers, encircle me with apples, for I grow languid with love (*amore*)."[134] Therefore, just as there does not appear to be any hardness or any firmness in liquids or in liquefied things, but they yield to every hard and rigid object without difficulty, and just as we see nothing of their own liveliness in languid people, no trace of innate strength, but their whole life depends entirely on another's will, likewise they who reach this third degree of love (*amoris*) no longer do anything on account of their own will, nor do they leave anything at all to their own decision. Rather, they commit all things to God's managing: all of their wants and all of their desires hang upon the divine good pleasure; they look to the divine will. And just as the first degree wounds feelings and the second binds thinking, thus the third entwines action so that one cannot be concerned with anything, unless the nod of the divine will draws or impels them to it.

42. Therefore, when the soul has in this manner been melted away in the divine fire, inwardly softened and thoroughly liquefied, what then will remain except that "the good will of God, pleasing and perfect,"[135] be displayed to the soul, as if that divine will were a certain mold of consummate virtue to which it might be shaped? For when metals have been liquefied and the molds have been set up, the metalworkers shape any image through a decision of their will and produce whatever vessels they wish in accordance with the proper shape and intended form. So, too, does the soul in this state easily adapt itself to every wish of the divine will, nay, rather it adapts itself with spontaneous desire to each of God's decisions and forms its every wish in accordance with the measure of divine benevolence. And just as a liquefied metal easily flows down into whatever passage is open to it, running toward the things that lie below, thus the soul in this state voluntarily humbles itself to every act of obedience and bends itself freely to every humiliation according to the divine arrangement.

43. And so in this state the form of the humility of Christ is displayed to such a soul, and these words are also said to it, "Have this mind in yourselves which also was in Christ Jesus, who, although he was in the form of God, did not judge equality with God a thing to be grasped, but emptied himself, taking the form of a slave, made in the

likeness of a man, and was found in the condition of a man; he humbled himself, becoming obedient to the point of death, even to a death on the cross."[136] Everyone who wishes to touch the highest degree of consummated love ought to conform himself to this pattern of the humility of Christ, "for greater love has no man than to lay down his life for his friends."[137]

44. And so those men who are able to lay down their life for their friends reach the highest height of love and now are placed in the fourth degree of love; now they fulfill the apostolic injunction: "Be imitators of God just like the dearest children, and walk in love (*dilectione*) just as Christ also loved you and surrendered himself for you, a sweetly-scented offering and sacrificial victim to God."[138] And so in the third degree the soul is glorified into God; in the fourth it is humbled for the sake of God. In the third degree the soul is conformed to the divine brightness; in the fourth it is conformed to Christian humility. And although in the third degree the soul was in some way "in the form of God," still, in the fourth degree it begins "to empty itself, taking on the form of a slave and again being found in the condition of a man."[139] And so in the third degree the soul is in some way put to death in God; in the fourth it is in a way reawakened into Christ. Therefore, he who is in the fourth degree can truly say, "It is now not I that live, but Christ lives in me."[140] And so he begins to walk in newness of life[141] since from now on "to live is Christ and to die is gain."[142] He is hemmed in on two sides: "he desires to be dissolved and to be with Christ, which is much better, but necessity leads him to remain in the flesh for our sake,"[143] "for the love of Christ compels him."[144]

45. And so this type of man becomes a new creature: "the old things have passed away and, behold, all things have been made new."[145] For in the third degree he has been killed; in the fourth, as it were, rising from the dead, "he dies no more; death no longer has dominion over him, for insofar as he lives, he lives for God."[146] Therefore, in this degree the soul is made in some way immortal and impassible. How could the soul be mortal, if it cannot die? How could it die, if it cannot be separated from him who is life? We know well enough whose words these are: "I am the way, the truth, and the life."[147] Therefore, how could one die who cannot be separated from him? "I am determined," he says, "that neither death, nor life, nor angels, nor archangels, nor principalities, nor powers, nor virtues, nor things present, nor things to come, nor strength, nor height, nor depth, nor any created thing will be able to separate us from the love of God, which is in Christ Jesus."[148] And is

it not the case that a man who does not feel the injuries borne against him can seem in some way impassible—a man who always rejoices in every injury and turns to his glory whatever punishment is inflicted upon him, just as in that sentence of the apostle: "Gladly will I boast of my infirmities, so that the power of Christ may dwell in me"?[149] For he who is content in his sufferings and reproaches for the sake of Christ remains, as it were, impassible. "On account of these things, I rejoice," he says, "in infirmities, in reproaches, in needs, in persecutions, in hardships for the sake of Christ."[150]

46. He who is in this degree can say confidently, "I am able to do all things in him who strengthens me,"[151] because he knows "how to be satisfied and to be hungry, and to be rich and to suffer want."[152] In this degree "love endures all things, believes all things, hopes for all things, and sustains all things."[153] In this degree "love is long-suffering, it is kind, it is not ambitious, it does not seek after what belongs to it,"[154] and it does not know how "to return evil for evil, nor curse for curse, but on the contrary it blesses."[155] He who ascends to this degree of love without a doubt exists in a state of love (*amoris*) wherein he is truly able to say, "I have become all things to all men, so that I might bring about salvation for all."[156] In the end this type of man desires "to be made anathema from Christ for the sake of his brothers."[157] What then will we say? Does it not seem that this degree of love (*amoris*) turns a man's mind to madness, as it were, when it will not allow him to hold a limit or measure to his jealous love (*emulatione*)? Does it not appear to be the height of madness to spurn true life, to reject the highest wisdom, and to resist omnipotence? Does he not reject life who desires to be separated from Christ for his brothers, just like the man who says, "Either forgive them this sin or blot me out from the book that you have written?"[158] Does he not appear to reject wisdom or rather wish to teach it, who says to the Lord, "May it be far removed from you to do this thing, and to slaughter the just with the impious, and make the just become like the impious. This is not your way. You who judge the whole earth, by no means will you make such a judgment."[159] Does a man not try to resist omnipotence, dare to soften the wrath of the omnipotent, and even prevail, when the ruling has already gone forth from the Lord, when the fires are already raging, and that man casts himself amid the raging fires "and stands amid the living and the dying,"[160] imposing a limit to necessity?

47. Behold into what great boldness of pious presumption the consummation of love often raises the mind of a man; behold how it makes

a man dare to be more than a man. Therefore, what he dares concerning the Lord, what he does on behalf of the Lord, that he lives in the Lord— all of these things appear to be almost entirely more than human. Altogether marvelous, altogether astounding: as much as he dares concerning God, that much further he casts himself down on behalf of God. As high as he ascends through his daring, that much further he descends through humility. Just as that to which he ascends through faith is above the human, similarly above the human is that to which he descends through patient endurance. And so in the first degree, as has been said, the mind returns to itself, in the second it ascends toward God, in the third it crosses into God, and in the fourth it descends beneath itself. In the first and second it is lifted up; in the third and fourth it is transfigured. In the first it ascends toward itself, in the second it transcends itself, in the third it is conformed to the brightness of God, and in the fourth it is conformed to the humility of Christ. Again, in the first it is led back, in the second it is carried over, in the third it is transfigured, and in the fourth it is reawakened.

NOTES

1   Song of Songs 2:5 (Old Latin).
2   Song of Songs 8:7 (Vulg).
3   Song of Songs 2:5 (Old Latin).
4   Eph. 3:19.
5   John 12:25; Luke 14:26.
6   Song of Songs 4:9.
7   Hos. 11:4.
8   Song of Songs 5:8.
9   Ps. 118:81 (Vulg).
10 Eccles. 4:12.
11 On this threefold gift, see Richard of St Victor, *Arca Moys*. 3.10, 11 (Aris, 67–68 [PL 196.120C–121A, 121C]; tr. Zinn, 237–38); *Adnot. Psalm. 118* (PL 196.350A); Achard of St Victor, *Sermo* 13.32 (Châtillon, 165; tr. Feiss, 248–49).
12 Eccles. 4:12.
13 Jer. 5:5.
14 Ezek. 20:34.
15 Eph 4:8.
16 1 Cor. 6:18.
17 Ps. 141:5 (Vulg).
18 Prov. 13:8.
19 Richard of St Victor, *Adnot. Psalm. 118* (PL 196.345AB).
20 Ps. 37:11 (Vulg.); 54:5 (Vulg).
21 Richard of St Victor, *XII patr.* 6 (Châtillon, 106 [PL 196.5D]; tr. Zinn, 58–59); *XII patr.* 85 (Châtillon, 330–32 [PL 196.61B]; tr. Zinn, 143–44).
22 Eccles. 1:8.
23 Richard of St Victor, *Arca Moys*. 5.18 (Aris, 147 [PL 196.191A]; tr. Zinn, 341–42).
24 Luke 7:15.
25 Matt. 3:9; Luke 3:8.
26 Tob. 13:2.
27 Richard of St Victor, *Statu* 1.9 (Ribaillier, 72 [PL 196.1122BC]).
28 Exod. 9:24.
29 Richard of St Victor, *Arca Moys*. 4.15 (Aris, 105 [PL 196.152D]; tr. Zinn, 284–85); *Trin.* 3.2 (Ribaillier, 136; tr. Zinn, 474–75, and tr. Evans, VTT 1:248–49;) Hugh of St Victor, *Eulogium* 2 (PL 176.97C; tr. Feiss, VTT 2:125).
30 Song of Songs 8:7.
31 Song of Songs 8:6.
32 Song of Songs 8:7.
33 Song of Songs 8:6.
34 Ps. 17:2 (Vulg).
35 Ps. 136:6 (Vulg).
36 Ps. 76:3–4 (Vulg).
37 Ps. 115:12 (Vulg).
38 Rom. 8:35.
39 1 Cor. 13:8.
40 Ps. 62:9 (Vulg).
41 Phil. 3:8.
42 Phil. 1:21.
43 Phil. 1:23.
44 Deut. 6:5; Matt. 22:37; Mark 12:30; Luke 10:27.
45 Hos. 7:11.

46   Deut. 32:28.
47   John 12:25.
48   Sir. 18:30.
49   Ps. 110:1 (Vulg).
50   Ps. 118:10 (Vulg).
51   Ps. 118:20 (Vulg).
52   Ps. 117:6 (Vulg).
53   Ps. 111:7–8 (Vulg).
54   Hos. 2:19–20 (Vulg).
55   Jer. 3:14, 19.
56   1 Cor. 6:17.
57   Isa. 26:18.
58   Song of Songs 2:17.
59   Song of Songs 4:8.
60   Song of Songs 8:3.
61   Gal. 4:19.
62   Song of Songs 4:5.
63   Richard distinguishes the four degrees of violent love here by speaking of thirst for God (accusative object), toward God (*ad* + accusative), in(to) God (*in* + accusative), and for the sake of or on account of God (*propter* + accusative). *In* + accusative means "into" and that is the connotation Richard gives in this passage. For a similar play on prepositions see Bernard, *Sermo De diversis*, 115 (SBO 6/2.392 [PL 183.741]).
64   Isa. 26:9.
65   Ps. 41:3 (Vulg).
66   Ps. 62:2 (Vulg).
67   Ps. 118:20 (Vulg).
68   Ps. 33:9 (Vulg).
69   Isa. 33:17.
70   Gen. 32:30.
71   2 Cor. 12:2.
72   Phil. 2:21.
73   John 6:38.
74   Richard reiterates the Augustinian theme that one rises to contemplation of God by first entering into oneself; see Richard of St Victor, *XII patr.* 83 (Châtillon, 330–32 [PL 196.59D]; tr. Zinn, 141–42); *Arca Moys.* 4.15 (Aris, 105–7 [PL 196.152D–154A]; tr. Zinn, 284–86).
75   Sir. 24:27 (Vulg.); Song of Songs 4:11.
76   Ps. 144:7 (Vulg). The Douay-Rheims translation reads, "'They shall publish the memory of thy sweetness." The literal meaning of the verb, "eructabunt," is "regurgitate."
77   Matt. 12:34; Luke 6:45.
78   Wisd. 16:20.
79   Apoc. 2:17.
80   1 Pet. 2:2.
81   Hos. 2:14.
82   Hos. 2:14.
83   Richard of St Victor, *Exterm.* 1.6 (PL 196.1077B); *Super exiit* 1 (Châtillon, 10) and 2 (Châtillon, 46).
84   Ps. 77:25 (Vulg).
85   Deut. 32:13.
86   Joel 3:18 (Vulg).
87   Ps. 106:10 (Vulg.); Luke 1:79.
88   Exod. 40:32 (Vulg).
89   Richard of St Victor, *XII patr.* 1 (Châtillon, 92 [PL 196.1C]; tr. Zinn, 53–54).
90   Ps. 96:2 (Vulg).

91 Sir. 24:7 (Vulg).
92 1 Cor. 13:12.
93 Ps. 118:135 (Vulg).
94 Exod. 33:13.
95 Matt. 7:7; Luke 11:9.
96 Ps. 12:1 (Vulg).
97 Matt. 7:8; Luke 11:10.
98 Ps. 26:8 (Vulg).
99 1 Cor. 2:9.
100 1 Cor. 2:10.
101 Gen. 28:12; John 1:51.
102 Gen. 32:30 (Vulg).
103 Ps. 42:3 (Vulg).
104 Isa. 60:8.
105 Ps. 54:7 (Vulg).
106 Isa. 40:31. Richard of St Victor, *XII patr.* 83 (Châtillon, 332 [PL 196.59C]; tr. Zinn, 141–42); *Arca Moys.* 1.3 (Aris, 8 [PL 196.66D]; tr. Zinn, 155); 4.10 (Aris, 97 [PL 196.145AC]; tr. Zinn, 273); 4.21 (Aris, 118 [PL 196.164B]; tr. Zinn, 301); 5.4 (Aris, 128 [PL 196.173BC]; tr. Zinn, 315); Godfrey of St Victor, *Microcosmus* (Delhaye, 207–24, 227–45; tr. Feiss, VTT 2).
107 Phil. 3:20.
108 2 Cor. 12:2. Richard of St Victor, *XII patr.* 74 (Châtillon, 302–4 [PL 196.53BC]; tr. Zinn, 131–32); *Arca Moys,* 3.8 (Aris, 65–66 [PL 196.118BC]; tr. Zinn, 233–34); *Adnot. Psalm. 121* (PL 196.365B), *Adnot. Psalm. 2* (PL 196.271A); *Trin.,* prol. (Ribaillier, 83, with further references [PL 196.890AC]; tr. Evans, VTT 1:210–11).
109 Richard of St Victor, *Arca Moys.* 3.8 (Aris, 65–66; tr. Zinn, 233–34); 3.10 (Aris, 68 [PL 196.119D–121A]; tr. Zinn, 236–37).
110 Ps. 141:6 (Vulg).
111 Isa. 60:20.
112 Isidore of Seville, *Etym.* 7.5.24–25 (ed. Lindsay).
113 Ps. 18:7 (Vulg).
114 Isa. 60:19.
115 Eccles. 11:7.
116 Ps. 83:11 (Vulg).
117 Ps. 75:11 (Vulg).
118 1 Tim. 6:15–16.
119 2 Cor. 12:2.
120 Richard of St Victor, *Arca Moys.* 4.15 (Aris, 106 [PL 196.153C]; tr. Zinn, 284–86); 4.22 (Aris, 119 [PL 196.165BC]; tr. Zinn, 302–4); other references in Dumeige, ed. *Ives, Epître,* 166 note (a).
121 Ps. 67:19 (Vulg).
122 Apoc. 8:1.
123 On "alienatio mentis" see Dumeige, ed., *Ives, Epître,* 190–91.
124 Richard of St Victor, *Arca Moys.* 4.23 (Aris, 121 [PL 196.168A]; tr. Zinn, 305); 5.14 (Aris, 143 [PL 196.187B]; tr. Zinn, 336).
125 Richard of St Victor, *Arca Moys.* 4.15 (PL 196.153C); *Trin.* 6.14 (Ribaillier, 245–46 [PL 196.978D]; tr. Evans, VTT 1:334); *Apoc.* 7.3 (PL 196.864D). On the analogy of iron plunged into fire and transformed into fire, see, for example, Basil, *Contra Eunomium,* 3.2 (PG 29.659B); Cyril of Jerusalem, *Catechesis* 17.14 (PG 33.985CD); Bernard, *De diligendo Deo,* 10.28 (SBO 3.143 [PL 182.991BC]); Hugh of St Victor, *In Eccl.* 1 (PL 175.117BD).
126 Luke 24:32.
127 2 Cor. 3:18.
128 Song of Songs 5:6 (Vulg).

129   2 Cor. 12:4.
130   Ps. 50:8 (Vulg).
131   1 Cor. 2:10.
132   1 Cor. 6:17.
133   Song of Songs 5:6 (Vulg).
134   Song of Songs 2:5.
135   Rom. 12:2.
136   Phil. 2:5–8.
137   John 15:13.
138   Eph. 5:1–2.
139   Phil. 2:6–7.
140   Gal. 2:20.
141   Rom. 6:4.
142   Phil. 1:21.
143   Phil. 1:23–24.
144   2 Cor. 5:14.
145   2 Cor. 5:17.
146   Rom. 6:10.
147   John 14:6.
148   Rom. 8:38–39.
149   2 Cor. 12:9.
150   2 Cor. 12:10.
151   Phil. 4:13.
152   Phil. 4:12.
153   1 Cor. 13.7.
154   1 Cor. 13:4–5.
155   1 Pet. 3:9.
156   1 Cor. 9:22.
157   Rom. 9:3.
158   Exod. 32:31–32.
159   Gen. 18:25.
160   Num. 16:48 (Vulg).

GODFREY OF ST VICTOR

MICROCOSM

(CHAPTERS 203–227)

INTRODUCTION AND TRANSLATION
BY HUGH FEISS OSB

INTRODUCTION

This introduction has two parts: (1) a sketch of what is known about Godfrey of St Victor and his writings; (2) a summary Godfrey's *Microcosm,* especially the chapters that are not translated here (1–202, 228–41).

THE MAN AND HIS WORKS

As is the case with the other twelfth-century Victorine writers, we do not know very much about the biography of Godfrey of St Victor (ca. 1125/1130–d. p. 1195). On the basis of autobiographical references in the *Fountain of Philosophy* one may deduce the following account.[1] Godfrey studied the arts in Paris from 1144–55 at the school on the Petit Pont founded by Adam of Balsham. Then Godfrey studied and taught theology. His theological training inclined him toward reading the Bible and the Fathers, rather than to using the techniques of dialectic being developed in the schools, although he was well acquainted with

---

[1] Godfrey's career and writings have been greatly clarified by the studies of Françoise Gasparri; see especially, "Textes autographes d'auteurs victorins du xiie siècle," *Scriptorium* 35 (1981) 277–84; "Observations paléographiques sur deux manuscrits partiellement autographes de Godefroid de Saint-Victor," *Scriptorium* 36 (1982): 43–50; "Godefroid de Saint-Victor: Une personalité peu connue du monde intellectuel et artistique parisien au xiie siècle," *Scriptorium* 39/1 (1985): 57–69, and "Philosophie et cosmologie: Godefroid de Saint-Victor," in *Notre-Dame de Paris: Un manifeste chrétien (1160–1230),* ed. Michel Lemoine, Rencontres médiévales européennes 4 (Turnhout: Brepols, 2004), 119–44, which cite her earlier studies. See also, Gilbert Ouy, "Manuscrits entièrement ou partiellement autographes de Godefroid de Saint-Victor," *Scriptorium* 36 (1982): 29–42. An earlier investigation is Philippe Delhaye, *Le Microcosmus de Godefroy de Saint-Victor: Étude théologique,* Mémoires et travaux par les professeurs des Facultés catholiques de Lille, fasc. 56 (Lille: Facultés catholiques, 1951), 13–49. To distinguish this study from Delhaye's edition of the *Microcosmus,* (Lille: Facultés catholiques, 1951), Delhaye's study will be referred to as *Étude.* The editions of Godfrey's two poetic works are Godefroy de Saint-Victor, *Fons Philosophiae,* ed. Pierre Michaud-Quantin, Analecta mediaevalia Namurcensia 8 (Louvain: Nauwelaerts/Namur: Godenne, 1956), tr. Edward Synan, *The Fountain of Philosophy* (Toronto: Pontifical Institute of Mediaeval Studies, 1972); "The *Preconium Augustini* of Godfrey of St Victor," ed. Philip Damon, *Mediaeval Studies* 22 (1960): 92–107. On Godfrey's sermons see Philippe Delhaye, "Les sermons de Godefroy de Saint-Victor," *Recherches de théologie ancienne et médiévale* 21 (1954): 194–210.

them.[2] Like his friend Stephen of Tournai, to whom he dedicated the *Fountain of Philosophy* (*Fons philosphiae*), he may have studied law at Bologna. He entered St Victor about 1155–60, at a time of turmoil under the incompetent Abbot Ernisius. Godfrey's humanistic outlook may have displeased Walter of St Victor who succeeded Richard as prior in 1173.[3] In any case, Godfrey was assigned to a priory. He returned to the Abbey in 1185–86,[4] and served there as *armarius*, in which capacity he was responsible for the production and preservation of the abbey's manuscripts, particularly those used in the liturgy. He functioned as archivist as well. He was a poet and a musician, a preacher and a theologian, more artist than speculative thinker. Two of his works, *Fountain of Philosophy* and *Microcosm* (*Microcosmus*) display the same encyclopedic interests manifest in Hugh of St Victor's *Didascalicon* and Richard of St Victor's *Book of Notes* (*Liber exceptionum*). Thirty-two of his sermons survive, most of them unpublished.[5]

The *Microcosm* is an encyclopedic work that makes generous use of allegory. In Delhaye's edition it is divided into 241 chapters distributed in three books. In the prologue to the *Microcosm*, Godfrey writes that he is old. In earlier times, his words, writings, and examples had been respected by others. Then he came on troubled times and spent some time in a solitary place, where he wrote the *Microcosm*. In it he makes use of the talents the Lord has given him, not with momentary sounds but with writing that speaks in perpetuity (1).[6] About one-third of the chapters discuss love, and so Godfrey's work deserves a place in this collection of Victorine writings about love. At the outset, Godfrey addresses to the reader a word about love: "The reader should not judge what he has read once until he has understood what he has read, because perhaps he will not yet understand in one reading the things which once understood he will love the more."[7] Godfrey concludes his

2   See, for example, the paired objections and response at chaps. 216 and 218, and especially 189 in the summary below and the note attached to it.

3   Delhaye, *Étude*, 27–32; 243–51. In his *Contra quatuor labyrinthos Franciae*, 4:2 (Glorieux, 270), Walter was particularly hostile to Seneca, whom he thought worse than the other pagan authors ("Sed et ipse Seneca peior ceteris convincitur"). Godfrey wrote approvingly of Seneca in the *Fountain of Philosophy*, 409–12 (Michard-Quantin, 49; tr. Synan, 54).

4   Delhaye, *Étude*, 187–98; Gasparri, "Godefroid," 63–67.

5   Delhaye, "Les sermons," 191–210; Delhaye, *Étude*, 231–43.

6   References to chapters in the *Microcosmus* usually will be placed in the text. Because the chapters are short, except for direct quotations it does not seem necessary to give the page and line numbers in Delhaye's edition.

7   Chap. 2 (Delhaye, 32.7–9): "Non iudicet lector semel lecta donec fuerint intellecta quia forsitan semel lecta nondum intelliget que semel intellecta magis diliget."

book with a resounding affirmation of human dignity and an exhortation to his readers to complete in themselves what has been realized in
the humanity of Christ until there will be one body under one Head
united by the love that is the Holy Spirit (239–40).[8]

The allegorical application of the Hexaemeron or biblical account
of the six days of creation[9] to human psychology had precedents in
Christian tradition, though earlier authors did not develop this theme
in such detail as Godfrey does. His concern is primarily theological
rather than philosophical. Speaking of the human being as a microcosm, he focuses on the human soul rather than the body, though he
has great esteem for the human body.[10] In the *Microcosm*, Godfrey is
not at all interested in the Platonic forms and divine ideas.[11] His concern is the human being living in time and space, whose nature equips
him for life in this world while grace draws him toward the world to
come. Although Godfrey's understanding of human being is Augustinian, he avoids notions of the body as a prison, a mere instrument of the
soul, or a sin-prone enemy; body and soul are partners in life, death,
and eternity.

SUMMARY OF THE *MICROCOSM*, CHAPTERS 1–202

Godfrey begins Book I with an explanation of the word "microcosm" (2) and says that from the word one can learn the great dignity
of human beings (3). He responds to those who would object that human beings are worm-like (4–5) by distinguishing three divine works
regarding the human body: nature, justice, and grace, the works respectively of divine goodness, justice, and mercy. The first work is past
and vital, the second is present and mortal, the third is future and immortal (7–8).[12] For the just, the body's mortality and experience of

---

8   Delhaye, *Étude*, 53–60, contrasts Godfrey's optimistic humanism with the pessimistic strain
     in Augustinian theology.
9   Gen. 1:1–31.
10   Delhaye, *Étude*, 137–77. Among those whom Delhaye lists as Godfrey's predecessors are
     Origen, *Hom. in Gen.* 1; Augustine, *Conf.* 13; and Eriugena, *De divisione naturae*, 3–4.
11   Delhaye, *Étude*, 149. In *The Fountain of Philosophy*, 217–28 (Michaud-Quantin, 42–43;
     tr. Synan, 47), Godfrey devotes some lines to the megacosm/microcosm and to the archetypal
     world of the divine ideas.
12   In his distinction between the natural endowments of human beings and the gifts of grace,
     Godfrey draws on the distinction Hugh of St Victor's makes between the work of creation

suffering are penitential garments (10). God came to the humble human body to raise it to God (16). However, it is primarily with reference
to his spirit that a human being is called a "world." When they refer to
the human being as a "microcosm," philosophers look at the natural
endowments, while theologians turn their attention to gifts of grace
(18). For example, philosophers see the parallel between the four elements and the four elements of the human spirit: sensation, imagination, reason, and intelligence (19). Godfrey will discuss such parallels
by a close commentary on the six days of creation (20), seeing in the
first three the natural gifts that are the concerns of the philosopher, and
in the last three the gifts of grace.

The creation of light on the first day symbolizes the creation of the
senses (21). The division of the firmament from the waters parallels the
way discretion divides the movements of the imagination (31). The
waters divided into four parts according to the four directions of the
compass, paralleling the four founts of imagination: inventiveness (*in-
genium*), memory, concupiscence, and anger, which in turn are gov-
erned by the four cardinal virtues (36–37). The book Godfrey is writing
is an example of an ascent from the east through the use of prudence
(39). Ascent from the west, from memory, occurs when, with the aid
of temperance, "the invisible things of God are seen and understood
from the creation of the world through the things that have been
made."[13] Such ascents move from external dispersion to internal recollection (43).[14]

The work of the third day corresponds to the turning of the spirit
inward to reason and understanding. When the land brings forth green
plants and fruit-bearing trees, the first signifies good works, the second

---

(*opus conditionis*) and the work of restoration (*opus restaurationis*); e.g., in *Sacr.* 1.1.3 (PL
176.188–89).

[13]   Chap. 40, citing Rom. 1:20. Godfrey goes on to say that "When they diligently consider the
human spirit, they find that it naturally has the capacity for, and knowledge and willing of
something good, and that the summit of all beatitude consists in the highest possession of
these three, indeed, that nothing can be more blessed than their creator, and through these
they find he who is supremely powerful, knowing and willing or good, which is the blessed
Trinity, the one God" ("Diligenter itaque considerato spiritu humano, invenerunt eum naturaliter aliquid boni posse, scire, velle, et in horum trium summa adeptione tocius beatitudi-
nis summam consistere, porro creatore suo nichil beatius esse ac, per hec, ipsum summe
potentem, scientem, volentem sive bonum esse, que est beata trinitas unus deus," Delhaye,
61.21–27). This passage recalls Hugh of St Victor's *On the Three Days* (translated in VTT 1).

[14]   Ascents from four compass points have a prominent place in Hugh of St Victor's *Libellus* 4–6
(Sicard, 140–51).

meritorious works done through divine grace in charity (53). Two rivers that irrigate the land are the mechanical and practical arts (55–58).[15] Then Godfrey discusses at some length philosophy and the liberal arts (66–73).

Book II discusses the fourth, fifth, and sixth days of creation, which parallel the gifts of grace that are the subject matter of the theologian. By grace a human being is similar to God and the dwelling place of God, greater than every other creature and so greater than this world (77). God created the world for human beings (77), who though less than angels by nature, are greater than they by grace (79). Grace anoints the microcosms that are the church universal and each of the elect. Grace is threefold: illumination for truth, affection for virtue, and capacity (*facultas*) for action. In humankind's natural endowment, power (*posse*) comes first, knowing second, and willing third. In the gifts of grace, the order is: knowing (*sapienta*), the fourth day; willing, the fifth day; and power, the sixth day (82–83). Christ is the sun; the moon is the church; each Christian is a star. Christ bestows faith; in the mysteries of his resurrection, birth, death, ascension, and the Eucharist, he is a sacramental sign for believers (88–103).

The fifth day concerns human affections.[16] These can bring merit or demerit or they can be neutral. The latter are natural movements of the heart (e.g., sorrow, joy, fear, hope, love, hate, shame, and confidence) connected with desiring or not desiring something; they arise from images of exterior things now perceived or retained in the memory (105). Affections that bring demerit are movements of the heart, unsavory or deformed because of lack of grace, desiring or not desiring something inordinately or immoderately (106). Meritorious affections begin with the grace of healthy sorrow for sin (107–10). Next, the Holy Spirit creates healthy fear and hope (111–114). Then Godfrey discusses wholesome hatred of evil. One should try to extinguish in oneself, or others for whom one has responsibility, inclinations (*vicia*) that can lead to evil, but if that is not possible, one should control them (116–128).[17] This is followed by a discussion of relevant passages in the Apocalypse (120–136), and other biblical books (137–138).

---

[15]   The comparison of the arts to a river occurs in *The Fountain of Philosophy*, 25–64 (Michaud-Quantin, 27–28; tr. Synan, 40–41).

[16]   Delhaye, *Étude*, 127–28, draws parallels between Godfrey's division of human feelings and desires (*affectiones*) and Richard of St Victor's treatment of the affects in *On the Twelve Patriarchs*. On these "affectiones," see also St Thomas Aquinas, *Sum. theo.* 1–2.22–48.

[17]   Unlike most theologians of his century, Godfrey did not think that such spontaneous im-

From hatred of evil, Godfrey turns to the impulse or feeling (*affectio*) of love for the good (*amor boni*) that is the companion of hatred of evil (139). The Holy Spirit can dispose this emotion of love (and joy and hope also) to accomplish great effects, even enabling it to fly upward to imageless contemplation and a foretaste of eternal beatitude (140). Love of the good, proceeding from reason, is natural to every man. The Holy Spirit can form and firm it to be stronger than death, that is, to be charity (141). Charity is never idle; it either acts to help a neighbor or to honor God. It is fourfold: of what is above ourselves, of ourselves, of what is alongside us, and for what is beneath us (142). It is to charity that Godfrey will devote Book III to which he now turns.

At this point, Charity comes to greet the author and invites him to a meal (143–44).[18] After the meal she leads her guests to a place set aside for conversation.[19] Thus, through the ministry of charity, rumination and conversation follow sacred reading.[20] Charity explains that she

pulses, desires, and feelings were sinful until they were consented to. In this he sided with Gilbert Porreta against Peter Lombard. For this see Delhaye, *Étude*, 67 note 5. St Thomas Aquinas' position in *Sum. theo.* 1-2, q. 24, is the same as Godfrey's.

[18] Such visions, often associated with a dream, are common in medieval literature. See Delhaye, *Étude*, 70, and the translation below, note 4; also A. C. Spearing, *Medieval Dream-Poetry* (Cambridge: Cambridge University Press, 1976).

[19] Although the most probable source for this idea is Prov. 9:1–6, which describes a feast prepared by Wisdom, one is reminded also of Plato's *Symposium*, which describes a party at which the participants philosophize about love.
The way Godfrey has Charity's guests move from a meal to a place set aside for "collatio" might reflect the evening schedule at St Victor, where a "collatio" followed the evening meal: see *Liber ordinis* 36 (Jocqué, 174–75). Hugh of St Victor, *Archa Noe* 1.1 (Sicard, 618 [PL 176.617–18]) describes one such "collatio": "Cum sederem aliquando in conventu fratrum, et illis interrogantibus, meque respondente, multa in medium prolata fuissent . . . in qua collatione" ("One time when I was sitting in the community of the brothers, and they were asking questions and I was answering, many things were brought up. . . . In that *collatio* . . ."). "Collatio" had a fairly wide range of meanings in the Middle Ages: conversation, gathering, address, grant, or the evening meal in a monastic community, during or after which the *Collationes* [*Conferences*] of Cassian might be read. Sicard, *Diagrammes*, 9–20, 261–62, concludes that the "collatio" from which *On the Ark of Noe* derived was the "hora locutionis" ("speaking hour") between None and Vespers (see *Liber ordinis* 34 [Jocqué and Milis, 163–66]).

[20] Lists of activities beginning with reading and moving to meditation, prayer, action, contemplation, preaching (*lectio, meditation, oratio, operatio, contemplatio, predicatio*) occur fairly often in Victorine writings. Here are some examples: Hugh of St Victor, *Didasc.* 3.10 (Buttimer, 59.15–21), 5.9 (Buttimer, 109–10); *Meditatione* 2.1 (Baron, 46.16–19); Ps.-Hugh, *Exp. in reg.* 1 (PL 176.885A): "lectio," "oratio," "contemplatio"; 9 (PL 176.911D–912A): "oratio," "lectio," "operatio"); Richard of St Victor, *Apprehendet* (Haureau 5: 116–17); "Legendo et meditando metimus, orando et contemplando vindemiamus, operando et praedicando seminamus" ("By reading and meditating we reap; by prayer and contemplation, we gather; by action and preaching we sow"); LE 2.7.13 (Châtillon, 325.68–69); LE 2.13.2 (Châtillon, 481.18–22); *Arca Moys.* 4.14 (Aris, 104 [PL 196.151AC]); *Nonn. Alleg.* (PL 196.193A); *Causam* (Châtillon, 203.21–

rules the world as the mother of all riches and delights, some of which are common to all, others proper to some (146–47). It is Charity that reveals to the author what he teaches to others regarding the microcosm and helps him teach it (149). She warns against two opposed errors: presumption and fearful hesitation (*pusillanimitas*) (151). Charity invites him to kiss her. Then he touches her entire body and so learns about the various kinds of ordered love (153).

First, there is love of what is beneath us, that is, love of our bodies (154).[21] Soul and body are one person, one human being, and will be so forever, so they should love the same things (155). Since the body is heavy, it sometimes pulls the lower parts of the spirit, that is, sensation and imagination, downward. In ordered love, the spirit with the help of grace does not let the body pull it toward sin (*vicium*), but rather lifts the body upward beyond the limits of nature toward the Lord. Ordered love of the flesh, although tending upwards, sometimes descends down (*condescendit*) to the imagination or the flesh, nurturing it with good thoughts or feelings (156).[22] The author then uses five metaphors to describe the ordered love that the Spirit owes the flesh to which it is personally united (156)[23]: (1) their relationship is like that of man and wife, who render each other what they owe; (2) like someone living in a house, who builds it up, repairs it, decorates it; (3) like someone carried by a beast of burden to which he owes the rod to teach obedience, a burden to carry for exercise, and fodder for bodily and spiritual nourishment; (4) like traveling companions, restored to peace after sin had created discord between them; (5) coheirs of the kingdom

---

22); *Serm. cent.* 56 (PL 177.1066BC, 1067D); Walter of St Victor, *Sermones ineditos* 18.13 (Châtillon, 159.329–160.333). See also, St Anselm, *Orationes*, prol. (Schmitt, 3:4.2–12); *Ep.* 28 (Schmitt, 3:136.14–18); Guigo I, *Meditationes*, ed. A Wilmart (Paris: J. Vrin, 1936) 146; Guigo II, *Scala claustralum*, 1–12, ed. Edmund Colledge and James Walsh, SC 163 (Paris: Cerf, 1970): 82–108 (PL 184.476B, 482C–483C). Two additions Godfrey makes to this sequence are worthy of note. Here he has reading (*lectio*), meditation (*ruminatio*), and conversation (*collocatio*). His addition of conversation is perhaps a significant clue to his personality and his spirituality. Elsewhere in *Microcosm*, Godfrey gives a seemingly scrambled list: praying, meditating, psalmody, reading, and writing (224). The connection with liturgy (psalmody) is not so unusual, but none of the Victorine texts just listed include writing as one of the activities to which reading and meditation lead. Perhaps more than his predecessors, Godrey thought of himself as a writer.

21   It is odd that Godfrey does not speak of love of the natural word and the things within it. By entitling his work *Microcosmus*, he suggested an affinity between humankind and the natural world, and specifically between the human body and the rest of the material world.

22   See Hugh of St Victor, *Unione* (Piazzoni, 861–88 [PL 177.285A–289A]).

23   Later in chap. 214, the list of reasons for ordered love of the flesh will be expanded to six by the inclusion of the personal union of the spirit to the flesh.

of God, whose heavenly beatitude requires the presence of the other (236). Some might (or did) object to the notion of loving one's body or oneself by citing authorities[24] that seem to forbid such love or by reasoning that what comes so naturally need not be commanded. Godfrey responds to this objection by saying charity requires that all love be ordered, and the prohibitions of loving one's body or oneself refer to disordered or blind love (162–66). Moreover, Jesus did tell us to love our neighbor as ourselves.[25]

Ordered love of oneself is "the bond of love which out of charity we owe to ourselves" (168). It is a bond or chain because our desires can easily lead us astray into vanities and vain curiosity; they need limits. They are like water that will run downhill unless the warmth of the sun evaporates it so that it rises (167). Ordered love, the working of nature and grace, does not eliminate natural impulses, but orders them (169–70). It is actually much more difficult for a man to correct himself than another, so ordered love of self is more meritorious than love of neighbor (171).[26]

Love of neighbor can be natural, unnatural, or the work of charity. We are naturally social animals[27] and so we are naturally inclined to love our neighbors, our relatives, and our families. Such bonds of love are fostered by joint activity and they bring security and pleasure. Cicero and many others have written about them (172–74). Unnatural

---

[24]   One of the authorities is Gregory the Great, *Hom. Ev.* 17 (PL 76.1139): "No one is properly said to have charity toward himself, but love tends toward another so that it can be charity" ("Nemo proprie ad semetipsm caritatem habere dicitur sed dilectio se in alterum tendit ut esse caritas posit"). Richard of St Victor cited this at a crucial juncture in his *De Trinitate* 3.2 (Ribaillier, 136; tr. Evans, 248). Richard's argument was that perfect love requires an other; Godfrey's view is that perfect love, which certainly must include love of another, does not preclude love of oneself.

[25]   Matt. 19:19.

[26]   Augustine formulated the distinction between love of the body, which is beneath us, and love of the soul, which we are, in *Doc. Chr.* 1.23 (Martin, 18 [PL 34.27]). In distinguishing four objects of love—God above us, ourselves, those who are next to us, and what is beneath us—Augustine believed that love of self and one's body is a matter of instinct rather than of virtue, so only the other two kinds of love needed to be commanded. Godfrey let his narrator develop this fourfold division of love, but in that development he emphasized the need to have a proper love of one's body. Later, when Queen Charity offers an improved sixfold distinction, Godfrey is tacitly disagreeing with Augustine. Cf. Delhaye, *Étude*, 73 note 3. As Delhaye rightly observes (*Étude*, 94–101), the way of thinking that equates the self with the soul and sees the body as other was not congenial to Godfrey, although he used it since no other model (e.g., that of Aristotle's *De anima*) was available to him.

[27]   "sociale animal": Seneca, *De beneficiis*, 7.1.7 (ed. and tr. John W. Basore, Seneca, *Moral Essays*, 3 vols. (Cambridge, MA: Harvard University Press, 1964) 3:458). The same phrase occurs in chap. 26 (Delhaye, 236.4).

love of neighbor is a bond that enables people to work together to satisfy debased desires in sex, in partying, in crime, and in treachery (175). Ordered love of neighbor is an inclusive bond embracing both friends and enemies, but in a wise and discriminating way, giving to each what one ought, not just what the other deserves.[28] Nothing should be arranged in the whole body of the church without the concurrence of ordered love (176–77). Such love expands (*dilatatur*) to friends and enemies, the good and the evil, in prosperity and in adversity (178).

After the guests had discussed the lower and middle and right and left parts of the body of Queen Charity, and confident in her help, the author stretches his hand toward her head. She tells him to wait, while she brings order to his confidence (*confidencia*), which needs to be restrained with modesty (*verecundia*) (180). Like other human feelings (*hominum affectiones*) confidence and modesty can be virtues, but they can also be deformed if directed at the wrong things, or unformed if not suffused with charity (181).[29] Confidence and modesty need each other; otherwise they are not virtues (182).[30]

This brings Godfrey to the sixth day of creation (184), on which the earth was harmoniously populated, and on which grace of meritorious operation was added to the graces of knowing and willing (185). As a

---

[28] Delhaye, 197.21–22: "distribuens unicuique non ut meretur sed ut oportet" ("distributing to each not as he deserves but as one ought").

[29] In a play on words, Charity declares, "Confidence or any other virtue informed by me is beautiful, reflecting to all my image in itself, while the rest remain in their naturally unformed state or, what is worse, degenerate toward natural deformity" ("Formosa enim est illa que a me informatur fiducia vel etiam quelibet virtus alia, meam omnibus in se representans ymaginem, reliquis aut in naturali informitate remanentibus aut, quod deterius est, ad innaturalem deformitatem degenerrantbius" (Delhaye, 202.2–7). The formation of the virtues by charity was taught by Peter Lombard, *Sent.* 3.23.4 (Quaracchi, 656), Simon of Tournai, and other late twelfth-century theologians (see Delhaye, *Étude*, 132–33).

Toward the end of chap. 181, Godfrey uses the verb "contem(p)no," "to disdain" or "hold in contempt," "disparage," "regard as of little value." Specifically, "the church or the perfect soul, deprived of the bodily presence of her spouse, Christ, but faithfully waiting for him, disdains all love of this world, to the point that she is ashamed of every shameful attraction, and abhors with the most chaste modesty all the vices of the flesh" ("ecclesia vel perfecta anima corporali presentia sponsi sui Christi privata, fiducialiter eum expectans, omnem huius mundi amorem contempnit, usque adeo ut verecundetur ad omnem etiam illecebrosum atractum, castissima verecundia abhorrens universa carnis vitia" (Delhaye, 202.28—203.1). Godfrey does not use the terms "contemno" and "contempus" very often. The widely used phrases, "contemptus sui" ("contempt of self") and "contemptus mundi" ("contempt of the world") are ordinarily not part of his theological vocabulary. Cf. above, 201–204.

[30] Delhaye, *Étude*, 133 note 1, here referring to Peter Lombard, *Sent.* 3.36.1 (Quaracchi, 711): the virtues are interconnected by being informed by charity.

good will arises from good affections, so good deeds arise from sensory life.[31] Godfrey summarizes the progression by which the Spirit of God is given: first disordered or undisciplined love of the flesh is replaced by ordered love of flesh, a love that guards and cultivates it and draws it upward. This involves restraint of all the senses. "Natural gifts are not eliminated when grace supervenes, rather, they are helped."[32] Good works, though done bodily, are spiritual because they are animated by the Spirit of God and promote spiritual life (191). Three of the animals brought forth on the sixth day deserve special mention, for they stand for charity, humility, and fortitude (192). The "goad of the flesh," of which Paul spoke,[33] kept him humble (193). Job's troubles taught him fortitude (194). While the virtues of humility and fortitude need to be expressed in action only intermittently as the occasion arises, if possible charity should always be present both in habit and in act (195). While some enter religious life, others express active charity in lives of simple goodness and concern for the needy, without undertaking anything arduous or unusual on their way to God. By their innocent lives they gain salvation for themselves, and "they provide the whole church of God with many fitting things and much adornment" (196).[34] After discussing the story of Job and recommending Gregory the Great's exposition of its spiritual meanings (allegory and tropology) (198–201), Godfrey turns to the creation of humankind, made on the earth and from the earth in God's image and likeness, in whom God deigned to dwell eternally, not only spiritually but also bodily. Thus far we have seen how God gives his gifts to each of his elect. "Now we will teach how the whole living man, fully and perfectly formed in the image and likeness of God, goes forth following the lead of grace to which this whole work belongs" (202).[35]

---

[31]   In chap. 189, Godfrey raises a question: a good will is meritorious and the implementation of a good will in action is also meritorious. The same distinction holds for a bad will and its execution in act. Are these two different (de)merits or one? He leaves the question unanswered: "However that may be, we leave this question, as less pertinent to us, to scholastic disputations, while we turn our attention toward other things" ("Quomodocumque autem sit, nos hanc questionem tamquam minus ad nos pertinentem, scolasticis disputationibus relinquimus, ad alia nostram convertentes intentionem" (Delhaye, 210.16–19).

[32]   "Naturalia enim a superveniente gratia non eliminantur sed adiuvantur" (Delhaye, 212.10–11).

[33]   2 Cor. 12:7.

[34]   Delhaye, 216.11–12: "universe dei ecclesie multa commoda et multum ornatum prestant." Delhaye, *Étude*, 131, rightly points out that such a positive estimate of the lives of lay Christians was not common in writings by medieval religious.

[35]   "Deinceps qualiter homo totus vivus, ad ymaginem et similitudinem dei plene et perfecte formatus exeat duce gratia, cuius totum hoc opus est, docebimus" (Delhaye, 223.10–12). The

CHAPTERS 203–227

There follows a long discourse (204–224) given by Charity, who now makes a second appearance, this time in the form of a six-winged bird, each pair of wings symbolizing one stage of charity: love of one's own body and soul, love of friend and enemy, love of God and love of the God-man. This is the section translated here. Her speech will cover some of the same ground as her earlier discourse. This repetition can serve several purposes. It may be a pedagogical device, or Godfrey may be filling in the blanks or refuting criticisms or correcting his earlier ideas (e.g., introducing a sixfold understanding of Christian love in place of the Augustinian fourfold division he had cited earlier). If it is a corrective added later than the previous two books, it was not part of Godfrey's original plan.[36]

CHAPTERS 228–241

Having explained how Christ restores humanity to the likeness of God, Godfrey concludes the *Microcosmus* with some chapters on Christology and Eschatology. Christ came in the sixth age. He was perfect in all that pertains to human nature and grace, resplendent in creative and recreative power, wisdom, and goodness. Now in him grace has given way to glory (228–29). Preceded by ministering angels, on the seventh day (Holy Saturday) he freed those held captive in the underworld, and on the eighth day, he rose and then ascended to glory (230–31).[37] From there he exercises dominion over the earth, converting the violent or sending them to punishment (232–34). What has been personally consummated in Christ, the Head, still has to be consummated in us, his members, so that with gifts of his creation and recre-

---

verb "exeat" can also mean to die. Here Godfrey seems to be referring to self-transcendence in love of God.

[36] See Delhaye, *Étude*, 72–73, where Delhaye discusses the topoi of the "wings of the soul" and "the six-winged angel." Especially noteworthy for its parallels to Godfrey's work is Alan of Lille, *De sex alis cherubim* (PL 210.265ff.). Further references can be found in the Delhaye's edition, 225, and in note 7 to the translation below. Christian authors allegorized the six-winged Seraphim of Isa. 6:2 in various ways. See for example, Grover Zinn, "Hugh of St Victor, Isaiah's Vision, and the *De arca Noe*," in *The Church and the Arts*, ed. Diana Wood, Studies in Church History 28 (Oxford: Blackwell, 1995): 99–116.

[37] Hugh of St Victor allegorizes on the sacred triduum in *Tribus diebus*, 26–27 (Poirel, 62–70; tr. Feiss, 91–94).

ation, they may perfectly image the power, wisdom and goodness of God manifest in the God-man, who is the highest object of their love (235).

All of this Godfrey has presented so that the reader, seeing himself, will recognize himself and admire the self he has recognized. Godfrey has shown that the human being is a microcosm by nature and grace and the eternal dwelling place of God. The soul will eternally see her Creator; the body will eternally see its Redeemer. Then all humankind will be a *microcosm*, God's eternal kingdom (236). In both body and soul humankind (*homo*) is personally united to God, which is true of no angel. This is true of both men and women, Mary above all (237). Now it remains for human beings to complete in their persons what Christ completed in their nature, so that "he who assumed your nature into his person will also assume your person into his nature."[38] Then there will be one body, united under one Head, animated by the love that is the Spirit (239–40). No love could be greater than the love that moved the Son of God to assume fallen human nature. Therefore, although Creator and Recreator are same, if one could be compared to another, we would owe more love to the Recreator than to the Creator (241).

---

[38]   "... is qui assumpsit naturam tuam in personam suam, assumat et personam tuam in naturam suam" (Delhaye, 261.16–17).

203. That perfect love of the creator is the consummation of a human being.

God's supreme work (*manus*) of a man's consummation consists in perfect love of what is above him, perfect, I mean, first in the mode of this life, and finally in the mode of his homeland (*patria*). For, according to the things said above, man was created through grace, first toward ordered love of what is beneath him, then toward ordered love of what he himself is, and thirdly toward ordered love of what is next to him. He is to have practiced these three so that it is easy for him to act on whatever each of these three loves suggests. Then, after he is established in this way, the grace of God adds the supreme work, when to all these previous achievements he adds the exercise of ordered love of what is above him toward consummation, first forming him according to the grace of merit, then consummating him according to the grace of reward. This is the consummated state of the human spirit made according to the image and likeness of God. The human soul could in no way reach a state of such dignity, unless established according to the previous order, raised to this dignity little by little as though from earth to heaven it flew by the wings of love like a heavenly animal.

204. Here begins a treatment of the spiritual ascent of the human being from earth to heaven, in which the adornment of the microcosm is consummated.

This reference to the wings of his love, which wondrously made us but more wonderfully remade us,[1] was made so that I might enkindle both myself and my neighbor to love of him. When I was still on the earth in which Queen Charity had established me long ago for the building up of my neighbor, suddenly moved in spirit,[2] I saw above me a great flying creature like an eagle with great wings, overshadowing me with its extended wings. I heard a voice saying to me, "Recollect yourself[3] and come up here." When I had heard this and thought about what was being said, I soon understood both who was speaking and what she was saying. But it was not as easy for me to do what was said as it was to understand it. I was hindered in two ways, for neither was it easy for me to collect my thoughts, nor once they were collected, to ascend.

And I said, "To will is at hand, but I do not find a way to actually do it."[4] And she said, "Where are your comrades to whom I very recently commended you?" Since they had been present, they were not far off. As soon as they were present, so too was the strength to do both. However, I did the first very sluggishly, because my scatterings were many. Some were outside of me, others were within me—outside of me through the senses, within me through imaginings. Of those that were outside of me through the senses, some were beneath me, some above me, some to the right, others to the left, some before, others behind, so that I was distracted whichever way the wind blew. The things within me were, however, within me in a certain wondrous way, and nevertheless they were as diffuse externally as the seas are on the earth. After sending out a speedy messenger, notably my desire of ascending, I collected them quickly into one as I had hoped.

When these had been collected into one, the eagle shading me from above sent down one of her wings onto the earth. She had six wings.[5] I was told to climb up upon this wing. I climbed up from here with the help of desire and of trust with shame: with desire, because of my eagerness to ascend; with trust, because of the kindness of the one calling; with shame (*verecundia*)[6] because of my unworthiness. As soon as I was lifted up from the earth, I began to waver on account of the unfamiliar foundation on which I was standing. I was told, "Why are you wavering? The footing on which you are resting is solid, although unfamiliar." When this voice spoke, the wing on which I stood was spread out (*dilatata*) in a wondrous way and then solidly compacted, while the other wings around it were in the same manner spread and then compacted with each other. And it happened that there was a single very broad and very pleasant walkway, like a firmament around the body of the flying eagle, formed in a circle in every part out of its six joined and spread wings.[7]

205. HOW NECESSARY IS THE VIRTUE OF CIRCUMSPECTION.

When I had seen this, I became more secure and ready; I was standing bravely and looking around (*circumspiciebam*).[8] And behold there appeared to me in the place of the eagle's head, the well-known face of Queen Charity. Then I was unable to contain myself because my joy. I began to run to her in order to hold her and kiss her head. I understood that she was this great flying creature, born, to be sure, from the waters, but raised up into the air by her strength.

But she said, "What are you doing? Alas, once again you comport yourself too confidently, since you come to me without modesty. But I forgive you because passionate love (*vehemens amor*) for me seized you. Such love does not always conduct itself as circumspectly as it rightly ought to do, but standing completely on confidence that is also present, for a little while forgets modesty, especially when confidence draws the person forward forcefully and overpowers the modesty that pulls it back. Therefore, I will first take care to teach you here something about circumspection that will perhaps be helpful for you. In fact, I just saw you looking circumspectly, but, as soon as you saw me, as though forgetful of circumspection, you began to rush at me.

"You should know that circumspection is a great virtue. We read that in praise of it, the holy animals of God are said to be 'full of eyes both front and rear.'⁹ Because by the holy animals the perfect are signified, whose every body, that is, every work, grace looks after and guards so that they do not offend in deed or in speech, one can understand that the perfect do not always need human circumspection, because the divine eye never fails, especially in situations of necessity where the human eye is lacking. Hence, even the Lord himself taught his apostles, whom he himself had already advanced toward perfection, to count human circumspection for little, saying, 'When you stand before kings and rulers, do not think about how or what you are going to speak.' And adding then the reason for counting human circumspection for little, he said, 'For it is not you who speak, but the spirit of your Father who speaks in you,'¹⁰ as if to say, You have no need of human circumspection, because circumspect divine grace guards you not only in every deed but also in every word. However, this pertains only to the perfect, whom I have nurtured like chicks and with extended wings took up to fly when they were still weak and taught them until they could fly on their own. And now the holy animals of God have mature wings as you see I have, who am the mother of them all.

"However, you, who are still a chick, scarcely covered with feathers and unable to fly, still need motherly circumspection, so that, except in case of necessity, you will not act without suitable circumspection and rush to the precipice. For this reason, just now I looked out for you climbing up over my wings and wavering. I spread them out and compacted them into one, so you would not waver and tumble down headlong, for you were not able to look out for yourself."

206. THAT CHARITY ADVANCES ITS OWN IN DIFFERENT WAYS.

"So now, sit humbly upon my wings and like a bird's chick taking food from the mouth of its mother, receive the words of my mouth with the open mouth of your heart. Nurtured by them, you will fledge into a heavenly animal able to fly. Up to now, I have nurtured you to walk like an earthly animal on the lower elements. Now, because you have mentioned my wings, which however you have not seen, I sense that you are striving toward higher things and so I wish to nurture you now like a heavenly animal set to fly. For this reason I appear to you here in this form for in regard to place and time I conform myself in various ways to good and devout desires of all of those striving in various ways toward the Lord. For if you look carefully at it, not only my words, but even this my very form will further your intention, and it will help you come to the point of touching in a orderly way my head, which you wished to touch precipitously a second time."

207. THE DOCTRINE OF CHARITY.

At this point, having heard these things, I sat down, devout and intent upon the words of her mouth. But she, opening her mouth taught me thus, saying, "First, I will show you about this my form, what it aims to signify (*sibi velit*). In this form of mine, in which I now appear to you, I am teaching what I wish you to be.

"Thus, formerly, God—wishing to present visibly his invisible form to corporeal eyes insofar as that was possible—created the body of the sun so that he, who formerly had shown his invisible image to invisible creatures in themselves, in the sun also would show his visible image to visible creatures. Thus, to hint to those who diligently looked where and how they ought to proceed, he made the sun,[11] in itself round, shiny and warm. In the sun, which is superior to all visible creatures in these three attributes—for nothing in visible creatures is more round, brighter, or warmer than the sun—in the highest roundness is shown his omnipotent eternity or eternal omnipotence; in its highest brightness, his highest wisdom; in its highest warmth, his supreme goodness. In this way he suggests, in a wonderful way, to all rational creatures who were outside, where they ought to be heading: inside, that is, toward omnipotent eternity, wisdom, and goodness. And so that all might know by what way and how they were to do this, God the Father placed another wonderful sacrament in the sun when he created it traversing the heavens with circular motion and not departing from the heavens, and gave it such magnitude and strength that when just its ray was sent to earth, it illumined everything, and when its heat had been diffused everywhere, it vivified all things. It signified by its magnitude and power God's power governing all things without departing from the infinity of his eternity. In the ray sent to earth he announced his wisdom coming personally into the flesh and in it illumining all things and showing the way by which one could travel upward toward the invisible. Its heat, diffused everywhere through its ray, signified the love and ardor of the Spirit vivifying all things, diffused through the earth by means of Wisdom, but drawing all things upward by its own power.[12]

"What the highest trinity proclaimed to all by the natural example of the sun's heat, I propose to you in this form of mine, as a grace-given example of the same trinity, the supreme good, for you alone and in you for all. As I sometimes show myself as an earthly animal to those cultivating their land, and as an aquatic animal to those seeking purity of heart, now I show myself as a heavenly animal to you and to those who are like you. Moses, the servant of God symbolized (*figuravit*) this in the figure of an eagle expanding his wings and taking his chicks up on them.[13] The Lord symbolized this in the figure of a hen gathering her chicks under her wings.[14] Finally, in the Apocalypse, John, among the rest of the four animals,[15] symbolized it in himself, namely, that all who are rapt higher than others by love of spiritual things become spiritual birds. For the rest, who are without the contagion of mortal sin and are occupied for the Lord's sake with earthly activities and exercise the works of virtues that they can in the active life, are earthly animals of God walking with the man-God on the earth, and can fittingly be called birds or oxen or domestic beasts or something else of this kind according to the diverse activities of diverse virtues about which you also spoke above. Hence, that same John,[16] concerning whom I just now proposed to you as an example, and the rest of the four holy animals in the shape of a man, an ox, and a lion, according to different actions befitting these figures, pictured the actions of the God-man walking upon earth. However, John, who was dedicated to contemplation of the divine and rapt higher by love of spiritual things and wrote about the nature of the Son of God, depicted himself—and those similar to himself, who were fashioned by me—in the figure of a heavenly animal.

"This I now depict in this my form for you, and for those like you, wishing you to understand in me what I do in those who are mine, and

I say that I am what I make my own to be. Thus, the apostle says that I work in those who work through me: 'The Spirit asks for them with unutterable groanings,'[17] that is, he makes them ask. Such I make all of my own who have been rapt higher through contemplation by love of spiritual things."

208. On the mystery of her wings.

"And this is the not contemptible (*contempnenda*) meaning (*ratio*) of this my form. But now listen to the meaning, no more contemptible, regarding this mystery—notably the number and order or disposition of my wings. This is the mystery of my wings. You know that from virtues proceed works of virtues, and especially from charity proceed the works of charity. Charity is never idle; it either increases or decreases. Besides, as I remember, you enumerated above some kinds of ordered love; that is, ordered love of what is beneath you, ordered love of that which you are, ordered love of him who is next to you, ordered love of him who is above you. You said that these are part of my body, and you spelled out some other things about these as you liked, since, with the exception of my head, I allowed you to discuss my body as you liked. But because not every aspect of my body was present then, you discussed it as it was. Because it did not appear to you then in the form which it appears now, I allow you to treat the rest of it now. Moreover, where you do not grasp the mysteries of my members even when you touch them, I will reveal by the clearer light of my teaching, so that you may learn more fully in what order you ought to touch my head."

209. Regarding the first wing.

"Therefore, as you yourself have testified, the members of my body are virtues, just as the wings proceeding from those members are general works of virtues. The individual feathers of the wings are specific works or acts of virtues.[18] For example, ordered love of the flesh, that is, love ordered for the Lord of what is beneath you, as you yourself assert, is the lower member of my body. This love cannot be idle. If it exists, it does great things, namely, it controls the five senses. If this is done for the Lord, the Lord himself shows how great it is when he compares it with the five prudent virgins entering the wedding with the bridegroom. Its effect is the control of the palate, tongue, lust, and finally all illicit movements of the flesh. Not only does it constrain the members of the body from evil deeds, but it also is active in good deeds.

Hence the mortification (*maceratio*) of the lusting flesh by means of through frequent fasts, vigils, prayers, bodily disciplines, and many other afflictions of the body, which ordered love of the flesh devises in order to make what is heavy light and take it more easily to the heights with itself. Why so many? I could still list for you many works of virtues proceeding from this ordered love of the flesh, but I pass through these more briefly now because earlier you spelled out some truths about these things that were in harmony with my teaching. Therefore great is the wing of this part of my body, which loses[19] from itself almost as many feathers as it gives birth to works of virtues."

210. REGARDING THE SECOND WING.

"Again, as you state, ordered love of what you are is the middle part of my body. This love works greater things than the previous one—for just as the interior man is greater than the exterior, so the works of this wing are greater than the works of the one that went before. It cleanses unclean thoughts and feelings (*affectiones*), cuts off those that are superfluous, orders those that are unstable, gives birth to good thoughts and feelings, and nurtures, guards, perfects, and preserves them. That is what you said earlier about this wing, and it need not be repeated, because you have already spoken well about it. This love sends out from itself as many feathers by which the interior man is lifted above, as it performs deeds of virtue in the interior man. So this wing set on the right side of my body opposite the first is great. For you can now see for yourself, this is the right and this is the left part of my body."

211. CORRECTION OF A CERTAIN DISTINCTION MADE EARLIER REGARDING THE PARTS OF THE BODY OF CHARITY.

"However because, above, you placed the ordered love of the flesh on the lower part of my body, and love of yourself in the middle part of it, I wish to distinguish the members of my body for you a little differently. As is commonly done, you distinguish them into four, whereas I earlier distinguished them for you into three. Next I distinguish each of the three into two. Thus ordered love of self, ordered love of neighbor, and ordered love of God are all different. However, one kind of ordered love of self is love of the flesh; another is of the spirit. For what you, doing what is commonly done, divided into love of what you are and love of that which is beneath you, for convenience of distinguishing my wings I propose to you as one love. I think it is unworthy that the whole human being come to be divided from any part of himself, rather than divide the parts among themselves. Not that your division, made with the considered opinion of the one doing the dividing, is to be reproached, but rather that this distinction of mine fits better with my teaching now and is more congruent with the truth. Truly, a man consists of soul and body, nor strictly speaking does he come into division with any of his parts, nor with reference to them is he superior or inferior to himself, but the parts are divided among themselves, one inferior, another superior. Therefore, as I said, with the parts divided among themselves, there are ordered loves of self, of the flesh, and of the spirit. Ordered love of neighbor is either of a friend or of an enemy. Ordered love of God is one thing when it concerns God alone, another when it concerns the God-man. And so from the three members of my body six wings proceed, placed opposite each other on the right and the left, and from each of the members, two emerge, one on one side, the other on the other side."

212. How necessary is the number of her wings.

"The sixfold number of my wings is very necessary, since, if one of them is taken away, the others would remain completely useless. For if ordered love of the flesh is taken away, what could love of the spirit accomplish? If by loving your flesh inordinately, you were to seek only the pleasures of the flesh, how would you serve the spirit? If by loving the spirit inordinately and completely neglecting the flesh, you pursued only the pleasures of the spirit, how would you satisfy the needs of the flesh? It is not at all possible for one of these to be loved inordinately without the other being loved, though not in an orderly way. One should think in exactly the same way regarding love of friend and enemy, and love of God and the God-man. It is not possible that one of these be— much less be useful—without the other, and so as the number cannot be decreased, so it cannot be increased. It allows nothing superfluous; it suffers no diminishment. Therefore this number of my wings is perfect, not only by the divine reason by which God made everything six-fold, but also by human reason by which the sixfold is said to consist of its parts."

213. On their order and arrangement.

"Moreover, their order and arrangement is unchangeable. You cannot, without confusion, make the second or third from the first, nor the third from the second or the first, nor the first from the third or the second. The first is to be merciful to yourself so that you may please God; the second is to be merciful to your neighbor so that you may please God and the neighbor, the third is to refer everything to God. This is the order of charity that the spouse arranged (*ordinavit*) in his bride when she had been led into the wine cellar. Hence, she glories exultantly in the song of love: 'The king led me into the wine cellar; he ordered charity in me.'[20] Clearly, the wine cellar signifies the church, in which is contained that gospel wine made from water at the wedding, a wine that was served last but which was, in the judgment of the chief steward, better than the first. It was a wine that inebriated the perfect soul in the love of God, so that she forgot the order of human love and was made learned in the order of divine love. Once these two—the number and order of my wings—are brought together, a third, the circular arrangement, necessarily emerges. For whoever has charity ordered in himself in this way is without doubt raised up, like a heavenly animal, and moves in the direction of eternity. So, to show this more carefully will not be useless for those moving upward."[21]

214. HOW SHE FLIES ON THESE WINGS AND WHERE SHE BEGINS.

"Let all those who are eager to move toward the Lord listen regarding whence they must begin and whence they are to take up for themselves feathers for flying. The beginning of striving toward God is the motion of my first wing. Its motion is the work of ordered love of the flesh, that is, loving one's flesh in an ordered way. It is so necessary that one begin to fly from here, that if you could have one hundred wings and move all of them without this one, you could do nothing. How could someone who loved his flesh inordinately, rise up toward something good, much less fly? How can someone lying in the mud fly? But whence are feathers born for this wing so that it can move itself? Undoubtedly from the things which you yourself carefully listed above— which at my inspiration you foresaw in your understanding when it ran ahead, even before you had seen these wings of mine, before you had learned anything about this kind of flight—that is, from continual consideration of those things the spirit owes to its flesh out of charity, either because it is personally united to her,[22] or because it is married to her as though to a wife, or because it serves in her like a soldier in his tent, or because she carries it like its beast of burden, or because with her as a companion it hastens from exile toward its native land, or most especially because with her as a coheir it looks forward to eternal participation in its paternal inheritance. These to be sure are the six feathers born for ordered love of the flesh from its very self by which the spirit moves to love its flesh in an ordered way and through this to rise above it. So, whoever has ordered love for its flesh but does not yet have the wing that is born from it should hurry to consider diligently the things just said and little by little he will sense the wing being born for him from the multiplication of feathers of this kind."

215. That one does not fly with one wing but with a pair of wings, and that feathers of the second wing are born from the same place where those of the first are born.

"When these feathers have been born, multiplied, and matured in you, you then have one wing, which, although it suffices to move itself, is not sufficient for flying. Flying requires not just one wing, but at least one pair of wings. But where are feathers born for this latter wing so that it can move itself, if not from the same place where feathers were born for the former wing? For, since the first and second wings are one pair, just as they are born from the one same root, so it is necessary that their feathers be born from the same root and cause at the same time. For in one pair of wings, one does not develop plumage before the other, but just as they grow at the same time so also they develop plumage at the same time, although what can come to be at the same time cannot be said at the same time. Therefore, as feathers are born to the spirit—from continuous consideration of the things the spirit owes its flesh—to move itself for ordered love of the flesh, so are born to her—from consideration of those things the flesh owes her spirit, with reciprocal love—feathers, by which to move herself for ordered love of the spirit. When these have been born and grown to adulthood, you now have one pair of wings, suitable, insofar as it lies within them, not only to move but also to fly. However, the capacity to act is not achieved unless you have the other two pairs of wings. If you do not have the former you cannot fly, although if the former are at rest, you can fly with the latter. So after having done enough regarding the first pair of wings, you need to have the second and the third."

216. Concerning the second pair of wings and whence feathers are born for them.

[Objection] "But someone will say to me, 'Whence can feathers for flying be born for the second pair of wings? Or, how are ordered love of a friend and ordered love of an enemy born from the same root so that from one root similar feathers are born for both? For if one could see to some extent from what root feathers ought to be born for ordered love of a friend, this would in no way enable one to see whence must be born either ordered or disordered love of an enemy. For the most ancient command of the natural law declared, "You shall love your friend and hate your enemy."[23] Hence, he seems to have directly contradicted the natural law when he said, "But I say to you, love your enemies, do good to those who hate you.'"[24]

[Reply][25] "However, those who tell themselves this have not yet learned through grace to distinguish between nature and nature. For those who have been illumined by grace have learned this: they know the law of created nature is one thing; the law of corrupted nature is another.[26] Nature as created knew no enemy, and for this reason never received any commandment regarding hating one's enemy. For man was created as a social animal[27] but, illumined by grace, insofar as it was in his power he regarded no one as an enemy.

"Only corrupted nature made and had enemies for itself. However, the corruption of nature is a falling (defectus)[28] from created nature, which, when for itself it trusted in itself and turned away from the grace offered it, fell—in itself and from itself. It was made inferior to itself and moreover fell from itself to such an extent that it was almost blinded and dead so that it could neither see nor feel its failure (defectum) and sickness. Hence, it came about that, although it was neither healthy nor whole, it counted as nature the vices to which it had grown accustomed by long-lasting habit and accepted those things as a law, which men called natural, regarding love of neighbor and hatred of enemies. However, that nature that never fell from its creation, and which remade what had fallen through grace, rightly said, 'Love your enemies, etc.'[29] He was speaking to those whom he had restored through grace to their created nature, not because such as they consider others enemies, but because they are considered enemies by those not yet restored.

"Therefore, if you look not at nature that is falling, but at nature that is advancing, you will see how ordered love of a friend and ordered love of an enemy are born from a single root. Neither nature nor grace know inordinate love of friend or enemy, but for its part, the fallenness of nature (defectus nature), that is, vice (vitium),[30] connects the two insofar as it can. For when created nature had fallen in itself, because it found no help in itself, it was compelled to seek outside and in some fashion made friends for itself. Those it could not make friends it found were enemies—when it could not be in harmony with them regarding what is good, and it did not want to be out of harmony with them because of what was evil.[31] Thus, therefore, ordered love of both the enemy and the friend are born from the place where love of neighbor is born. For, since every human being is neighbor to you, none is to be considered your enemy, even if someone considers you his enemy. You ought not harbor hatred for anyone, provided you have been restored to your nature through grace, although someone who is not yet restored may harbor hatred for you. Hence, when the one who gave the command to love one's enemy began, 'Love your enemies,'[32] he added, not 'do good to those whom you hate,' but 'who hate you,'[33] knowing that those restored by him to their original nature, or rather promoted to greater things through grace, hate no one, although they are hated by many, because surely that shows greater virtue than if having no enemy they hated nobody."

217. THE ONE ROOT OF LOVE OF NEIGHBOR IS TWOFOLD: THE COMMAND AND THE EXAMPLE OF THE LORD.

"Let me be silent about natural love of neighbor with which the commandment is not concerned; let me put far from my teaching the evil (*viciosum*) love of neighbor which is prohibited and so utterly unworthy of my recollection. There is one root of ordered love of neighbor that is the concern of the command to love one's friend and also one's enemy. This root is so tenacious that if there were no other, no force could pull it out, because he who gave the command regarding both also gave an example.[34] The authority of his command was so great that it could not be disdained (*contempni*) with impunity, even if it stood alone, but from his great love he wished to become neighbor of human beings (for he was not yet such when he was God) so that what he had established in a commandment by divine authority he could also confirm in example by divine charity. He went so far in confirming this by example that no one could fail to be amazed by such an example, even if he failed to imitate it."

218. OBJECTION TO THE THINGS JUST SAID.

[Objection] "But here again someone will say to me, 'He commanded both, but how did he give an example of both, who is said to have given his life (*animam ponere*) only for his friends? He said, "No one has greater love than this, that he lay down his life for his friends."[35] In this saying, he declared not only that he was dying for his friends, but also that it showed greater love to die for one's friends than for one's enemies.'

[Reply] "But that is what I said above: because he never fell[36] from nature as created, but rather progressed in grace, he harbored hatred for no one and not only called back to their created nature his own who had fallen from their created nature, but also raised them through grace to things greater than what was theirs by nature. For this reason he most rightly declares that he died not for enemies but for friends. For how could he rightly be said to have given up his life for his enemies, when he, insofar as he could, considered no one hateful, but even to the extent of dying for them made those who hated him his friends. To the extent he loved and from that love gave his life for his friends and was greater than any who loved him, his love was greater than every other human love. Nevertheless, the statement (*dictum*) 'greater love no one has,'[37] could also be correctly understood in another way, namely if the noun 'love' is taken to mean 'sign of love.' Certainly, no sign of love can be greater than death freely accepted of behalf of someone. In that case, the emphasis of the statement (*vis dicti*) does not lie in what is added: 'for his friends.'"

219. ANOTHER TWOFOLD ROOT OF LOVE OF NEIGHBOR.

"There is one ineradicable (*inevulsibilis*) root of both loves, that is, of friend and of enemy. As was said, the command and equally the example of so great a source (*autoris*), even if taken by itself, could suffice by itself to put feathers on this pair of wings. Now, however, there is also another root which is older and no less sufficient, namely, because all human beings (*homines*) are born as siblings (*fratres*) from one earthly father, all can become coheirs of the one heavenly Father of the Son and coheirs of eternal beatitude. In fact, many, who through grace merited to receive them, have already received the promises of that heavenly Father as pledge and betrothal-gift (*arras*) of that so great inheritance. By the debt of fraternal love, they are obliged to make every effort to call, draw, and compel to sharing in that great happiness those who have not yet merited to receive any earnest or pledge regarding it. If they do that, they are taking care of themselves and their coheirs. However, if they have neglected to do it, they perish on account of their neglect of themselves and their coheirs. Therefore, who does not now see that that loving consideration of these things gives birth to great feathers for this pair of wings, nurtures them, and makes them able to fly?"

220. WHITHER ONE FLIES WITH THE FIRST PAIR OF WINGS.

"From what has been said already, it is now clear whence feathers for flying are born for the first two pairs of my wings. Now I will teach you more carefully about how far they can fly, although in what has gone before there are already hints about it. The first pair, if it is well covered with feathers, lifts the soul and body to such a high dignity that they do not fear to be separated for a time from each other. The spirit willingly puts off the flesh for a time, and the flesh willingly consents to this with the spirit. They do so because of the beauty (*species*) of a more happy union, which each promises to the other. Hence, as long as they are bound together, they are patiently more than willingly joined and, when they are separated, they are more willingly than patiently separated.

"This may happen in a crucial time of necessity, when the spirit is compelled either to deny him whom it loves or to expose the flesh to the persecutor. At such a time the spirit urges this on the flesh, and the flesh willingly consents to the spirit in the matter. Or it may happen without any pressing necessity, but by the desire of a burning mutual will by which the spirit 'desires to be dissolved and to be with Christ— the flesh, however, to rest in hope.'[38] The spirit advises it, saying, 'My flesh—born, nurtured, and grown to adulthood with me, my beloved, the companion of my exile, the sharer of my journey, the future coheir of the communal reign of our common Lord—behold now how long we have lived together, walked together, worked together, shared happy and sad things; we now burn with a vision of our common Lord, but we cannot now reach him at the same time. Moreover, this companionship of ours is a burden to both of us. I grumble in the interim that you are opaque, muddy, and sordid to me; and you grumble that I am harsh, heavy, and insupportable to you when I starve you with fasts, consume you with vigils, punish you with sighs, drown you with tears, afflict you with corporal disciplines, and now calmly suffer this union, burdensome to us both, to be dissolved, so that I may fly ahead of you and precede you to the common Lord. And behold, I promise you that at the appointed time I will return to you and take you up again, no longer opaque but clear, no longer muddy but solid, no longer dirty but clean.

And you will receive me back, but I will be no longer hard, but gentle, no longer burdensome but light, no longer unsupportable but bearable (*tractabilem*) in every way. Then both of us, happily and inseparably joined, will be placed before the common Lord and so we will glory together forever in our common vision of him.'

"When, at my instigation, the spirit suggests these things to the flesh, the flesh accedes to the spirit, and both of them, raised up on the feathers of ordered love—the spirit by desire, the flesh by consent—are prepared for the dissolution of this cohabitation which is burdensome to them, so that—with the spirit raised up through desire and the flesh through consent—on behalf of both of them the spirit says to him in whom they are raised up, 'My soul thirsts for you, my God, and in many ways my flesh [longs for you].'"[39]

221. THAT FLYING UPWARD IN THIS WAY THE SPIRIT STILL BURNS WITH DESIRES FOR ITS FLESH.

"Very often God soon grants what they wanted to happen to them, so that the spirit flies up all the way 'to under the altar of God,'[40] helped by wings of ordered love, both of its flesh and of itself. And, settled there, it cannot forget its flesh, whose other raised-up wing is at rest. Nor can it consider itself completely liberated, however much it has achieved happiness, until it receives the companion of its exile and the coheir of its joy, which is still sleeping in the dust. Burning with desire, it cries to him who freed it to hasten the liberation of the flesh. But 'when one robe had been given, the one shouting was bidden to rest' in expectation of the other stole, 'until the number of its brothers is completed.'[41] The first martyrs heard this answer given to them from heaven. As John says, with this pair of well-feathered wings they flew up 'under the altar of God'[42] when, under the press of necessity by which either the flesh would perish temporally or the spirit would perish eternally, the flesh and the spirit agreed out of love that they would hand the flesh to the persecutor so that the spirit might fly up free. All, whether those who have no subjects whom they rule or prelates by whom they are well ruled, if they fly up by this pair of wings, are made kings over themselves: their spirit commands the flesh in an ordered way, their flesh obeys the spirit in an ordered way. As a result, by the equal movement of these wings, for the time being, one flies up to 'under the altar of God'[43] until it takes up the other again and carries it before the gaze of God."

222. How and how far one flies with the second pair of wings.

"With the first pair of my wings, one flies like a turtle dove, or a solitary, or someone flying with only one companion but, with the second pair, one flies in a flock like a dove until it reaches the same goal with the first one. Whoever, by the free flight of my primary, well-feathered wings, raises himself higher from the earth and is strengthened by their agility, fears less about his own fall. He sometimes goes on to move my second wings and to make use of them in fight. When they are spread right and left, far and wide, some of those whom they find on both sides, who are placed beneath them, they shade and protect;[44] others they even raise above themselves. They shade and protect the terrestrial animals of God who are not strong enough to fly. I mean that they shade them from the heat of carnal desires, from the heat of troubles. From temptations and from the scoffing of unclean spirits, they protect those who are involved with earthly activities and wearied by this sort of heat and assault. They continually ask for a share of divine protection, saying, 'Guard me, Lord, like the apple (*pupillam*)[45] of your eye; protect me under the shade of your wings.'[46] Although such as these are not able to fly, because they 'dwell in the help of the most high and stay in the protection of the God of heaven,' they experience what is promised to them in Psalm 90: 'He will shade you with his arms, and you will hope under his wings (*pennis*).'[47]

"Further, when those striving toward higher things and wanting to fly exert themselves in these my second wings and have been raised up, he first puts them on my first wings so that on them they may first grow strong enough to fly by themselves, just as I now raise you upon my first wings. When they have grown strong on them, he then transfers them to the second, if he sees that they are suitable to fly for others. For this is the proper task of these wings of mine, to fly for others, not for themselves, just as the duty of the first wings is to fly for themselves and not for others. For whoever flies at will through the first wings that are sufficient for him, has no need for help from the second wings; rather, others are helped by them. So, whoever wishes to exercise with these second wings of mine should know that he has accepted them not for his own needs, but for the needs of others; namely, to shade and protect those who cannot fly or to raise up those who can fly. If they see any one of either sort in danger, they are even prepared 'to give up their life for them.'[48] This, then, is the high point of the flight of this pair of my wings, namely 'to give up one's life for one's brothers,'[49] who are future coheirs of one and the same king. This is especially so of those established in their ruling office (*regimine*); they owe them this flight by reason of their office. For it is not enough for anyone established in an office to fly with the first pair of my wings, however readily, if he does not exert himself sufficiently and continuously in the second."

223. THAT THE SON OF GOD HIMSELF, WHO BECAME A BIRD FOR US, EXERTED HIMSELF MORE IN THIS PAIR OF WINGS.

"The Son of God was established in a ruling position by the Father, as he himself testifies about himself in the second Psalm, where he says, 'I, however, established as king, etc.'[50] He became neighbor of humankind in the flesh that he assumed for the sake of humankind. In that same flesh he showed himself to human beings not only as a man by living reasonably among them, but also as a calf by offering himself to death for the sake of the dying, and by rising as a lion on behalf of those who were going to rise, and as an eagle by ascending for those who were going to ascend.[51] This figure of the eagle,[52] which by its celibate way of life also is flying higher than all the flying creatures of heaven, also has six wings, like the other holy living creatures of God. However, in this pair of my wings he exerts himself more energetically (*virilius*) than all the others, for, 'challenging its chicks to fly and flying over them, he expanded his wings and lifted up and carried on his shoulders'[53] the ones he found were ready to fly. However, those that he found were not yet ready he protected for the time being 'under the shade of his wings'[54] until they too were ready, if not to fly with this pair of wings, at least to fly with the first pair. This was not unjustified, for the one who first gave the command regarding this pair of wings ought also before all others to give an example. I mean an example not just of how they might fly, but also of where they should fly to, that is, all the way 'to giving one's life for one's brothers. For no one has greater love than this.'[55] To describe his death[56] I do not know which I may say more truthfully: example or command. However, I think it is example. The number and greatness of the 'eagles [that] gather at his body'[57] afterwards is exemplified by the number and greatness of the pastors of souls found in the church of God. All fly with these wings to the point[58] that they are prepared 'to give their lives for their brothers.' Although not all of them are found to have given their lives for their brothers, by their readiness to do so, all those flying in a flock with the souls whom they raised up with themselves arrive all the way 'under the altar'[59] of God. For he who was here for them as a protecting eagle and raised them with his wings becomes there for them an altar, protecting them with its horns[60] from heat and from rains, until 'all are brought to perfection in one perfect man,'[61] and are 'handed over' by him 'to God the Father as a kingdom.'"[62]

224. How after these things the aforesaid vision disappeared.

Mistress (*magistra*)[63] Charity discussed with subtlety these things and many like them regarding the two parts of her wings. She also very clearly corrected the distinction which I, according to my lights, had made above regarding the parts of her body. I was still sitting, devoutly inhaling the words of her mouth like a baby inhaling food served to it from the mouth of its mother. I was nourished like a chick by the power of her lively speech so that each syllable of her words became for me like individual feathers for flying. Such was the power of her speech that the efficacy of what she said also engendered in me an understanding of the things to be said. So it happened that, when she seemed to be preparing herself for future discourse regarding the remaining third of her wings, my mind warmed to pursue the rest of her first discourse like a chick, which, already well feathered and disdaining the food of its mother, longs to fly by itself to its food sources.

When she noticed this, she looked at me more carefully and said, "I see that it is not in vain that I have prolonged my speech to you to this point. Now you not only hold my words in your memory, you also, with anticipatory cleverness, see what is to be said. But remember the word, which you yourself uttered earlier about the four parts of my body, namely, when you were speaking about four kinds of ordered love. If anyone has practiced well the first three of those which are two pairs of my wings, as you now see, so that it is easy for him to activate whichever one it occurs to him to use, then finally when he is so positioned, the grace of God stretches out its supreme hand. Then to all these things that he already has, he adds ordered love of that which is above him and brings him to consummation. Only by grace does anyone become fit to touch my head. Because you did not yet have this grace when you were saying this, for you were still inexperienced in the first three which you did not know are my wings, I therefore appeared to you in this form, so that, instructed in the first two pairs of my wings, you could first exercise them, and thus be made worthy of the granting of the supreme grace. However, this exercise consists not solely in the power of the tongue on which you presume, but rather in virtue of heart and hand. If, therefore, you have become proficient in all these, it is well; fly up wherever you wish."

Then, not without tears and sobbing (*singultuosis*) sighs, I said, "My 'Lady (*domina*),[64] you know'[65] very well my knowing, willing, and capacity; 'before you is all my desiring.[66] Have mercy on me, because my soul trusts in you.'"[67]

She said to me, "I indeed know you better than you know yourself, but I wanted you to show the devotion of your heart by the confession of your mouth.[68] Hence, although it is premature, I give you permission to fly up because in my estimate your willing is loftier than your ability. Come forward now and touch my head so that your capacity may be increased and your willing may be effective."

She had not yet finished her words when I flew up and touched her head, kissing it once, twice, and a third time. When I had done this, she said to me, "What are you feeling?" And I replied, "The turtle dove has found a nest for herself, where she can place her chicks."[69] She said, "Behold, you have found what you wanted. Fly up now as you wish, and return to your nest as you wish, and put your chicks there as you wish."

And having said this, the vision disappeared. I, however, "found myself"[70] in the church "next to the altar"[71] of my Lord whom I was serving continually. Then, "returning to myself,"[72] I reflected back on what I had seen and heard, and I understood what else Mistress Charity wished me to do. She wanted me to persevere in the ordered love of my Lord, who is her head and my head, which I had learned about from her, so that I would direct all[73] my strivings and all my flights toward him, and finish in him the strivings toward difficult things, the flights toward easy things, the strivings toward humble things, the flights toward sublime things, that is, so that whatever I began to do—in order to strive upward by praying, meditating, psalmody, reading, writing,[74] or whatever other thing I began to do in order to strive upward—all of it I would refer to him, all of it I would place in that very nest like chicks. Also, if I could benefit any neighbors in these or other ways, I would also nurture them like chicks in this nest. So, admonished by these things, let us press on by ordered love of what is above us, which is the third pair of the wings of charity, confident in his help and flying up above ourselves.

225. What is Ordered Love of That Which is Above Us

Let us see therefore[75] what is this ordered love of what is above us. Raised up by its wings, the spirit of a human being is advanced to such a great dignity that the whole new man formed in the "image and likeness of God"[76] and, as it were, a kind of world—that is, a microcosm— is made worthy to have God dwell with him. For this reason, indeed, the human spirit is called a microcosm by the theologian, because he is made worthy to have God dwell with him unto eternity.

This love (*amor*) is the bond of sweetest affection (*dilectionis*) by which the human soul is conveyed above itself by grace and bound to God, adhering to God immediately, ineffably, and inseparably. I say "immediately," because the soul that loves its Lord perfectly sets no intermediary between itself and the Lord for the sake of which it loves the Lord. I call it a mutual bond, because [she is] beloved (*dilecta*) and lover (*diligens*) and, in a wonderful way, beloved before she is lover, because she is loved from eternity, but loves in time; she is loved that she might love, not loving so that she is loved. No perfect[77] soul that has not experienced it can know how very sweet is this bond of love. Moreover, she who experiences it cannot express it as it is, because there is nothing similar to it in human affections, because it is the Holy Spirit.[78] Nevertheless, the holy soul that experiences it and wishes to express the experience does so as far as she can do so under the figure (*tipo*) of a bride aglow with desire for her husband:[79] "Let him kiss me with the kiss of his mouth."[80] But after the attainment of the one she desires, she expresses, as far as it is possible, how much sweetness there is in that attainment, when she adds, "For better than wine are your breasts, shining with the finest ointments,"[81] not because this is comparable to so great a reality, but because in human affections nothing more similar to it can be found. For what in human affections is sweeter than the love of bridegroom and bride? For this reason, God himself, wishing to express his mutual love with a soul of this kind, condescended to human custom and did not refuse to be called the spouse of such a soul.

In fact, to more explicitly commend his mutual love for us, he deigned to unite himself personally to our nature, taking up (*assumens*) the whole human being, that is, body and soul, to himself in person, the soul immediately and the flesh through the mediation of the soul. He did this so that our double nature no longer would adhere as a bridegroom does to his bride through a spiritual union as at the very beginning of the marriage, but as a husband clings to his wife indissolubly through carnal union in a consummated marriage. And so in our head the bond of mutual love between the Lord and humankind is made consummated and indissoluble, so that in him—the eternal indwelling God—humankind is made blessed. But in his members the consummation is still awaited. In no other human being living on earth except in Christ is this bond of mutual love made so indissoluble that it deserves the name of marriage. Meanwhile, the bride is still sighing and groaning over the delay of the marriage. She has only received betrothal gifts (*arras*) of it. She awaits the fulfillment of the divine espousal by which God drew her to himself. Meanwhile out of intense love he gradually "emptied himself, accepting her form"[82] so that he could fill her through mutual love, imprinting on her a form, his "image and likeness."[83] Thus, after a fashion, God—out of love—falls into humankind, so that humankind in some fashion might—out of love—advance into God.

226. NOTE THAT HUMANKIND IS DRAWN INTO GOD BY A DOUBLE BOND OF LOVE.

From this, one gathers that humankind is drawn by a twofold bond of love, which is the third pair of the wings of charity: by the one, because he is God; by the other, because on humanity's account he became man; by the one by which he created him out of love, by the other by which he re-created him out of love; by the one by which he made him capable of his good things, by the other by which he made him full of his good things. Moreover, this did not happen without, so to speak, injury[84] to himself—because by his emptying,[85] he made humanity full of his good things. From this it follows that humankind is drawn to God by a greater love because he is the God-man than because he is God. For one of these is natural,[86] the other freely given grace (*gratuitus*);[87] by what is natural he tends toward God, by what is freely given grace he tends toward the man-God. What is natural is less; what is freely given gift is greater. By natural love man was formed "in the image of God"; by freely given love he is reformed "in the likeness of God."[88]

227. BOTH THE IMAGE AND THE LIKENESS OF GOD CONSIST OF THREE THINGS.

Both of these consist of three things,[89] so that in both the creative Trinity and the re-creative Trinity, the created Trinity and the recreated Trinity are found: the creative Trinity, which is highest power, highest wisdom, and highest goodness, created humankind naturally powerful, wise, and good, that is, a created trinity and "image of God."[90] Again, there is the re-creative Trinity—the highest wisdom, the highest goodness, the highest power—which, by freely given grace, created humankind supremely wise, supremely good, and supremely powerful—which is the re-created trinity and the "likeness of God."

NOTES

1   "Deus qui humanae substantiae dignitatem mirabiliter condidisti et mirabilius reformasti" ("O God, who wondrously formed the dignity of humankind and more wondrously reformed it"). These words were part of a Christmas oration in the *Sacramentum Veronense*, and later were incorporated into the "offertory" prayers of the Roman rite. Cf. Gerhard Ladner, *The Idea of Reform* (Cambridge: Harvard University Press, 1959), 284–85.

2   "factus in spiritu": this phrase occurs in several later accounts of a vision experienced by a Carthusian monk. See *Bücher: Bibliotheken und Schriftkultur der Kartäuser: Festgabe zum 65. Geburtstag von Edward Potkowski*, Contubernium, Tübinger Beiträge zur Universitäts- und Wissenschaftsgeschichte 59, ed. Sönke Lorenz (Stuttgart: Franz Steiner, 2002), 301.

3   "Collige dispersiones tuas": The inspiration for this expression seems to be Ps 146:2 (Vulg.); Godfrey uses it several times in the subsequent sentences. I take it to refer to thoughts and impulses. Cf. Hugh of St Victor, *Libellus* 5 (Sicard, 148–50). Sicard also cites a *sententia* (#312) which O. Lottin (*Psychologie et morale aux XIIᵉ et XIIIᵉ siècles*. Vol. 5: *Problèmes d'histoire littéraire: L'école d'Anselme de Laon et de Guillaume de Champeaux* [Gembloux: J. Duculot, 1959], 246.26–39) attributes to the school of Anselm of Laon and William of Champeaux. The *sententia* says that as a result of sin humankind's simple essence fell into confusion. Its memory fell on a sharp rock and was completely broken.

4   Rom. 7:18.

5   Isa. 6:2; Apoc. 4:8. There are a number of medieval comments on the six wings of the cherubim. For example, Alan of Lille, *De sex alis cherubim* (PL 210.265ff); Pseudo-Rhaban Maur, *Allegoriae in Sacram Scripturam* (PL 112.856–57).

6   Most often it seems best to translate Godrfrey's use of the word *verecundia* as "modesty." It can also mean "shyness" and also "shame," which seems to be the primary connotation in this sentence.

7   Delhaye's edition refers here to the entry "aquila" (eagle) in Warner of St Victor, *Gregorianum* 2.2 (PL 193.69A–71A). Warner (Garnerius) was subprior of St Victor at his death in 1170. His *Gregorianum* is an encyclopedia of Biblical terms. Unfortunately Warner's text does not make clear what exactly Godfrey means by this convoluted description of the bird's anatomy.

8   "circumspectio": the English word "circumspection" conveys the meaning of this Latin word, which is closely related to "discretio." The probably Victorine *De contemplatione et eius speciebus* devotes several pages to it: "Circumspection is a form of prudence, looking ahead to what is to be done and maintaining caution in speaking. However, when circumspection is specified in relation to contemplation, it is said to be the exploration of the mind (*animi*), by which the mind contemplates amid earthly things with understanding, counsel, and delight. The mind traverses earthly things with understanding; deliberates and inquires about them with counsel; and discerns and chooses among them with delight" ("Circumspectio namque species prudentie dicitur, provida gerendorum vel sermonum cautela. Quoniam vero circumspectio a contemplatione specificatur, anima exploratio dicitur, qua animus intellectu, consilio et delectu inter mundana contemplatur. Animus enim intellectu per mundane discurrit; consilio, de mundanis deliberat et inquirit; delectu, inter ipsa discernit et elegit" [Baron, 44.16–21]).

9   Apoc. 4:6.

10 Matt. 10:18–20.

11 Ambrose, *Homiliae in Hexaemeron*, 4.1.2 (PL 14.201); Pseudo-Rhaban Maur, *Allegoriae in Sacram Scripturam* (PL 112.1057); Warner of St Victor, *Gregorianum* 1.5 (PL 193.37B); Plato, *Republic*, 508a–e.

12 Godfrey here makes use of the appropriation of power, wisdom, and goodness to Father, Son, and Holy Spirit respectively, which Hugh of St Victor pioneered in *On the Three Days* (ed. Poriel; tr. Feiss, VTT 1).

13 Deut. 32:11; Exod. 19:4.

14   Matt. 23:37.
15   Apoc. 4:6–8: "Around the throne, and on each side of it, are four living creatures, full of eyes in front and behind. The first living creature is like a lion; the second is like an ox; the third has a face like a human face, and the fourth is like a flying eagle. And the four living creatures, each of them with six wings, are full of eyes all around." The author of the Apocalypse is drawing on Ezek. 1:1–14; 10:1–22. In Christian tradition, the four living creatures mentioned in this passage were interpreted as symbols of the four evangelists. The eagle was assigned to John because his gospel opens with the lofty theology of the divine Word. See, for example, Irenaeus, *Adv. haer.* 3.11.8 (tr. ANF 1:428–855); Augustine, *De consensu evangelistarum* 1.6.9. (PL 34.1046–47; tr. NFPF 6:80–81); Jerome, *Commentariorum in Evangelium Matthaei, prol.* (PL 26.19B–20A); Gregory, *Hom. in Ezek.* 1.4.1 (PL 76.315AC). These representations of the four evangelists appear frequently in the Book of Kells; e.g., fols. 27v, 129v, 290v, reproduced in *The Book of Kells*, intro. Peter Brown ([New York: Alfred A. Knopf, 1980); also, Bernard Meehan, *The Book of Kells* (New York: Thames and Hudson, 1994), 36–43.
16   Apoc. 4:7.
17   Rom. 8:26.
18   Alan of Lille, *De sex alis cherubim* (PL 210.276–77); Pseudo-Hugh of St Victor, *Misc.* 4.87, "On the six wings of the Seraphim," 4.89, "On the four feathers of the living creatures," 4.90, "On the six wings of the living creatures of the New Law" (PL 177.739D–740A).
19   "amittit": "loses," perhaps by disciplining the flesh. However, the next paragraph has "emittit," "sends out," which could be the proper reading here as well.
20   Song of Songs 2:4 (Vulg).
21   In par. 207, Godfrey wrote that roundness signifies eternity.
22   In Latin, "spirit" (*spiritus*) is masculine and "flesh" (*caro, carnis*) is feminine. In this sentence, I have translated pronouns referring to "spirit" as neuter ("it"), and those referring to "flesh" as feminine ("she").
23   Matt. 5:43.
24   Matt. 5:44; Luke 6:27.
25   Here and elsewhere in the *Microcosmus* (especially chaps. 162–64, see Delhaye, *Étude*, 22 note 3), Godfrey makes use of the techniques of emerging Scholasticism. Here he raises an objection based on an apparent contradiction and in his reply solves it by distinguishing several meanings of "nature."
26   Pseudo-Hugh of St Victor, *Quaestiones in epistolas S. Pauli, ad Ephesios*, q. 11 (PL 175.570); *Misc.* 1.168 (PL 177.561). These two passages distinguish three meanings of human nature: that nature before the Fall, what remains of the good of that nature after the Fall, nature as corrupted by sin.
27   "sociale animal": Seneca, *De beneficiis*, 7.1.7 (Basore, 3:458). The same expression occurs in chap. 172 (Delhaye, 192.7).
28   In what follows Godfrey is going to use the verb "deficere" and the noun "defectus" often. In this context the verb means "to fail or fall," and the noun means "failing, failure, lack."
29   Matt. 5:44; Luke 6:27, 35.
30   "vitium": In modern English, "vice" means a habit of sin ("he fell into the vice of avarice") and thus is the opposite of "virtue," or it means moral squalor ("a den of vice"). In twelfth-century Latin, the meaning varies; often *vitium* is used to refer to the inclinations that are the roots of sin. This usage goes back through Cassian to Evagrius, the fourth-century monk and theologian who spoke in a systematic way of "eight thoughts" that must be controlled by the Christian who seeks self-mastery (Evagrius' *apatheia*) and purity of heart (Cassian's term), that is to say, "ordered love." Although these became known as the "seven deadly sins," they are not so much sins as imperfect dispositions or inclinations, which may or may not develop into habits of sin.
31   Delhaye, 236.27–29: "inimicos invenit dum eis nec in bono concordare potuit nec a malo discordare voluit."

[32] Matt. 5:44.

[33] Cf. Matt. 5:46; Luke 6:32; John 15:19.

[34] John 13:15; 1 Pet. 2:21.

[35] John 15:13.

[36] Reading "deficit" for "defecit."

[37] John 15:13.

[38] Phil. 1:23; Ps. 15:9 (Vulg).

[39] Ps. 62:2 (Vulg).

[40] Apoc. 6:9.

[41] Apoc. 6:11. Translation based on Ronald A. Knox, tr. *The New Testament* (1945; reprinted Springfield, IL: Templegate, 1997), 267.

[42] Apoc. 6:9.

[43] Apoc. 6:9.

[44] Isa. 31:5.

[45] "pupillam": a diminutive of "pupa" (girl, damsel), that can mean "girl," "pupil of the eye," or "eye." "The apple of one's eye" means not just someone one loves very much, but the pupil of the eye in which that beloved is reflected. According to http://www.phrases.org.uk, King Alfred used the expression in his Anglo-Saxon translation of Gregory's *Pastoral Rule*.

[46] Ps. 16:8 (Vulg).

[47] Ps. 90:1–2, 4 (Vulg). "Sheltered under his arms, under his wings nestling, thou art safe" (*The Old Testament*, tr. Ronald A. Knox [New York: Sheed and Ward, 1950] 2:864. In Latin, *penna* (alt. *pinna*) means feather, but by metonymy it can mean wing. Heretofore it has been translated as "feathers," since Godfrey contrasts it to "ala" (wing).

[48] John 15:13; 1 John 3:16.

[49] John 15:13; 1 John 3:16.

[50] Ps. 2:6.

[51] Warner of St Victor, *Gregorianum* 3.11 (PL 193.101D-102A) makes the same application of the four faces of the four living creatures alluded to in Ezek. 1:10, which, like the Cherubim of the *Microcosmus*, had three pairs of wings. See note 15 above.

[52] Warner of St Victor, *Gregorianum* 2.1 (PL 193.65).

[53] Deut. 32:11.

[54] Ps. 16:8 (Vulg).

[55] John 15:13.

[56] "ad cuius mortis": the Latin text is peculiar; I have chosen to correct "mortis" to "mortem."

[57] Matt. 24:28.

[58] John 15:13. The reference to good pastors articulates a major concern of the canons of twelfth-century St Victor. On this, see Margot Fassler, *Gothic Song: Victorine Sequences and Augustinian Reform in Twelfth-Century Paris*, Cambridge Studies in Medieval and Renaissance Music (New York: Cambridge, 1993); Hugh Feiss, "Preaching by Word and Example: Pastoral Reform and Practice at Twelfth-Century St Victor," forthcoming.

[59] Apoc. 6:9.

[60] The "horns of the altar" were projections at each corner of a stone altar: see, for example, Exod. 27:2; Exod. 29:12; Lev. 4:7; 1 Kings 1:50. On Hugh's references to the "horns of the altar" in his *Archa* and *Libellus*, see Conrad Rudolph, *"First, I Find the Center Point": Reading the Text of Hugh of Saint Victor's The Mystic Ark* (Philadelphia: American Philosophical Society, 2006) 30–31 and note 69.

[61] Eph. 4:13.

[62] 1 Cor. 15:24.

[63] "magistra": the feminine of "magister," teacher, master.

[64] "domina": feminine of "Lord."

[65] Correcting "nostri" to "nostis." John 21:17.

[66] Ps. 37:10 (Vulg).

[67] Ps. 56:2 (Vulg).
[68] "confessio oris": In medieval theology, "confessio oris" (confession of the mouth) was most often associated with "contritio cordis" (contrition of the heart) and "satisfactio operis" (work of satisfaction) to form the three parts of sacramental confession or penitence. The phrase "confessio oris" occurs in Rom. 10:10, but there it means confession of faith.
[69] Ps. 83:4 (Vulg).
[70] "inventus sum": Acts 8:40.
[71] "iuxta altare": see, for example, Lev. 6:10.
[72] Acts 12:11.
[73] Correcting "omnis" to "omnes."
[74] See introduction, note 20.
[75] This section is one of the most profound and moving passages in Victorine literature. There is much to say about it, some of which has been said in the introduction. It would be worthwhile to trace its most noteworthy ideas back to the writings of Hugh of St Victor and in other Victorine authors. Among those ideas are the following: The human being is a microcosm of the entire created universe made in the image and likeness of God. The soul is beloved and therefore a lover. The marital love that unites spouses is a unique human expression of the love of God and the soul. Christ emptied himself and became incarnate by assuming a human nature ("assumptus homo"). The distinction between consummated and unconsummated marriage, important in medieval marriage law and theology, has an application to the relationship between the soul and God. The union of Christ with the soul is immediate, ineffable, and inseparable.
[76] Gen 1:26; 5:1.
[77] "perfecta": one might correct this to "perfecte" ("perfectly"), so that it modifies the verb "know."
[78] Peter Lombard, *Sent.* 1.17.1–2 (Quarrachi, 106ff.); Hugh of St Victor, *Sacr.* 2.13.12 (PL 176.547); Pseudo-Hugh of St Victor, *Allegoriae in Novum Testamentum, Rom.* 6 (PL 175.900 BC).
[79] "sponse sponsi desiderio estuantis": Hugh of St Victor, *Soliloquy on the Betrothal Gift of the Soul* and *The Praise of the Bridegroom*, both translated in this volume; Bernard, SCC, 72 (PL 183.1133).
[80] Song of Songs 1:1 (Vulg).
[81] Song of Songs 1:1–2 (Vulg).
[82] Phil. 2:7.
[83] Gen. 1:26; 5:1.
[84] Correcting "inuiria" to "iniuria."
[85] "inanicione": See Phil. 2:7: "semet ipsum exinanivit formam servi accipiens" ("He emptied himself, accepting the form of a slave").
[86] "Natural" here means "by divine creation," apart from the further gift of restorative and elevating grace. Cf. Osborne, *Love of Self,* 6.
[87] "gratuitus": neither "gratuitous" nor "gracious" fully captures the meaning of this term; hence I translate it, "by freely given grace."
[88] Gen 1:26; 5:1.
[89] The triad, power-wisdom-goodness, loomed large in the works translated in the first volume of this series, particularly in Hugh of St Victor's *On the Three Days*. Here, however, the triad is not explicitly appropriated to the three persons (Father-power; Son-wisdom; and Holy Spirit-goodness). Moreover, when he here introduces the Incarnation (which is the topic of the rest of the *Microcosmus*), Godfrey varies the order of the attributes to wisdom-goodness-power, which may signify that that Incarnate Wisdom reveals to humankind the path of goodness, which leads to the Father. Regarding the divine attributes of power, wisdom, and goodness, Delhaye adds another to the texts discussed VTT 1: Pseudo-Hugh of St Victor, *Misc.* 5, 67 (PL 177.794CD): "The countenance of the Father is power; that of the Son is wisdom; that of the Holy Spirit, kindness. The light of the countenance is memory, understand-

ing, and will. Humankind fell from memory into forgetfulness; from understanding into ignorance; from will into the abuse of rectitude. But God sent His Son who brought faith, hope, and charity. By these, this image, this countenance, is signed upon us, that is, impressed on our reason. Faith drives away forgetfulness by restoring memory. Hope puts ignorance to flight by cleansing the understanding. Charity extinguishes the abuse of righteousness by lifting up the will. Therefore, the countenance of the Trinity *in charity* is power, wisdom, and kindness. Through power he created all things; through wisdom he arranged all things; through kindness he governs and fosters all things. But because we cannot advance to see his face, we have the light, that is, the image and likeness. Through the image, that is, through memory, understanding, and will, we apprehend him. Through the likeness we express him in ourselves, that is, through faith, hope, and charity" ("Vultus Patris est potentia; Filii, sapientia; Spiritus sancti, benignitas. Lumen vultus est memoria, intelletus, voluntas. De memoria cecidit homo in oblivionem; de intellectu in ignorantiam; de voluntate in rectitudinis abusionem. Sed Deus misit Filium suum qui attulit fidem, spem, charitatem. Quibus haec imago, hic vultus signatur super nos, id est, rationi imprimitur. Fides pellit oblivionem, memoriam restituendo; spes ignorantiam fugat, intellectum purgando; charitas rectitudinis abusionem extinguit, voluntatem relevando. Vultus itaque Trinitatis in charitate est potentia, sapientia, benignitas. Per potentiam cuncta creatvit; per sapientiam cuncta disposuit; per benignitatem cuncta gubernat et fovet. Sed quia ad vultum videndum accedere non possumus, habemus lumen, id est imaginem et similitudienm. Per imaginem ipsum apprehendimus, id est, per memoriam, intellectum, et voluntatem. Per similitudinem eum nobis exprimimus, id est, per fidem, spem, et charitatem").

90   Gen. 1:26; 5:1.

BIBLIOGRAPHY

Primary Sources

Victorine Authors

Gilduin of St Victor. *Libellus de accentibus cum prologo*. Ed. Luc Jocqué and Dominique Poirel, "De Donat à Saint-Victor: un 'De accentibus' inédit." *La tradition vive. Mélanges d'histoire des textes en l'honneur de Louis Holtz*. Ed. Pierre Lardet. Turnhout: Brepols, 2003. Pp. 181–92.

Liber ordinis Sancti Victoris Parisiensis. Ed. Lucas Jocqué and Ludovicus Milis. CCCM 61. Turnhout: Brepols, 1984.

Hugh of St Victor. *Chronicon vel de tribus maximis circumstantiis gestorum* (Partial ed. W. M. Green, "Hugo of St Victor *De tribus maximis circumstantiis gestorum*." *Speculum* 18 (1943): 484–93. Partial ed. G. Waitz. "Chronica quae dicitur Hugonis de Sancto Victore." *Monumenta Germaniae Historica, Scriptores*, 24. Hanover, 1879. Pp. 88–97. Partial ed. Roger Baron. "Hugues de Saint-Victor lexicographe," *Cultura neolatina*, 16 (1956): 109–45 [Partial tr. Mary Carruthers. "The Three Best Memory Aids." In *The Medieval Craft of Memory: An Anthology of Texts and Pictures*. Ed. Mary Carruthers and Jan M. Ziolkowski. Philadelphia: University of Pennsylvania, 2002. Pp. 32–40.

_____. *De archa Noe, Libellus de formatione arche*. Ed. P. Sicard. Corpus Christianorum Continuatio Mediaevalis 176. Turnhout: Brepols, 2001.

_____. *De tribus diebus*. Ed. D. Poirel. Corpus Christianorum Continuatio Mediaevalis 177. Turnhout: Brepols, 2002. Pp. 3–70. *On the Three Days*. Tr. Feiss. VTT 1: 61–102.

_____. *Didascalicon: De studio legendi*. Ed. Charles Henry Buttimer. The Catholic University of America, Studies in Medieval and Renaissance Latin, vol. 10. Washington: The Catholic University Press, 1939. Tr. Jerome Taylor. *The Didascalicon of Hugh of St Victor*. Records of Western

Civilization Series. New York: Columbia University Press, 1991. Ed. and tr. Thilo Offergeld. Hugo von Sankt Viktor, *Didascalicon de Studio Legendi/Studienbuch.* Fontes Christiani 27 Freiburg: Herder, 1997. Tr. Michel Lemoine. Hugues de Saint-Victor, *L'Art de lire/Didascalicon.* Sagesses chretiennes. Paris: Cerf, 1991.

——————————. *Didascalicon, I doni della promessa divina. L'essenza dell'amore. Discorso in lode del divino amore.* Tr. Vincenzo Liccaro. Milan: Rusconi, 1987.

——————————. "Diligens scrutator sacri eloquii: An Introduction to Scriptual Exegesis by Hugh of St Victor Preserved at Admont Library (MS 671)." Ed. Ralf Stammberger. In *Manucripts and Medieval Culture: Reform and Renewal in Twelfth-Century Germany.* Ed. Alison I. Beach. Medieval Church Studies 13. Turnhout: Brepols, 2007. Pp. 272–83.

——————————. *The Divine Love. The Two Treatises* De laude caritatis *and* De amore sponsi ad sponsam *by Hugh of St Victor.* Tr. A Religious of the C.S.M.V. [Sr. Penelope Lawson] London: A. R. Mowbray, 1956.

——————————. "Le *Liber Magistri Hugonis.*" Ed. D. van den Eynde. *Franciscan Studies* 23 (1963): 268–99.

——————————. *On the Sacraments of the Christian Faith (De Sacramentis) of Hugh of Saint Victor.* The Mediaeval Academy of America Publications 58. Tr. Roy Deferrari. Cambridge: The Mediaeval Academy of America, 1951.

——————————. *L'oeuvre de Hugues de Saint-Victor* 1. Ed. H. B. Feiss and P. Sicard. Tr. (French) D. Poirel, H. Rochais, and P. Sicard. Intro. and notes D. Poirel. Sous La règle de saint Augustin. Turnhout: Brepols, 1997.

——————————. *L'oeuvre de Hugues de Saint-Victor* 2. Ed. and tr. B. Jollès. Sous La règle de saint Augustin. Turnhout: Brepols, 2000.

——————————. *Opera omnia.* PL 175–77. Ed. J. P. Migne. Paris, 1854.

——————————. *Opera Propaedeutica.* Ed. R. Baron. Notre Dame, IN: University of Notre Dame Press, 1966.

——————————. "Quelques recueils d'écrits attribués à Hugues de Saint-Victor." Ed. O. Lottin. RTAM 25 (1958): 248–84.

——————————. "Questions inédits de Hugues de Saint-Victor." Ed. O. Lottin. RTAM 26 (1959): 177–213; 27 (1960): 42–60.

——————————. *Selected Spiritual Writings.* Tr. a Religious of C.S.M.V. [Sr. Penelope Lawson] London: Faber and Faber, 1962.

_____. *"Sententiae magistri Hugonis Parisiensis."* Ed. L. Ott. RTAM 27 (1960): 29–41.

_____. *Six opuscules spirituels.* Ed. and tr. Roger Baron. SC 155. Paris: Cerf, 1969. [Earlier translations of the same texts in. *Textes spirituels de Hugues de Saint-Victor.* Tr. Roger Baron. Tournai: Desclée, 1961.]

_____. *I tre giorni dell'invisibile luce; L'unione del corpo e dello spirito.* Tr. Vincenzo Liccaro. Classici della Filosofia Cristiana 6. Forence: Sansoni, 1974.

_____. "Ugo di San Vittore 'auctor' delle *Sententiae de divinitate.*" Ed. A. Piazzoni. *Studi Medievali, 3rd series.* 23 (1982): 861–955. Tr. Christopher P. Evans. VTT 1:103–77.

Adam of St Victor. *Sequentiae.* Ed. G. Dreves and Clemens Blume. *Analecta Hymnica*, vols. 54 and 55 (Leipzig: 1915, 1922). Ed. Jean Grosfillier. *Les sequences d'Adam de Saint-Victor: Étude littéraire (poétique et rhétorique). Textes et traductions, commentaires,* Bibliotheca Victorina 20. Turnhout: Brepols, 2008. Pp. 252–481. Ed. E. Misset and P. Aubry. *Les proses d'Adam de Saint-Victor, texte et musique.* Paris: 1900. Ed. and tr. Bernadette Jollés. *Quatorze proses du xiie siècle à louange de Marie,* Sous la Règle de saint Augustin. Turnhout: Brepols, 1994. Ed. and tr. Digby Wrangham. Adam of St Victor. *Liturgical Poetry,* 3 vols. London: Kegan Paul, Trench, 1881.

Achard of St Victor. *De discretione animae, spiritus et mentis.* Ed. G. Morin, "Un traité faussement attribué à Adam de Saint-Victor." *Aus der Geisteswelt des Mittelalters*, BGPTMA, Supplementband 3/1 (Münster: Aschendorff, 1935), 251–62. Ed. N. M. Häring, "Gilbert of Poitiers, Author of the 'De discretione animae, spiritus et mentis' commonly attributed to Achard of Saint Victor." MS 22 (1960): 148–91. Tr. Hugh Feiss. *On the Distinction of Soul, Spirit and Mind.* Achard of Saint Victor. *Works.* CS 165. Kalamazoo: Cistercian Publications, 2001. Pp. 353–74.

_____. *De unitate Dei et pluralitate creaturarum.* Ed. and tr. E. Martineau. Saint-Lambert des Bois: Franc-Dire, 1987. Tr. Hugh Feiss. *On the Unity of God.* Achard of Saint Victor. *Works.* CS 165. Kalamazoo: Cistercian Publications, 2001. Pp. 375–480.

_____. *Sermons inédits,* ed. Châtillon, TPMA 17. Paris: J. Vrin, 1970. Tr. Hugh Feiss, *Works,* CS 165. Kalamazoo: Cistercian Publications, 2001. Pp. 59–351.

Richard of Saint-Victor. *De arca Moysi* [*De arca mystia; De contemplatione; Benjamin major*] Ed. Marc-Aeilko Aris. *Contemplatio. Philosophische Studien zum Traktat Benjamin Maior des Richard von St. Victor.* Fuldaer Studien 6. Frankfurt: Josef Knecht, 1996. Pp. [4]–[148]. PL 196.63–202B. Tr. Grover A. Zinn. *The Twelve Patriarchs, The Mystical Ark, and Book Three on the Trinity.* The Classics of Western Spirituality. New York: Paulist, 1979. Pp. 149–370.

_____. *De quatuor gradibus violentae caritatis.* Ed. and tr. Gervais Dumeige. In *Ives, Épître à Séverin sur la charité. Richard de Saint-Victor. Les quatre degrés de la violente charité.* TPMA 3. Paris: J. Vrin, 1955.

_____. *De questionibus regule sancti Augustini solutis.* Ed. M. L. Colker. "Richard of Saint Victor and the anonymous of Bridlington." *Traditio* 18 (1962): 181–227.

_____. "*De statu interioris hominis.*" Ed. J. Ribaillier. *Archives d'histoire doctrinale et littéraire du moyen-âge* 34 (1967): 7–128.

_____. *De Trinitate.* PL 196.887–992. Tr. Hans Urs von Balthasr. *Die Dreieinigkeit.* Christliche Meister 4. Einsiedeln: Johannes Verlag, 1980.

_____. *De Trinitate.* Ed. J. Ribaillier. TPMA 6. Paris: J. Vrin, 1958. Tr. Christopher P. Evans. VTT 1:195–382.

_____. *La Trinité.* SC 63. Ed. and tr. G. Salet. Paris: Cerf, 1959.

_____. *Les douze Patriarches ou Benjamin Minor.* Ed. and tr. Jean Châtillon and M. Duchet-Suchaux. SC 419. Paris: Cerf, 1997. Tr. Grover A. Zinn. *The Twelve Patriarchs, The Mystical Ark, and Book Three on the Trinity.* Classics of Western Spirituality. New York: Paulist Press, 1979. Pp. 51–147.

_____. *L'Édit d'Alexandre ou les trois processions.* Sermons et opuscules spirituels inédits 1. Ed. Jean Châtillon and W. J. Tulloch. Tr. J. Barthélemy. Paris: Desclée de Brouwer, 1951.

_____. *Liber exceptionum.* Ed. Jean Châtillon. TPMA 5. Paris: J. Vrin, 1958.

_____. *Omnia opera.* PL 196.

_____. *Opuscules théologiques.* Ed. J. Ribaillier. TPMA 15. Paris: J. Vrin, 1967.

_____. *Selected Writings on Contemplation.* Tr. Clare Kirchberger. London: Faber and Faber, 1957.

_____. *Sermones centum*. PL 177.901–1210. [Among works of Hugh of St Victor].

_____. *Trois opuscules spirituels de Richard de Saint-Victor: Textes inédits accompagnés d'études critiques et notes*. Ed. Jean Châtillon. Paris: Études Augustiniennes, 1986.

_____. *The Twelve Patriarchs, The Mystical Ark, and Book Three on the Trinity*. The Classics of Western Spirituality. Tr. Grover A. Zinn. New York: Paulist, 1979.

Pseudo-Hugh of St Victor. *Questiones et decisiones in Epistolas D. Pauli*. PL 175.431B–634A.

_____. *De bestiis*. PL 177.14–164D.

_____. *Expositio super Regulam S. Augustini*. PL 176.881–924A.

De contemplatione et eius speciebus. Ed. Roger Baron. Monumenta Christiana selecta 2. Tournai: Desclée, 1955.

Godfrey of St Victor. *Fons philosophiae*. Ed. Pierre Michaud-Quantin. Analecta mediaevalia Namurcensia 8. Louvain: Nauwelaerts/ Namur: Godenne, 1956. Tr. Edward Synan. *The Fountain of Philosophy*. Toronto: Pontifical Institute of Mediaeval Studies, 1972.

_____. *Microcosmus*. Ed. Philippe Delhaye. Lille: Facultés catholiques, 1951.

_____. "Praeconium Augustini." Ed. Philip Damon, MS 22 (1960): 92–107.

_____. *Sermo in generali capitulo*. Ed. Helmut Riedlinger. In *Die Makellosigkeit der Kirche in den Lateinischen Hoheliedkommentaren des Mittelalters*, BGPTMA 38/3. Münster: Aschendorff, 1958. Pp. 188–93.

_____. *Sermo de omnibus sanctis et specialiter de Sancto Victore*. Partially ed. Philippe Delhaye. *Le Microcosmus de Godefroy de Saint-Victor. Étude théologique*. Lille: Facultés catholiques/Gembloux: J. Duculot, 1951. Pp. 232–33.

_____. *Sermo in die omnium sanctorum*. Ed. Philippe Delhaye. *Le Microcosmus de Godefroy de Saint-Victor, Étude théologique* Lille: Facultés catholiques/Gembloux: J. Duculot, 1951. Pp. 233–43.

Walter of St Victor. *Contra quatuor labyrinthos Franciae*. Ed. P. Glorieux. "Le *Contra quatuor labyrinthos Franciae* de Gauthier de Saint-Victor." *AHDLMA 19* (Année 1952). (Paris, 1953): 105–335.

————. *Sermons*. Ed. Jean Châtillon. *Galteri a Sancto Victore et quorundam aliorum, Sermones ineditos tringinta sex*. CCCM 30. Turnhout: Brepols, 1975.

Maurice of Saint Victor. *Sermones*. Ed. Jean Châtillon. *Galteri a Sancto Victore et quorundorum aliorum, Sermones ineditos tringinta sex*. CCCM 30. Turnhout: Brepols, 1975.

Warner of St Victor, *Gregorianum*. PL 193.13–462A.

Classical Authors

Catullus. *Carmina*. Texts available at http://en.wikipedia.org/wiki/Poetry_of_Catullus

Juvenal. *Satirae*. Ed. C. F. Hermann. Leipzig: Teubner, 1883.

Seneca. *Moral Essays*. 3 vols. Ed. John W. Basore. Loeb Classical Library. Cambridge, MA: Harvard University Press, 1964.

Virgil. *Eclogues, Georgics, Aeneid I–VI*. Ed. G. P. Goold. Loeb Classical Library. Cambridge, MA: Harvard University Press, 1999.

Editions of the Bible

Biblia sacra cum glossa interlineari ordinaria. . . . Venice, 1588.

Biblia sacra iuxta Vulgatam versionem. Ed. Robert Weber, et. al. 4th ed. Stuttgart: Deutsche Bibelgesellschaft, 1994.

Bibliorum sacrorum Latinae versions antiquae seu Vetus Italica. Ed. P. Sabatier. 3 vols. in 6. Paris: Franciscus Didot, 1751.

Cantici canticorum vetus latina translatio a S. Hieronymo ad graecum textum hexaplarem emendata. Ed. Albertus Vaccari. Rome: Storia e Letteratura, 1959.

Douay-Rheims (online: www.drbo.org).

Knox, Ronald A. *The Old Testament*. 2 vols. New York: Sheed and Ward, 1950. *The New Testament*. Springfield, IL: Templegate, 1997.

Commentaries on the Song of Songs

Origen. *In Canticum canticorum commentarium. In Canticum canticorum homiliae*. Ed. W. Baehrens. GCS 33. 1925. Tr. R. P. Lawson. ACW 26. New York: Newman/Paulist, 1957.

Philonis Carpasii. *Commentarium in Canticum canticorum, ex antiqua versione latine Epiphanii Scholastici*. Ed. Aldo Ceresa-Gastaldo. Corona Patrum. Turin: Società Editrice Internazionale, 1979.

Apponius. *Explanatio in Canticum canticorum.* PLS 1.799–1031. *Commentaire sur le Cantique des Cantiques.* Ed. and tr. B. Vregille and L. Neyrand. 3 vols. SC 420, 421, 430. Paris: Cerf, 1997–9.

Bede. *In Cantica canticorum.* Ed. D. Hurst. CCL 119B. Turnhout: Brepols, 1983.

Robert of Tumbalenia. *Super Cantica canticorum.* PL 79.471–548A.

Paterius. *Expositio veteris et novi testamenti.* PL 79.683–1136D.

Alcuin. *Compendium in Canticum canticorum.* PL 100.639–666D = PL 83.1119–1132C.

Angelôme of Luxeuil. *Enarrationes in Cantica canticorum.* PL 115.551–628D.

Haimo of Auxerre. *Enarratio in Canticum canticorum.* PL 117.295–358D = PL 70.1055–1106C.

Anselm of Laon. *Enarrationes in Cantica canticorum.* PL 162.1187–1228B.

Bruno of Segni. *Expositio in Cantica canticorum.* PL 164.1233–1288B.

Rupert of Deutz. *Commentaria in Canticum canticorum.* Ed. Rhaban Haacke. CCCM 26. Turnhout: Brepols, 1974.

Glossa ordinaria In Canticum canticorum. Ed. Mary Dove, *Glossa ordinaria.* Part 22. CCCM 170. Turnhout: Brepols, 1997.

Philip of Harveng. *Commentaria in Cantica canticorum.* PL 203.181–490B.

Thomas the Cistercian. *Cantica canticorum.* PL 206.15–862.

Geoffrey of Auxerre. *Expositio in Cantica canticorum.* Ed. Ferruccio Gastaldelli. Temi e Testi 19. Rome: Storia e Letteratura, 1974.

John of Mantua. *In Cantica canticorum.* Ed. Bernhard Bischoff and Burkhard Taeger. Spicilegium Friburgense 19. Fribourg, Switzerland: Universitätsverlag, 1973.

Patristic Authors

Physiologus. Tr. Michael J. Curly. Austin: University of Texas Press, 1939.

Acta Johannis. Ed. Eric Junod and Jean-Daniel Kestli. Corpus Christianorum Scriptorum Series Apocryphorum 1–2. Turnhout: Brepols, 1983.

Origen. *Homiliae in Genesim.* Ed. W. A. Baehrens. GCS 29. Leipzig, 1920. Tr. Ronald Heine. FOC 71. Washington, DC: Catholic University of America Press, 1982.

Basil of Caesarea. *Contra Eunomium.* PG 29.497–669.

Cyril of Jerusalem. *Catecheses.* PG 33.331–1180.

Ambrose. *Homiliae in Hexaemeron.* PL 14.123A–274A.

_____. *De spiritu sancto.* Ed. Faller. CSEL 79. Vienna, 1964.

Jerome. *Commentariorum in Evangelium Matthaei.* CCL 77. Edited by D. Hurst and M. Adriaen. Turnhout: Brepols, 1969 (PL 26.15–218).

—————. *Liber interpretationis Hebraicorum nominum.* Ed. P. de Lagarde. CCL 72. Turnhout: Brepols, 1969. Pp. 58–161.

—————. *Selected Letters.* Ed. and tr. F. A. Wright. Loeb Classical Library. Cambridge, MA: Harvard University Press, 1975.

—————. *Tractatus sive homiliae in Psalmos. In Marci evangelium. Alia varia argumenta.* Ed. G. Morin, et al. CCL 78. Turnhout: Brepols, 1958.

Augustine. *Confessiones.* Ed. Pius Knöll. CSEL 33. Vienna: F. Tempsky, 1896. Ed. L. Verheijen. *Confessionum Libri XIII.* CCL 37. Turnhout: Brepols, 1990. Pp: 1–273. Ed. J. J. O'Donnell. *Confessions.* 3 vols. Oxford: Clarendon, 1992. Tr. Maria Boulding. Hyde Park, NY: New City Press, 1997. Tr. H. Chadwick. New York: Oxford, 1991.

—————. *Contra Faustum Manichaeum.* PL 42.207–518. Tr. Roland Teske. *Answer to Faustus, A Manichee.* FOC 71. Washington, DC: Catholic University of America Press, 1982.

—————. *De catechizandis rudibus.* Ed. G. Combès and J. Farges. *Le magistère Chrétien.* Oeuvres de saint Augustin 11. Paris: Desclée de Brouwer, 1949. Pp. 28–147. Ed. I. B. Bauer. *De fide rerum invisibilium, et alia.* CCL 46. Turnout: Brepols, 1969. Tr. Raymond Canning. *Instructing Beginners in Faith.* Hyde Park, NY: New City Press, 2007.

—————. *De civitate Dei.* Ed. B. Dombart and A. Kalb. CCL 47–48. Turnhout: Brepols, 1955. Tr. H. Bettenson. *The City of God.* New York: Penguin, 1986. Tr. R. W. Dyson. New York: Cambridge, 1998.

—————. *De consensu evangelistarum.* PL 34.101–1239.

—————. *De diversis quaestionibus LXXXIII.* Ed. Almut Mutzenbecher. CCL 44A. Turnhout: Brepols, 1975. Pp. 3–249 (PL 40.11–100). Tr. Boniface Ramsey. *Responses to Miscellaneous Questions.* Hyde Park, NY: New City Press, 2008.

—————. *De doctrina Christiana.* Ed. J. Martin. CCL 32. Turnhout: Brepols, 1962. Pp. 1–167. Ed. G. Combès and J. Farges. *Le magistère chrétien.* Pp. 168–541. Tr. Edmund Hill. *Teaching Christianity.* Hyde Park, NY: New City Press, 1996.

—————. *De fide et symbolo.* Ed. J. Zycha. CSEL 41. Vienna: F. Tempsky, 1900. Ed. J. Rivière. *Exposés généraux,* 8–75. Ed. and tr. E. P. Meijering. Amsterdam: J. C. Gieben, 1987.

Tr. in *On Christian Belief*. Hyde Park, NY: New City Press, 2005.

_____. *De Genesi ad litteram*. Ed. J. Zycha, CSEL 28.1. Vienna: F. Tempsky, 1894. Pp. 1–456. Tr. Edmund Hill. *The Literal Meaning of Genesis*. In *On Genesis*. Hyde Park, NY: New City Press, 2002. Pp. 155–506.

_____. *De libero arbitrio*. Ed. W. Green. CCL 29. Turnhout: Brepols, 1970. Tr. Mark Pontifex. *The Problem of Free Choice*, ACW 22. Westminster, MD: Newman, 1955.

_____. *De spiritu et littera*. Ed. C. Urba and J. Zycha. CSEL 60. Vienna: F. Tempsky, 1913.

_____. *De Trinitate*. Ed. W. J. Mountain and F. Glorie. CCL 50, 50A. Turnhout: Brepols, 1968. Tr. Edmund Hill. *The Trinity*. Hyde Park, NY: New City Press, 1991.

_____. *De vera religione*. Tr. K.-D. Daur. CCL 32. Turnhout: Brepols, 1962. Pp. 171–260. Tr. J. H. S. Burleigh. *On True Religion*. Chicago: Henry Regnery, 1968. Tr. Boniface Ramsey, in *On Christian Belief*. Hyde Park, NY: New City Press, 2005.

_____. *Enarrationes in Psalmos*. Ed. E. Dekkers and J. Fraipont. CCL 38–40. Turnhout: Brepols, 1956. *Expositions of the Psalms*. Tr. Maria Boulding. 6 vols. Hyde Park, NY: New City Press, 2000–2004.

_____. *Enchiridion ad Laurentium de fide, spe et caritate*. Ed. J. Rivière. *Exposés généraux de la foi*. Oeuvres de saint Augustin 9. Paris: Desclée de Brouwer, 1947. Pp. 102–327. Ed. E. Evans. CCL 46 Turnhout: Brepols, 1969. Tr. Bruce Harbert. *The Augustine Catechism: The Enchiridion on Faith, Hope, and Love*. Hyde Park, NY: New City Press, 2008.

_____. *Epistolae*. Ed. A. Goldacher. CSEL 34, 44, 57, 58. Vienna: F. Tempsky, 1895–1923. Ed. J. Divjak. *Epistolae ex duobus codicibus nuper in lucem prolatae*. CSEL 88. Vienna: Hoelder-Pichler-Tempsky, 1981. Tr. Roland Teske. *Letters*. 4 vols. Hyde Park, NY: New City Press, 2001-5.

_____. *In Johannis evangelium tractatus*. Ed. R. Willems. CCL 36. Turnhout: Brepols, 1954. Tr. John W. Rettig. *Tractates on the Gospel of John*. FOC 78, 79, 88, 90, 92. Washington, DC: The Catholic University of America, 1988–95.

_____. *In Primam epistolam Joannis*. Ed. P. Agaësse, *Commentaire de la Première Épître de S. Jean*. SC 75. Paris: Cerf, 1994. Tr. John W. Rettig. *Tractates on the First Epistle of John*.

FOC 92. Washington, DC: The Catholic University of America, 1995. Pp. 97–277.

—————————. *Soliloquia*. Ed. Pierre de Labriolle. Oeuvres de saint Augustin 1/5. Paris: Desclée de Brouwer, 1948. Tr. Thomas F. Gilligan. Works 1. FOC. 5. New York: CIMA, 1948.

Peter Chrysologus. *Sermones*. PL 52.183–666D.

Gregory of Tours. *Historia Francorum*. Ed. W Arndt and Br. Krush. Monumenta Germaniae historica. Rerum Merov. 1. Hanover: Hahn, 1885.

Gregory the Great. *Dialogues*. Ed. A. de Vogüé. SC 160, 265 (Paris; Cerf, 1979–80). Tr. Odo Zimmerman. FOC 39. Reprint. Washington, DC: Catholic Univeristy of America Press, 2002.

—————————. *Homiliae in Evangelia*. Ed. R. Étaix, CCL 76. Turnhout: Brepols, 1999.

—————————. *Homiliae in Hiezechielem*. Ed. M. Adriaen. CCL 142. Turnhout: Brepols, 1971. Ed. and tr. Charles Morel. *Homélies sur Ézékiel*. SC 327, 360. Paris: Cerf, 1986–90.

—————————. *Moralia in Iob*. M. Adriaen. CCL 143, 143A, 143B. Turnhout: Brepols, 1979–85. *Morales sur Job*, 1–2. Ed. and tr. Gillet. SC 32bis. Paris: Cerf, 1989. *Morales sur Job*, 11–14. Ed. and tr. A. Bocognano. SC 212. Paris: Cerf, 1974. *Morales sur Job*, 15–16. Ed. and tr. A. Bocognano, SC 221. Paris: Cerf, 1975. *Morales sur Job*, 28–29. Ed. and tr. M. Adriaen et al., SC 476. Paris: Cerf, 2003. *Morales sur Job*, 30–32. Ed. and tr. M. Adriaen, et al., SC 525. Paris: Cerf, 2009.

—————————. *Registrum epistolarum*. Ed. P. Ewald and L. M. Hartmann. Monumenta Germaniae historica. Epist. 1–2. Berlin, 1877–99.

Medieval Authors

Adam Scot. *Soliloquium de instructione animae*. PL 198.843–72.

Aelred of Rievaulx. *Opera ascetica*. Ed. A. Hoste and C. H. Talbot. CCCM 1. Turnhout: Brepols, 1971. Tr. Lawrence Braceland. *Spiritual Friendship*. Ed. Marsha Dutton. CF 5. Collegeville, MN: Cistercian Publications, 2010.

Alan of Lille. *De sex alis cherubim*. PL 210.265–280C.

Anselm of Canterbury. *Opera omnia*. 6 vols. Ed. F. S. Schmitt. Edinburgh: T. Nelson, 1938-61. Translations ed. Brian Davies and

G. R. Evans. Oxford World's Classics. *The Major Works.* Oxford: University Press, 1998.

Arno of Reichersberg. *Scutum canonicorum.* PL 194.1493–1528D.

Bernard of Clairvaux. *Opera.* Ed. Jean Leclerq *et al.* 9 vols. Rome: Editiones Cisterciensis, 1957–98.

——————. *The Steps of Humility and Pride.* Tr. M. B. Pennington. Kalamazoo: Cistercian Publications, 1989.

——————. *On the Song of Songs.* 4 vols. Tr. K. Walsh and Irene Edmonds. CF 4, 7, 31, 40. Kalamazoo: Cistercian Publications, 1971–83.

Bonaventure. *Soliloquium.* Ed. A. C. Peltier, *Opera omnia.* Paris: Vivès, 1868.

Boethius. *Philosophiae consolatio.* Ed. and tr. J. F. Stewart. E. K. Rand, and S. J. Tester. Loeb Classical Library. Cambridge: Harvard University Press, 1973.

Contemplations of the Dread and Love of God [*Fervor amoris*]. Ed. M. Connolly. Early English Text Society, Original Series, 303. Oxford: Oxford University Press, 1993.

Crapillet, Pierre. *Le 'Cur Deus homo' d'Anselme de Canterbury et le 'De arrha animae' d'Hugues de Saint-Victor.* Ed. Robert Bultot and Geneviève Hasenohr. Université catholique de Louvain. Publications de l'Institut d'études médiévales 2/6. Louvain-la-Neuve, 1984.

Dante Alighieri. *The Divine Commedy of Dante Alighieri. Vol. 1: Inferno.* Ed. and tr. Robert M. Durling. New York: Oxford, 1996.

Guigo I. *Meditationes.* Ed. A. Wilmart. Paris: J. Vrin, 1936.

Guigo II. *Scala claustralum.* Ed. Edmund Colledge and James Walsh. SC 163. Paris: Cerf, 1970 [PL 184.475–84]. Tr. E. Colledge and J. Walsh. *The Ladder of Monks and Twelve Meditations.* CS 48. Kalamazoo: Cistercian Publications, 1981.

Hildegard of Bingen. *Liber vitae meritorum.* Ed. A. Carlevaris. CCCM 90. Turnhout: Brepols, 1995. Tr. Bruce Hozeski. *The Book of the Rewards of Life.* New York: Oxford, 1994.

——————. *Ordo virtutum,* Ed. P. Dronke. Hildegard of Bingen, *Opera minora.* CCCM 226. Turnhout: Brepols, 2007. Pp. 479–521. Tr. Audrey Ekdahl Davidson. *The Ordo Virtutum of Hildegard von Bingen.* Kalamazoo, MI: Medieval Institute Publications, Western Michigan University, 1984.

——————. *Scivias.* Ed A. Führkötter and A. Carlevaris. CCCM 43A. Turnhout: Brepols, 1978). Tr. Columba Hart. Classics of Western Spirituality. New York: Paulist, 1990.

Jacobus de Voragine. *Golden Legend*. Tr. William Granger. 2 vols. Princeton: Princeton University Press, 1993.

John Scotus Eriugena. *Periphyseon (De divisione naturae)*. Ed. Édouard Jeauneau. CCCM 161–65. Turnhout: Brepols, 1996–2003.

Peter Damian. *Lettre sur la toute-puissance divine*. Ed. A. Cantin. SC 191. Paris: Cerf, 1972.

Peter Lombard. *Sententiae in IV libris distinctae*. SB 4–5. Grottaferrata: Editiones Collegii S. Bonaventurae ad Claras Aquas, 1971–81.

Pseudo-Augustine. *Soliloquia*. PL 40.863–98.

Pseudo-Bernard. *Meditationes*. PL 184.485–508.

_____. *Soliloquium*. PL 184.1157B–1168B.

Pseudo-Rhaban Maur. *Allegoriae in Universam Sacram Scripturam*. PL 112.849D–1088C.

Rhaban Maur. *Expositio in librum Esther*. PL 109.635–65.

Thomas à Kempis. *Opera omnia*. Ed. Henricus Sommalius. Rev. Eusebius Amort. 3 vols. Cologne: Krakamp, 1759.

Thomas Aquinas. *On Love and Charity: Readings from the "Commentary on the Sentences of Peter Lombard."* Tr. Peter A. Kwasniewski, Thomas Bolin and Joseph Bolin. Washington, DC: Catholic University of America Press, 2008. *Supplement to On Love and Charity*. Washington, DC: Catholic University of America Press, 2008. Published online at cuapress.cua. edu/Books.

_____. *Summa theologiae*. Ed. Petrus Caramello. 3 vols. Turin: Marietti, 1952. *Summa Theologica*. Tr. Fathers of the English Dominican Province. 3 vols. New York: Benziger, 1947.

William Langland. *Piers Plowman*. Ed. George Economou. *Piers Plowman: The C Version*. Philadelphia: University of Pennsylvania Press, 1996.

SECONDARY SOURCES

Andrès, Pierre. "Marriage et vie chrétienne," *DS* 10:361–64.

Astell, Ann W. *The Song of Songs in the Middle Ages*. Ithaca, NY: Cornell University Press, 1990.

Baron, Roger. "La pensée mariale de Hugues de Saint-Victor." *Revue d'ascétique et de mystique* 31 (1955): 249–71.

_____. "Note sur la succession et la date des écrits de Hugues de Saint-Victor." *Revue d'histoire ecclésiastique* 57 (1962): 88–118.

_____. "Notes biographiques sur Hugues de Saint-Victor." *Revue d'histoire ecclésiastique* 51 (1956): 920–34.

_____. "Rapports entre Saint Augustin et Hugues de Saint-Victor. Trois opuscules de Hugues de Saint-Victor." *Revue des études augustiniennes* 5 (1959): 391–429.

_____. "Textes spirituels inédits de Hugues de Saint-Victor." *Mélanges de science religieuse*, 13 (1956): 157–78.

_____. *Études sur Hugues de Saint-Victor.* N.p.: Desclée de Brouwer, 1963.

Berry, Wendell. *Life Is a Miracle: An Essay against Modern Superstition.* Berkeley: Counterpoint, 2000.

Bogumil, Karlotto. *Das Bistum Halberstadt im 12. Jahrhundert.* Mitteldeutsche Forschungen 69. Cologne: Böhlau, 1972.

Bonnard, Fourier. *Histoire de l'abbaye royale et de l'ordre de chanoines réguliers de Saint-Victor de Paris.* 2 vols. Paris: Arthur Savaète, 1904–7.

The Book of Kells. Intro. Peter Brown. New York: Alfred A. Knopf, 1980.

Bourke, Vernon J., ed. *The Essential Augustine.* New York: Mentor, 1964.

Bücher: Bibliotheken und Schriftkultur der Kartäuser: Festgabe zum 65. Geburtstag von Edward Potkowski. Contubernium. Tübinger Beiträge zur Universitäts- und Wissenschaftsgeschichte 59. Ed. Sönke Lorenz. Stuttgart: Franz Steiner, 2002.

Bultot, Robert. "A propos du 'contemptus mundi' dans l'école de Saint-Victor." *Revue de sciences philosophiques et théologiques* 51 (1967): 3–22.

Bynum, Caroline Walker. "The Spirituality of Canons Regular in the Twelfth Century." In *Jesus as Mother: Studies in the Spirituality of the High Middle Ages.* Berkeley: University of California Press, 1982. Pp. 22–58.

Cabassut, André, and Michel Olphe-Galliard. "Cantique des Cantiques: Histoire de l'interpretation spirituelle." DS 2 (1953): 86–109.

Cacciapuoti, Pierluigi. "*Deus existentia amoris.*" *Teologia della carità e teologia della Trinità negli scritti di Riccardo di San Vittore († 1173).* Bibliotheca Victorina 9. Turnhout: Brepols, 1998.

Callahan, John F. *Augustine and the Greek Philosophers.* N.p.: Villanova University Press, 1967.

Canning, Raymond. "*Uti/frui.*" In *Augustine through the Ages: An Encyclope-dia.* Ed. Allan D. Fitzgerald, Grand Rapids, MI: Eerdmans, 1999. Pp. 859–61.

Carruthers, Mary. *The Book of Memory: A Study of Memory in Medieval Cul-ture.* 2nd ed. Cambridge: Cambridge University Press, 2008.

————. *The Craft of Thought: Meditation, Rhetoric, and the Making of Images, 400–1200.* Cambridge: Cambridge University Press, 1998.

Cary, Philip. *Outward Signs: The Powerlessness of External Things in Augustine's Thought.* New York: Oxford, 2008.

Châtillon, Jean. "Cordis affectus au moyen âge." DS 2:2288–2300.

————. "La Bible dans les écoles du xiie siècle." In *Le Moyen Âge et la Bible* Ed. Pierre Riché and Guy Lobrichon. Paris: Beauchesne, 1984.

————. "Les quatres degrés de la charité d'après Richard de Saint-Victor." *Revue d'ascétique et de mystique,* 20 (1939): 237–64.

————. "*Quidquid convenit Filio Dei per naturam convenit Filio hominis per gratiam.*" *Divinitas* 11 (1967): 715–28 (=*Miscel-lanea André Combes*) [Rome, 1967] 2:319–31.

————. *D'Isidore de Séville à saint Thomas d'Aquin: Études d'his-toire et de théologie.* London: Variorum, 1985.

————. *Le mouvement canonial au moyen âge: reform de l'église, spiritualité et culture.* Ed. Patrice Sicard. Bibliotheca Vic-torina 3. Turnhout: Brepols, 1992.

————. *Théologie, spiritualtié et métaphysique dans l'oeuvre oratoire d'Achard de Saint-Victor.* Études de Philosophie Médié-vale, 58. Paris: Vrin, 1969.

Church, Society and Monasticism. Ed. E. López-Tello García and B. S. Zorzi, Studia Anselmiana 146. Analecta Monastica 9. Rome: Pontificio Ateneo S. Anselmo, 2009.

Constable, Giles. *"Love and Do What You Will." The Medieval History of an Augustinian Precept.* Morton W. Bloomfield Lecture 4. Kalamazoo: Medieval Institute Publications, Western Michigan University, 1999.

Consuetudines Floriacenses saeculi tertii decimi. Ed. Anselmus Davril. Corpus Consuetudinum Monasticarum 9. Siegburg: Franciscus Schmitt, 1976.

Coulter, Dale M. *Per visibilia ad invisibilia: Theological Method in Richard of St Victor (d. 1173)*. Bibliotheca Victorina 19. Turnhout: Brepols, 2006.

Courcelle, Pierre. "La culture antique d'Absalon de Saint-Victor." *Journal des Savants* (année 1972): 270–91.

Cousins, Ewart. "A Theology of Interpersonal Relations." *Thought* 45 (1970): 56–82.

——————. *The Notion of Person in the De Trinitate of Richard of St Victor*. Ph.D. diss. Fordham University, 1966.

Croydon, F. E. "Notes on the Life of Hugh of St Victor." JTS 40 (1939): 232–53.

Dardis, Brendan M. *Eulogium sponsi et sponsae*. M.A. diss. St Benedict, OR, Mt. Angel Seminary, 1985.

De Bruyne, D. "Les anciennes versions latines du Cantique des cantiques." RBen 38 (1926): 97–122.

De Ghellinck, Joseph. "La table des matières de la première édition des oeuvres de Hugues de Saint-Victor." *Recherches de science religieuse* 1 (1910): 270–89, 385–96.

——————. *Le mouvement théologique du xiiᵉ siècle*. 2nd ed. Paris: Desclée de Brouwer, 1938.

de Lubac, Henri. *Medieval Exegesis: The Four Senses of Scripture*. Vol. 3. Grand Rapids, MI: Eerdmans, 2009.

De Rijk L. M. "Some Notes on the Twelfth-Century Topic of the Three (Four) Human Evils and of Science, Virtue and Techniques as their Remedies." *Vivarium* 5 (1967): 8–15.

Delhaye, Philippe. "Les sermons de Godefroy de Saint-Victor." *Recherches de théologie ancienne et médiévale* 21 (1954): 194–210.

——————. *Le Microcosmus de Godefroy de Saint-Victor. Étude théologique*. Mémoires et travaux par les professeurs des Facultés catholiques de Lille, 56. Lille: Facultés catholiques, 1951.

DeYoung, Rebecca Konyndyk, Colleen McCluskey, and Christina Van Dyke. *Aquinas's Ethics: Metaphysical Foundations, Moral Theory, and Theological Context*. Notre Dame, IN: University of Notre Dame Press, 2009.

Dideberg, Dany. *Saint Augustin et la Première Épître de saint Jean: Une théologie de l'agapè*. Théologie historique 34. Paris: Beuchesne, 1975.

Dubus III, Andre. *House of Sand and Fog*. New York: Norton, 1999.

Dumeige, Gervais. *Richard de Saint-Victor et l'idée chrétienne de l'amour.* Paris: Presses Universitaires de France, 1952.

Dunn, James D. G. *The Theology of Paul the Apostle.* Grand Rapids: Eerdmans, 1998.

Ebner, Joseph. *Die Erkenntnislehre Richards von St. Viktor.* BGPTMA 19.4. Munich: Aschendorff, 1917.

Ehlers, Joachim. *Hugo von St. Viktor: Studien zum Geschichtsdenken und Geschichtsschreibung des 12. Jahrhunderts.* Frankfurter historische Abhandlungen 7. Wiesbaden: Steiner, 1973.

Fassler, Margot. "Who Was Adam of St Victor? The Evidence of the Sequence Manuscripts." *Journal of the American Musicological Society* 37 (1984): 233–69.

───────────. *Gothic Song: Victorine Sequences and Augustinian Reform in Twelfth-Century Paris.* New York: Cambridge University Press, 1993.

Feiss, Hugh. "Heaven in the Theology of Hugh, Achard, and Richard of St Victor." In *Imagining Heaven in the Middle Ages: A Book of Essays.* Ed. J. S. Emerson and H. B. Feiss. New York: Garland, 2000. Pp. 145–63.

───────────. "*Dilation*: God and the World in the Visions of Benedict and Julian of Norwich." *American Benedictine Review* 55 (2004): 55–73.

───────────. "Preaching by Word and Example: Pastoral Reform and Practice at Twelfth-Century St Victor" [forthcoming]

───────────. "The Grace of Passion and the Compassion of God: Soundings in the Christian Tradition." *American Benedictine Review,* 41 (1990): 141–56.

───────────. *Learning and the Ascent to God in Richard of St Victor.* STD diss., Rome, Pontifical Athenaeum of Sant' Anselmo, 1980). A shortened version was privately published under the same title: St Benedict, OR: [Mount Angel Abbey, 1979].

Fitzgerald, Allan D., ed. *Augustine through the Ages: An Encyclopedia.* Grand Rapids: Eerdmans, 1999.

Gantier, Louis-Marie. "Le pape et l'évêque dans l'ecclésiologie monastique d'Abbon de Fleury (vers 950–1004)." *Church, Society and Monasticism.* Ed. E. López-Tello García and B. S. Zorzi. Studia Anselmiana 146. Analecta Monastica 9. Rome: Pontificio Ateneo S. Anselmo, 2009. Pp. 131–49.

Gasparri, Françoise. "Godefroid de Saint-Victor: Une personalité peu connue du monde intellectuel et artistique parisien au XIIe siècle." *Scriptorium* 39/1 (1985): 57–69.

_____. "Observations paléographiques sur deux manuscripts partiellement autographes de Godefroid de Saint-Victor." *Scriptorium* 36 (1982): 43–50.

_____. "Philosophie et cosmologie: Godefroid de Saint-Victor." In *Notre-Dame de Paris: Un manifeste chrétien (1160–1230).* Ed. Michel Lemoine. Rencontres médiévales européennes 4. Turnhout: Brepols, 2004. Pp. 119–44.

_____. "Textes autographes d'auteurs victorins du XIIe siècle." *Scriptorium* 35 (1981) 277–84.

Gilson, Etienne. *The Christian Philosophy of Saint Augustine.* Tr. L. E. M. Lynch. New York: Random House, 1960.

Giraud, Cédric. *Per Verba magistri. Anselme de Laon et son école au XIIe siècle.* Biblothèque d'histoire culturelle du Moyen Âge 8. Turnhout: Brepols, 2010.

Goy, Rudolf. *Die Überlierferung der Werke Hugos von St. Viktor.* Monographien zur Geschichte des Mittelalters 14. Stuttgart: Anton Hiersemann, 1976.

_____. *Die handschriftliche Überlieferung der Werke Richards von St. Viktor im Mittelalter.* Bibliotheca Victorina 18. Turnhout: Brepols, 2005.

Griffiths, Fionna. *The Garden of Delights: Reform and Renaissance for Women in the Twelfth Century.* Philadelphia: University of Pennsylvania Press, 2007.

Grosfillier, Jean. *Les sequences d'Adam de Saint-Victor: Étude littéraire (poétique et rhétorique). Textes et traductions, commentaires.* Bibliotheca Victorina 20. Turnhout: Brepols, 2008.

Guimet, Fernad. "*Caritas ordinata* et *amor discretus* dans la théologie de Richard de Saint-Victor." *Revue de Moyen Âge latin,* 4 (1948): 225–36.

Hardarson, Gunnar. *Littérature et spiritualité en Scandinavie médiévale: La traduction norroise du De arrha animae de Hugues de Saint-Victor.* Bibliotheca Victorina 5. Turnhout: Brepols, 1995.

Harkins, Franklin T. *Reading and the Work of Restoration. History and Scripture in the Theology of Hugh of St Victor.* Studies and Texts 167. Toronto: Pontifical Institute of Mediaeval Studies, 2009.

Hauréau, Barthélemy. *Notices et extraits de quelques manuscripts de la Biblio-thèque Nationale*. 6 vols. Paris: Klincksieck, 1890–3.

Hazo, Robert G. *The Idea of Love*. Concepts in Western Thought. New York: Praeger, 1967.

Herde, Rosemarie. "Das Hohelied in der lateinischen Literatur des Mittelalters bis zum 12. Jahrhundert." *Studi Medievali* 8 (1967): 957–1053.

Herdt, Jennifer A. *Putting on Virtue: The Legacy of the Splendid Vices*. Chicago: University of Chicago Press, 2008.

Hesbert, R.-J. *Corpus Antiphonalium Officii*. Rerum Ecclesiasticarum Docu-menta. Series Maior. Fontes 9. Rome: Herder, 1968.

Hollywood, Amy. *The Soul as Virgin Wife: Mechthild of Magdeburg, Marguerite Porete, and Meister Eckhart*. Notre Dame: University of Notre Dame Press, 1995.

Ilkhani, Mohammad. *La philosophie de la création chez Achard de Saint-Victor*. Bruxelles: Ousia, 1999.

Illouz, Eva. "Love and Its Discontents: Irony, Reason, Romance." *Hedgehog Review*, 12/1 (Spring 2010): 18–32.

Kingsmill, Edmée. *The Song of Songs and the Eros of God: A Study in Biblical Intertexuality*. Oxford: Oxford University Press, 2010.

Kraebel, A. B. "*Grammatica* and the Authenticity of the Psalms-Commentary attributed to Bruno the Carthusian." *Mediaeval Studies* 71 (2009) 63–98.

——————. Ed and tr. *The Sermons of William of Newburgh*. Toronto: Pontifical Institute of Mediaeval Studies for the Centre for Medieval Studies, 2010.

Ladner, Gerhard. *The Idea of Reform*. Cambridge: Harvard University Press, 1959.

LaFleur, Richard A. *Scribblers, Sculptors, and Scribes*. New York: Collins, 2010.

Lanham, Carol Dana. *Salutation Formulas in Latin Letters to 1200*. Münchener Beiträge zur Mediävistik und Renaissance-Forschung 22. Munich: Arbeo, 1975.

Lauritzen, Paul. "Intellectual Street Fighter: Gilbert Meilaender's Ethics of Everyday." *Commonweal*, 137/10 (May 21, 2010): 13–17.

Lazzari, F. *Il "contemptus mundi" nella scuola di S. Vittore*. Naples: Istituto Italiano per gli Studi Storici, 1965.

Leclercq, Jean. "Écrits monastiques sur la Bible aux xiᵉ–xiiᵉ siècles." *Mediaeval Studies*, 15 (1953): 98–104.

_____. *Love of Learning and the Desire for God*. Trans. Catharine Misrahi. New York: Fordham University Press, 1974.

Lemoine, Michel, ed. *Notre-Dame de Paris: Un manifeste chrétien (1160–1230)*. Rencontres médiévales européennes 4. Turnhout: Brepols, 2004.

Lerner, Robert E. "The Image of Mixed Liquids in Late Medieval Mystical Thought." *Church History* 40 (1971): 397–411.

_____. "New Light on the *Mirror of Simple Souls*." *Speculum* 85 (2010): 91–116.

Liccaro, Vincenzo. *Studi sulla visione del mondo di Ugo di San Vittore*. Università delgi studi di Trieste. Facoltà di magisterio 12. Udine: Del Bianco, 1969.

Lienhard, Joseph T., "Friendship, Friends." In *Augustine through the Ages: An Encyclopedia*. Ed. Allan D. Fitzgerald. Grand Rapids: Eerdmans, 1999. Pp. 372–73.

Lottin, Odon. *Psychologie et morale aux XIIᵉ et XIIIᵉ siècles*. Vol. 5: *Problèmes d'histoire littéraire. L'école d'Anselme de Laon et de Guillaume de Champeaux*. Gembloux: J. Duculot, 1959.

_____. "Quelques recueils d'écrits attribués à Hugues de Saint-Victor." *RTAM* 25 (1958): 248–84.

_____. "Questions inédits de Hugues de Saint-Victor." *RTAM* 26 (1959): 177–213; 27 (1960): 42–60.

Louth, Andrew. *St John of Damascus: Tradition and Originality in Byzantine Theology*. Oxford Early Christian Studies. New York: Oxford, 2002.

Luckmann, Harriet, and Linda Kulzer, eds. *Purity of Heart in Early Ascetic and Monastic Literature*. Collegeville, MN: Liturgical Press, 1999.

Matter, E. Ann. "*Eulogium sponsi de sponsa*: Canons, Monks, and the Song of Songs." *The Thomist* 49 (1985): 560–64.

_____. *The Voice of My Beloved: The Song of Songs in Western Medieval Christianity*. Philadelphia: University of Pennsylvania Press, 1990.

McGinn, Bernard. "The Abyss of Love." In *The Joy of Learning and the Love of God: Essays in Honor of Jean Leclercq*. Ed. R. Elder. Kalamazoo: Cistercian Publications, 1995. Pp. 95–120.

_____. "*Visio Dei*: Seeing God in Medieval Theology and Mysticism." In *Envisaging Heaven in the Middle Ages*. Ed. C. Muessig and A. Putter. London: Routledge, 2007. Pp. 15–33.

McGuire, Brian Patrick. *Friendship and Community: The Monastic Experience, 350–1250.* Cistercian Studies 95. Kalamazoo, MI: Cistercian Publications, 1988.

Meehan, Bernard. *The Book of Kells.* New York: Thames and Hudson, 1994.

Miethke, Jürgen. "Zur Herkunft Hugos von St. Viktor." *Archiv für Kulturgeschichte* 54 (1972): 241–61.

Miquel, Pierre. *Le vocabulaire latin de l'expérience spirituelle dans la tradition monastique et canoniale de 1050 à 1250.* Théologie historique 17. Paris: Beauchesne, 1989.

Negri, L. "Lettura stilistica di Ugo di San Vittore, 'De arrha animae.'" *Convivium* 24 (1956): 129–40.

Németh, Csaba. "*Videre sine speculo:* The Immediate Vision of God in the Works of Richard of St Victor." *Annual of Medieval Studies at the Central European University* 8 (2002): 123–37.

Newman, Barbara. *From Virile Woman to WomanChrist: Studies in Medieval Religion and Literature.* Philadelphia: University of Pennsylvania Press, 1995.

Noonan, John T. "Marital Affection in the Canonists." *Studia Gratiana* 12 (1967): 479–509.

Norris, Richard, tr. *The Song of Songs Interpreted by Early Christian and Medieval Commentators.* The Church's Bible. Grand Rapids, MI: Eerdmans, 2003.

Ohly, Friedrich. *Hohelied Studien. Grundzüge einer Geschichte der Hoheliedauslegung des Abendlandes bis um 1200.* Schriften der wissenschaftlichen Gesellschaft an der Johann Wolfgang Goethe Universität, Frankfurt am Main. Geisteswissenschaftliche Reihe 1. Wiesbaden: Franz Steiner, 1958.

Osborne, Thomas M., Jr. *Love of Self and Love of God in Thirteenth-Century Ethics.* Notre Dame: University of Notre Dame Press, 2005.

Ostler, Nicholas. *Ad Infinitum: A Biography of Latin.* London: Harper, 2007.

Ott, Ludwig. "Hugo von St. Viktor und die Kirchenväter." *Divus Thomas* (Fribourg) 27 (1949): 180–200; 293–332.

—————. "*Sententiae magistri Hugonis Parisiensis.*" RTAM 27 (1960): 29–41.

—————. *Untersuchungen zur theologische Briefliteratur der Frühscholastik unter besonderer Berücksichtigung des viktoriner Kreises.* BGPTMA 34. Münster: Aschendorff, 1937.

Ouy, Gilbert. *Les manuscripts de l'abbaye de Saint-Victor. Catalogue établi sur la base du répertoire de Claude de Grandrue (1514).* 2 vols. Bibliotheca Victorina 10. Turnhout: Brepols, 1999.

_____. "Manuscrits entièrement ou partiellement autographes de Godefroid de Saint-Victor." *Scriptorium* 36 (1982): 29–42.

Pascher, Joseph. *Das liturgische Jahr.* Munich: Max Hueber, 1963.

Pellegrino, Michele. *Le Confessioni di Sant' Agostino.* Cultura 15. Rome: Editrice Studium, 1972.

Pierre, Teresa Olsen. "Marriage, Body, and Sacrament in the Age of Hugh of St Victor." In *Christian Marriage: A Historical Study.* Ed. Glenn W. Olsen. New York: Crossroad, 2001. Pp. 218–27.

Poirel, Dominique. "*Hugo Saxo.* Les origins germaniques de la pensée d'Hugues de Saint-Victor." *Francia. Forschungen zur westeuropäischen Geschichte* 33/1 (2006): 163–69.

_____. *Hugues de Saint-Victor.* Paris: Cerf, 1998.

_____. "Love of God, Human Love: Hugh of St Victor and the Sacrament of Marriage." *Communio* 24 (Spring 1997): 99–109.

Poppenberg, E. *Die Christologie des Hugo von St. Viktor.* Hiltrup, 1937.

Reinhardt, Elizabeth. "Das Theologieverständnis Richards von Sankt Viktor." In *What is "Theology" in the Middle Ages? Religious Cultures of Europe (11th–15th Centuries) as refleted in their Self-Understanding.* Ed. Mikolaj Olszewski. Archa Verbi, Subsidia 1. Münster: Aschendorff, 2007. Pp. 85–103.

Rice, Nicole. *Lay Piety and Religious Discipline in Medieval English Literature.* Cambridge: Cambridge University Press, 2008.

Riedlinger, Helmut. *Die Makellosigkeit der Kirche in den lateinischen Hoheliedkommentaren des Mittelalters.* BGPTMA 38/3. Münster: Aschendorff, 1958.

Robinson, Marilynn. *Absence of Mind: The Dispelling of Inwardness from the Modern Myth of the Self.* New Haven: Yale, 2010.

Rochais, H.-M. "Enquête sur les sermons divers et les sentences de saint Bernard." *Analecta Sacri Ordinis Cisterciensis* 18 (1962): 141–42.

Rorem, Paul. *Hugh of St Victor.* New York: Oxford University Press, 2009.

Rousselot, Pierre. *Pour l'histoire du problème de l'amour au Moyen Âge.* BGPTMA 6/6. Münster; Aschendorff, 1908. Tr. Alan Vincelette, *The Problem of Love in the Middle Ages:*

A Historical Contribution. Marquette Studies in Philosophy 24. Milwaukee: Marquette University Press, 2001.

Rudolph, Conrad. *"First I Find the Center Point": Reading the Text of Hugh of Saint Victor's The Mystic Ark.* Philadelphia: The American Philosophical Society, 2004.

Saint Mary of Egypt: Three Medieval Lives. Tr. Hugh Feiss and Ronald Pepin. Cistercian Studies 209. Kalamazoo, MI: Cistercian Publications, 2005.

Schlette, Heinz-Robert. *Die Nicthigkeit der Welt: Der philosophische Horizont des Hugos von St. Viktor* Munich: Kösel, 1961.

Schütz, Christian. *Deus absconditus, Deus manifestus. Die Lehre Hugos von St. Viktor über die Offenbarung Gottes.* Studia Anselmiana 56. Rome: Herder, 1967.

Schwartz, Daniel. *Aquinas on Friendship.* Oxford: Clarendon, 2007.

Sheridan, Mark. "Mapping the Intellectual Genome of Early Christian Monasticism." *Church, Society and Monasticism.* Ed. Eduardo López-Tello García and Benedetta Selene Zorzi. Studia Anselmiana 146. Analecta Monastica 9. Rome: Pontificio Ateneo S. Anselmo, 2009. Pp. 324–40.

Sicard, Patrice. *Diagrammes médiévaux et exégèse visuelle: Le Libellus de formatione arche de Hugues de Saint-Victor.* Bibliotheca Victorina 4. Turnhout: 1993.

——————. *Hugues de Saint-Victor et son école.* Turnhout: Brepols, 1991.

——————. "Repertorium Sententiarum quae in saeculi XII Hugonis de Sancto Victore operum codicibus inveniuntur." *Sacris erudiri* 32 (1991): 171–221.

Sloan, Thomas O. "Rhetoric and Meditation: Three Case Studies." *Journal of Medieval and Renaissance Studies* 1 (1971): 45–58.

Smalley, Beryl. *The Study of the Bible in the Middle Ages.* First paperback ed. Notre Dame, IN: University of Notre Dame Press, 1964.

Spearing, A. C. *Medieval Dream-Poetry.* Cambridge: Cambridge University Press, 1976.

Stewart, Columba. *Cassian the Monk.* Oxford Studies in Historical Theology. New York: Oxford University Press, 1998.

Taylor, Jerome. *The Origin and Early Life of Hugh of St Victor: An Evaluation of the Tradition.* Texts and Studies in the History of Mediaeval Education 5. Notre Dame, IN: University of Notre Dame Press, 1957.

The Vatican Mythographers. Ed. and tr. Ronald E. Pepin. New York: Fordham University Press, 2008.

Turner, Denys. *Eros and Allegory: Medieval Exegesis of the Song of Songs.* Cistercian Studies 156. Kalamazoo: Cistercian Publications, 1995.

Vaccari, A. "Latina Cantici canticorum versio a S. Hieronymo ad Graecam Hexaplarem emendata." *Biblica* 36 (1955): 258–60

——————. "S. Hieronymi in Canticum." *Gregorianum* 42 (1961): 728–29.

Van 't Spijker, Ineke. "Exegesis and Emotions: Richard of St Victor's *De Quatuor Gradibus Violentae Caritatis.*" *Sacris Erudiri* 36 (1996): 147–60.

——————. *Fictions of the Inner Life: Religious Literature and the Formation of the Self in the Eleventh and Twelfth Centuries.* Turnhout: Brepols, 2004.

——————. "Learning by Experience: Twelfth-Century Monastic Ideas." In *Centres of Learning: Learning and Location in Pre-Modern Europe and the Near East.* Ed. J. W. Drijvers and A. A. MacDonald. Leiden: Brill, 1995. Pp. 197–206.

Van Bavel, T. J. "Love." In *Augustine through the Ages: An Encyclopedia.* Ed. Allan D. Fitzgerald. Grand Rapids: Eerdmans, 1999. Pp. 509–16.

Van den Eyne, Damien. *Essai sur la succession et la date des écrits de Hugues de Saint-Victor.* Spicilegium Pontificium Athenaeum Antonianum 13. Rome: Pontificium Athenaeum Antonianum, 1960.

——————. "Le *Liber Magistri Hugonis.*" *Franciscan Studies* 23 (1963): 268–99.

Van Engen, John. *Sisters and Brothers of the Common Life: The Devotio Moderna and the World of the Later Middle Ages.* Philadelphia: University of Pennsylvania Press, 2008.

Vrudny, Kimberly. "Medieval Fascination with the Queen: Esther as Queen of Heaven and Host of the Messianic Banquet." *ARTS* 11/2 (1999): 36–43.

——————. "Medieval Treatment of the Queen: Austrian Manuscripts and the Quest for Esther." *ARTS* 8/1 (1995): 14–21.

Wack, Mary F. *Lovesickness in the Middle Ages: The* Viaticum *and Its Commentaries.* Philadelphia: University of Pennsylvania Press, 1990.

Waddell, Chrysogonus. "The Song of Songs in the Stephen Harding Bible." *Liturgy OCSO* 18/2 (1984): 28–32.

Wadell, Paul. *The Primacy of Love: An Introduction to the Ethics of Thomas Aquinas.* New York: Paulist, 1992.

Watson, Nicholas. "Conceptions of the Word: The Mother Tongue and the Incarnation of God." *New Medieval Literatures* 1 (1997): 85–124.

_____. *Richard Rolle and the Invention of Authority.* Cambridge: Cambridge University Press, 1992.

Weisweiler, Heinrich. "Die Arbeitsmethode Hugos von St. Viktor: Ein Beitrag zum Entstehen seines Hauptwerkes *De sacramentis.*" *Scholastik* 20–24 (1949): 59–87, 232–67.

Wilmart, A. "L'ancienne version latine du Cantique I–II." RBen 28 (1911): 11–36.

Zinn, Grover. "Hugh of St Victor, Isaiah's Vision, and the *De arca Noe.*" *The Church and the Arts.* Ed. Diana Wood. Studies in Church History 28. Oxford: Blackwell, 1995. Pp. 99–116.

INDEX OF SCRIPTURE REFERENCES*

Old Testament

---

* Latin Vulgate version. References to notes are to the page on which the note occurs and to the number of the note.

New Testament

INDEX OF ANCIENT
AND MEDIEVAL AUTHORS*

VICTORINE WRITINGS

---

* This index is divided into four sections: Victorine Writings; Classical Authors; Early and Medieval Christian Authors; Medieval Commentaries on the Song of Songs.

PSEUDO-HUGH OF ST VICTOR

ADAM OF ST VICTOR

Achard of St Victor

Richard of St Victor

Pseudo-Richard of St Victor

Godfrey of St Victor

MAURICE OF ST VICTOR

WARNER (GARNIER) OF ST VICTOR

WALTER OF ST VICTOR

ANONYMOUS

CLASSICAL AUTHORS

EARLY AND MEDIEVAL CHRISTIAN AUTHORS

MEDIEVAL COMMENTARIES ON THE SONG OF SONGS

SUBJECT INDEX*

1 John 197–200

Abbey of La Lucerne 75
Abbey of St Victor 9–10, 70–71; necrology
    186 (n. 4)
Achard of St Victor 75; on love 75–83
Adam of St Victor 71 (n. 195), 325 (n. 1); on
    love 70–75
Adler, Mortimer 99 (n. 359)
aemulatio 58 (n. 112), 155 (n. 10), 275, 282,
    284, 295
affectus, affectio (see Feeling)
Altruism and eudaemonism 50–51, 61, 90,
    102, 108, 111–112, 141
Angels 180–181, 248, 253–254, 257 (n. 18),
    313
anima (see Soul and body)
Anselm of Laon 50
appetitus 85
arrha (see Love)
Aristotle 105, 107–108
Asceticism 89, 160, 321
Augustine of Hippo 42; influence on Vic-
    torines 101–103, 154; on love 51–62

Beatitude 54, 56 (n. 102), 64, 135 (n. 21),
    145, 162, 182 (n. 2)
Beauty 101, 123, 142, 203–204, 205–207,
    230 (n. 12, 20); of the bride 127–128,
    161, 194, 216; of the bride contrasted
    with prostitute 196, 198–199, 209,
    217–220; vocabulary for 229 (n. 9)
Bee 140

Benedict of Nursia 204
benevolentia 58–59 (n. 111)
Bernard of Clairvaux 269–270
Berndt, Rainer 11
Bethany 249, 254

Cassian 338 (n. 3)
Catullus 39
Châtillon, Jean 11
Christ; following of 106; homo assumptus
    248, 251, 334; humanity of Christ has
    by grace what his divinity has by na-
    ture 248, 251, 257(n. 6, 26), 313; humil-
    ity 293–294, 306; obedience of
    254–255; teacher 49 (n. 69); triduum
    134 (n. 16), 313
Christian 219, 231 (n. 37), 249, 254
Church 307; Body of Christ 57–58, 66, 82
    (n. 262), 99, 102, 122, 130, 199, 248, 313;
    bride 73 (n. 201, 204, 205); laity 312;
    three orders 232 (n. 42); unity, ce-
    mented by charity 66 (n. 162), 78
circumspectio 316–317, 337 (n. 8)
collatio 308 (n. 19)
Compunction 87, 201, 223, 231 (n. 30)
Compassion 61, 76, 80, 81–83, 87, 90–92,
    101, 268, 287, 294–296
condilectus 93
confessio 224–225, 231 (n. 44),, 340 (n. 68)
confidentia 311, 317
Constantine the African 40
Contemplation 82, 90–91, 104, 135 (n. 28),
    179, 258 (n. 42), 261, 267–269, 288–
    291, 320, 334

---

* Footnote references indicate number of footnote and page where it is to be found. Latin
    terms, without capitals, and titles of books are in italics.